Evolution of a Revolution

Selections from the Writings of Albert Ellis Ph.D.

Edited by James McMahon, Psy.D., Ph.D., Sc.D.
& Ann Vernon, Ph.D., Sc.D.

Published by Barricade Books Inc.
185 Bridge Plaza North
Suite 309
Fort Lee, NJ 07024

www.barricadebooks.com

ISBN 13: 978-1-56980-434-6
ISBN: 1-56980-434-6

10 9 8 7 6 5 4 3 2 1

Library of Congress Cataloging-in-Publication Data

Ellis, Albert, 1913-2007.
  [Selections. 2010]
  Evolution of a revolution : selections from the writings of Albert Ellis / edited by James McMahon & Ann Vernon.
     p. cm.
  ISBN 978-1-56980-434-6
  1. Rational emotive behavior therapy. 2. Personality. 3. Sex (Psychology) I. McMahon, James, 1937- II. Vernon, Ann. III. Title.
  RC489.R3E468 2010
  616.89'14--dc22

                          2009052799

Manufactured in the United States of America

TABLE OF CONTENTS

Table of Contents

PREFACE

During the fiftieth year of its founding, ideas concerning how to memorialize and pay tribute to the life and work of Albert Ellis were discussed by the Trustees of the not-for-profit Albert Ellis Institute (AEI). It was decided by the Trustees, also known as the Board, to undertake certain publishing goals to support the work of the Institute and to provide scholarships given in the name of Albert Ellis for use at the AEI. The Trustees further decided to undertake the preparation of an Ellis reader.

As a companion to this first Albert Ellis reader, it is anticipated that six other readers will be published in the areas of philosophy, education, addictions, sex-marriage-family, religion, and research. The companion readers will have input from Board members as well as from experts such as Raymond DiGiuseppe, Windy Dryden, Kristene Doyle, Daniel David, F. Michler Bishop, and Steve Johnson, all of whom have been associated with the Albert Ellis Institute for many years. It is anticipated that the Albert Ellis reader will be available in summer 2010, with the companion readers coming at various later dates.

Albert Ellis was a prolific writer, as evidenced by the fact that he was author or coauthor of more than sixty books and over seven hundred articles that were published in journals, in magazines, and as chapters in texts. It is the AEI Board's hope that the Ellis reader and later companion readers will pay tribute to the Institute's founder and benefactor who launched the monumental cognitive revolution in psychotherapy in the mid-fifties. In addition, the readers will synthesize Ellis' writings in order to demonstrate the evolution of Albert Ellis' thinking from 1955 until his death in 2007.

New York, 26 February 2010

Jeffrey Bernstein, President, Board of Trustees of the Albert Ellis Institute.

INTRODUCTION

Early Background

Albert Ellis was born in Pittsburgh in 1913, but lived most of his life in New York City, where he died in 2007 at age 93. He was the eldest of three children in an upper-middle-class Jewish family whose parents eventually divorced. As a child, Albert had various health problems, including a kidney ailment that necessitated lengthy hospitalizations. He was a very bright student who began writing essays at age twelve. Albert was also an avid reader and claimed to have read the works of Immanuel Kant by the time he was sixteen. He struggled with social phobia throughout his childhood and teen years, and became quite anxious about dating. However, he forced himself to overcome this anxiety by asking one hundred women he had targeted at the Botanical Gardens for a date. That "shame attack," as he would later call it, enabled him to work against his fear of being rejected.

After completing high school in the Bronx, he went on to attend the Baruch School of Business in New York. His goal upon graduation was to become rich, and he took a job as a clothing salesman while writing fiction on the side. He actually penned a half million words on Marx and the social philosophy of communism as well, but gave it up by concluding that the whole radical socialist project would eventually become top heavy with bureaucracy and implode itself. He also attempted to write many plays which he hoped would make it to the Great White Way but none did.

In the 1930s, Ellis claimed to have read thousands of articles on sex, dating, courting, and marriage. Because he was interested in romantic and sexual relationships, he began to give advice to friends and family, and he eventually formed an organization called LAMP—an acronym for Love and Marriage Program. A lawyer he consulted advised him to get a degree in clinical psychology so that his capacity to give amative advice would have more credibility. Although he considered becoming a famous psychiatrist, he opted for a master's degree in clinical psychology from Columbia University Teachers College and continued there in the doctoral program. For his doctoral dissertation, Ellis proposed, and the faculty accepted, that he would study the sex lives of Columbia coeds. However, the Administration of the University overruled the faculty with the logic, purportedly, that were the parents of the Columbia women to learn what their daughters were doing, the results might cause parents to withdraw their daughters from Columbia. Purportedly, that negative publicity could have had dire consequences for Columbia's fiscal support. Instead, Ellis undertook a more doctrinaire study; namely, the use of MMPI and other tests for clinical prediction. A summary of his dissertation was published in *Psychological Bulletin*. That move did not endear Ellis to the faculty at Columbia since many of them had not published in that then most prestigious of psychological journals.

Even before being awarded the doctorate in 1947, Albert Ellis had been working for the State of New Jersey as psychologist with myriad duties at its Sex Offenders Clinic. He would then see a few people at night in Manhattan from which he commuted. He rose to become Chief of Psychology for the State of New Jersey. After receiving his doctorate, Ellis decided to study psychoanalysis. He spent two years in intense analysis and then worked under supervision with his own clients. At that time in New York, psychoanalysis and psychoanalytic revisionism were the strong suits of psychotherapy, whereas nondirective psychotherapy propounded by another graduate of Teachers College (Carl Rogers in 1931) was gaining momentum. Behavioral techniques from Watson, Skinner, and others were being amalgamated into eclectic interventions, including Dollard and Miller's attempt to wed psychoanalysis and behaviorism. Later, Truax would refer to psychoanalysis as a behavioral technique during which "uh huh" responses by an analyst or psychoanalytically-oriented therapist would act to reward a conclusion that the therapist wished to hear. Well before Truax, Ellis had reached the same conclusion! He resigned his job in New Jersey to devote himself toward building a private practice in psychotherapy in Manhattan. He had a penchant for efficiency and tried to operationalize some of the psychoanalytic concepts. Although he realized that some psychoanalytic concepts were dogmatic, they were integral to the theory. He also learned in due course that many of the tenets of psychoanalysis—even if they worked from a clinical perspective—could not be tested. In the period during which he trained, for example, sessions between the therapist (or analyst) and patient or client (or analyst and) could not be observed by a supervisor. It was the student therapist's report that was important, however inaccurate or biased it might have been.

The more Ellis exposed himself to the theory, the more disillusioned he became. Then one day in 1953 he was working with a female patient who had failed to get a job she had interviewed for with a male interviewer. She attributed her poor performance to fear of males since men in authority reminded her of her father who had beaten the patient when she was a child. Ellis quipped to her (perhaps in frustration), "But your father is dead." The patient then purportedly replied, approximately: "You mean it is not my father who is frightening me today but it is what I am saying right now about the past that is frightening me?" Ellis replied, "Yes, and you keep telling yourself that over and over again so that you are propagandizing yourself into the false belief even more strongly." At that moment, between the patient and Albert Ellis, the cognitive revolution in psychotherapy was born.

After working on the implications of what he had experienced with his patient, Ellis presented it as his theory to the American Psychological Association annual meeting in 1955. There, he outlined his theory and predicted that some day it would replace psychoanalysis and nondirective psychotherapy in popularity. In 1957, especially in consideration of his long-standing interests in relationships, he wrote *How to Live with a Neurotic*. That book explained some of his techniques, which he then called Rational Therapy. Later, he thought that label to have been a major mistake since it opened the way for criticism of his work as surface therapy that missed profound possibilities of intervention: the word *rational* was understood by some to mean rationalization or excuse making.

After his APA presentation in 1955 in Chicago, Ellis continued writing and working for sexual liberation. He wrote texts concerning incest as taboo, the *Art and Science of Love*, and he lauded the work of Alfred Kinsey. Ellis joined the editorial board of a leading journal in sexology and he wrote about an American sexual tragedy.

In 1959, Ellis and his brother and several friends incorporated the Institute for Rational Living in the State of New York. Its goal was the advancement of scientific psychology, and the original charter took pains to eschew dogma of any kind. The incorporation followed another milestone in New York; namely, licensing of psychologists—the very first time that happened at a statewide level (1957). The Institute was run from Ellis's apartment before the not-for-profit organization purchased the building that was and is its home at 45 East 65th Street on the Upper East Side of Manhattan.

In addition to articles, presentations, and texts on sex, love, and marriage, especially *Creative Marriage* with Robert Harper in 1961, Ellis and Harper wrote *A Guide to Rational Living*, which was published in 1961 (and republished about fifteen years later). It sold over one million copies. In 1962, he published his magnum opus, *Reason and Emotion in Psychotherapy*. That text was revised in 1994. The text gave the background for his theory, it coupled reason to emotion (so important to the theory when it was first presented in Chicago in 1955). and it argued for the ABC theory of personality. These last two points had become critical for the balance of Ellis's work, as did his arguments for unconditional self-acceptance, plus the rejection of absolutes that demanded that life be different than the way it was.

Later, in 1976, after Ellis read Michael Mahoney's book, *Scientist as Subject,* he realized that any observer would influence the outcome of psychotherapy so that objectivity in reporting was more myth than fact. Further, he learned that the past did not cause the present since that would countenance a logical fallacy called, *post hoc ergo proter hoc.* Thomas Reid, the Scottish philosopher and cleric, chastised David Hume when the latter invoked the fallacy, and Reid gave an example: just because night follows day does not mean that day causes night. Rules for causality involve much more than temporal sequence. Reid concluded, then, that Hume had no explanation at all with his arguments for past events causing present circumstances. Freud contributed to that same logical fallacy, but on the grand scale. Ellis not only disputed absolutism for its role in generating or maintaining neurotic thinking, but he disputed psychoanalysis. He quipped that if people treated in psychoanalysis got better, it was in spite of the psychotherapy and not because of it.

Nothing in the previous paragraph, however, was an argument against *learning* from the past. Ellis argued that when a past, emotionally loaded memory was treated as if it were happening now—or invested with emotion anew—then the person got stuck with the idea that past was prologue. Because psychoanalysis spent so much time on past memories, however, Ellis argued that the patient might become distracted to the point that s/he would not ever see that what was driving behavior was driving it now. Investments into past events were being made anew to keep old emotionally invested material alive. Break the emotional investment reasoning, Ellis argued, and the chain of events causing or contributing to disturbance would fall.

Both Freudians and Rogerians wanted to know about emotional investments, or how a patient felt about situations or events—or even about past emotions as matters of experience. Ellis went another way, and for good reason. He argued that we lived in language and that some language was rational in that it conformed to reality, while other language was irrational in that it exaggerated reality. All language, whether rational or irrational he argued, was logical. Thus, if a patient believed that were s/he able to sail out far enough, s/he might fall off the earth, that was irrational because the world was round and the laws of gravity would hold the boat on the surface of the water. On the other hand, the statement was logical: if the earth were flat (which it was not) it would be logical to believe that one could sail out far enough to fall off.

But Ellis went further. In his 1955 explication of his theory, and in his 1961 text with Harper and in his *magnum opus,* Ellis argued that a thought and feeling seldom could be separated. He allowed that there could be pure thoughts and pure feelings but that they were rare. The vast majority of the time, he argued, a thought could not be separated from a feeling, and vice versa. Emphasizing this argument, which turned out to be supported by neurophysiology, Ellis came up with the term rational-emotive (note the hyphen) to show the more or less constant conjunction of the two.

Like Robert Woodworth before him in experimental psychology at Columbia in 1918 or so, Ellis accorded great importance to the connection. If the thought or activating event (A) was invested with emotion or consequence (C), Ellis argued that the hyphen (B) either tied the two together positively or negatively. If the tie-together was an irrational demand than life be different that it was with should, ought, must, have to, need to, awful, or other connections, then negative emotions were sure to follow. This process argued for the ABC model in Ellis's psychotherapy outline. Some sentence example might help to make this argument more meaningful to the reader.

I am in an airplane (with attendant turbulence) and I feel anxious.

Let us call the first sentence A, or the memory or event, and the second the emotional consequence-feeling or C statement. Ellis argued and neurophysiology has shown that A does not cause C in the brain: they are not directly connected. Ellis argued that an irrational statement or evaluation or demand or unconscious belief or childish tantrum was involved with the hyphen or B statement very, very quickly.

A. I am in an airplane (with attendant turbulence)
B. and the airplane shouldn't fly this way; it might crash and kill me and that would be awful and so
C. I feel anxious.

Ellis continued the argument, which comported with research concerning childhood self statements. If one observed children, all elements of the ABC would be present, such as he took my ball and he shouldn't have done that because now I am angry. Were one to dispute or replace the "B" statement with an emotionally unloaded, more rational appraisal, chances are that calmness would follow.

Introduction

A. I am in an airplane (with attendant turbulence)

B. but making myself scared will not help. I know it is not the airplane that is scaring me because it is just metal and plastic, and it is not the turbulence because if it were all planes would be grounded and no pilot would be rational enough to fly the plane. Where does it say in the laws of physics that planes should not fly my way during turbulence? And, is this ride awful—full of awe—the worst plane ride in the history of aviation? It might be uncomfortable, but it is hardly awful.

C. I feel less anxious.

Under less anxious conditions, the patient can learn these disputes and to anticipate or change emotionally laden memories and to see them as inconveniences and even very unfortunate situations from the past that need not drive current events. To invoke such memories just like they were experienced is to live life in the past and to be victim of that tyranny. Karen Horney was more pointed about it: she argued for the tyranny of *should* statements.

Suppose, however, that a person said that s/he understood that the plane ride objectively was not awful, and that there could be something worse such as *two* similar plane rides. The person reasoned, however, that it was awful "to me"—or subjectively awful. That individual, Ellis argued, moved from calm to total negative emotional investment (or from 0 level of stress to 10 level of stress in one swoop). He worked with his patients through disputation and imagery to feel and see themselves as 5-level and below so that the investment was not going in the direction of subjectively making oneself overwhelmed.

Ellis argued that to dislodge heavily loaded emotional appraisals at B would be difficult since they were usually long held. However, through practice, he further argued that a person could learn not to demand that life be different than it was. If one truly wished to change one's circumstances, then, s/he would calm down and work toward a plan that involved reasonable change.

This whole process, as simple as it sounded, was not simplistic. To round it out, Ellis introduced his arguments for self-worth. While his argument was that self was a matter of personal definition, there is abundant evidence that self as an owner of roles (executive self) and that seems to many observers to be more biological than learned. Further, there seems to be an automatic ability of the nervous system to organize itself (autopoeisis).

However, at the cultural level where much about self is learned as either a stalwart individual, a believer, a skeptic, or as a team player—or comes from a combination of some or all of these learned clusters, Ellis's arguments had great merit. The gist of his conclusions about self were that to think that self could be added to or detracted from meant that the individual would be up-down emotionally in the face of every success and failure s/he experienced in any role. To evaluate a role made great sense to Ellis for the performance of a role could then be improved, dropped, or left neutral. To rate the whole self, however, was surely a waste of time since it would mean rating all past roles, present roles, and roles in the future: it could not be done.

Thus, Ellis saw the elegant solution as self-acceptance. For a person unconditionally to accept him- or herself meant that mistakes and successes would not add to or take from self, but both could add to or take from a role. Generally, for a patient to experience unconditional self-acceptance (and not unconditional positive regard from Rogers, where role mistakes are unconditionally accepted) would mean that s/he was both neurosis and psychosis free. That person was not a megalomaniac demanding superiority of self, or person with fragmented character who believed that social class determined one's worth. A person's worth was equated by Ellis to mean that s/he was alive. In that sense, all people were equal. Role performance or lack thereof made for marketplace evaluations of talent so that one could potentially reap greater rewards for more talent in a given role, or less reward for lackluster talent in some role. Suffice it to say that the notion of self-acceptance is yet another way that distinguishes this theory from others.

The preceding pages presented a brief overview of the development of rational-emotive behavior therapy and its basic tenets. The *Ellis Reader* chronicles this development in greater detail through selected writings that have been organized in three phases as subsequently outlined.

The introductory chapters clearly argue the fact that Albert Ellis could have been referred to as a sexual libertine for much of his professional life. The first chapters of the *Ellis Reader* indicate that he carried through with his LAMP interests from the 1930s. Furthermore, when he was in graduate school at Columbia Teachers College, Ellis learned how to evaluate the research and techniques then available. He was quite skeptical about projective techniques, structured and nonstructured, and he learned the newest statistical techniques (including factor analysis) to help shape his outlook. Ellis was an activist concerning human rights according to his own writings, but scant information seemed available concerning personal relationships with people outside of the racial mainstream then in New York.

The middle chapters of Ellis's writing presented here show a philosophical shift away from positivism (or logical empiricism as some Americans called this philosophy of science) toward pragmatism. For sure, Ellis was a consummate humanist: he saw human beings as the center of civilization. Evaluating the work of human beings and stating their worth followed positivist thinking: if information did not come through the senses, it was probably nonsense (literally)—except for humankind's ability to use poetry, literature, music, and other cultural pursuits that helped people to think about thinking. He agreed with Arnold Lazarus that large aspects of human behavior were beyond behavior therapy and could not be analyzed by those techniques. As mentioned, Ellis's philosophy of science shifted to permit more individual and social construction of behavior, so much so that John Dewey's mutualism began to play a role in Ellis's thinking. Dewey, a longtime faculty member at Columbia, argued for relational interaction and respect for others, almost along the lines echoed by Leviticus and Jesus that human beings love their neighbors as they loved themselves. This type constructivism really argued for reorganization of thinking-feeling than it did for radical construction for all human activity. The shift by the early 1990s endeared Ellis's work to more theorists and practitioners (Mahoney and O'Hanlon, for example), while others (Wessler, for example) thought Ellis to have thrown out the baby with the bathwater since his arguments could not be pinned down.

Still, the middle chapters selected for this manuscript open the way for dealing with thinking-feeling, anxiety, depression, and other neuroses, as well as psychosis and character disorders. He not only emphasized his ABC model in refined ways, but Ellis was open to new arguments from DiGiuseppe, Dryden, and others regarding hot and cold emotions, discomfort anxiety-LFT, and how to overcome life changes or habits such as procrastination in order to be happier. In addition, Ellis began applying the model to young children as evidenced by the establishment of the Living School on the premises, where children and their parents were taught rational principles. Consequently, some attention was directed to applications of the model with young children.

A last shift for Albert Ellis involved his views of religion. Whereas he had considered himself a non-absolute atheist (did not think much of arguments for the existence of God or the practice of religion), he more or less thought many religious practices to be silly, distractions, and wastes of time. He changed that view, unlike Freud who considered religion to be a grand neurosis, so much so that he argued that religious adherence and observance could be reinforcing when used with his thinking-feeling methods. Concerning this argument, his theory-therapy moved from rational therapy to rational-emotive therapy over time. Two decades ago, Ellis added, at the behest of some professional interlocutors of sound professional reputation, the word behavior to the description: hence, rational-emotive behavior therapy. The term was not as inclusive as Arnold Lazarus's BASIC-ID (behavior, affect, sensation, imagery, cognition, interpersonal relations, drugs), but it came close in its eclecticism. The ABC model, to some extent, was more architecture than it was exact formula. Some cognitive scientists (Daniel David and Mircea Miclea, for example) argued that B-C in the ABC model were so intertwined that when one was disputed, so was the other.

The final chapter in this manuscript represents an alpha-omega summary of where Ellis had come from and what he argued for throughout his lifetime. Additionally, at the end of the 1980s, the American Psychological Association reported that Ellis was cited more often as a source for research and application than any other living psychologist except Carl Rogers. After Rogers died at the end of the 1980s, Ellis was the then most quoted and cited living American psychotherapist. Of course, the hegemony of psychoanalysis and its myriad schools, revisions, and applications overwhelms the literature compared to REBT, but even those schools of thought have integrated ideas from the monumental revolution that Ellis brought to bear on mental health—first in New York, then throughout America, and now worldwide.

A final thought concerns tolerance for diversity, contradictions, and ambiguities. A chapter has been selected which will make itself evident to the reader. One can see Ellis's vast writings as contradictory from time to time, or, as these writers would prefer, see them as a tribute to his diversity. He wrote so much that sometimes cause did become effect and vice versa. On balance, however, his work has lent itself to applications and solid outcome research for the betterment of humankind. The reader him- or herself can judge if this text achieves its goal of presenting a broad overview of Ellis's writings to justify this betterment conclusion. The chapters then demonstrate the evolution of a revolution by Albert Ellis, one that has changed the face of psychotherapy worldwide.

New York, 1 March 2010

James McMahon Psy.D., Ph.D., Sc.D.
Ann Vernon, Ph.D., Sc.D.

CHAPTER 1

THE ORIGINS OF RATIONAL-EMOTIVE PSYCHOTHERAPY

EDITOR'S COMMENTARY:

Albert Ellis began a classical psychoanalysis in the very early 1950s at the Horney Institute in Manhattan. From other sources, it was known that his analyst's name was Heulbeck. Upon completion of his training, Ellis saw patients in a classical way, for example three times per week with the analyst sitting out of view and behind the patient. According to Ellis, patients reported that they understood insights but seemed often not to carry those insights into consequent sessions. Therefore, he started to experiment by shortening the number of interventions per week, usually to one session. Ellis also sat face-to-face with his patients so that he was ready to be active. Ellis concluded that less was better: when he saw patients less often, they seemed to do better (he offered some percentage estimates of improvement).

A shift by Ellis from psychoanalysis and psychoanalytically oriented psychotherapy took place when he used the analogy of learning theory. He saw that psychoanalysis was based upon a conditioning model, and so Ellis went to it directly.

Apparently, he arrived at this conclusion about five years before Truax did, according to the counseling literature. He also saw how avoidance was a reinforcement for neurosis in his patients. Yet, Pavlov's theory did not fit most human experiences since dogs were not advantaged with human language. It was human language, argued Ellis, that could serve as a vehicle to transport reward or punishment cues. By 1954, Ellis had concluded that humans could learn fear cues from their own language self-signaling, and that signaling often represented the opinions of other people, parents, teachers, chance meetings, and the like. Instead of the unconscious clueing humans to be negatively auto-suggestive, Ellis argued that a negative or neurotic style resided within auto-suggestive language that, with some work, could be made conscious. Thus, learning theory was an interim step in theory development between psychoanalysis and rational-emotive interventions.

Ellis also began to see clearly the attachment children developed toward irrational appraisals of life and its changes, thanks to parents and others who functioned within a given child's scope of reference. Not only did children learn to invest their learned behavior within language with negative emotions, but they stubbornly and steadfastly clung to them. It was the re-indoctrination of self-defeating irrationalities, however, that kept a person disturbed into his or her adult years, and this factor often loomed as more important in terms of disturbance than the originally learned disturbance. Therefore, people could make themselves disturbed at any age, but they hardly did so on purpose. In a case example where a woman did not get along with her husband (she had attributed the lack of getting along to having been deprecated by her father when she was younger), Ellis showed the patient that her lack of feeling good about herself came from her belief that she had been a rotten person. Ellis argued that she could have been role rotten, but not a totally rotten person, and the woman changed her beliefs and started to feel better. It was the patient who concluded that she kept telling herself unavoidable negative sentences so that it was her own sentences that continued to disturb her and not her father, her husband, or her relationship. The patient felt better when she disputed and replaced her own indoctrinating sentences. By the beginning of 1955, then, the theory of rational-emotive therapy had been pretty well formulated.

Excerpted from *Reason and Emotion in Psychotherapy,*
Lyle Stuart, Inc. 1962

Rational-emotive psychotherapy (often called, for short, rational therapy or RT) was born the hard way. My original training as a psychotherapist had been in the field of marriage, family, and sex counseling: where treatment largely consists of helping individuals with specific marital and sexual problems by authoritatively giving them salient information about how to handle each other, how to copulate effectively, how to rear their children, and so on. This kind of therapy seemed to work fairly—and sometimes surprisingly— well. But it had its obvious limitations, since it quickly became clear to me that in most instances disturbed marriages (or premarital relationships) were a product of disturbed spouses; and that if people were truly to be helped to live happily with each other they would first have to be shown how they could live peacefully with themselves.

So I embarked on a course of intensive psychoanalytic training. I had been highly conversant with all of Freud's main works, and with many of those of his chief followers, ever since my early years in college (when I had practically lived in the old Russell Sage Library at 22nd Street and Lexington Avenue, a block away from the downtown branch of the City College of New York, where I was then a student).

Although, from the very start, I had many reservations about Freud's theory of personality (since, even at the age of seventeen, it was not too difficult for me to see that the man was brilliantly *creating* clinical interpretations to make them fit the procrustean bed of his enormously one-sided Oedipal theories), I somehow, perhaps by sheer wishful thinking, retained my belief in the efficacy of orthodox psychoanalytic technique.

I believed, in other words, that though nonanalytic methods of psychotherapy were often helpful and much less time-consuming than classical analytic methods, the latter were indubitably deeper, more penetrating, and hence considerably more curative. So I very willingly underwent an orthodox psychoanalysis myself, with a highly respectable training analyst of the Horney group, who had been a Freudian analyst for twenty-five years prior to his affiliation with the Horney school, and who also had sympathetic leanings toward some of the main Jungian teachings. For all his theoretical eclecticism, however, his analytic technique was almost entirely Freudian; with the result that I spent the next three years on the sofa, with my analyst for the most part sitting silently behind me, while I engaged in free association, brought forth hundreds of dreams to be interpreted, and endlessly discussed the transference connections between my childhood relations with my mother, father, sister, and brother, on the one hand, and my present sex, love, family, professional, and analytic relations on the other.

Both I and my analyst considered my analysis to have been successfully completed; and at his suggestion I went on to complete several control cases: that is, to work, under the supervision of a training analyst, with my own patients, with whom I consistently employed the sofa, free association, extensive dream analysis, and resolution of the transference neurosis. During this period, although I saw some marriage and family counseling clients with whom I did not attempt psychoanalysis, I routinely put all my regular psychotherapy patients on the sofa and proceeded with them in a decidedly orthodox psychoanalytic way.

Unfortunately, the miracle of depth therapy, which I had confidently expected to achieve through this analytic procedure, never quite materialized.

I think that I can confidently say that I was a good young psychoanalyst at this time. Certainly, my patients thought so and kept referring their friends and associates to me. And my therapeutic results were, as far as I could see, at least as good as those of other New York analysts.

Most of my patients stayed in treatment for a considerable period of time (instead of leaving early in the game, as many psychoanalytic patients do); and about 60 per cent of my neurotic patients showed distinct or considerable improvement as a result of being analyzed (Ellis, 1957b). These results, as Glover (1940), Phillips (1956), and other investigators have shown, are better than average for classical psychoanalytic treatment.

I soon had honestly to admit to myself, however, that something was wrong. First of all, on my patients' side, serious resistance to the psychoanalytic method was frequently encountered. Free association, in the true sense of the term, was most difficult for many of my patients to learn; and some of them never really learned to do it effectively. Where some analysands dreamed profusely and had no trouble relating their dreams to me, others rarely dreamed and often forgot what they did dream.

Long, unhelpful silences (sometimes for practically the entire analytic session) would frequently occur, while I (in accordance with classical technique) sat idly by with a limply held pencil. Quite consistently, although I did my best to hold them with their backs rooted to the sofa, patients would want to jump up and pace across the room, or sit up and look at me, or do everything but stare reflectively at the ceiling. Every so often, they would bitterly turn on me, complain that I wasn't doing anything to help them, and say that that was just about all they could stand of this kind of nonsense. I, of course, dutifully and cleverly interpreted that they were, by their refusal to go along peaceably with the analytic rules, resisting the transference relationship and resisting getting better. Often, I convinced them of just that; but I myself more and more wondered.

I also wondered about my own role in the therapeutic process. Interpreting my patients' free associations and dreams, and particularly connecting their present problems with then-past memories, I at first found to be great fun. "Detectiving" I privately called it; and I often thought how lucky I was to be able to be paid for engaging in delightful brain-picking.

Being an old hand at creative writing, I found this kind of true-life detectiving even more enjoyable than figuring out surprise endings to my own or others' stories. When I would convince a patient that he really was angry today not because his boss cursed him or his wife gave him a hard time in bed, but because he actually hated his father or his mother, and was unconsciously getting back at him or her by his present outbursts, and when my patient would excitedly agree: "Yes, that's right! I see it all so clearly now!" I would feel wonderfully pleased and would be absolutely certain that, now that I had supplied him with this brightly shining key to his basic problems, this patient would unquestionably get better in short order.

I soon found, alas, that I had to honestly admit to myself (and sometimes to the patient as well) that I was usually dead wrong about this. For the same individual who just yesterday had screamed in triumph, as he wildly pounded my desk and almost unmoored my lovely alabaster lamp, "You're right! You're absolutely right! I do hate my father. I hate, hate, hate him very much, and have always hated him, even though I never wanted to admit it before, to myself or anyone else. Yes, you're perfectly right!"—this very individual, after his powerfully abreactive insight, and his jubilation over his finally being able to see why he couldn't get up in the morning and go to work, would come in the very next day, and the day after, and the week and the month after, and *still* not be able to get out of bed to go to the office.

Then he would pitifully, desperately ask: "How come? Why is it, Doctor Ellis, that I saw it all so clearly yesterday, and I still see it so clearly today, and I now admit that I really hate the old bastard, and I still can't get out of bed, still haven't changed a bit in my behavior? Why? Why is it?" And I (strictly, still, in the light of psychoanalytic theory, though wondering more and more about the validity of that very therapeutic theory) would be forced to reply: "Yes, I know. You have had some significant insight, and I'm sure it will help you yet. But I guess that you don't *really* see it clearly enough; or there's something else, some other significant insight, that you still don't see, though you probably are approaching seeing it; and if we just keep on patiently, until you *really* see what's troubling you, then you'll be able to get up and go to work in the morning or do anything else which you are now neurotically unable to do."

Usually, again, the patient was reassured (or at least temporarily stopped in his tracks) by these words. But not—no, never entirely—I. I still wondered, wondered. . . .

Other points of classical psychoanalytic technique I also inwardly questioned. Why, when I seemed to know perfectly well what was troubling a patient, did I have to wait passively, perhaps for a few weeks, perhaps for months, until he, by his own interpretive initiative, showed that he was fully "ready" to accept my own insight? Why, when patients bitterly struggled to continue to associate freely, and ended up by saying only a few words in an entire session, was it improper for me to help them with several pointed

psychological theory of behavioristic learning theory, which in turn stems largely from Pavlovian conditioned response theory. This theory holds that, just as Pavlov's dogs had their unconditioned hunger drives thoroughly conditioned to the ringing of a bell by the simple process of the experimenter's ringing this bell in close association with the presentation of food (so that the dogs began to salivate as soon as they heard the bell, before the food was even presented to them), a human being is conditioned early in his life to fear something (such as his father's anger) by threatening or punishing him every time he acts in a certain disapproved manner (for example, masturbates or lusts after his mother).

Since, according to this theory, the individual (like Pavlov's dogs) is *taught* to fear something (such as parental disapproval), and since he was taught to do so when he was very young and didn't even realize what he was learning, the fairly obvious solution to his problem is to show him, in the course of psychoanalytic therapy, exactly what originally transpired. Knowing, therefore, that he has been taught to fear, and also realizing that he is *not* now a child and that he *no longer* needs to fear this same thing (such as, again, parental disapproval), this individual's conditioned fear (or neurosis) presumably will vanish. His insight into the early conditioning process, in other words, will somehow nullify the effects of this process and give him the freedom to recondition himself.

This seemed to me, in my early years as a therapist, a most plausible theory. I became one of those psychologists who thought that a rapprochement between Freudian (or at least neo-Freudian) psychoanalysis and behavioristic learning theory was close at hand, and that everything possible should be done to aid this rapprochement.

Espousal of learning theory helped my therapeutic efforts in at least one significant respect. I began to see that insight alone was not likely to lead an individual to overcome his deep-seated fears and hostilities; he *also* needed a large degree of fear- and hostility-combatting *action*.

I got this idea by extrapolating from Pavlov's *de*conditioning experiments. For when the great Russian psychologist wanted to decondition the same dogs that he had conditioned by ringing a bell just before he fed them every day, he merely kept ringing the same bell, time after time, but *not* feeding them after it rang. After a while, the dogs learned to extinguish their conditioned response—that is, they no longer salivated at the sound of the bell alone.

This kind of deconditioning gave me [and apparently a good many other psychotherapists, such as Salter (1949) and Wolpe (1958)], the idea that if disturbed human beings are continually forced to do the thing they are afraid of (such as be in the same room with an animal or ride in a subway train) they will soon come to see that this thing is *not* as fearful as they erroneously think it to be, and their fear will thereby become deconditioned or extinguished.

So I began to try, as a therapist, not only to show my patients the origins of their fears, and to get them to see that they need no longer fear these things (such as parental rejection) no matter how much they *once* may have appropriately feared them; but also, and just as importantly, I tried to encourage, persuade, and impel them to *do* the things they were afraid of (such as *risking* actual rejection by their parents or others) in order more concretely to *see* that these things were not actually fearsome. Instead of a truly psychoanalytically-oriented psychotherapist, I thereby started to become a much more eclectic, exhortative-persuasive, activity-directive therapist. And I found that this type of therapy, although it still had its definite limitations, was distinctly more successful with most patients than my previous psychoanalytic methods.

Still, however, I kept running into many exasperating situations, known alas to therapists of all hues and stripes, where the patients simply refused to do virtually anything to help themselves, even after they had obviously acquired a remarkably large degree of insight into their disturbances.

One of my notable therapeutic failures, for example, was with a girl who refused to go out of her way to meet new boyfriends, even though she desperately wanted to marry. She knew perfectly well, after scores of sessions of therapy with me and two other highly reputable analysts, that she had been specifically taught to be afraid of strangers (by her overly fearful parents and relatives); that she was terribly afraid of rejection, because she was always told that she was uglier and less lively than her younger married sister; that she was petrified about assuming the responsibilities of marriage which she was certain (largely, again, because of family indoctrinations) that she would not be able to live up to successfully; and that she was over-attached to her father, and didn't want to leave his safe side for the lesser safety of marriage. In spite of all this self-understanding, she still utterly refused to meet new boyfriends and found every possible flimsy excuse to stay at home.

The question which I kept asking myself, as I tried to solve the mystery of the inactivity of this fairly typical patient, was: "Granted that she *once* was taught to be terribly afraid of rejection and responsibility in love and marriage, why should this 33 year old, quite attractive, intelligent girl *still* be just as fearful, even though she has suffered greatly from her fears, has succeeded at several other significant areas of her life, and has had years of classical analysis, psychoanalytically-oriented therapy, and now activity-directive eclectic therapy? How is it possible that she has learned so little, in this sex-love area, and still insists on defeating her own ends *knowing*, now, exactly what she is doing?"

My first answer to this question was in terms of Pavlovian-type conditioning and the normal laws of human inertia. "If," I said to myself, "this patient has been so strongly conditioned to be fearful during her childhood and adolescence, and if she is a human being who normally finds it easier to repeat an old action rather than to learn a new one, why should she *not* remain fearful forever?"

But no, this did not quite make sense: since there *was* a good reason why fear, no matter how strongly it may originally be conditioned, should at least eventually vanish in seriously troubled patients such as this one: namely, lack of pleasurable reinforcement and concomitant amassing of highly unpleasurable punishment. For, according to Pavlovian and behaviorist learning theory, the dog originally becomes conditioned to the sound of the bell when it is rung just before he is fed because *(a)* he naturally or unconditionedly *likes* meat and *(b)* he is reinforced or rewarded by this meat every time he hears the bell. It is not, therefore, the meat *itself* which induces him to respond to the bell which is rung in conjunction with it, but the *rewardingness* of the meat to the dog.

Similarly when the deconditioning experiment is done, and the bell is rung continually without any meat being presented to the dog, it is not the absence of the meat, *per se*, which disturbs the dog and induces it to respond no longer to the bell, but the lack of reward or reinforcement which is attendant upon the absence of the meat.

Presumably, then, human beings should act pretty much the same way as Pavlov's dogs reacted in conditioning and deconditioning experiences. If they are conditioned, early in their lives, to fear or avoid something (such as rejection by their parents), they should theoretically be gradually reconditioned or deconditioned when they find, as the years go by, that the thing they were conditioned to fear really is *not* so terrible. This should especially be true of people with psychological insight: who, once they can consciously tell themselves, "I learned to fear rejection during childhood, but I can see that there is really nothing to fear *now*" should presumably overcome their fear in short order and no longer have to be beset by it.

Unfortunately, cures of intense fears and hostilities rarely occur in this manner. Whether or not people acquire considerable insight into the early origins of their disturbances, they seldom automatically extinguish their fears, even though life experiences continue to show them *(a)* that there really *is* nothing to be afraid of, and *(b)* that as they remain afraid they will acquire and maintain seriously punishing and handicapping neurotic symptoms. In spite of the enormous dysfunctional influences of their early-acquired fears, they still persist in maintaining most inconvenient behavioral consequences of these fears.

Noting this, and noting the dogged way in which so many of my patients kept holding on to their self-sabotaging fears and hostilities, I continued to ask myself: "Why? Why do highly intelligent human beings, including those with considerable psychological insight, desperately hold on to their irrational ideas about themselves and others? Why do they illogically and intensely continue to blame themselves (thus creating anxiety, guilt, and depression) and unforgivingly blame others (thus creating grandiosity, hostility, and resentment) even when they get such poor results from these two kinds of blaming?"

Finally, in 1954, I began to put all my psychological and philosophical knowledge together in a somewhat different way than I had previously done and started to come up with what seemed to be a good part of the answer to these important questions. Human beings, I began to see, are not the same as Pavlovian dogs or other lower animals; and their emotional disturbances are quite different from the experimental neuroses and other emotional upsets which we produce in the laboratory in rats, guinea pigs, dogs, sheep, and other animals. For human beings have one attribute which none of the other living beings that we know have in any well-developed form: language and the symbol-producing facility that goes with language (Cassirer, 1953; Whorf, 1956). They are able to communicate with others and (perhaps more importantly, as far as neurosis and psychosis are concerned) with themselves in a manner that is infinitely more complex and variegated than is the signaling of other animals.

This makes all the difference in the world, I was soon able to see. For, whereas the Pavlovian dog is obviously able to signal himself on some rudimentary level, once the bell is rung in juxtaposition with the meat that he enjoys eating, and to convince himself that the sound of the bell equals eating time (and, in the extinguishing process, that the sound of the bell *without* the presentation of food equals non-eating time), his self-signaling tends to be very limited and largely to be at the mercy of *outside* circumstances.

It is relatively easy for the experimenter, therefore, to show the dog that under condition *b* (presentation of the bell without the food) it is wise for him to stop salivating. It is less easy, but still possible, for the experimenter to show the dog that under condition *a* (presentation of food with a noxious stimulus, such as a painful electric shock) it is wise for him to avoid eating, while under condition *b* (presentation of food without any noxious stimulus) it is better for him to resume eating again. This is presumably because the dog's self-signaling processes are fairly rudimentary or primary and he doesn't have what Pavlov called the complex or secondary signaling processes which man, alone of all the animals, seems to have. Consequently, it is easy for him to make the simple equations: food plus electric shock equals *avoid eating*, and food minus electric shock equals *eat*.

As soon, however, as man's complex or secondary self-signaling processes arise, a new factor comes into play that may enormously change the simple going-toward or avoidance equations made by lower animals. This factor may be called self-consciousness or thinking *about* thinking.

Thus, the Pavlovian dog may signal himself: "This meat is good," and he may go toward it or salivate in connection with it. Or he may signal himself: "This meat plus this electric shock is bad," and he may avoid the meat plus the shock. He probably never, however, signals himself, as a human being may well do: "I am aware (conscious) that I am thinking that this meat is good" or "I can see (understand) that I am telling myself that this meat plus the electric shock is bad and I'd better stay away from it."

The dog perceives and to some degree thinks about things outside himself (the meat and the electric shock) and even about himself (his own preferences for the meat or annoyance at being shocked). But he does not, to our knowledge, think about his thinking or perceive his own mental processes. Consequently, he has little ability to *define* external stimuli as good or bad and is largely limited to his concrete pleasant or noxious *sensations* about these stimuli.

The dog, in other words, seems to be telling himself (or, more accurately, signaling himself, since he does not have our kind of language) something along the line of: "Because this food *tastes* good, I like it and shall keep going toward it," and "Because this food plus this electric shock *feels* bad, I dislike it and shall keep avoiding it." He regulates his behavior largely because his *sensations* are reinforced (rewarded) or punished.

A human being, on the other hand, can be rewarded or punished by his sensations, and can accordingly draw conclusions about going toward or avoiding certain situations; but, more importantly, he can *also* be rewarded or punished by all kinds of symbolic, non-sensate processes, such as smiles, critical phrases, medals, demerits, etc., which have little or no connection with his sensing processes. And he can also be rewarded or punished by his *own* thinking, even when this thinking is largely divorced from outside reinforcements and penalties.

A man, for example, may force himself to volunteer for service in the armed forces, which he may ardently dislike and consider very dangerous (especially in wartime), because he feels that, even though his friends or associates will not literally harm him in any way if he refuses to enlist (that is, they will not boycott him, fire him from his job, or actually punish him with any noxious stimuli), they will *think* he is unpatriotic and will (silently and covertly) *feel* that he is not as good as are enlisted men. Although, in a case like this, there are actually very few and minor disadvantages (and probably several major advantages) for this man's staying out of the armed forces, he will *define* or *create* several huge "penalties" for his doing so, and will either drive himself to enlist or refrain from enlisting but force himself to be exceptionally guilty and self-hating about his not enlisting.

Similarly, although a woman's parents may be living thousands of miles away from her and have little or no contact with her, or although they may actually be deceased, she may force herself to be terribly guilty and unhappy over some of her behavior (or even contemplated behavior), such as her having premarital sex relations, because if her parents *were* at hand they probably *would* disapprove of her actions (or thoughts), even though they quite probably would take no overt actions against her performing these acts (or thinking these thoughts).

Here, especially, we have a clear-cut case in which an act (fornication) has no actual disadvantages (assuming that the woman and her current friends and associates disagree with her parents and do approve of the act), and probably has considerable advantages; and yet this woman fearfully refrains from the act (or performs it with intense guilt) because she essentially *defines* it (or her absent or dead parents' reaction to it) as reprehensible.

Dogs, in other words, fear real noxious stimuli, while human beings fear *imagined* or *defined* as well as real unpleasant stimuli. To some degree, it is true, lower animals can imagine or define the obnoxiousness of a situation. Thus, as Skinner (1953) has shown, pigeons and other animals can become "superstitious" and can fear a certain corner of a cage (or of similar cages) because they were *once* punished in that corner, even though they thereafter receive no punishment in this situation. Even in these instances, however, the pigeon *once* had to be concretely punished; and it now avoids the situation in which it was punished because of overgeneralization, rather than by pure definition.

Humans, however, merely have to be *told* that it is horrible or awful for others to disapprove of them; and they easily, without any real noxious evidence to back this propaganda, can come to believe what they are told;

and, through this very belief, *make* disapproval thoroughly unpleasant to themselves.

Still another way of expressing the main point I am trying to make here is to say that lower animals can easily be conditioned to fear physically punishing effects, and through their physical fears also learn (in the case of some intelligent animals, such as dogs) to fear others' gestures and words (as a dog first fears being punished for doing something and then learns to dread a scowling look from his master when he does this same thing, even though he is not always directly punished for doing it).

Man, in addition to being deterred by physical punishment and by the words and gestures of others that signify that such punishment is likely to follow, also deters himself by *(a)* heeding the negative words and gestures of others even when these are *not* accompanied by any kind of direct physical punishment, and by *(b)* heeding his *own* negative words and gestures about the possible negative words and gestures of others (or of some hypothetical gods). Man, therefore, often becomes fearful of *purely* verbal or other signaling processes; while lower animals never seem to be able to become similarly fearful. And human neuroses, in consequence, are qualitatively different from animal neuroses in some respects, even though they may overlap with animal disturbances in certain other respects.

To return to my patients. I began clearly to see, during the year 1954, that they not only learned, from their parents and other people and means of mass communication in our society, to fear words, thoughts, and gestures of others (in addition to fearing sensory punishments that might be inflicted on them by these others), but that they also were able, because of their facility with language (or their ability to talk to others *and* themselves), to fear their *own* self-signalings and self-talk.

With these uniquely human abilities to fear others' and their own gestures and verbal communications, the patients were beautifully able to *imagine* or *define* fears that actually had no basis in physical or sensory punishment. In fact, virtually all their neurotic fears were defined fears: that is, anxieties that were originally defined to them by others and then later carried on as their *own* definitions. More specifically, they were first told that it was terrible, horrible, and awful if they were unloved or disapproved; and they then kept *telling themselves* that being rejected or unapproved was frightful. This twice-*told* tale, in the great majority of instances, constituted their neuroses.

What both the Freudians and the behaviorist-conditioning psychologists are misleadingly doing, I clearly began to see, is to leave out a great deal of the *telling* or *language* aspects or human neurosis. Not entirely, of course: for they both tacitly, if not too explicitly, admit that children are told, in one way or another, by their parents and other early teachers, that they are worthless and hopeless if they say or do the wrong things (especially, lust after their mothers or hate their fathers); and that they thereby acquire too strong consciences or (to use a Freudian term) superegos and therefore become disturbed.

While admitting, however, that philosophies of life that are language-inculcated have *some* neurosis-producing power, the classical psychoanalysts and the conditionists also stress the supposedly nonverbal or subcortical early influences on the child and often seem to think that these "nonverbal" influences are even more important factors in creating emotional disturbance than are language indoctrinations. In this, I am quite convinced, they are wrong: as the limitations of the kind of therapy they espouse partially seem to indicate.

More to the point, however, even when Freudians and conditionists seem fully to admit the enormous influence of verbal indoctrinations in the *creation* of neurosis [as, for example, Dollard and Miller (1950) clearly admit], they almost all sadly fail as scientists and clinicians when it comes to admitting the exceptionally important influence of verbal self-indoctrinations in the *maintenance* of emotional disturbance. And this, as I saw when I did both classical psychoanalysis and psychoanalytically-oriented psychotherapy, has even direr consequences for their therapeutic effectiveness.

For, as Bernheim (1887), Coué (1923), and many other psychological practitioners have seen for at least the last 75 years, man is not only a highly suggestible but an unusually *auto*suggestible animal. And probably the main reason, I would insist, why he *continues* to believe most of the arrant nonsense with which he is indoctrinated during his childhood is not merely the influence of human laws of mental inertia (which quite possibly serve to induce lower animals to keep repeating the same dysfunctional mistake over and over again), but because he very actively and energetically keeps verbally reindoctrinating himself with his early-acquired hogwash.

Thus, a child in our culture not only becomes guilty about lusting after his mother because he is quite forcefully taught that anyone who behaves in that manner is thoroughly blameworthy; but he also *remains* forever guilty about this kind of lusting because *(a)* he *keeps* hearing and reading about its assumed heinousness, and *(b)* he *continues* to tell himself, every time he has an incestuous thought, "Oh, my God I *am* a blackguard for thinking this horrible way." Even if *a* were no longer true—if this child grew up and went to live in a community where incest was thought to be a perfectly fine and proper act—the chances are that, for many years of his life and perhaps to the end of his days, *b* would still hold true, and he would keep thinking of himself as a worthless lout every time he had an incestuous idea.

This is what I continued to see more and more clearly, as I worked my way from psychoanalytically-oriented toward rational-emotive psychotherapy: that my patients were not *merely* indoctrinated with irrational, mistaken ideas of their own worthlessness when they were very young, but that they then inertly or automatically kept hanging on to these early ideas during their adulthood. Much more to the point: they (as *human* beings normally will) most actively-directively *kept* reindoctrinating themselves with the original hogwash, over and over again, and thereby creatively *made* it live on and on and become an integral part of their basic philosophies of life.

This energetic, forcible hanging on to their early-acquired irrationalities was usually something that they did unwittingly, unawarely, or unconsciously—though not always, since sometimes they quite consciously kept repeating to themselves the "truth" of the nonsense they had originally imbibed from their associates and their society. But consciously or unconsciously, wittingly or unwittingly, they definitely *were* making themselves, literally forcing themselves, to continue believing in many unrealistic, purely definitional notions; and *that* was why they not only remained neurotic in spite of the great disadvantages of so being, but why they also so effectively resisted my (or any other therapist's) best efforts, and also resisted their own efforts, to give up their neuroses.

I had finally, then, at least to my own satisfaction, solved the great mystery of why so many millions of human beings not only originally became emotionally disturbed, but why they persistently, in the face of so much self-handicapping, remained so. The very facility with language which enabled them to be essentially human—to talk to others and to talk to themselves—also enabled them to abuse this facility by talking utter nonsense to themselves: to *define* things as terrible when, at worst, these things were inconvenient and annoying.

In particular, their talking and their self-talking abilities permitted people to forget that their real needs, or necessities for human survival, were invariably of a physical or sensory nature—that is, consisted of such demands as the need for sufficient food, fluids, shelter, health, and freedom from physical pain—and permitted them illegitimately to translate their psychological *desires*—such as the desires for love, approval, success, and leisure—into *definitional needs*. Then, once they defined their desires or preferences as necessities, or accepted the false definitions of their parents or others in this connection, their self-talking abilities beautifully enabled them to *continue* to define their "needs" in this nonsensical manner, even though they had no supporting evidence to back their definitions.

Still more precisely: I discovered clinically, when I realized how important talk and self-talk was to neurotics and psychotics, that a disturbed individual almost invariably takes his preference to be loved or approved by others (which is hardly insane, since there usually *are* concrete advantages to others' approving him) and arbitrarily defines and keeps defining this preference as a dire need. Thereby, he inevitably becomes anxious, guilty, depressed, or otherwise self-hating: since there is absolutely no way, in this highly realistic world in which we live, that he can thereafter *guarantee* that he *will* be devotedly loved or approved by others.

By the same token, a disturbed person almost invariably takes his preference for ruling others, or getting something for nothing, or living in a perfectly just world (which again are perfectly legitimate desires, if only one could possibly achieve them) and *demands* that others and the universe accede to his desires. Thereby, he inevitably becomes hostile, angry, resentful, and grandiose. Without human talk and self-talk, *some* degree of anxiety and hostility might well exist; but never, I realized, the extreme and intense degrees of these feelings which constitute emotional disturbance.

Once I had clearly begun to see that neurotic behavior is not merely externally conditioned or indoctrinated at an early age, but that it is also internally reindoctrinated or autosuggested by the individual to himself, over and over again, until it becomes an integral part of his presently held (and still continually self-reiterated) philosophy of life, my work with my patients took on a radically new slant.

Where I had previously tried to show them how they had originally become disturbed and what they most actively now do to counter their early-acquired upsets, I saw that I had been exceptionally vague in these regards: and that, still misled by Freudian-oriented theories, I had been stressing psychodynamic rather than philosophic causation, and had been emphasizing what to undo rather than what to un*say* and un*think*. I had been neglecting (along with virtually all other therapists of the day) the precise, simple declarative and exclamatory sentences which the patients once told themselves in creating their disturbances and which, even more importantly, they were *still* specifically telling themselves literally every day in the week to maintain these same disturbances.

Let me give a case illustration. I had, at this period of my psychotherapeutic practice, a thirty-seven year-old female patient whom I had been seeing for two years and who had made considerable progress, but who remained on a kind of therapeutic plateau after making this progress. When she first came to therapy she had been fighting continually with her husband, getting along poorly at her rather menial office job, and paranoidly believing that the whole world was against her. It quickly became clear, in the course of the first few weeks of therapy, that her parents (both of whom were rather paranoid themselves) had literally taught her to be suspicious of others and to demand a good living from the world, whether or not she worked for this living. They had also convinced her that unless she catered to their whims and did almost everything in the precise manner of which they approved, she was ungrateful and incompetent.

With this kind of upbringing, it was hardly surprising that my patient thought that her husband never really did anything for her and that, at the same time, she herself was essentially worthless and undeserving of having any good in life. She was shown, in the course of psychoanalytic-eclectic therapy, that she had been thoroughly indoctrinated with feelings of her own inadequacy by her parents (and by the general culture in which she lived). She was specifically helped to see that she was demanding from her husband the kind of unequivocal acceptance that she had *not* got from her father; and that, after railing at him for not loving her enough, she usually became terribly guilty, just as she had become years before when she hated and resisted her parents when she thought they were expecting too much from her.

Not only was this patient shown the original sources of her hostility toward her husband and her continual self-depreciation, but she was also encouraged to actively decondition herself in these respects. Thus, she was given the "homework" assignments of *(a)* trying to understand her husband's point of view and to act toward him as if he were not her father, but an independent person in his own right, and of *(b)* attempting to do her best in her work at the office, and risking the possibility that she might still fail and might have to face the fact that she wasn't the best worker in the world and that some of the complaints about her work were justified.

The patient, in a reasonably earnest manner, did try to employ her newly found insights and to do her psychotherapeutic "homework"; and, during the first six months of therapy, she did significantly improve, so that she fought much less with her husband and got her first merit raise for doing better on her job. Still, however, she retained the underlying beliefs that she really was a worthless individual and that almost everyone with whom she came into contact recognized this fact and soon began to take undue advantage of her. No amount of analyzing her present difficulties, or of tracing them back to their correlates in her past, seemed to free her of this set of basic beliefs.

Feeling, somehow, that the case was not hopeless, and that there must be *some* method of showing this patient that her self-deprecatory and paranoid beliefs were ill-founded, I persisted in trying for a therapeutic breakthrough. And suddenly, as I myself began to see things rather differently, this long-sought breakthrough occurred.

The following dialogue with the patient gives an idea of what happened. Like the other excerpts from actual sessions included in this book, it is slightly abridged, grammatically clarified, and cleared of all identifying data. Verbatim transcripts, though giving more of a flavor of what happens in therapy, have been found to be unwieldy, discursive, and (unless carefully annotated) somewhat unclear. A subsequent *Casebook of Rational-Emotive Psychotherapy* will include verbatim transcripts, with considerably more annotation than there is space for in the present volume.

"So you still think," I said to the patient (for perhaps the hundredth time), "that you're no damned good and that no one could possibly fully accept you and be on your side?"

"Yes, I have to be honest and admit that I do. I know it's silly, as you keep showing me that it is, to believe this. But I still believe it; and nothing seems to shake my belief."

"Not even the fact that you've been doing so much better, for over a year now, with your husband, your associates at the office, and some of your friends?"

"No, not even that. I know I'm doing better, of course, and I'm sure it's because of what's gone on here in these sessions. And I'm pleased and grateful to you. But I still feel basically the same way—that there's something really rotten about me, something I can't do anything about, and that the others are able to see. And I don't know what to do about this feeling."

"But this 'feeling,' as you call it, is only your belief—do you see that?"

"How can my feeling just be a belief? I really—uh—feel it. That's all I can describe it as, a feeling."

"Yes, but you feel it *because* you believe it. If you believed, for example, really believed you were a fine person, in spite of all the mistakes you have made and may still make in life, and in spite of anyone else, such as your parents, thinking that you were not so fine; if you really *believed* this, would you then feel fundamentally rotten?"

"—Uh. Hmm. No, I guess you're right; I guess I then wouldn't feel that way."

"All right. So your feeling that you are rotten or no good is really a belief, a very solid even if not too well articulated belief, that you are just no good, even though you are now doing well and your husband and your business associates have been showing, more than ever before, that they like you well enough."

"Well, let's suppose you are right, and it is a belief behind, and—uh— causing my feelings. How can I rid myself of this belief?"

"How can you *sustain* it?"

"Oh, very well, I'm sure. For I do sustain it. I have for years, according to you."

"Yes, but what's the *evidence* for sustaining it? How can you *prove* that you're really rotten, no good?"

"Do I have to prove it to myself? Can't I just accept it without proving it?"

"Exactly! That's exactly what you're doing, and have doubtlessly been doing for years—accepting this belief, this perfectly groundless belief in your own 'rottenness,' without any proof whatever, without any evidence behind it."

"But how *can* I keep accepting it if, as you say, there is no proof behind it?"

"You can keep accepting it because—" At this point I was somewhat stumped myself, but felt that if I persisted in talking it out with this patient, and avoided the old psychoanalytic clichés, which had so far produced no real answer to this often-raised question, I might possibly stumble on some answer for my *own*, as well as my patient's, satisfaction. So I stubbornly went on: "—because, well, you're human."

"Human? What has that got to do with it?"

"Well—" I still had no real answer, but somehow felt that one was lurking right around the corner of the collaborative thinking of the patient and myself. "That's just the way humans are, I guess. They *do* doggedly hold to groundless beliefs when they haven't got an iota of evidence with which to back up these beliefs. Millions of people, for example, believe wholeheartedly and dogmatically in the existence of God when, as Hume, Kant, and many other first-rate philosophers have shown, they can't possibly ever prove (or, for that matter, disprove) His existence. But that hardly stops them from fervently believing."

"You think, then, that I believe in the 'truth' of my own rottenness, just about in the same way that these people believe in the 'truth' of God, without any evidence whatever to back our beliefs?"

"*Don't* you? And aren't they—the theory of God and of your own rottenness—really the same kind of definitional concepts?"

"Definitional?"

"Yes. You start with an axiom or hypothesis, such as: 'Unless I do perfectly well in life, I am worthless.' Or, in your case, more specifically: 'In order to be good, I must be a fine, self-sacrificing daughter, wife, and mother.' Then you look at the facts, and quickly see that you are not doing perfectly well in life—that you are not the finest, most self-sacrificing daughter, wife, and mother who ever lived. Then you conclude: 'Therefore, I am no good—in fact, I am rotten and worthless.'"

"Well, doesn't that conclusion follow from the facts?"

"No, not at all! It follows almost entirely from your definitional premises. And, in a sense, there are no facts at all in your syllogism, since all your 'evidence' is highly biased by these premises."

"But isn't it a fact that I am *not* a fine, self-sacrificing daughter, wife, and mother?"

"No, not necessarily. For, actually, you may well be as good a daughter to your parents as most women are; in fact, you may be considerably better than most in this respect. But your premise says that in order to be good, you must be practically *perfect*. And, in the light of this premise, even the fact of how good a daughter you are will inevitably be distorted, and you will be almost bound to conclude that you are a 'poor' daughter when, in actual fact, you may be a better than average one."

"So there are no real facts at all in my syllogism?"

"No, there aren't. But even, if there were—even, for example, if you were not even an average daughter or wife—your syllogism would still be entirely tautological: since it merely 'proves' what you originally postulated in your premise; namely, that if you are not perfect, you are worthless. Consequently, your so-called worthlessness or rottenness, is entirely definitional and has no existence in fact."

"Are all disturbances, such as mine, the same way?"

"Yes, come to think of it—" And, suddenly, I *did* come to think of it myself, as I was talking with this patient, "—all human disturbances seem to be of the same definitional nature. We *assume* that it is horrible if something is so—if, especially, we are imperfect or someone else is not acting in the angelic way that we think he *should* act. Then, after making this assumption, we literally *look* for the 'facts' to prove our premise. And invariably, of course, we find these 'facts'—find that we *are* or someone else *is* behaving very badly. Then we 'logically' conclude that we were right in the first place, and that the 'bad' behavior we found conclusively 'proves' our original assumption. But the only real or at least unbiased 'facts' in this 'logical' chain we are thereby constructing are our own starting premises—the sentences we tell ourselves to begin with."

"Would you say, then," my patient asked, "that I literally tell myself certain unvalidated sentences, and that my disturbance stems directly from these, my own, sentences?"

"Yes," I replied with sudden enthusiasm. "You give me an idea, there. I had not quite thought of it that way before, although I guess I really had, without putting it in just those terms, since I said to you just a moment ago that it is the sentences we tell ourselves to begin with that start the ball of definitional premises, semi-definitional 'facts,' and false conclusions rolling. But, anyway, whether it's your idea or mine, it seems to be true: that every human being who gets disturbed really is telling himself a chain of false sentences—since that is the way that humans seem almost invariably to think, in words, phrases, and sentences. And it is these sentences which really *are*, which *constitute* his neuroses."

"Can you be more precise? What are my own exact sentences, for instance?"

"Well, let's see. I'm sure we can quickly work them out. You start by listening, of course, to the sentences of others, mainly of your parents. And their sentences are, as we have gone over many times here, 'Look, dear, unless you love us dearly, in an utterly self-sacrificing way, you're no good, and people will find out that you're no good, and they won't love you, and that would be terrible, terrible, terrible.'"

"And I listen to these sentences of my parents, told to me over and over again, and make them mine—is that it?"

"Yes, you make them yours. And not only their precise, overt sentences, of course, but their gestures, voice intonations, critical looks, and so on. These also have significant meaning for you: since you *turn them*, in your own head, into phrases and sentences. Thus, when your mother says, 'Don't do that, dear!' in an angry or demanding tone of voice, you translate it into, 'Don't do that, dear—or I won't love you if you do, and everyone else will think you're no good and won't love you, and that would be terrible!'"

"So when my parents tell me I'm no good, by word or by gesture, I quickly say to myself: 'They're right. If I don't love them dearly and don't sacrifice myself to them, I'm no good, and everyone will see I'm no good, and nobody will accept me, and that will be awful!'"

"Right. And it is these phrases or sentences of yours that create your *feeling* of awfulness—*create* your guilt and your neurosis."

"But how? What exactly is there about my own sentences that creates my awful feeling? What is the false part of these sentences?"

"'The last part, usually. For the first part, very often, may be true. The first part, remember, is something along the lines of: 'If I don't completely love my parents and sacrifice myself for them, many people or some people, including my parents, will probably think that I'm a bad daughter—that I'm no good.' And this part of your sentences may very well be true."

"Many people, including my parents, *may* really think that I'm no good for acting this way—is that what you mean?"

"Yes. They actually may. So your *observation* that if you are not a perfect daughter various people, especially your parents, won't approve of you, and will consider you worthless, is probably a perfectly sound and valid observation. But that isn't what does you the damage. It's the rest of your phrases and sentences that do the damage."

"You mean the part where I say 'Because many people may not approve of me for being an imperfect daughter, I *am* no good'?"

"Exactly. If many people, even all people, think that you're not a perfect daughter, and that you *should* be a perfect daughter, that may well be their true belief or feeling—but what has it really got to do with what *you* have to believe? How does being an imperfect daughter *make* you, except in *their* eyes, worthless? Why, even if it is true that you are such an imperfect child to your parents, is it *terrible* that you are imperfect? And why is it *awful* if many people will not approve of you if you are a poor daughter?"

"I don't have to believe I'm awful just because *they* believe it? I can accept myself as being imperfect, even if it is true that I am, without thinking that this is awful?"

"Yes. Unless your *definition* of 'awful' and 'worthless' becomes the same as *their* definition. And that, of course, is exactly what's happening when you get upset about your parents' and others' view of you. You are then *making* their definition of you *your* definition. You are *taking* their sentences and making them your own. And it is this highly creative, *self*-defining act on your part which manufactures your disturbance."

"I have the theoretical choice, then, of taking their definition of me as worthless, because I am an imperfect daughter, and accepting it or rejecting it. And if I accept it, I make their definition mine, and I upset myself."

"Yes, you illogically upset yourself."

"But why illogically, necessarily? Can't they be right about my being an imperfect daughter making me worthless?"

"No—only, again, by definition. Because, obviously, not every set of parents who have an imperfect daughter considers her worthless. *Some* parents feel that their daughter is quite worthwhile, even when she does not completely sacrifice herself for them. Your parents obviously don't think so and make or define your worth in terms of how much you do for them. They are, of course, entitled to define you in such a way. But their concept of you is definition; and it is only tautologically valid."

"You mean there is no absolute way of proving, if they consider me worthless for not being sufficiently self-sacrificing, that I actually am worthless?"

"Right. Even if everyone in the world agreed with them that your being insufficiently self-sacrificing equaled your being worthless, that would still be everyone's definition; and you still would not *have* to accept it. But of course, as we have just noted, it is highly improbable that everyone in the world would agree with them—which proves all the more how subjective their definition of your worth is."

"And even if they and everyone else agreed that I *was* worthless for being imperfectly interested in their welfare, that would still not mean that I would have to accept this definition?"

"No, certainly not. For even if they were right about your being worthless to *them* when you were not utterly self-sacrificing—and it is of course their prerogative to value you little when you are not doing what they would want you to do—there is no connection whatever, unless you *think* there is one, between your value to them and your value to yourself. *You* can be perfectly good, to and for yourself, even though they think you perfectly bad to and for them."

"That sounds all very well and fine. But let's get back to my specific sentences and see how it works out there."

"Yes, you're quite right. Because it's those specific sentences that you have to change to get better. As we said before, your main sentences to yourself are: 'Because they think I am worthless for not being utterly self-sacrificing to them, they are right. It *would* be terrible if they continue to think this of me and don't thoroughly approve of me. So I'd better be more self-sacrificing—or else hate myself if I am not.'"

"And I have got to change those sentences to—?"

"Well, quite obviously you have got to change them to: 'Maybe they are right about *their* thinking I am worthless if I am not a much more self-sacrificing daughter, but what has that really got to do with *my* estimation of myself? *Would* it really be terrible if they continue to think this way about me? *Do* I need their approval that much? *Should* I have to keep hating myself if I am not more self-sacrificing?'"

"And by changing these sentences, my own versions of and belief in *their* sentences, I can definitely change my feelings of guilt and worthlessness and get better?"

"Why don't you try it and see?"

This patient did keep looking at her own sentences and did try to change them. And within several weeks of the foregoing conversation, she improved far more significantly than she had done in the previous two years I had been seeing her. "I really seem to have got it now!" she reported two months later. "Whenever I find myself getting guilty or upset, I immediately tell myself that there *must* be some silly sentence that I am saying to myself to cause this upset; and almost immediately, usually within literally a few minutes of my starting to look for it, I find this sentence. And, just as you have been showing me, the sentence invariably takes the form of 'Isn't it terrible that—' or 'Wouldn't it be awful if—' And when I closely look at and question these sentences, and ask myself '*How* is it really terrible that—?' or '*Why* would it actually be awful if—?' I always find that it isn't terrible or wouldn't be awful, and I get over being upset very quickly. In fact, as you predicted a few weeks ago, as I keep questioning and challenging my own sentences, I begin to find that they stop coming up again and again, as they used to do before. Only occasionally, now, do I start to tell myself that something would be terrible or awful if it occurred, or something else is frightful because it has occurred. And on those relatively few occasions, as I just said, I can quickly go after the 'terribleness' or the 'awfulness' that I am dreaming up, and factually or logically re-evaluate it and abolish it. I can hardly believe it, but I seem to be getting to the point, after so many years of worrying over practically everything and thinking I was a slob no matter what I did, of now finding that *nothing* is so terrible or awful, and I now seem to be recognizing this in *advance* rather than *after* I have seriously upset myself. Boy, what a change that is in my life! I am really getting to be, with these new attitudes, an entirely different sort of person than I was."

True to her words, this woman's behavior mirrored her new attitudes. She acted much better with her husband and child and enjoyed her family relationship in a manner that she had never thought she would be able to do. She quit her old job and got a considerably better paying and more satisfying one. She not only stopped being concerned about her parents' opinion of her, but started calmly to help them to get over some of their own negative ideas toward themselves, each other, and the rest of the world. And, best of all, she really stopped caring, except for limited practical purposes, what other people thought of her, lost her paranoid ideas about their being against her, and began to consider herself worthwhile even when she made clear-cut errors and when others brought these to her attention in a disapproving manner.

As these remarkable changes occurred in this patient, and I began to get somewhat similar (though not always as excellent) results with several other patients, the principles of rational-emotive psychotherapy began to take clearer form; and, by the beginning of 1955, the basic theory and practice of RT was fairly well formulated.

Since that time, much more clinical experience has been had by me and some of my associates who soon began to employ RT techniques; and the original principles have been corrected, expanded, and reworked in many significant respects. RT theory is by no means static and continues to grow—as any good theory doubtlessly should. Struck with the proselytizing bug, I also began to write a good many papers and give a number of talks on RT, mainly to professional audiences; so that now a number of other therapists espouse the system or have incorporated parts of it into their own psychotherapeutic methods.

Much opposition to RT has also been expressed during the past few years, sometimes by those who do not seem to understand fully what it is, and who accuse rational therapists of believing in and doing all kinds of things in which they are not in the least interested. Others, who better understand RT, oppose it because they say that its theories sound plausible and that perhaps they work clinically, but that there is no experimental or other scientific evidence to support them.

To satisfy this latter group of critics, many of whose points are entirely justified and should be answered with attested fact rather than more theory, I have been gathering a mass of experimental, physiological, and other scientific evidence and will eventually present this as at least partial validation of the basic RT theories. There has proven to be, however, so much of this confirmatory material available, that it will take some time yet to collate it and to present it in a series of theoretical-scientific volumes.

In the meantime, many clinicians who admittedly do not understand RT and who would very much like to do so have kept asking for a book that would summarize and go beyond the papers on the subject that have already been published in the professional literature. It is mainly for these readers that the present book has been written. In this book, I have made an attempt to gather some of the most important papers and talks on RT that I have written and delivered during the past five years and to present them in a fairly integrated way.

The materials in the present volume, then, are *not* intended to be an adequate substitute for those which will ultimately appear in a series of more definitive volumes on RT. The pages of this book only briefly outline the theory of rational-emotive psychotherapy and make no attempt to bolster it scientifically. They do try to present the clinician with some of the main clinical applications of the theory and to enable him (on partial faith, if you will) to try these applications on some of his own counselees or patients. By so doing, he may get some indication of the potential validity of RT. But it must of course always be remembered, in this connection, that no matter how well a theory of therapy works in practice, and no matter how many improved or "cured" patients insist that they have been benefited by it, the theory itself may still be of unproven efficacy, since something quite different in the patient-therapist relationship (or in some outside aspect of the patient's life) may have been the real curative agent.

In any event, rational-emotive psychotherapy has, in even the few brief years of its existence, so far proven to be a highly intriguing and seemingly practical theory and method. It is hoped that the publication of this introductory manual will bring it to the attention of many more individuals than those who are now conversant with its approach and that it will spur discussion and experimentation that will help develop its principles and its applications.

CHAPTER 2

RECOGNIZING AND ATTACKING
NEUROTIC BEHAVIOR

EDITOR'S COMMENTARY:

This chapter comes from Ellis and Harper's A Guide to Rational Living. In an original (1961) and revised text (New Guide to Rational Living, 1975), Robert Harper, a very well-known psychologist from Washington, DC, joined Ellis in another of their ventures to popularize rational-emotive psychotherapy. The text itself has an introduction that explains E-Prime Language. Korzybski, an instructor at the University of Florida, noted that when students were upset or under too much stress that was not facilitative, they did not earn grades up to their academic potential. Korzybski asked one group of students to eliminate the infinitive and verb forms of to be *from their vocabulary, whereas a second group continued to use "I am," "You are," "They are" statements as usual. For example, instead of saying, "I am depressed," a student was asked to eliminate that emotionally-primed verb and to say something else, such as, "I feel depressed when . . .," or "I tend to make myself depressed about . . ." To use the infinitive* to be *means that a person is born that way, so that "is" or "are" statements mean that the negative emotion is part of one's human nature by birth instead of the negative emotion having been learned. Korzybski showed that students who did not generalize by using that infinitive to be increased in their performance by one full letter grade (e.g., from a 2.0 to a 3.0 GPA on a 4.0 scale).*

Concerning this chapter on recognizing and attacking neuroses, the authors started with two case vignettes, one about a dental student who wanted to drop his courses, and a second about a promiscuous female who condemned herself. Freud saw neurosis as an imbalance in the dynamics or interaction between id (native biology), superego (culture and society's rules) and ego (human ability to balance id demands with superego constraints). Contrarily, Ellis and Harper saw neurosis as stupid behavior by people who were not stupid. Simply, people kept repeating the same behavior with the hope of achieving a different result. To undermine preceding or activating events, Ellis and Harper explicated three levels of insight—that concept itself having come from depth therapy. Further, they summarized each case using a syllogism, a form of stating a problem as had been done originally by Aristotle. An example would be the faulty conclusion from the syllogism, Children learn from their parents who could have been disturbed; I have learned from my parents; therefore, I am disturbed (not only a faulty conclusion, but also a faulty generalization that violated the teachings of Korzybski). The authors also gave attention to self-downing, or rating total self as a result of some performance issue. They offered alternative statements instead of self-rating statements, these last which they judged to be not only neurotic but potentially emotionally immobilizing since a person was questioning his or her very being or right to exist. The chapter concluded with two themes: Ellis and Harper returned to their then strong suit of working with a couple and using rational-emotive techniques, and a vignette within the chapter by Robert Moore. Moore presented work with a couple where one spouse blamed the other with the familiar but erroneous, "you caused me to feel the way I did." The example Moore presented reinforced rational-emotive theory and therapy to achieve positive results.

Excerpted from *New Guide to Rational Living,*
Wilshire Books,
1961 & 1975

Clear thinking, we contend, leads to appropriate emoting. Stupidity, ignorance, and disturbance block straight thinking and result in serious degrees of over- or underemotionalizing. When people function inhibitedly or practically foaming at the mouth, and when they do *not* appear stupid, we usually call them neurotic. Let us consider a couple of examples.

A twenty-two-year-old male says that he does not want to finish his dental training because he dislikes some of his subjects and has a difficult time studying them. In consequence, he concludes, he would just as soon go into business.

When we probe his motivations more deeply, we soon discover that he really would like dentistry but fights it because (1) his parents keep pressuring him to finish school and he loathes their pressuring; (2) he doesn't get along too well with his classmates and feels unpopular; and (3) he doubts that he has the manual dexterity and manipulative ability required of a good dentist.

This individual keeps sabotaging his own desires because he has no insight into, or seems ignorant of, his basic, unconscious motives. He starts with the conscious premise that he "naturally" dislikes certain of his subjects. But after some direct questioning (one of the main techniques of rational-emotive therapy) he quickly admits (first to the therapist and, more importantly, to himself) that he terribly fears domination by his parents, failing to win the esteem of his classmates, and ultimately failing as a dentist. His "natural" dislike for some of his subjects stems, therefore, from his highly "unnatural" underlying philosophy: "Oh, my Lord! What a weak poltroon I will always remain if I do not achieve outstanding independence, popularity, and competence!"

When, in the course of RET, this individual understands his rational beliefs; and when, perhaps more importantly, he questions and challenges these fears, he usually decides to return to school and to work through his parental, social, and self-induced difficulties. Thus, this youth can ask himself: "*How* can my parents actually dominate me, if I refuse to let them do so? And why need I find it *awful*, why must I consider myself a *slob* if I continued to let them dominate me?" And he can dispute his horribilizing: "Why need I define it as horrible if I fail in popularity at school or never get acknowledged as the best dentist that ever existed? Granted, that might prove inconvenient, but what would make it horrible?" By this kind of disputing, challenging, and questioning of his own irrational (and empirically unconfirmable) beliefs, he can stop his stupid thinking and the overemotionalized reactions—such as his needless anxiety and flight—to which it leads.

A female client had a similar problem but more insight. This twenty-year-old woman knew that she wanted to teach and also knew that she had made no effort to do so because she had thought she couldn't. She also suspected that she often tried to punish herself for some promiscuous sex activity in which she had engaged a year previously. Even though she presumably had insight into her underlying beliefs, she continued to defeat herself and to behave in a neurotic manner.

This client did *not* realize that her self-downing and her sex guilt stemmed from ignorance and faulty thinking. She originally put herself down because she accepted the hypercritical views of her older sister, who jealously did not want her to think well of herself. Then the client, working on the unquestioned assumption that she had little scholastic ability, began to avoid her schoolwork and thereby to "prove" to herself that she actually had none—thus reinforcing her original sister-aided lack of confidence.

This woman's sexual promiscuity, moreover, largely stemmed from her same lack of confidence. Feeling worthless and that boys would not care for her, she took the easiest way of winning them by bartering her body for their attentions. She based her guilt about her promiscuity on the arbitrary notion, also taken over from her sister, that she would prove wicked for having premarital relations and would commit a particularly heinous offense if she behaved promiscuously.

Even though she seemed to know that she condemned herself for her sex behavior and therefore sabotaged her desire to teach, she actually had only partial insight into her neurosis. She did not see her two basic premises and realize their falseness and irrationality: (1) that she could not do well scholastically and that all people who do poorly in this area have no worth; and (2) that she deserved punishment for wickedly engaging in promiscuity.

A fuller understanding of her self-defeating behavior led to far-reaching changes in her thoughts and actions. First, I (A.E.) helped her to question the connection between scholastic success and so-called personal worth and to see that no such connection really exists. She began to understand that we have no way of accurately rating the totality, the essence, of a human; and that, in making such a global rating, we harm rather than help ourselves. Thus, she could accept herself (merely because she *decided* to do so) *whether* or *not* she succeeded at school. And she could enjoy herself considerably even when she failed. Ironically, as usually happens, seeing and acquiring this kind of unconditional self-acceptance helped her to concentrate much better on her schoolwork (since she still found it *desirable* though not *necessary* to do so) and to achieve better grades.

Secondly, I helped my client to challenge the so-called wickedness of her promiscuity and to understand that although she may have made mistakes (by having affairs with males whom she did not really enjoy as lovers), this hardly made her a *louse* who deserved damnation for these errors. By surrendering her philosophy of lousehood and self-condemnation, she removed her remaining motives for sabotaging her own endeavors and helped herself work toward her goal of teaching.

The case of this client, as perhaps of most individuals who come for therapy, exemplifies the differences between what we call Insight No. 1, Insight No. 2, and Insight No. 3. We mean by Insight No. 1 the fairly conventional kind of understanding first clearly postulated by Freud: knowledge by the individual that he or she has a problem and that certain antecedents cause this problem. Thus, the young dentist in training whose case we observed at the beginning of this chapter knew that he had a problem with his career, but thought it stemmed from his dislike of certain subjects and not from his anxiety about social and vocational failure. Not knowing the antecedents of his problem, he did not really have any reasonable amount of "insight."

The young teacher in training had more insight, since she not only recognized her failure at her chosen career, but also knew or suspected that (1) she lacked confidence and (2) she kept trying to punish herself for her previous sexual promiscuity. Knowing, therefore, some of her motives for her ineffective behavior, she had a considerable amount of "insight"—or what we call Insight No. 1. She only vaguely, however, had Insight No. 1, since she *knew* that she lacked confidence but didn't clearly see that this lack of confidence consisted, more concretely, of her telling herself: "My older, hypercritical sister views me as inadequate. How absolutely terrible if she correctly sees me this way! Perhaps she does. In fact, I feel sure she sees me correctly and that I never *can* perform adequately!"

This young woman also knew that she felt guilty and self-punitive about her previous premarital affairs. But she did not specifically see that her guilt and self-punishment resulted from her internalized sentences: "Many people view promiscuity as wicked. I have behaved promiscuously, Therefore I must see myself as wicked." And: "People often agree that those who do mistaken acts deserve punishment for their sins. I have committed such acts by having sex with males for whom I did not really care. Therefore I should punish myself by not trying to succeed in the career, teaching, in which I would like to succeed."

Although, then, this client definitely had a good measure of Insight No. 1, she had it in such a vague and indefinite manner that we could well call it only partial insight. As for Insight No. 2, she had little. For Insight No. 2 consists of seeing clearly that the irrational ideas that we create and acquire in our early lives still continue, and that they largely continue because we keep reindoctrinating ourselves with these ideas—consciously and unconsciously work fairly hard to perpetuate them. Thus, this client kept telling herself, over and over again, "I *should not* have had those promiscuous relations. And in order to expunge my sins and lead a happy life today, I *have to* keep punishing myself for behaving the way I did and thereby continue to cleanse myself." Without this kind of constant self-reinforcement, her early ideas (including those taken over from her sister) would almost certainly extinguish themselves. So Insight No. 2—which she did not have to any degree at the start of her therapy with me—consisted of her clearly seeing that she had not let herself go through this extinguishing process and that she still actively blocked it.

Insight No. 3 remained far from this client's horizon. For No. 3 consists of the wholehearted belief, "Now that I have discovered Insights No. 1 and

2, and fully acknowledge the self-creation and continued reinforcement with which I keep making myself believe the irrational ideas that I have believed for so long, I will most probably find no way of eliminating my disturbances than by steadily, persistently, and vigorously working to change these ideas."

More concretely, when my client acquired Insight No. 1 and No. 2, she could then go on to No. 3: "How fascinating that I have kept convincing myself that I *should not* have had promiscuous sex and that I *have to* keep punishing myself for my errors. As long as I keep believing this hogwash, how can I feel anything *but* self-downing and depressed? Well, I'd better keep strongly disputing and challenging these nutty beliefs until I give them up!" She and I working together in therapy helped her to achieve these three important insights; and by using them and following them up with other hard therapeutic work during the next year, she finally solved her main problems. She not only got a teaching job and did quite well at it during this period but also continued to have the kind of nonmarital sex for which her sister severely criticized her, to enjoy it considerably, and to feel no guilt about it.

We contend, in other words, that almost all neurotic or self-sabotaging behavior results from some kind of basic ignorance or lack of insight on the part of the disturbed individual. Although humans may behave neurotically because of certain biophysical conditions (such as severe hormonal imbalances or by their going sleepless for many nights on end), they don't often do so purely for these reasons. Under more usual conditions, they create their disturbances by their own *ideas*, which they may consciously or unconsciously hold.

Thus, as in the two cases cited in this chapter, people may know that they resist going to school because they fight against parental pressure. Or they may unconsciously resist going to school without clear awareness that rebellion against parental pressure lies at the bottom of this resistance. Or they may know they punish themselves for some sex guilt. Or they may punish themselves without realizing they do so because of this kind of guilt.

In any event, whether or not people consciously know their irrational ideas, they would hardly act neurotically without such ideas. Thus, in the instances given in this chapter, if the young dental student had not made himself so irrationally fearful of parental domination and vocational failure that he gave up studying and flunked out of school, we would find nothing inappropriate in his wanting to leave school and would conclude that he clearly saw the facts of life and acted in sane accordance with them. And if the student of education *rationally* accepted her sister's view of her worthlessness and *sensibly* kept punishing herself for her promiscuity, we would conclude that she had better give up teaching and practice, say, prostitution.

But we cannot justify pronounced feelings of failure, beliefs in worthlessness, unthinking acceptances of others' condemnation and self-damning tendencies. Not because they emerge as absolutely wrong or wicked, or because they contradict the laws of God or the universe. But simply because, on good pragmatic grounds, they almost always prove self-defeating and needlessly prevent us from getting many of the things we desire.

Moreover, self-downing beliefs and emotions stem from unrealistic overgeneralizations that we cannot scientifically verify. They contain magical, demonizing formulations that remain definitional and unprovable. If you say to yourself, for example, "I have failed at this task [e.g., winning the love of another person or succeeding at a job] and I find that disadvantageous and unfortunate," you make a statement (or hypothesis) that you can empirically validate or disprove: for you (and others) can observe whether you really have failed and what disadvantages (in regard to certain of your personal goals) will probably follow from your failing.

If you say to yourself, however, "Because I have failed at this task, I find it *awful* and it makes me a *rotten person*," you make a statement (or hypothesis) that you cannot empirically validate or disprove. For *awfulness*, an essentially undefinable term, does not really mean *very disadvantageous*. It means *more than* 100 percent disadvantageous, unfortunate, obnoxious, or inconvenient. And how can anything in that category really exist? Your finding it *awful* when you fail, moreover, means that you *can't stand* failing and that you *shouldn't* fail. But, of course, you *can* stand failing; and the universe hardly insists that you *should* not or *must* not fail!

The hypothesis, again, that failing makes you a *rotten person* means that (1) you unfortunately have failed; that (2) since you have intrinsic, essential rottenness, you will *always* and *only* fail; and that (3) you deserve damnation (roasting in some kind of hell) for failing. Although we can empirically substantiate the first of these three meanings, the second and third meanings seem unprovable—except by arbitrary definition.

Although, therefore, we can confirm your *failing* at something (or at many things), we cannot confirm your all-inclusive label as a *failure*. You may devoutly call yourself a failure (even with a capital F!). But that label constitutes a misleading, pernicious overgeneralization.

Stated differently: Inappropriate, self-destructive emotion—such as your feeling severe anger, depression, guilt, or anxiety—results from your (consciously or unconsciously held) prejudiced, childish, senseless ideas and almost inevitably leads to inefficient, self-sabotaging behavior which we call neurosis. When you display neurotic behavior, you can employ several palliative methods to help overcome your disturbance. Thus, you can change your job or your marital status; take a vacation; develop a vital interest in some area; work at succeeding at professional or avocational pursuits; consume sufficient quantities of alcohol, marijuana, heroin, tranquilizers, psychic energizers, or other drugs; devote yourself to a new church or creed; or try various other diversionary approaches.

Almost any or all of these kinds of diversions may temporarily work. For they essentially induce you, when irrationally attached to some set of disturbance-provoking ideas (which we may call x), to divert yourself to some other set of ideas (which we may call y). As long as you keep thinking of y instead of x ideas, you may not feel too troubled.

Unfortunately, this kind of diversion rarely solves your basic problems. For no matter how vigorously or often you may divert yourself to y ideas, you still really believe in and have not given up x ideas. So you strongly keep tending to return to the neurotic behavior caused by x ideas.

Take Mrs. Janus, for example. People viewed her, at the age of thirty-eight, as a still beautiful and talented woman. When she did not lie in bed all day with a horrible migraine headache or did not fight viciously with her husband and two teen-age children, she showed herself as a charming companion, hostess, and club woman. So, to keep herself unangry and relatively free from migraine, Mrs. Janus drank heavily, gobbled tranquilizers, and passionately devoted herself to a New Spiritism group which believed in reincarnation and taught that life in this sorry vale of tears serves as a prelude to an infinity of Real Lives to come.

It almost worked. Getting half crocked most of the time, and intently proselytizing for her spiritist views, Mrs. Janus found relatively little time to upset herself, to act terribly angry at others, and to retreat into her migraine headaches. But when the liquor lost some of its effectiveness, and she found life in the afterworld wanting in solving her problems in this world, Mrs. Janus's neurotic symptoms returned full blast. In fact, she felt so unable to contain her anger against her associates that even her newly found spiritist friends began to look askance at her behavior and to ease her out of some of the high positions that they at first delighted in giving her. Seeing even this new group desert her, Mrs. Janus grew angrier and began to verge on a complete breakdown.

Came the dawn. And, more by brute force than gentle persuasion, her husband dragged Mrs. Janus into therapy by telling her that unless she did something to help herself, he and the children would pack and leave. It required only a few sessions to reveal that she profoundly believed that because her parents had both acted strictly and punitively during her childhood, the rest the world owed her a completely opposite kind of living. All her close associates, especially her husband and children, she thought absolutely *should* lean over backward to make life easy for her and thereby compensate for her unduly hard life during childhood.

When, in the normal course of human events, Mrs. Janus found that her close relatives and friends somehow did not feel the way she did about catering to her, she felt inordinately angry, viewed them as treating her unethically, and did her best to ram their "rank injustices" down their throats. When everything went her way—which of course it rarely did—she felt fine. But when balked or frustrated, she felt miserable and tried to divert herself by making others equally miserable.

Alcohol and tranquilizers often made Mrs. Janus "feel good" for a short while—at which time all life's "injustices" would not seem so unjust. And her spiritistic views, which promised her the best of all possible afterworlds, also temporarily diverted her from her injustice collecting. But such diversions, naturally, could not last. Nor did they change her devout beliefs that the world *should* prove a kinder, easier place and that her close associates *should* make up for the horrors of her past by catering to her in the present.

In the course of a year and a half of both individual and group rational psychotherapy, I (R.A.H.) helped Mrs. Janus first acquire Insight No. 1: namely, that her extreme hostility and migrainous upsets stemmed from her own behavior, rather than that of others, and followed from the irrational philosophy: "Because I suffered in the past, people *should* treat me with utter kindness today."

After helping Mrs. Janus to see the real causes of her neurotic behavior, I then (with the help of the members of her therapy group) led her to Insights No. 2 and 3: "Now that I see that *I* create my disturbances with *my* often-repeated internalized sentences about the 'injustice' of it all, I'd better keep disputing, questioning, challenging, and changing these sentences. For I not only keep convincing myself that people treat me unkindly and unfairly—which at times they really may—but that such unfairness *shouldn't* exist and I find it *horrible* when it does. Well, what *makes* it horrible? Nothing, of course. Unfortunate, yes—because I don't keep getting what I want. But horrible? Only if I define it so!

"And why *shouldn't* people treat me the unkind way they often do? I can see no reason why they shouldn't—though I can think of many reasons why I would like them not to! If people don't cater to me the way I prefer, tough!

But I'd better convince myself that I can still lead a good and happy existence, mainly by catering to myself!"

When she began to get Insights No. 2 and 3—that she kept reiterating her demanding philosophy and that she'd better keep working at changing it and the damaging emotions to which it led, Mrs. Janus reduced her drinking to a cocktail or two a day, threw away her tranquilizers and felt remarkably unangry, with her husband, children, and friends, even when (as fallible humans) they *did* act unjustly or unfairly to her. The more she accepted reality, and refused any longer to make it as grim as she had made it, the less spiritistic and devoutly believing in reincarnation she grew. As she said at one of her closing therapy sessions: "Why do I have to worry about highly hypothetical afterlives when I now know how to make *this* life so enjoyable?"

ADDITIONAL THOUGHTS ON RECOGNIZING AND ATTACKING NEUROTIC BEHAVIOR

By Robert H. Moore
Florida Branch, Institute for Rational Living, Inc.
Clearwater, Florida 33516

Does neurotic behavior always consist of illogical thinking? No exactly. In many ways, you behave quite *logically*, even though you may act neurotically.

How so? Well, even substantially neurotic behavior seldom results from completely illogical thinking. You generally do *what you believe* serves your best interest. As a member of the human race, when you react to a particular set of conditions you do essentially what we all do: At point A (your Activating experience), you gather, with all your sensory apparatus, as much relevant information as you can. At point B (your Belief system), you process that information, weigh it, consider it, think it over. At point C (your emotional or behavioral Consequence), you react with your gut and tend to take some action about your Activating experience.

As an example, I (R.H.M.) had a woman client, when I practiced psychology in Pennsylvania, who told me during one of her earlier sessions that her nineteen-year-old daughter had just written to her from a distant state to announce her pregnancy (point A). She and her husband then had sat up most of the evening arguing about whether or not the girl might have gotten pregnant before her wedding day, which had taken place several months earlier, and about how awful it would prove if such premarital conception had occurred (point B). My client got herself into a considerable lather about it all and prepared to write her daughter angry words about what people do who take marriage vows so lightly (point C).

Now, did my client react *logically*? She most certainly did. Given her daughter's pregnancy a few months after marriage, and given the values through which she processed this information, how could she have "logically" reacted other than she did? I used her reaction to point out that even disturbed feelings (like moral condemnation of or anger toward her daughter) *logically* stem from the evaluative process (at point B). My client very clearly *believed* premarital sex wrong—and this belief *determined* that she react as she did to her suspicion about her daughter's pregnancy. For her to have *believed differently*—for instance, that premarital sex has a legitimate place in the lives of young lovers—would have caused her, again *logically*, to react quite differently to the same suspicion about her daughter.

To get back to you: even when you behave from your "gut," or you prefer to rely upon what you call "intuition," or you as impulsively, without considering all the available evidence, you so behave because you have *judged*, rightly or wrongly, that you can allow yourself to react in these ways. You have *decided* that guessing seems better than careful consideration; and you therefore have chosen to act "intuitively" or "impulsively."

Virtually all your instantaneous or "spontaneous" emotional responses arise in the same way. At point A, you perceive what goes on around you. At B, you evaluate how likeable or dislikeable you find this situation at A. But you do your evaluations at B quickly, with the almost lightning speed that comes from your having rehearsed the scene many times before, if only in your mental imagery. *Then* you react emotionally at C.

Though you may not like to admit this, you basically remain a thinker, a calculator. And you devote much of your thinking to bringing about or preserving comfort, pleasure, or freedom from pain: to the pursuit of either short or long range hedonism. How, then, do you manage—in this seemingly "logical" manner—to behave, often, so neurotically? Have you inferior intelligence? Or have you suffered some brain impairment?

Not likely! Like other so-called neurotics, you rarely have innate retardation or brain impairment; and you can reason capably from premise to conclusion. Your fundamental premises, moreover, appear quite O.K.: for you probably start with the same basic values or goals that almost all humans start with—to stay alive and to feel reasonably happy and free from needless pain. Then you typically sabotage these basic goals (as Dr. Maxie C. Maultsby Jr. has observed) in one or more of several important ways.

1. You perceive reality inaccurately.
2. You seriously jeopardize your own safety.
3. You impede your own progress toward your chosen goals.
4. You often experience more inner turmoil than you can comfortably bear.
5. You create needless conflict between yourself and other members of your community.

Look these criteria over carefully and they will help define for you self-defeating or neurotic behavior. But why do you, when you act neurotically, do these self-damaging things—especially if you think clearly and act so well in so many other respects? Who puts you up to this?

You do. How? In, again, several specific ways:

1. Regarding your inaccurately perceiving reality: In the exercise your natural tendency to behave logically—meaning, to link things over, to draw conclusions, and to act in accordance with these conclusions—you start with some "bad" data, or misinformation. You then unwittingly reason—straight as an arrow!—from a false premise to an almost inevitably faulty conclusion. Thus, by believing the false premise that someone close to you must always and only favor you, and by observing that he or she sometimes does not, you may erroneously conclude that this person intends to do you in, even to cause you bodily harm in some way. You thereby behave logically (self-preservingly), but at the same time unrealistically and neurotically when you defend yourself against this imagined "attack" against you.

Don't we all do this at times—jump from misinformation or false premises to wrong conclusions? Right! But then we usually discover our mistake, shift our gears, and recalculate. We unneurotically replace our faulty premise, correct our thinking, and revise our plan of action accordingly.

When you act as a real "neurotic," however, you change your behavior only with difficulty—because you generally accept little or no new information upon which to reason. Moreover, you often see reality in such a prejudiced light that you do not understand why everyone else does not reason as you do to reach the same conclusion. And you so successfully avoid a careful examination of some of your own false assumptions that you resist changing your behaviors even when their "logical" conclusions lead you to behave in obviously self-sabotaging ways.

When you behave neurotically, again, you "see" considerably more or less than an objective viewer would see on an instant replay of a perceived event. You view as fact what the rest of us speculate about—such as others' motives for their behaviors. You escalate probabilities into certainties. You often fail to distinguish a person, place, or thing from your evaluation of it. And you typically make dogmatic judgments about the goodness and rightness of many things that cross your path.

2. Regarding the neurotic jeopardizing of your own safety: When you appear seriously accident prone, smoke yourself half to death, overeat to the extent of taxing your heart and other vital organs, keep driving your car at speeds well above the traffic limits, or make an actual suicide attempt, you frequently exhibit foolish or neurotic behavior. Not that self-maiming or suicide always prove irrational or insane. Occasionally, they don't. But if your bents run strongly in these directions, you'd better at least seriously consider the *possibility* that emotional disturbance darkens your existence; and I'd advise you to beat a hasty path to the nearest rational-emotive therapist!

3. Regarding the impeding of your own progress toward your chosen goals: Does this kind of neurotic behavior have logical elements, too? Indeed, it does. For the unmitigated pursuit of achievement, or even of vital recreational pursuits, may prove highly stressful; and your setting up some barriers to this kind of stress may indeed show some method in your "madness." When you act neurotically, however, you tend to set up such enormous barriers, in this respect, that you progress toward your important goals at something like a snail's pace—and completely forestall your reaching some of them.

I had a friend and colleague some years ago, Debbie P., who had earned a Phi Beta Kappa key at a major university—definitely a sign of ability and goal-orientation—but who thereafter organized her pursuits with the greatest difficulty. She not only had trouble establishing goals for herself, but she particularly sabotaged those goals related to her job as a social worker. Although ostensibly interested in building her skills in this area, her fears and anxieties so debilitated her that she often could not bring herself to schedule an interview at the clinic where she worked. She avoided having a social life and, when asked to address a group of people at a meeting, she went into a freeze. Once, in my presence, she bolted and ran, panic-stricken, from a room in which someone had "threatened" to take her picture with a camera.

Many neurotic individuals, like Debbie, weave for themselves such a consistent fabric of inactivity and inhibition that only with great difficulty can we ascertain that at one time they had notable goals and ambitions.

4. Concerning your experiencing more inner turmoil than you can comfortably stand: Instead of neurotically withdrawing from the goals, jobs, and relationships you get upset about, you may plunge into all these kinds of activities—but pay, as you plunge, a considerable (and unnecessary) toll in personal conflict and inner turmoil. Thus, while aspiring to a professorship or the presidency of a business concern, you can neurotically make yourself prone to constant feelings of quick anger, deep hurt, enormous anxiety, vicious hatred, profound anguish, and overwhelming depression.

Then, instead of expressing intense anxiety, anger, depression or other emotional upset, you may take out your disturbances on your body and may develop some psychosomatic condition—such as ulcers, high blood pressure, fainting spells, skin rashes, migraine headaches, allergic reactions, or debilitating fatigue. You can also rope yourself into the risky business of temporarily quelling your feelings of disturbance by getting yourself addicted to alcohol, pills of various sorts, temper tantrums, overabsorption in work, compulsive promiscuity, or various other forms of escapism.

5. In regard to your creating needless conflict between yourself and other members of your community: When you do, for any reason, feel upset emotionally, you tend to find it almost impossible to have such feelings in isolation, but almost always share them—all too willingly!—with your friends and associates. Your mate, lover, and other intimates get involved with, and to some extent victimized by, your neurotic feelings and behaviors. Whereupon, disliking these behaviors, and often having emotional difficulties of their own, they interact poorly with you—and both you and they get penalized thereby.

When your family members and friends do get substantially involved with your problems, you often identify them as "causing" these problems. You tend to believe that your upset feelings or self-defeating behaviors flow directly from your interaction with them or from their "wrong" or "stupid" acts. You then commonly feel cheated or abused by them and conclude that your disturbances (depressions, anxieties, hostilities, etc.) got created by their "abusiveness." And even though you sometimes may correctly diagnose their neuroses, you foolishly believe that these difficulties give you a good excuse for acting disturbedly yourself.

"But how can I feel anything but depressed, with him out drinking all the time?" a young woman recently asked me. "If he didn't drink like that, I'd never get depressed!"

"Of course I drink," replied her husband. "Who wouldn't when your wife flirts outrageously with other men right in front of you, with half the people we know in the community watching her do so? Wouldn't any man who cared for his wife so much and who kept getting treated like that by her take to drink—or even worse?"

The couple had come to me on the brink of separation, after fighting almost continuously through two of their three years of marriage. Both considered their reactions to the other's outlandish behavior perfectly "natural." She firmly believed that her husband's drinking caused her to get depressed. He believed that his wife's public flirtations drove him to drink. Each devoutly held that the other's performances would have to change in order that he or she feel or behave any differently. And, expectably, they had gotten heavily into damning each other for their own neurotic reactions. They felt almost doomed to divorce when they came to me for counseling.

Neither of these two recognized, before they came for rational-emotive help, that a partner's poor behavior can not actually reach out and command anyone to respond neurotically. Both had accepted the popular—but still highly erroneous—belief that *you* cause *my* emotional problems. And this belief put them, quite understandably, into regular conflict—a fairly typical example of neurotic behavior incorporating or feeding upon an element of its environment, in this case, a spouse.

Similarly, when you act neurotically you can easily blame non-human elements in your environment. When things don't work the way they presumably *should*. When planes don't take off on schedule. When your car that you have just spent a great deal of money on suddenly, for no good reason, sputters and balks. When the Internal Revenue Service refuses to accept your indubitably proper explanation for taking a large business or health deduction. When music blares out in public places in spite of your allergy to such noises. In all these instances, and in many more, you can cavalierly condemn the fates or powers above for their totally unfair attitudes toward you. And when you do, you neurotically not only upset yourself about some original hassles, but also make yourself so irate and temper-ridden that your reaction itself actively increases your difficulties with others and often gets you into much more trouble than the first problem that presented itself.

Neurosis, then, commonly strikes you in many different forms and shapes. If you recognize its various manifestations as neurotic, and fully accept the fact that you (and not others, social conditions, or the unkind fates) *make yourself* disturbed, you have an excellent chance of understanding and undoing your disturbance, instead of lamely excusing or needlessly living with it. Copping out proves easy. Coping with neurosis seems a damned sight harder—but also infinitely more rewarding.

CHAPTER 3

THE CONTEXT AND CAUSES OF
MARITAL DISTURBANCE

EDITOR'S COMMENTARY:

The authors begin the chapter on neurosis in marriage with a case example of a vocational counselor who came to psychotherapy because his wife made demands of him. As it turned out, Ellis and Harper showed the patient that he played a large role in the marriage disturbance by insisting that his wife not act the way she did. The more he insisted by neglecting her, the more she persisted. When he learned to accept her as the human being he married, even while he disliked some of her nagging, her nagging softened and the relationship improved. That said, the authors then moved on to reinforce their definition of neurosis as part and parcel of learned behavior from society (including parents, significant others, and even by happenstance). As neurotic thinking helped to shape the society-culture in which we lived, the society-culture helped to fragment our thinking-feeling since they were learned within that society-culture. Even so, the thinking-feeling could be recognized within relationships through five dire needs that the authors presented and about which they gave examples. In the last section of the chapter on causes of marital disturbance (or relationship disturbance in general), the authors explained five dire demands made by individuals as irrational ways to form emotional bonds. Strikingly, they referred to working with a couple as a dyad rather than as individuals as "unusual." Today, the evidence—especially as reported by John Gottman—shows that the most long-lasting results for marriage happiness come from working with a couple. The authors indicated that working with couples was akin to working with a small group, so that the dynamics or influences of one person on the other person as a source of learning became evident. Even for the reader who generally is not interested in working with couples, everyone is engaged in relationships on a day-to-day basis by virtue of the language we use and have learned from other people. These two selections reinforce that point of view, as well as show how the theory and applications of rational-emotive psychotherapy help solve both individual and small group problems (and by inference to help redirect society and its culture with good examples).

Excerpted from *Creative Marriage*
Lyle Stuart, Inc. 1961

Most couples who enter marriage today expect two main things from their relationship: regular sex satisfaction and the enjoyments of secure and intimate companionship and love. They normally get neither. Why?

Take the case of the sexually frustrated vocational counselor who came to see me recently. "I know a great deal about problems of marriage," he said at the start of his first session. "In fact, even though I mainly deal with people's vocational difficulties, I am always getting into their married lives, too. You know—people don't come to work on time, or keep losing jobs, and that sort of thing because their wives keep them up all night quarreling or things like that. You know how it is."

"Yes," I said. "And just as your vocational counseling takes you into marital areas, so does my marriage counseling take me, frequently, into people's job and business problems."

"I can well imagine that it does. Anyway, the thing's damned aggravating! Here it's my business, you know, and I do it practically all the time, patching up my clients' squabblings with their wives and that sort of thing, and, well damn it all, I can't do a thing with my own wife. Not a thing!"

"You mean——?"

"I mean sexually. Yes, that's what I mean: sexually! Not a thing."

"She doesn't satisfy you that way?"

"Satisfy me? Oh, no; that's not the problem at all. I'm satisfied, all right. Too satisfied, in fact! But she—never. Day and night she keeps after me. This morning, for instance. Wouldn't let me out to get to work. Held me up until I almost missed the train. Hugging and kissing and pressing up against me. God, like a cat in heat! Constantly. Never satisfied. And I was always reasonably good at sex. Still am, I think. Not that *she* thinks so!"

This thirty-five-year-old husband then went on to state that his thirty-year-old wife nagged him considerably, neglected their three children, made great financial demands on him, and was most unreasonable in many other ways. Once he had begun his tirade against his wife, he could not be stopped; and he even kept ignoring most of my questions and comments as he self-righteously assailed his wife in one outburst after another. I finally managed to get in a few words edgewise:

"But *do* you ever satisfy your wife sexually?"

"Well, frankly, I'm so disgusted, these days, by her inordinate demands that I hardly have the heart to do it at all."

"But how about previously, when you first married? Did you satisfy her then?"

"I tried to. But it was always impossible. As I said, I'm really not bad at sex. Had a reputation, in fact, before I married. But she's really something! I can do it, well, say twice a week. But she wants it every night. Or more! What can you do about a thing like that?"

"Don't you know?"

"Satisfy her, you mean, in other ways? Without having . . . well, without——"

"Yes, apparently you do know. Without having actual intercourse. You know perfectly well, apparently, that you can satisfy a woman, whether you yourself are sexually interested or not, without having penile-vaginal coitus. So even if your wife wants sex relations more than you desire them, you can still satisfy her thoroughly."

"Oh, yes. I realize that. I read your books, *Sex Without Guilt* and *The Art and Science of Love*. I have even recommended them to some of my clients who have sex problems."

"What's the trouble, then? Why *don't* you satisfy your wife sexually, if that is what, according to your own story, is upsetting her so much? Why can't you spend five or ten minutes, every night in the week if necessary, giving her an orgasm—or three or four of them, if that is what she thinks she needs?"

"Well—uh—look. It's—You see, it's like this——"

And this husband went on, in beautifully evasive language, to explain that he didn't *feel* like satisfying his wife when she was acting the way she was; that her non-sexual demands also disgusted him and made him sexually unresponsive; that she didn't *really* seem to love him, even though she wanted him sexually all the time; and so on. It was quite clear, after he had been talking for a few more minutes, that sex, really, was *not* his main marital problem.

What actually bothered him, as I then started to show him, was his own thoroughly *unrealistic expectations* of marriage. He expected, merely because he *was* married, that his wife would be completely loving, exactly attuned to him sexually, financially undemanding, a wonderful mother, a devoted daughter-in-law to his mother, a thoroughly well-adjusted person in her own right, etc. When, because of her all-too-human (and quite expectable) fallibility, his wife did not measure up to this highly idealized picture that he thought she *should* attain, my client immediately started to go on a little sit-down strike of his own. He kept telling himself that his wife did not *deserve* to be satisfied sexually; and thereby appreciably helped to make matters between them immeasurably worse.

"Granting," I said, "that your wife may have all the deficiencies that you have been listing during the last half hour, is there anything that *you* are doing to help her overcome them?"

"Like what?"

"Like satisfying her sexually, for example, so that she'll have an incentive to try to please you in other ways. Like being unusually nice and calm when she is nagging you. Like asking her tactfully and encouragingly to try to be a little nicer to your mother. Like helping her with the children when she is having a difficult time handling them. Do you ever do any things like these to try to better her situation and yours?"

"But look at what she is doing to me!"

"Yes, but isn't that exactly the same sentence that she's saying to herself many times a day: 'Look at what he's doing to *me*'?"

"I guess you're right. I suppose she is."

"And, anyway, do two wrongs make a right?"

"No; I know they don't."

"You 'know' it; but you don't seem to act on that knowledge. Your real problem, as I said before, is your *own* unrealistic expectations. Because you think that your wife *ought to be* different from the way she is—when you really mean that *you would like it better* or that *it would be preferable* if she were—you keep beating her over the head when she fails to live up to your idealized views. She then resentfully goes into a dive and makes even more sexual and other demands on you—thus causing your expectations to be that much more unrealistic and, in fact, unrealizable as long as you continue to employ your self-defeating and wife-defeating tactics."

"You suggest, then, that I force myself to be nice to my wife and thereby try to get her to lessen her sex demands on me?"

"Yes, but not *just* that. I suggest, even more importantly, that you change your *own* attitudes toward your wife and what you think *ought to be* expected of her. Then, instead of having to try to force yourself, against the grain as it were, to be nice to her, you will easily and almost automatically treat her better. If you, because of *your* changed attitudes, no longer think of her as a bitch who is depriving you of your 'just' and 'natural' husbandly due, but as a woman who is perhaps doing her best, under very difficult and sexually-deprived circumstances, to come to terms with you and the children, then you will *want* to be nice to her. For both her sake and your own. Then you will *want* to satisfy her sexually. With that kind of an attitude well established on your part, it will be very difficult *not* to have a much better marriage than you and your wife are now having."

It would be nice if I could say that, after this first-session presentation of what seemed to be some of the real problems of his marriage, my client immediately went home and started acting much differently toward his wife. He didn't; and several more marriage counseling sessions, as well as several with his wife, were required before he was able to start changing his attitudes and his marital behavior. Eventually, however, he did stop pitying himself and made a real attempt to satisfy his wife sexually, and their marriage noticeably improved.

The point to be emphasized here is that there are two expectations with which most people today go into marriage—the hope for regular sex satisfaction and the enjoyments of secure and intimate companionship and love. These two goals are not only intimately related to each other but to the *general* personality patterns and life expectations of the married partners. People go into marriage (or premarital affairs) with a basic set of assumptions, beliefs, attitudes, or philosophies of living. If their basic assumptions are objective, open-minded, and rational, their behavior, both in and out of marriage, will likewise tend to be reasonable and undisturbed. If, as is alas! usually the case in our society, either (or both) marriage partner's basic beliefs are prejudiced, unrealistic, and illogical, his or her marital behavior will also tend to be unreasonable and disturbed.

But this is only the beginning. Since marriage is that kind of relationship where two people ceaselessly intercommunicate and interact, if one of them behaves erratically or negatively, his or her behavior will have some significant effects on the actions and feelings of the other. In most instances, the other partner will react by behaving equally or more erratically or negatively. Then, of course, the first badly behaving partner in turn will be re-affected by the thoughts and doings of the first partner, and so on, in an endless vicious circle.

Premarital emotional disturbance, in other words, almost invariably leads to marital disturbance, which then leads to still further disturbance. By the time the mutual negativism of the partners has reverberated against each other several times, the fact that either or both partners were *originally* irrational or neurotic is quite lost from sight. Each becomes convinced that it is the other, or the marriage, which is causing the enormous upset that now exists.

My vocational counselor client, for example, was quite convinced, when he first came to see me, that he had been a perfectly normal, well-adjusted individual prior to his marriage. He was certain that only his wife's inordinate sexual and other demands had caused him to become tense, disgusted, and unhappy. When I finally was able to convince him that it was his *own* attitudes *toward* his wife's demands, rather than those demands themselves, that were causing his unhappiness, and that he had had similar unrealistic attitudes before he ever met his wife, he was much more willing to work toward changing these attitudes as well as to improve his marriage.

This same client, of course, freely admitted that his wife had been a very disturbed individual before their marriage—even though, at that time, he had not realized how disturbed she was. But, as I again showed him, he did not in any manner *accept* his wife's disturbance, or consider it a characteristic *to be worked on*. Instead, as is usually the case with individuals who are intimately associated with neurotics in our society, he incessantly *blamed* his wife for *being* neurotic; and thereby, of course, helped to make her more self-blaming and even more neurotic. When he was able to look into his own heart and stop blaming his wife, he enabled her to relieve considerable of her negative pressure on herself, and thereby to become less disturbed.

Most people in our culture, then, *enter* engagement and marriage with their full share of irrational ideas and neurotic behavior. They are relatively *blind* to both their own and their mate's disturbances. When they finally see these neurotic manifestations, they stubbornly refuse to *accept* them. Instead, they *blame* the other for being troubled and *pity themselves* for having to live with such a troubled person. They thus help intensify both their own and their partner's original neuroses; and the net result is a marriage that is a veritable hotbed of emotional upsets. Talk of the blind trying to lead the blind! Or the blaming trying to lead the blamed.

Only by having a fairly detailed view of some of the how's and why's of individual and societal disturbances today is one likely to be well prepared for the experience of felicitously entering and lovingly sustaining a good marital relationship. . . .

What are some of the main factors causing frequent marital disturbance in our society?

First, the whole of modern social life, of which marriage is an integral part, is today in such a state of rapid change and complex confusion that many personal goals and desires tend to be swept away in the general cultural storm. Since every couple and every marriage are part of the large society in which we live, and since this society is notoriously in a state of severe turmoil, it would be strange indeed to find that most people today were living in a state of effortless marital bliss.

Most of us are aware that modern social conditions produce many dramatic problems, such as war, crime, delinquency, overpopulation, urban and suburban monotony, poverty, and racial strife. But we less often realize that much of the deep-seated unhappiness and the neurotic symptoms of the "average" man and woman of our civilization are insidious but still statistically "normal" tolls of our wayward modes of living. In an ideal society, it may be possible to have thoroughly unneurotic individuals and couples; but ours is hardly that ideal.

As both of the authors of this book frequently stress to their clients and patients: "Do your best, by all means, to understand the society in which you live, and to make suitable allowances for its flaws and idiocies in raising your children in it. But let's have no illusions: since you live in an imperfect culture, you are bound, to some degree, to have imperfect selves and imperfect offspring. No matter how sane and intelligent may be your own modes of child-raising, your children will suffer from other less sane and intelligent influences: from contacts with their friends, their teachers, books, movies, TV shows, etc. Tough! But these are the facts and you must, to some degree, accept them—or else become a hermit. Make all the allowances you will for your culture; but you still can't completely escape it. Sick people are in large degree—though not completely—a product of a sick society. Be forewarned."

A second reason why marriages or the people in them tend to be so emotionally warped today is because people tend to use them as dumping grounds for problems acquired in other aspects of their lives. Not only do most husbands and wives inflict difficulties on each other which they acquired originally in their parental homes, but they also tend to project daily confusions, conflicts, and frustrations which originate from their non-marital relationships. Most men, for example, meet with various problems at their work. There they are not free to express openly aggressive feelings which they engender in themselves by not realistically accepting work frustrations. So they often bring these feelings home and express them against their wives.

Similarly, most wives have grievances of their own in relation to careers which they may have away from home or to the demanding routines of homemaking and care of their children. They fail to see realistically, temporarily accept, and then planfully do something effective about the frustrations of their careers or their homes. Instead they irrelevantly bring these frustrations—or the negative emotions which they allow to surround them—into the relatively relaxed, intimate, personalized relationship with their husbands. The dumping of such extraneous problems into the marriage breeds still more problems. These, still again, are not squarely faced and tackled but are "resolved" by self- and marriage-destroying outbursts of temper and hostility.

A third main reason for widespread upset in marital relationships is the fact that our customs concerning both courtship and marriage are, to a considerable extent, distinctly conducive to the growth of illogical, inflexible, self-defeating thoughts and actions. Although our society is now a little less Puritanical in its outlook toward sex than it was in earlier periods, the sexual side of courtship and marriage is still clouded with considerable super-romanticism and antisexualism.

Love, especially what is vaguely referred to as "true love," is represented as somehow entirely separate from the "baser" sex impulses and is supposed to follow various ethereal and unrealistic channels as described in our movies, television scripts, magazine stories, and other sources of romantic beliefs.

As Dr. Karen Horney, among others, frequently pointed out, *should's, supposed to's, ought's,* and *must's* are the inevitable equipment of disturbed individuals. The neurotic particularly believes that (a) he himself *should* act in a perfectionistic, wholly moralistic way and that (b) everyone else also *should* behave in this idealistic manner. From the first of these unrealistic beliefs he acquires anxiety, guilt, and self-doubt; and from the second, suspiciousness, hostility, and self-righteousness. He then, of course, carries these unrealistic *should's* into his premarital and his marital relationships. He ends up, as is only to be expected, loathing himself and his mate.

During courtship, irrational expectations may never come up against a serious showdown. It is relatively easy to hide from reality in the high romantic grass of young unmarried love. But, comes the marriage, and truth will out. This man or this woman to whom you are married cannot possibly measure up to your unrealistic expectations. And your mate is bound to meet with similar frustrations of his or her expectations of you. While it is possible for you both to learn to face the realities of married life, or to restructure your expectations so that they conform to reality, the evidence is overwhelming that a majority of present-day married couples do not actually do this. They respond to reality in illogical, inflexible, self-defeating ways; in short, they develop or perpetuate their own neuroses.

Which brings us, once again, to the very core of most serious marital disturbances: the emotional disturbance of the married partners. A simple definition of neurosis is the one stated in one of our previous books, *How to Live with a Neurotic:* stupid behavior by non-stupid people. Neurotic behavior consists of self-defeating thoughts and actions. It is the process of rendering oneself unhappy in a situation where all the necessary attributes actually exist and could be realized. But the neurotic individual shortsightedly does *not* take advantage of his own intelligence and planning ability; on the contrary, he sabotages his own ends.

In no set of human relationships are neurotic patterns more observable and more pernicious than in marriage and family life. For not only do married neurotics execrably influence each other and make themselves two or three times as unhappy as they need be, but they also pass on their patterns of disturbance to their children—who, in turn, later marry, raise their own families, and thus perpetuate similar self-defeating modes of living.

As we noted previously, human disturbance almost always results from the individual's mistaken, unrealistic, or illogical beliefs, or philosophies. Since the symptoms of his disturbance—for example, his fears, guilts, and depressions—take on what is generally called an "emotional" tone, and since they usually lead to physical feelings and consequences—such as feelings of nausea or pain and symptoms of high blood pressure, ulcers, or migraine headaches—it is easy to forget, or to fail to see in the first place, that these disturbed "emotions" are actually the result of early-ingrained and later self-repeated and sustained ideas or attitudes. But they are.

Human beings, for the most part, talk to themselves in simple declarative sentences. And when these sentences are rational and logical—when the individual tells himself something like, "Jones doesn't like me; that's too bad; now let's see what I can calmly do to get him to like me better."—his "emotions" are appropriate and undisordered. But when he tells himself irrational and illogical sentences—such as, "Jones doesn't like me; it's absolutely terrible and awful that he doesn't like me; I can't stand his not liking me; and this proves that Jones is a blackguard."—his "emotions" are inappropriate, negative, and self-defeating.

If, in other words, an individual is theoretically capable of acting in a non-self-defeating way, and he actually defeats himself and brings needless anxiety and hostility into his relationships with himself and others, he must be thinking unclearly, illogically. He must have some unrealistic value system which blocks his potential of thinking, feeling, and acting in a reasonable manner. If a person is to be helped to think clearly and do away with his unrealistic value system, he must be shown (a) that he is irrational, (b) exactly how he is repeating nonsensical ideas to himself, (c) where and how he originally learned to do this kind of illogical thinking (or was indoctrinated with silly ideas), (d) that there is a good possibility of his becoming rational, (e) exactly how he can attack his illogical ideas and replace them with more realistic ones, and (f) how he can finally build generalized rational philosophies of living, so that he will ultimately automatically think, for the most part, in sane and undefeating ways.

This process of showing a disturbed individual exactly how he has learned and is now himself sustaining nonsensical ideas, which (consciously or unconsciously) lie behind and keep sustaining his "emotional" disturbances or his neurotic symptoms, is called rational psychotherapy. In their professional writings, the authors of this book have developed the theory and practice of rational therapy and are continually working to perfect it.

As applied to marital problems, rational analysis largely consists of showing each spouse that his or her disturbed behavior (in or out of marriage) arises from underlying unrealistic beliefs or philosophies. The client is then shown what these beliefs are and how they are producing individual and marital upsets. Thirdly, he or she is given some understanding of how the irrational value system originally arose and how it is being (wittingly or unwittingly) sustained and reinforced. Finally, the counselee is helped to replace his or her self-defeating ideas and attitudes with more rational and more effective philosophies. This change in the value system of the client is achieved not only by discussion in the counseling situation but by his being induced to think for himself when he is outside the session and by fear-removing and hostility-dispelling actions that he is induced to take under the therapist's guidance.

In this book we are trying to help people with problem marriages to undergo a similar process. Although we obviously cannot listen to their particular problems and thereby discover the special set of irrational beliefs that are causing their neurotic interactions with their mates; fortunately this is not absolutely necessary (even though it is highly desirable). This is because there are actually only a limited number of patterns of self-defeating marital behavior. In outlining and unraveling some of these main patterns, we shall almost inevitably uncover at least some of those which exist in any individual instance.

Take, for instance, a case which one of us presented at a symposium on Neurotic Interaction in Marriage, which was sponsored by the Counseling Division of the American Psychological Association, and on which both authors of this book were panelists.

A husband and wife who had been married for seven years came for marriage counseling because the wife was terribly disturbed about the husband's alleged affairs with other women and the husband was "fed up" with his wife's complaints and general unhappiness and thought it was useless going on. It was quickly evident that the wife was a neurotic individual who believed that she had to be greatly loved and protected; hated herself thoroughly for her incompetency; severely blamed everyone, especially her husband, for not loving her unstintingly; and felt that all her unhappiness was caused by her husband's lack of affection.

The husband, at the same time, was a moderately disturbed individual who believed that his wife should be blamed for her mistakes, particularly the mistake of unjustly thinking he was having affairs with other women. He also believed that it was unfair for his wife to criticize and sexually frustrate him when he was doing the best he could, under difficult circumstances, to help her.

In this case, the somewhat unorthodox procedure of seeing both husband and wife together at all counseling sessions was employed. I often find this method to be time-saving, in that the main difficulties between the mates are quickly arrived at. I have observed, too, that the witnessing of one mate's emotional reeducation by the other spouse may serve as a model and incentive for the second spouse's philosophic reorientation. The husband-wife-therapist group, in this sense, becomes something of a small-scale attempt at group therapy.

Because the husband, in this case, was less seriously disturbed than the wife, his illogical assumptions were first brought to his attention and worked upon. He was shown that, in general, blame is an irrational feeling because it does neither the blamer nor his victim any good; and that, in particular, although many of his complaints about his wife's unrealistic jealousy and other disturbances might well have been justified, his criticizing her for this kind of behavior could only serve to make her worse rather than better—thus bringing more of the same kind of behavior down on his head.

The husband was also shown that his assumption that his wife *should* not berate or sexually frustrate him was erroneous; since why *should* not disturbed individuals act in precisely this kind of manner? He was led to see that, even though his wife's actions were mistaken, two wrongs do not make a right—and his reaction to her behavior was equally mistaken. For, instead of getting the results he wanted, he was only helping make things worse. If he really wished to help his wife—as he kept saying that he did—then he had better, for the present, *expect* her to act badly, stop inciting himself to fury when she did so, and spend at least several weeks returning her anger and discontent with kindness and acceptance. Thereby he would give her leeway to tackle her own disturbances.

The husband, albeit with some backsliding at times, soon began to respond to this realistic approach to his wife's problems; and, in the meantime, her irrational assumptions were tackled by the counselor. She was shown how and why she originally acquired her dire need to be loved and protected—mainly because her mother had not given her the love she required (or thought she required) as a child—and how necessarily self-defeating it was for her, as an adult, to continue to reinfect herself with this nonsensical belief. Her general philosophy of blaming herself and others was ruthlessly revealed to her and forthrightly attacked. She, like her husband, was shown just how such a philosophy is bound to alienate others, rather than win their approval or get them to do things in a different and presumably better manner.

Finally, the wife's notion that her unhappiness was caused by her husband's lack of affection was particularly brought to conscious awareness and exposed to the merciless light of rationality. She was shown, over and over again, how her unhappiness could come only from within, from her own attitudes toward external events such as her husband's lack of love, and that it could be expunged only by her facing her own part in creating it.

As the husband in this case started accepting his wife's neurosis more philosophically, she herself was more easily able to see, just because he was not goading and blaming her, that she was the creator of her own jealousies, self-hatred, and childish dependency. She began to observe in detail the sentences she kept telling herself to make herself unhappy.

On one occasion, when the counselor was explaining to the husband how he kept goading his wife to admit she was wrong, and how the husband ostensibly kept trying to help his wife think straight but actually kept showing how superior he was to her, the wife interrupted to say:

"Yes, and I can see that I do exactly the same thing, too. I go out of my way to find things wrong with him, or to accuse him of going with other women, because I really feel that I'm so stupid and worthless and I want to drag him down even below me." This, in the light of her previous defensiveness about her jealousies, was real progress.

After a total of twenty-three joint sessions of counseling, the fate of the marriage of this couple was no longer in doubt and they decided to go ahead with having a child, which they had previously avoided because of their mutual uncertainties. They also solved several other major problems which were not necessarily related to their marriage but which had previously proved serious obstacles to happy, unanxious living.

This is a fairly typical example of how a couple with a severe marital problem may be treated by a rational therapeutic approach to marriage counseling. It indicates some of the main irrational beliefs—such as the belief that one must be loved for oneself, no matter how badly one acts toward one's mate —which keep constantly cropping up to make people, and especially married couples, disturbed.

There are many other similar irrational beliefs, but most of them can be placed under ten or twelve major headings. As far as neurotic interaction in marriage is concerned, as a matter of fact, the basic unrealistic philosophies which upset people can fairly adequately be listed under five major headings:

1. *The dire need for love.* One of the major irrational assumptions that many persons in our society acquire is the notion that it is a dire necessity for an adult human being to be approved or loved by almost everyone for almost everything he does; that what others think of one is more important than gaining one's own self-respect; and that it is better to depend on others than on oneself. Applied to marriage, this means that the illogical and neurotic individual firmly believes that, no matter how he behaves, his mate, just because she *is* his mate, *should* love him; that if she doesn't respect him, life is a horror; and that her main role as a wife is to help, aid, succor him, rather than to be an individual in her own right.

When *both* marriage partners believe this nonsense—believe that they *must* be loved, respected, and catered to by the other—they are not only asking for what is rarely accorded an individual in this grimly realistic world, but are asking for unmitigated devotion from another individual who, precisely because he demands this kind of devotion himself, is the *least* likely candidate to give it. Under such circumstances, a major marital disaster is almost certain to occur.

The idea that one has to be thoroughly loved, admired, and liked by others, particularly by one's mate, is particularly beaten into almost all our heads in this society. Thus, we continually place an emphasis on the importance of getting consistently and unusually favorable responses from our associates and of feeling that one is somehow a failure, or worthless, whenever such responses are not forthcoming.

Actually, there are a great many other interesting and satisfying goals in life and in marriage than receiving affection. And it is difficult, if not impossible, to have intimate interaction with anyone over a period of time, especially in a domestic relationship such as marriage, without having your interests and desires interfere to some extent with the interests and desires of your mate; and vice versa. If, therefore, the fulfillment of a major pleasure is blocked by your spouse, however legitimately, it is idealistic nonsense to believe that you will love, admire, and like her wholeheartedly during the very moment that she frustrates you.

If you pretend that you ineffably love your marriage partner at the very moment when she is blocking your heartfelt desires, you are most likely to build up considerable resentment toward her. Even if you are not conscious of this resentment, it will probably come out indirectly, and perhaps all the more destructively, in other situations. If, however, you do not keep up this kind of pretense, then your spouse, if she is typically in the throes of the I-must-at-all-costs-at-all-times-be-adored philosophy of our culture, will almost certainly feel (that is, tell herself) that it is terrible that you have not given her your unconditional and permanent love, admiration, and acceptance. Either way, then, as a result of your mate's (or your own) holding this love-is-a-necessity policy, you are likely to sabotage whatever real feelings of love may originally exist in your marriage.

This over-emphasis in our culture on being loved is a prime example of how realistic *desires* can be easily and insidiously translated into neurotic *needs*. To some extent, young children *need* to be loved—that is, they require a certain amount of love and esteem, help and support, from the persons around them if they are to survive well physically and develop sufficient self-love, self-esteem, and self-confidence to become healthy and effective personalities. But, however necessary being loved may be for children (and there is some experimental evidence to indicate that even this may be exaggerated as a need after the child has passed the stage of early infancy), there is no evidence whatever that being loved or approved is absolutely necessary for adults. It is pleasant, nice, desirable for adults to be loved; but it is most questionable that it is really essential.

When one *believes*, however, that it *is* essential for one's happiness to be greatly loved, this very belief *makes* being loved a requisite for stability and happiness. Or, stated differently, when one *defines* one's well-being in terms of being accepted and approved by others, one makes it necessary, by that very definition, to be so accepted and approved. And when, in reality, one is *not* suitably loved, one will definitely, under these definitional circumstances, be miserable. Curiously enough, whenever this misery occurs, there is a tendency for most human beings to forget completely that it has been wholly caused *not* by the lack of love they receive but by their own *definition* of the "necessity" of their receiving this love.

The translation of the perfectly legitimate desire to be loved by one's mate into the idiotic and quite illegitimate so-called *need* to be adored by him or her is probably the most fundamental irrationality of millions of married individuals. This single unrealistic notion accounts for the highest percentage of serious neurotic interactions in marriage.

2. *Perfectionism in achievement.* A second major irrational belief which most disturbed people in our culture seem to hold is that a human being should or must be perfectly competent, adequate, talented, and intelligent in all possible respects and is utterly worthless if he or she is incompetent in any way. When married, these disturbed individuals tend to feel that, as mates, and particularly as sex partners, they should be utterly successful and achieving. The wife therefore berates herself because she is not a perfect housewife, mother, and bedmate; and the husband flays himself because he is not an unexcelled provider and sex athlete.

From this point on, things inevitably go from bad to worse. Becoming depressed because of their supposed inadequacies, both husband and wife may compulsively strive for perfection and almost kill themselves trying to keep up with what they consider their "normal" responsibilities.

Thus, the husband may try to have coitus with his wife every night, when he obviously is capable of doing so only once or twice a week. Or the wife may try to keep the house spotlessly clean at all times, even though she has two or three young children constantly helping to mess it up. Not only do such compulsive strivings foredoom themselves to failure; but, in addition, they tend to make the compulsively perfectionist mate abhor sex relations, housecleaning, or other aspects of marriage, and finally abhor marriage or the marital partner.

The other side of the coin of perfectionist strivings is equally dismal. Seeing that they cannot possibly attain the unrealistic marital goals that they set themselves, spouses frequently give up the battle completely, run out of the field, and actually *make themselves* into poor lovers or housemates. Thus, the husband who is perfectly capable of coitus twice a week, but not daily, may become so disgusted with himself for his "failure" that he eventually ceases all attempts at sex relations with his wife. Or the wife who cannot keep her home absolutely spotless, may give up and become slatternly, or a devoted clubwoman who is never at home, or even an adulteress who thereby stays away from her housewifely responsibilities.

3. *A philosophy of blame and punishment.* A third irrational assumption of most disturbed individuals is that one should severely blame oneself and

others for mistakes and wrongdoings; and that punishing oneself or others for errors will help prevent future mistakes.

Actually, blame or hostility toward oneself almost invariably serves to distract one from the real issue—"Now that I have made this mistake, how can I manage *not* to make it again?"—and to induce one destructively to focus on the false issue—"Now that I have made this mistake, how can I keep punishing myself and atoning for my great sin?" And blaming others carries one miles away from the practical problem—"Now that Smith has behaved badly toward me, how can I understand why he behaves in that manner and try to help him behave better in the future?"—and diverts one to the vicious circle of hostility—"Now that Smith has behaved badly toward me, how can I behave even worse toward him, so that he will hate me all the more and then behave still worse toward me?"

The married individual who blames others naturally tends to get upset by the mate's errors and stupidities, spends considerable time and energy trying to reform the spouse, and vainly tries to "help" a spouse by sharply pointing out the error of his or her ways. The expectable result is that the mate endeavors to act quite the same way, and brilliantly succeeds.

Because, as we previously have seen, emotionally disturbed human beings already have the tendency to blame themselves too much for their imperfections; because even healthy men and women tend to resist doing the so-called right thing when they are roundly criticized for doing the so-called wrong one; and because criticized humans tend to focus compulsively on their wrongdoings rather than calmly facing the problem of how they may *change* their behavior—for many reasons such as these, one partner's blaming another for the other's imperfections usually does immense harm.

Even counselors—who quite obviously are on their client's side—rarely can get away with blaming an individual. And spouses—who were often wed in the first place mainly because the bride or groom felt that he or she would *not* be criticized by this spouse—can virtually never do anything but the gravest harm to their relationships by criticizing their mates. But negative criticism is precisely what most disturbed individuals, by their basically false philosophies of living, are driven to make.

Married couples with self-blaming tendencies, moreover, ceaselessly continue to seek out their own "horrible" imperfections and to castigate and punish themselves mercilessly for their misdeeds. In so doing, they become irritable, depressed, and sometimes a victim of complete inertia. Naturally, under these circumstances, they rarely make good companions, bedmates, or parents. Their mates then tend to become equally distressed, and often blaming or self-blaming in their turn; and separation, divorce, or a continuing mock marriage impends.

4. *Catastrophizing frustrations.* A fourth idiotic assumption which underlies and causes emotional distress is the notion that it is terrible, horrible, and catastrophic when things are not the way one would like them to be; that others *should* make things easier for one, help conquer life's difficulties; and that one should not have to put off present pleasures for future gains. This is a typically childish philosophy of life; and when it is held by adults—which (look around you!) it obviously often is—it can only lead to disappointment, disillusionment, and hostility toward others and toward fate for *not* giving one the easy living one thinks is one's due.

In their marriages, individuals who consciously or unconsciously espouse this I-cannot-stand-frustration system of values invariably get into serious difficulties. For marriage, of course, *is* an exceptionally frustrating situation in many instances, involving considerable boredom, sacrifice, pleasure postponement, doing what one's mate wants to do, and so on. Children may be delightful members of a family in many instances; but child marriages, especially when the participants are technically adults, are generally disastrous. Childish mates bitterly resent their marriages and their spouses on numberless occasions; and, sooner or later, they clearly show this resentment. Then, often feeling that *they* are not loved or that they are being frustrated in *their* desires, the spouses of these childish wives and husbands get in a few or a few hundred counter-licks themselves, and the battle is again on. The ultimate result is invariably a hellish marriage—or a divorce.

5. *The belief that emotion is uncontrollable.* A fifth and final irrational belief which we shall consider here—since this is not primarily a book on neurosis itself but on irrationality in marriage—is the mythical supposition that most human unhappiness is externally caused or is forced on one by outside people and events and that one has virtually no control over one's emotions and cannot help feeling badly on many occasions. Actually, most human unhappiness is *self*-caused and results from invalid assumptions, and internalized sentences stemming from these assumptions, such as some of the beliefs which we have just been examining.

Once a married person is convinced, however, that his own unhappiness is externally caused, he inevitably blames his mate for his own misery; and, once again, he is in a marital stew. For the mate, especially if she is herself not too mature, will contend (a) that she does *not* cause his unhappiness; and (b) that he, instead, causes hers. Of such silly beliefs, again, is the stuff of separation made.

It is our staunch contention, then, that emotionally disturbed individuals possess, almost by definition one might say, a set of basic postulates which are distinctly unrealistic, biased, and illogical. Consequently, such individuals will find it almost impossible to be happy in an utterly realistic, everyday, down-to-earth relationship such as modern marriage usually is. Moreover, being unhappy, these easily upset mates will inevitably jump on their partners—who, if reasonably well adjusted, will tend to become fed up with the relationship and to want to escape from it; and, if somewhat neurotic themselves, will return their spouses' resentful sallies in kind, thus leading to neurotic interaction in marriage.

It should be stressed at this point that, no matter how irrational the beliefs of one spouse may be, it takes two disturbable people to make for true neurotic interaction in marriage. Suppose, for example, that a husband believes he must be completely loved by his wife, no matter how he behaves toward her. Suppose he also irrationally believes that he must be competent in all respects; that he should blame others, especially his wife, for errors and mistakes; that he must never be frustrated; and that all his unhappiness is caused by his wife's behavior and other outside events rather than by his own thinking and doing.

If the spouse of this severely disturbed husband had no similar illogical beliefs of her own, she would quickly see that her husband was disturbed, would not take his hostility toward herself with any resentment, and would either accept him the way he was, or would calmly try to see that he got professional help, or would quietly conclude that she did not want to remain married to such a disturbed individual and would divorce him. She would *not,* however, neurotically react to her husband herself, thus causing a mighty conflagration where there need only be a nasty, but still limited, flame.

Unfortunately, most disturbed husbands in our culture do not have completely sane wives, and most neurotic wives have equally irrational husbands. Therefore, instead of one mate's helping the other to overcome his or her difficulties, aggravation of these difficulties is the more usual procedure. The fact remains, however, and should never be lost from sight, that it is *not* the nagging, irresponsible, or depressed behavior of one marital partner that really causes the disturbance and negativism of the other partner. Rather, it is the *attitude* of the second partner *toward* the first—as well as, just as importantly, his attitude toward *himself.* If either one of two mates were truly rational and non-disturbed, this would not automatically lead to marital bliss in every instance; but it would definitely help prevent most of the extreme difficulties which are today so prevalent in marriage.

CHAPTER 4

WHEN ARE WE GOING TO QUIT STALLING ABOUT SEX EDUCATION?

EDITOR'S COMMENTARY:

The questions and comments raised and made by Ellis highlight his mind-set and hope for societal transition regarding sexual myths and mores. Yet, in spite of obvious changes during the fifty years from the time this chapter was first published, many of the questions still remain since there are so many sexual hang-ups that confront children, parents, and society in general. For example, Kinsey's studies about premarital sex showed numbers that today dwarf those original findings. Out of wedlock childbearing then was considered socially scandalous, whereas today, for example, more than 70% of African-American births take place outside of the marriage bond (but not necessarily outside of the bond of a couple residing together). Similarly, Caucasian births outside of marriage at the time constituted less than 5% of all births—even though abortion at the time was illegal in the United States and the pill had not yet been approved by the FDA—whereas today they constitute more than 35% of all such births. Nudity and partial nudity then were scandalous except as part of high culture in museums or troves of art treasure, whereas today distinctions are made between soft and hardcore porn for the consuming public. In this gem of a chapter, one that shows transition from study and comment to clinical pathology to follow, Ellis argued that to have good sex education demanded that there be good sex teachers. Of course, he included parents as good sex teachers, and he offered an outline on how to educate teachers, parents, clergy, and children. Given realities in the marketplace about sexual ideas and liberty in twenty-first-century America, Ellis's words still resonate since there are still school boards that veto sexual education, as well as parents who demand that they alone educate their children about physiology and the values attendant to reproduction. There are also countless organizations that shape guilt-filled behavior rather than seeing sex within a desired context such as love, or reproduction, or social responsibility (or as recreation, frankly).

Excerpted from *Sex Without Guilt*,
Lyle Stuart, Inc. 1958 & 1966

More nonsense is written about sex education than about virtually any other popular subject. In spite of these writings, or perhaps in some measure because of them, American sex attitudes, as I have shown in my books *The Folklore of Sex and The American Sexual Tragedy*, are thoroughly confused.

Thus, we heartily believe in sex education—and do little or nothing about it.

We say that we should go all out to teach our children the facts of life—and then, in our sex education materials, delete most of the realistic facts from life.

We put on determined sex education campaigns—and then see that our young people are so abysmally ignorant that they undergo innumerable unwanted pregnancies, unnecessary abortions, forced marriages, gruesome wedding nights, terrible sex fears, and needless divorces.

The truth is that our sex education today is bound to be emasculated; for the simple reason that our general sex beliefs and feelings are inconsistent and muddled. Most of us are not even aware of our now-you-see-them-and-now-you-don't sex attitudes, as their deepest roots are unconscious rather than conscious. Typically, we seem to think one way about sex—and actually think quite another.

For example, we consciously are horrified by the thought of premarital sex relations and adultery—and we unconsciously envy, laugh with, and even applaud fornicators and adulterers. Or we consciously think abortion is permissible—and unconsciously castigate ourselves for taking any part in one.

When, with our many open and underlying sex conflicts, we try to teach our children the objective and scientific facts of sex, we inevitably fumble pretty badly. We want to be oh so casual and cool about conveying the facts of life; instead, we tend to stammer, blush, look out of the window, paw restlessly at the floor with our feet, or otherwise avoid coming to direct, matter-of-fact terms with the subject we are trying to present. But children, of course, sense our feelings as well as our words. And telling them that sex is a perfectly natural and beautiful part of life while you are hum-hawing to beat all get-out is like trying to persuade them that you love your mother-in-law while you are using her picture as a spit target.

Let's face it: good sex education needs good sex teachers—teachers who are themselves free from irrational taboos; who think that sex is good clean fun; who have had a fine and abundant sex life themselves; and who can handle their own sex problems in much the same manner as they solve nonsexual life situations.

These teachers, whether they be parents or professionals, should of course present sex education in a global, total-pattern manner, as part of a unified picture of life. Human sex behavior cannot be divorced from emotion, personality, social living, economic affairs, and the other complex aspects of modern living. These teachers should not, under the guise of placing the facts of sex in the general context of life, instill irrelevant, guilt-producing notions that will deluge sexual science under a pietistic landslide.

No one, for example, would begin to teach a child homemaking tasks and responsibilities by beginning: "The home is a sacred place, and cooking and cleaning are beautiful God-given occupations which must always be carried out in a serious and sober manner, so that the fundamental purposes of life may be gloriously fulfilled." Yet, this is the kind of hokum with which our books and talks on sex education are commonly filled.

Naturally, when handed this type of "enlightenment," the bright child quickly begins to wonder what it is about sex that is so intrinsically filthy that mealy-mouthed words by the dozen are needed to help clean it up.

Once again: our children are virtually never taught that playing baseball is a worthy pastime—but that you must not talk about it publicly. Or that reading is an estimable occupation—but that *book*, *hero*, and *read* are nasty four-letter words which you must never say aloud. Or that playing chess is a wonderful sport—providing that you do not play it with your mother, father, sister, brother, other blood relations, any member of your own sex, and all but one single member of the other sex in your entire lifetime. Yet, while smugly assuring our youngsters that coitus is the finest and most beautiful thing in the world, we seriously caution them not to engage in, speak about, or ever privately think about it—except, perhaps, on any Fourth of July that happens to fall on Monday of a leap year. And then we wonder why, as adolescents and adults, they happen to have numberless sex problems!

What, then, is the answer?

Very frankly, as I point out in *The Case for Sexual Liberty* (1965a), there is no perfect, or even half-perfect, answer. Societal sex attitudes must be changed as a *whole* before we can reasonably expect *individual* sex education to be truly effective.

If you, for example, managed to surmount your own sex biases to some extent, and to present your child with objective, scientific sex viewpoints, you would be producing a youngster who would largely be out of step with his own community: since it is most unlikely that many of the other parents in your region would have given their children a similarly objective sexual frame of reference. The result would be that your youngster, while he might well be less sexually disturbed than his peers, would still tend to suffer from the disturbances of his environment: which is a sorry, and yet none the less incontrovertible, fact to contemplate.

Is the case of sex education in present-day America entirely hopeless then? No, not entirely. On the practical side, there are still a few things you can do to help along the cause of honest-to-goodness sex education in this and succeeding generations. Here are some suggestions:

1. Recognize your own sex ignorance and limitations and do not pretend that you know what you obviously do not know about sex and love.

2. Read as many scientific and factual books and articles on the subject as you can—and read everything that you do read most critically. Ignore all opinions that are moralistic or sectarian and try to draw conclusions from data rather than dogma.

3. Face your own sex problems squarely and honestly—and run, do not walk, to the nearest psychologist or marriage counselor when you are sexually disturbed.

4. As soon as your children begin asking sex questions, answer them in a direct, factual, down-to-earth manner. Teach them that sex, in virtually all its aspects, is a fine, pleasurable thing. But also teach them, prophylactically, that the world is presently full of bigots and ignoramuses who think otherwise and who will try to make them feel guilty about their sexuality. Tell them that, unfortunately, they will often have to obey against public display of nudity—but that as long as the laws and mores of these bigots—such as the laws that are discreet, they can, in the privacy of their own thoughts and boudoirs, guiltlessly keep their own counsels.

5. If you have any qualms about giving proper sex education to your children, do not hesitate to call on other qualified persons to help you do so. Psychologists, physicians, marriage counselors, teachers, and others who have specialized in sex education will be glad to be of service in this connection.

6. Above all, try to be as accepting, non-critical, and democratic about the

sex behavior of others as you can possibly be. Take the same attitudes toward sex ethics and morals as you would toward general ethics and morals. Work, in whatever way you can, for rules and laws which seek only to discourage sex acts whereby one individual needlessly, gratuitously, and distinctly harms another being, rather than statutes and mores which are based on superstition, ignorance, and sadistic sex "morality."

CHAPTER 5

DIFFERENCES AND DEVIATIONS
IN SEXUAL BEHAVIOR

EDITOR'S COMMENTARY:

Aside from a 1989 text about marriage intervention in which he was one of several authors, this first selection reflected Ellis as scientist, psychopathologist, and practitioner rather than sexual guru. These writings illustrated a transition to more clinical work by Ellis as the Institute that now bears his name had purchased a headquarters building where training and dissemination of information could be shared on a face-to-face basis in earnest. Ellis started this initial selection with the general idea of pathology, and that sexual pathology or any pathology for that matter could be approached statistically, biologically, morally, and psychologically. After examining each, and taking a peek through that particular lens, his emphasis centered on the psychological dimension. Ellis drew a parallel between a sexual neurotic and general neurotic, both of whom showed rigid behavior. While either type could logically favor a given behavior, the neurotic label applied when rigidity dominated in place of preference. To make the point clear, Ellis used an example of a woman with an eating disorder, noting that she might prefer salad over other foods, but to insist that this is the only type of food she could eat is rigid thinking. Following this line of reasoning, Ellis equated the term deviate to neurotic in that the rigid deviate refused to engage behaviors as matters of choice but only as matters of obsession and compulsion. In that sense, they deviated from choice makers. Ellis then likened fixed heterosexuals and homosexuals and bisexuals to his definition of rigid deviates or neurotics.

Concerning recognition of a person with emotional disturbance (especially oneself), Ellis gave a drop-bucket definition that such people acted irrationally, illogically, inappropriately, and childishly. Having said that, he also pointed out that the reader might not necessarily recognize neurotic behavior in self or others given the description. For example, if a person acts childishly when playing with the family dog or with his grandchildren, that is one thing. To have a temper tantrum during a business discussion as might a toddler is quite another, as is eccentricity compared to neurosis. Ellis then developed recognizable

71

differences highlighted by guilt and blame, feelings of inadequacy, genetic predisposition or heredity, hostility and resentment, a variety of defenses, rigidity and compulsiveness, shyness and withdrawal, antisocial and rule breaking behavior, psychosomatic symptoms and hypochondria, depression (compared to being blue or sad from time to time), narcissism and inability to love, inability to relax or to enjoy a hobby, overexcitement, inertia and lack of direction, striving with too much ambition, escaping into irresponsibility, and self-downing or lack of what today would be called unconditional self-acceptance.

Excerpted from *The Art and Science of Love,*
Lyle Stuart, Inc. 1960

It is surprisingly difficult to define exactly what is a sexual deviation. Sex books and discussions often devote large amounts of space and time to the so-called deviations, perversions, or abnormalities; and yet there is little agreement among the writers and discussants as to what, essentially, constitutes deviated behavior.

As I have shown in previously published papers and books (A. Ellis, 1952b, 1963a, 1963e, 1965a), various authorities have insisted that a sexually deviated or perverted act is one that is (a) statistically abnormal or infrequently resorted to by members of the general populace; (b) biologically or procreatively inappropriate; (c) psychologically unhealthy or immature; or (d) ethically or morally "bad" or "wrong." None of these criteria, I contend, is satisfactory because, in the last analysis, each depends largely on social norms or on culturally approved standards; and these norms and standards differ enormously from one community to another.

Thus, from a statistical standpoint, masturbation and petting are widely prevalent in our country; while instead, homosexuality seems more frequent among young Arabian males. Who, then, are we to call deviated or sexually abnormal—ourselves or the Arabs?

From the standpoint of mental health or emotional "maturity," it may be healthful and mature for a Scandinavian girl to have an "illegitimate" child but unhealthful and "immature" for a modern American girl to do likewise. And where it was relatively "healthy" for an ancient Greek male to be largely homosexual in his interests and acts, it is (as we shall show below) distinctly "unhealthy" or "neurotic" for a modern American male to be predominantly homosexual.

From a so-called biological or procreative standpoint, all acts which do not lead to childbearing, such as masturbation and petting, would have to be called perverse; while forcible rape or an adult male's being attracted exclusively to thirteen-year-old girls would have to be deemed perfectly "normal." A married couple's having intercourse with the use of contraceptives would also have to be viewed as abnormal or deviated behavior.

From a moral or theoretical point of view, a woman's having an orgasm in marital intercourse may be looked upon as wicked (as it actually is viewed in some communities, including some fanatical religious groups in our own country); while a woman's remaining with her husband when she does not have sex satisfaction may be seen as a virtual crime in other communities (as it seems to be viewed among some fanatical romantic groups among our avant garde liberals). Which of these women, the one who does or the one who does not have a climax in marital relations, are we to consider a pervert?

Although the usual definitions of sexual deviation would seem to be prejudiced and parochial, and none of them can be *absolutely* upheld, there does seem to be one that holds up fairly well for people living in our own society as well as for most individuals in most societies: namely, a psychosocial approach to deviation.

This definition starts with the assumption, which I first stated in *The American Sexual Tragedy* (1963e), that an individual who has no sexual defects (such as an injured penis or neuromuscular deficiencies) may be considered to be sexually deviated if he can *only*, under *all* circumstances, enjoy one special form of sexual activity: or if he is obsessively-compulsively fixated on a given mode of sex behavior; or if he is fearfully and rigidly bound to one or two forms of sexual participation.

This definition of sexual deviation—or sexual neurosis—is the only one that seems to be consistent with that which is usually given of a non-sexual deviation or neurosis. A non-sexual neurotic is an individual who, out of some kind of illogical fear, favors one kind of behavior (such as staying alone in his room) and disfavors another kind (such as going to social functions or riding on trains). A sexual neurotic or deviant, similarly, may be said to be an individual who, out of irrational anxiety, rigidly refrains from one kind of behavior (such as heterosexuality) and adheres exclusively to another kind (such as homosexuality or masturbation).

By the same token, a non-sexual neurotic often becomes obsessively-compulsively attached to a given form of conduct—such as touching picket fences, keeping his room inordinately clean and tidy, or remaining thoroughly attached to his mother. And a sexual neurotic or deviant becomes obsessively-compulsively attached to a given form of sex conduct—such as copulating with women who have small feet or who wear bloomers, or who whip him.

This does not mean that individuals cannot *logically* favor or prefer one kind of sexual (or non-sexual) conduct to another. They can (Kepner, 1959). Thus, it is possible for a woman to prefer staying by herself attending social functions or prefer being a Lesbian to being heterosexual—provided that she has, for a reasonable length of time, unprejudicedly *tried* both alternatives (that is, tried sociality *and* asociality or heterosexuality *and* Lesbianism) and then merely decided that she likes one mode better than the other.

If however, this same woman rarely or never tries, say, social functions or heterosexuality and still insists that they are worthless, pleasureless activities, we can only surmise that she has some irrational fear of these kinds of acts and that she is compulsively attached to other activities because of her fear. Under these circumstances, we would have to think of her as being neurotic.

Moreover: even if this woman tries social functions and heterosexuality and finds them relatively unsatisfactory as compared to staying at home and being homosexual, it would be suspicious if she *always*, under *all* circumstances, rigidly sticks to her preferences. Granted that she usually may dislike social affairs, why should she always find them distasteful—especially, say, when something is to be gained, such as a job promotion, by attending one? And granted that she prefers Lesbians, why should she, in the face of suffering possible grave penalties for being homosexual, always engage in Lesbian acts and refuse more safely available, albeit somewhat less satisfactory, heterosexual affairs?

If we forget about sex for a moment and transpose the problem of deviance and neurosis into, say, the analogous problem of eating, the core attitudes behind deviation will probably become much clearer.

Suppose, for instance, that an individual who is in good physical health and has no special allergic reactions tries all kinds of foods, eats at different hours, and uses several types of crockery. He finally decides that he prefers meat and potatoes to all other foods, that he likes to eat one large meal a day, at three in the morning, and that blue plates are best for him. Under these circumstances, many of us might think this individual peculiar; but we would have no scientific grounds for calling him neurotic or deviated.

Suppose, however, this same individual insists, after little or no experimentation, that he will eat *nothing* but meat and potatoes; or that he *only* will eat at three in the morning, even if he is starving; or that he must eat *exclusively* on blue plates and cannot eat on dishes of any other color. Or suppose, if meat and potatoes are arbitrarily banned in his community and a stiff jail sentence is given to anyone discovered eating them, he *still* insists on ingesting only this kind of food and refuses to touch any other kind of easily available victuals. Or suppose that he is utterly revolted by every other kind of food except meat and potatoes and winces with disgust every time he sees others eating these other foods.

Such an individual, obviously, has a distinct, illogical *fear* of most foods, or of different eating times, or of non-blue plates. From a psychological standpoint, he is clearly abnormal, fixated, compulsive, or neurotic.

Suppose—to use an opposite example that a person enjoys many kinds of foods but that, without really ever having tried meat and potatoes, or after trying them once or twice and finding them mildly unsatisfying, or after trying them only *after* he has convinced himself that they cannot be appetizing, he insists that these foods *must be* utterly revolting and he either never tries them again or occasionally tries them with great prejudice and keeps insisting that they are tasteless or disgusting. From a psychological standpoint, again, this person would have to be classed as distinctly phobic or neurotic.

So, too, are sexually fixated or compulsively driven people neurotic. Irrationally ignoring the *many* possible kinds of sex participation, they rigidly adhere to a single mode or two. Or, in some instances, they try a variety of sex acts (such as masturbation, homosexuality, exhibitionism, and peeping) but fearfully refrain from other common modes (such as heterosexuality).

If these people, without fear and after a fair trial, simply *preferred* one kind of sex behavior and *preferred* to eliminate another kind, that would be one thing. But when they are thoroughly *fixated* on one mode and *phobic* toward another, they are clearly afflicted with sexual deviation or neurosis (Ollendorf, 1966).

I am reminded, in this connection, of a story told to me by Donald Webster Cory, author of the excellent book, *The Homosexual in America*, and himself one of America's outstanding bisexuals, about the time when he was among a group of fixed homosexuals, one of whom was describing to the other members of the group an experiment that had been done to test the odor of used menstrual pads.

According to Cory, almost all the other members of the group turned visibly pale and showed extreme discomfiture; and several of them insisted that unless the speaker stopped his description, they would begin to retch. This is an excellent illustration, I feel, of the extreme ideological prejudice which a neurotic or deviate can acquire against even the thought of an irrationally feared object or event (in this case, the homosexual's fear of female genitals).

It is important, for the sake of scientific clarity, that we be utterly consistent in our definition of sexual deviation and that we eschew existing superstitions which are based on an erroneous view of animal sexuality. Thus, it is often held that, since lower animals only have heterosexual intercourse and rarely or never resort to such acts as masturbation or homosexuality, it is "unnatural" and "perverted" for man to do so. This is sheer nonsense: animals frequently masturbate and often resort to homosexuality. Besides, the argument, that, because man is an animal, he should necessarily do what other animals do is hardly a legitimate one.

The other end of this argument is equally fallacious; that because man has a mammalian heritage (as the Kinsey researchers accurately keep pointing out) and mammals engage in all kinds of sex acts, including homosexual behavior, when humans engage in these same acts they are only "normal" and are never "abnormal" or "perverted."

This argument is partially correct in that homosexual activity *in itself* is not abnormal or deviated, since its roots are well established in man's biological plurisexual heritage. But when an individual's homosexual acts become fixated, fear-impelled, or obsessive-compulsive then, we must again insist, they are just as deviant as would be his frantically or compulsively eating, running, or making noises—all of which are also part of our mammalian heritage.

At the same time, we must not fall into the unscientific trap of viewing as "perverted"—as the writers of the Old Testament did—any sex act which is non-procreative.

We know today, as the ancient Hebrews did not, that human sexuality is designed for fun and frolic, as well as for procreative ends. If non-procreative acts actually were deviated we would have to call millions of married individuals who use contraceptives, as we noted above, sex perverts.

Even so liberal a sexologist as Van de Velde (1926) makes the mistake of defining "normal" sex behavior as follows: "That intercourse which takes place between two sexually mature individuals of opposite sexes; which excludes cruelty and the use of artificial means for producing voluptuous sensations; which aims directly or indirectly at the consummation of sexual satisfaction, and which, having achieved a certain degree of stimulation, concludes with ejaculation—or emission—of the semen into the vagina, at the nearly simultaneous culmination of sensation—or orgasm—of both partners."

In this definition, he labels as "abnormal" any sex act which makes use of artificial means (such as a massaging device), which is even slightly sadistic, which is not always intended to end in orgasm, which is ever anything but heterosexual, which results in extra-genital orgasm for either partner, and which ends in penile-vaginal copulation but not in almost simultaneous orgasm.

On every one of these counts Van de Velde is wrong. Perfectly normal and non-perverted sex behavior may *at times* be homosexual, somewhat sadomasochistic, artificially aided, undirected toward orgasm, extra-genital, and non-productive of simultaneous climax. It is only when the sex participant invariantly resorts to some of the acts Van de Velde describes, and does so out of compulsive fear or hostility rather than out of moderate preference, that he can accurately be called abnormal or perverted.

If we eliminate unscientific and vague definitions of deviation, it should be clear that a human being's engaging in many acts which have frequently been labeled as "unnatural" or "perverse" may or may not constitute his being deviated.

Thus, if a male engages in homosexual activity during his teens, becomes heterosexually oriented by the time he is an adult, but occasionally (especially when he is isolated from females) re-engages in homosexual acts, we cannot justifiably call him a homosexual or deviant.

A fixed homosexual is one who, after reaching adulthood, *exclusively* or *mainly* lusts after members of his own sex and has little or no desire for members of the other sex.

A fixed homosexual is a deviant not because he engages in inverted acts but because, out of an irrational fear of heterosexuality, he does not desire heterosexual activities. If he were truly bisexual or ambisexual and had spontaneous, non-compulsive desires for members of both sexes he would not necessarily be sexually deviant or neurotic. He might, on other counts, however, be emotionally disturbed not for having but for giving in to his bisexual desires, just as a person might be neurotic not merely for having but chronically giving in to the desire to steal when he lived in a community which severely punished thieves.

Our typical Greenwich Village type homosexuals are deviant or neurotic because they not only engage in inverted sex acts, but usually are (a) compulsively homosexual; (b) irrationally afraid of or disgusted by members of the other sex; (c) rebelliously insistent on flouting their homosexuality, in spite of the legal penalties and other difficulties which are attendant upon such flouting; and

(d) exceptionally defensive about their homosexuality, usually will not admit that it is limited or neurotic, and often contend that they are better off than or superior to heterosexuals. The deviation of these homosexuals consists not in the kind of sex act they perform but the fearful and hostile manner in which they perform it.

As Alfred Adler pointed out many years ago (Ansbacher, 1958), the fixed homosexual who typically inhabits our metropolitan areas generally, by his entire way of living (rather than just by his sex acts), is expressing (a) an exaggerated psychological difference which he thinks exists between man and woman; (b) a more or less deep-seated revolt against adjustment to the normal sex role; (c) a tendency to depreciate females; (d) compensatory tendencies to alleviate the feeling of inferiority he feels in the face of the overrated power of woman; and (e) a display of increased oversensitivity, ambition, defiance, distrust of others, and the desire to dominate. McReynolds (1959), Cory (1958, 1963, 1964), and R. Harper (1959b), although apparently unaware of Adler's position heartily concur about the defensiveness, self-destructiveness and pseudo-creativeness of the vast majority of fixed homosexuals.

Once we define sexual deviation in the psychological manner in which we are now doing, we must be consistent and objective about whom we label as deviant. Just as we may call a person deviant because he is a fixed homosexual, so we may also, at times, have to term him deviant because he is a fixed and invariant heterosexual.

Thus, we have the cases of many heterosexuals who under no circumstances would consider forgoing their usual heterosexual activities for masturbatory or homosexual acts—even, for example, if they were imprisoned only with members of their own sex for thirty years. And we have many other heterosexuals who, in their marital relations, will adhere only to one form of activity, such as coitus with the male surmounting the female, and will under no conditions resort to petting, kissing, or other coital positions.

Such individuals, obviously, have some arbitrary or irrational *fear* of non-heterosexual or non-coital relations. Therefore, even though the form of their sex activity is perfectly "normal" their general sex outlook is deviated or abnormal.

Are we to conclude, then, that the only individual in society who is perfectly normal sexually is one who engages in *all* kinds of activity, including heterosexual, homosexual, and animal relations?

Naturally not: any more than we would contend that anyone who did not thoroughly enjoy *all* kinds of would be abnormal.

A *reasonable* restriction or constriction of one's sex desires and acts, in accordance with personal individuation, is only to be expected; and a reasonable channelization is also to be expected—especially in a country, such as our own, where the laws and mores actively propagandize the citizens against certain sex practices, such as homosexual activities, and in favor of other practices, such as heterosexual participations.

"The fact remains, however, that when an individual in our society *completely*, under *all possible* circumstances restricts himself to one, and only one, quite specialized form of sex behavior, and when he does so not out of mere preference, after first engaging in considerable experimentation, and not because of some unusual physical anomaly but out of an arbitrary, illogical, or fear-induced notion, then he is sexually deviated or neurotic.

By the same token, an individual who utilizes several kinds of sexual outlets but who will under no circumstances even try another common kind of outlet (such as masturbation, coitus, petting, or genital kissing), is to some extent deviated, though perhaps to a lesser degree than the person who rigidly adheres to a single outlet.

If the mode of sex behavior to which a deviant rigidly is attached is a broad one, as well as one which is socially approved in the community in which he resides, then he may be relatively little deviated or neurotic.

Thus, an individual in our society who only engages in heterosexual relations, including kissing, petting, and several different coital positions but who under no conditions will ever consider masturbating or having homosexual relations, may be considered a minor deviant.

By the same token, a person who masturbates, pets, and has several kinds of heterosexual coitus but who will under no circumstances try oral-genital relations (which today are becoming acceptable among educated persons) with his or her mate is also deviated; but probably to a minor degree.

On the other hand, an individual in our society who, under normal conditions, refuses to try sex relations with members of his own sex or with animals can hardly be called deviated: since these are still highly frowned upon and legally penalized activities. At the same time, if this individual refuses, under quite *abnormal* conditions (say, on a desert island, where there is no sexual alternative), to consider having homosexual or animal relations, then we may justifiably call him a deviate—though a minor one.

We are including in our concept of sex deviation, in other words, the concepts of both *fetichism* and *antifetichism*. If a person is irrationally driven or inordinately compelled to do a certain limited (and sometimes bizarre) kind of sex act in order to achieve satisfaction, he is a fetichist and hence deviated. If he is fearfully or arbitrarily biased against and repelled by any kind of sex activity, particularly one that is widely accepted in his community, then he is an anti-fetichist and also deviated.

We are also differentiating, in our concept of sex deviation, between (a) sexual deviants and non-deviants and (b) major and minor deviants. All sexual deviants, we are saying, irrationally and arbitrarily narrow down their potential sex activities and either fearfully under-perform or compulsively over-perform in certain sexual areas.

Minor deviants narrow down their potentially pleasurable experiences less than do major deviants. Thus, a minor deviant may practice several modes of sex conduct (including masturbation, homosexuality, and petting with females) but may fearfully refrain from one other mode (such as heterosexual coitus).

A major deviant will tend to limit himself to one particular act (such as exhibitionism, masturbation, or homosexual relations with young boys) and to refrain from all or most other acts.

We may also distinguish between sex deviants who commit statutory offenses and those who do not. Thus, an individual who only enjoys masturbation or who only becomes sexually excited when his heterosexual partners wear pink bloomers will not normally commit any offense if he follows his deviant proclivities; while an individual who exclusively engages in homosexuality or sex relations with animals will be a sex offender if he resides in the United States or most other civilized nations. Deviants who commit actual statutory offenses will tend to be more emotionally disturbed than those who commit no such offenses—since, by resorting to illegal acts, they are putting themselves in jeopardy and therefore acting in a self-defeating manner. Many exceptionally disturbed deviants, however, never commit any statutory offense.

One other kind of possible sex deviation should be considered and that is what might be called *disordered sexuality* or *general compulsive sexuality*.

Some authorities, such as Allen (1949), Kahn (1937), Karpman (1955), and Pollens (1938), have pointed out that sex deviates, particularly those who get arrested for committing sex offenses, frequently engage in several kinds of activities. Thus, on different occasions a man may be arrested for exhibitionism, peeping, and homosexuality; and this same individual may be married and have a record of many successful heterosexual participations. Obviously, he is not fetichistic or anti-fetichistic; but just as obviously, since he keeps getting into difficulties and is often driven to commit new sex offenses, he is hardly sexually normal.

In my own experience with these kinds of deviates, both in my work as Chief Psychologist of the New Jersey State Diagnostic Center (a special psychiatric facility for examining sex offenders) and in my private practice as a psychotherapist, I have found that this generalized type of sex deviate is quite disordered or compulsive and that his disorder stems from intellectual subnormality and/or extreme emotional disturbance.

Usually, these individuals are more or less psychotic; and, just as they are driven to perform all kinds of bizarre non-sexual acts (such as senseless thefts, arson, assault and battery, and even murder) they are also compelled by their thoroughly disordered thinking to commit several different kinds of sex acts which, in themselves, may be fairly harmless but which are banned by their communities.

This type of individual with generally disordered or compulsive sexuality is significantly different from the usual fetichistic or anti-fetichistic deviant in many respects. The common ground on which they meet is that of emotional disturbance; but the usual kind of deviate may be (though not necessarily is) considerably less disturbed than the general sex deviate.

Sexual deviation, then, stems from an individual's having some illogical, irrational, childish, fixated fetichistic (or anti-fetichistic), inflexible *ideas* about what he may or may not do sexually. As such, it does not necessarily refer to his *practicing* a given form of sex behavior but to his *wanting* to adhere to a deviant mode even when alternative modes are freely available.

A person who is exclusively homosexual because there are no women available is not necessarily a deviant; but one who exclusively desires sex relations with members of his own sex, even though he actually has no homosexual activity because he fears arrest or hasn't the courage to risk rebuff by other males is, actually, deviated. An overt deviant is one who puts his fear-impelled ideas into practice; a latent deviant is one who would like to do so but for one reason or another does not.

Many psychologists and psychiatrists, particularly those of Freudian orientation, talk of "latent homosexuality" in connection with individuals who consciously believe that they are heterosexual but who unconsciously are attracted to members of their own sex. This definition of latent homosexuality is exceptionally vague and loose: since virtually all so-called normal human beings have *some* unconscious homosexual urges. The mere fact that we are all biologically bisexual or plurisexual means that, in most instances, we will *sometimes* be sexually attracted to members of the same sex; and even, as the Kinsey figures show, that we will tend to have a few homosexual episodes during our lives.

Real latent homosexuality occurs, however, when an individual consciously feels that he is entirely or almost entirely heterosexual but when, unconsciously and actually, he has *considerable* or *almost exclusive* homosexual leanings. That such latent homosexuality exists in some individuals is certain, judging from clinical evidence; but that latent homosexuals, in the true sense of the term, frequently exist in our society is dubious.

Another classical psychoanalytical concept which unfortunately has taken wide root since Freud first expounded it (Freud, 1938) is the idea that human beings are "naturally" polymorphous perverse—meaning, that they are biologically plurisexual—and that they "normally" go through, first, the stage of masturbation, then homosexuality, and finally heterosexuality.

This theory contends that when individuals do not finally attain heterosexual orientation, but remain "fixated" on the polymorphous perverse or homosexual levels, they are deviates. It also holds that individuals have pregenital or partial sex instincts—such as those of desiring caressing, fondling, kissing, and anal contacts—and that when they remain fixated on the pregenital levels they again become deviates—such as homosexuals, sadomasochists, exhibitionists, etc.

Although this Freudian theory has some degree of validity—since human beings are biologically plurisexual and can become fixated on some aspect of their potential sexual range and thereby become deviated—it includes a whopping untruth: namely, that there are almost invariant "normal" stages of human sexual development and that the average person goes neatly through these stages.

Actually, as I have found with many individuals seen for intensive psychotherapy and as Pomeroy (1958) has observed, some people never experience certain stages (thus, never contemplate or engage in homosexual relations); others go through certain stages in reverse (for example, first have a homosexual and *then* a masturbatory phase); still others easily flip back and forth, from one so-called stage to another (for instance, first become heterosexual, then homosexual, then heterosexual again); and some follow different patterns.

Sexual deviation, therefore, does not consist of a regression to or fixation upon an early "normal" stage of sexual development; but rather a fixation upon a distinctly limited or disordered form of sexuality at *any* stage in the individual's life. It implies (a) biological plurisexualism or the *capacity* to experience sex satisfaction in several different ways at all ages in an individual's existence; and (b) psychological fetichism, anti-fetichism, or compulsivity.

In the last analysis deviation is an arbitrary, childish, fear-inspired renunciation of some of one's innate capacities for sexual enjoyment or an equally childish rebellion-impelled refusal to exert a reasonable degree of social control over one's sex drives. Sex deviation is thus a special kind of neurosis or psychosis.

Causes of sexual deviation. Although sex deviants have been clinically and experimentally studied for the last century and there is considerable agreement among authorities as to what the basic causes of deviation are, there is also considerable remaining disagreement, particularly in relation to the causes of homosexuality.

CHAPTER 6

THINKING–FEELING
POTENTIALS

EDITOR'S COMMENTARY:

In this selection, Albert Ellis claimed that RET (rational-emotive therapy) could be accomplished in far fewer visits than other therapies while being profound—to the consternation of depth psychotherapists who claimed just the opposite. Many changes, he claimed, were by-products of main events, particularly as clients learned how RET could intervene for them in their lives in general and not just for a specific problem which might have brought them into psychotherapy in the first place. While emphasizing homework and elegant solutions, Ellis complimented Carl Rogers for his work on positive regard—although both Rogers and like-minded practitioners argued for highly emotional transference processes to achieve results which were not as effective as the holistic acceptance taught by Ellis. Further, Ellis went on the offensive by arguing that Rogers and like-minded therapists did not attack the underpinning behaviors that generated neurotic misery. Next, Ellis argued for what he called a rigorous scientific approach, the heart of which in rational-emotive behavior therapy was his ABC model explicated at length. Ellis argued against what he called magical formulation, which today might be called logical fallacies (such as the past creating the present, which is called the fallacy of post hoc, ergo propter hoc). To round out this selection, Ellis pointed to the many studies then available supporting rational-emotive interventions for their effectiveness in helping to eliminate neurotic behavior and encourage unconditional self-acceptance.

Evolution of a Revolution

Excerpted from *Growth Through Reason*, Wilshire Books, 1971

Rational-emotive psychotherapy has many unique features that differentiate it from most other forms of psychotherapy. One of these in particular will be emphasized by the cases that are included in this book: namely, that it is not only a relatively short-term procedure (taking from one to thirty sessions in most instances, where the conventional forms of therapy take considerably longer), but it usually fosters gains within gains. That is to say, when a rational-emotive therapist is working with a client on a major problem—such as the typical symptom of feelings of severe inadequacy or worthlessness—there tends to occur (a) a significant diminution of this problem before the symptom is completely eliminated and (b) an amelioration of certain other of the client's emotional complaints, even though some of them may have hardly been mentioned during the therapy sessions.

This kind of treatment bonus, moreover, often occurs with startling rapidity. When I practiced psychoanalysis and psychoanalytic psychotherapy some years ago, I warned my clients that before they improved as a result of seeing me, they might well get worse. And I was frequently right! Many of them ultimately got better—but only after they had undergone considerable suffering concomitantly with, and quite probably as a direct result of, treatment. For revealing to an individual some of his hidden traits and motivations may finally do *him* some good, but in the short run it aggravates his suffering.

This can happen in rational-emotive therapy (RET, for short), too; but it usually doesn't. RET not only quickly reveals to the individual many important things of which he is, at best, only dimly aware; but it almost immediately begins to undercut and disembowel the conscious and unconscious irrational assumptions that make him and keep him emotionally disturbed. This is particularly true of his un-substantiable negative assumptions about himself, which create his "feelings" of inadequacy, worthlessness, anxiety, guilt, and depression. From the very first therapeutic session, the therapist is showing the client exactly what his self-defeating values and philosophies are, how these make him anxious and self-hating, and precisely what he can do to question and challenge them in order to minimize or exterminate their effects.

In the distinct majority of instances, then, RET begins to work promptly and to produce some beneficial results. This does not mean that all rational-emotive clients, or even the majority of them, become significantly improved or "cured" in a brief period of time. Not so! Some of them make little or no advance for many weeks. Others make progress but take a long time before they finally make important inroads against their basic self-sabotaging philosophies and thereby become better.

Nor is the rational-emotive therapist usually interested in what is called a "symptom cure"—although the so-called "depth" therapists like to think so ad nauseam. On the contrary, he normally tries for what he considers to be the most elegant cure imaginable: that is, a radical restructuring of the client's value system and the semiautomatic internalization by him of a scientific, logico-empirical attitude toward himself and the world that will effectively prevent him from ever becoming seriously disturbed again. Unless the client is in some special, restricted category—is, for example, very young or old, or of quite limited intelligence—the therapist vigorously endeavors to induce him to surrender some of his basic philosophic nonsense, and not merely his annoying symptoms. If this can't be accomplished, too bad; but almost always this is the rational-emotive therapeutic goal.

That is why the incidental, and often amazingly quick, gains achieved in RET are so startling: they are almost a by-product rather than a direct aim of the therapy process. In my own case, for example, I generally assume that my new client probably is capable of fundamental personality change rather than only relatively slight behavior modification. I also assume that although most individuals have great difficulty in changing their fundamental views and behaviors, this particular client may be one of the relatively few who is able to do so with some degree of ease and speed. If I am wrong, then he and I have lost little or nothing. If I am right, then we both are saved considerable time, and he gains a shortcut to release from pain. So why not experiment and see?

Experiment? Why, of course! One of the brightest aspects of psychotherapy, and the prime element in keeping it (at least for myself) from becoming a blasted bore, is the fact that each client is in many respects quite singular, different from the many others who have gone before him; and therefore there is no damned way of knowing, save clairvoyantly, how he is going to react to the same kinds of methods that the therapist has used many times before or to different techniques that he improvises for this current encounter. Even, therefore, when the therapy of choice is far from being eclectic and is based on a clear-cut theory and practice (as is RET), each session is still highly experimental. Although I have realized this to some degree for many years, I am grateful to Gerald C. Davison and his associates

(1970) at the State University of New York at Stony Brook for recently emphasizing this point in a more formal manner.

Anyway, as I experiment with the new client who is before me, I try many maneuvers to try to achieve a consistent goal: to see how quickly I can get him to see what is *really* bothering him, to understand exactly what he is doing to make this thing bothersome, and to discover what he can do to stop bothering himself. If I can get him to see these things, and then to act on them quickly, fine. If not, too bad. But almost always, if he works at all at helping himself along the lines I outline for him, he will improve to some extent, usually, within a short period of time.

That is what most of the cases in this book demonstrate: that rational-emotive psychotherapy tends not only to work, but to have fairly immediate as well as long-range effects. *Why* it works this well is, of course, open to various interpretations. Relationship-oriented therapists, such as Arbuckle (1967) and Patterson (1966, 1969), and psychoanalytically-oriented therapists, such as Greenwald (1967), tend to "explain" RET results by hypothesizing that it is not the rational-emotive therapist's didactic content and philosophic analysis that really affect the client, but rather it is his warmth, his relating, or his transference connections with the client. This is a little far-fetched, since, as will be seen in the cases in this book, he frequently has a minimum relationship and a maximum teaching alliance with his client. Moreover, if the RET "relationship" works so quickly, even when little or no effort is made to achieve it, how is it that the client-centered, experiential, existential, and psychoanalytically-oriented relationships work so slowly, even when therapists who subscribe to these schools take such great pains to establish them?

Other critics of RET, such as Pottash and Taylor (1967) claim that it really gets its good results because it is a kind of behavior therapy that conditions the client to react better and to surrender his symptoms. This is partly true since the rational-emotive therapist does reinforce the client's more efficient behavior, and he does make liberal use of *in vivo* homework assignments that help force the client to act differently. However, systematic desensitization, operant conditioning, and other forms of behavior therapy generally take a number of sessions to produce good therapeutic results (Wolpe and Lazarus, 1966), whereas RET may help create significant behavioral change in as little as one or two sessions. Moreover, as some of the less doctrinaire leaders in the field of behavior therapy have been increasingly pointing out, cognitive processes are really explicitly or implicitly included in most effective behavior therapy cases, and rational-emotive psychotherapy, in particular, is one of the best means for supplementing traditional desensitizing or operant conditioning methods (Davison & Valins, 1969; Eysenck, 1964; Lazarus, 1971).

Are cognitive processes and didactic teaching the core of the rational-emotive technique? Yes and no. Actually, as its name implies, RET is a truly comprehensive method of treatment, which includes cognitive-explicatory, evocative-emotive, and behavioristic-active-directive methods. As noted in the previous paragraph, it is strongly oriented toward homework assignments, as well as to other active-directive techniques, such as role-playing, assertion training, and conditioning and counter-conditioning procedures. It also makes use of many dramatic-emotive exercises, particularly in the course of group and marathon encounter therapy, including honest expression of feeling, direct confrontation, risk-taking experiences, uninhibited language, love experiences, and the use of unconditional positive regard. Its unique essence, however, especially when it is employed in individual psychotherapy and in marriage and family therapy, is a Socratic-type dialogue through which the client is calmly, logically, forcefully taught that he'd better stop telling himself nonsense, accept reality, desist from condemning himself and others, and actively persist at making himself as happy as he can be in a world that is far from ideal.

RET also differs from the vast majority of other schools of psychotherapy in that it consciously strives to help the client achieve the most elegant solution to the problem of human worth or self-acceptance. Theoretically, virtually all systems of therapy aim for the client's self-acceptance; but actually they tend to fall down sadly. Thus, Carl Rogers (1961, 1971) has done a great service to psychology by emphasizing the value of unconditional positive regard; and in this respect, as Bone (1968) incisively points out, client-centered and rational-emotive psychotherapy are oriented toward the same goals. In actual practice, however, almost all Rogerian and existentialist therapists seem to assume that their clients can only improve through highly conditional positive regard: through the therapist's relating warmly to the client and, by his existential encounter with the client, showing him that he is a worthy person *because* the therapist accepts him and *because*, presumably, others will therefore accept him as well. Consequently, the "successfully" treated Rogerian client normally gains "self-esteem" or "ego strength" by entering therapy with the irrational idea, "I am no good unless other people accept or love me," and leaving therapy with the slightly better but still basically insane idea, "I am now worthwhile because my therapist cares for me, and presumably others can care for me as well." It is exceptionally difficult to see how this client has gained any appreciable kind of unconditional positive self-regard.

Conditional self-acceptance is similarly achieved by the client in most other types of therapy—including experiential, basic encounter, sensitivity training, reality, Gestalt, Synanon, and operant conditioning therapy. For all these schools go along with the individual's basic irrational belief that it is not only preferable that others approve of him but that he absolutely needs this approval if he is to accept himself. Essentially, therefore, these forms of therapy "help" him by showing him better techniques of relating rather than disabusing him of the idea that he has to relate well in order to consider himself a worthwhile human being.

These schools, as well as several other systems of psychotherapy also do not forthrightly and unequivocally attack and uproot the individual's other important disturbance-creating notion: that is, the idea that he must achieve notably or perform well in life in order to have confidence in himself. Thus, Adlerian therapy (Adler, 1927, 1929, 1931; Ansbacher and Ansbacher, 1956) shows the client that he has to have considerable social interest if he is to be a worthy member of the human race. Branden's biocentric-objectivist approach (1969) bases the individual's self-esteem on the conviction that he is competent to deal with reality effectively and that he is morally worthy. Behavior therapy often teaches the client that he really can master certain situations at which he has a prior history of failure and that therefore he can have confidence in himself. (Bandura, 1969; Wolpe and Lazarus, 1966).

On the other side of the fence, RET now seems to be almost the only kind of psychotherapy that is based on the assumption that the individual can fully, unconditionally accept himself whether or not he is approved by others and whether or not he performs well in life; that clearly distinguishes between the client's *preference* and *need* to be popular and achieving; and that specifically teaches him that he doesn't have to rate or evaluate his *self* or his *being*, even though he'd better objectively perceive and measure his *traits* or his *abilities*. It sharply differentiates between the person's achievement-confidence and his approval-confidence, on the one hand, and his self-acceptance, on the other; and it presents a radical solution to his "ego" or "identity" problem by essentially eliminating his "ego" (Ellis, 1971a, 1971b, in press c).

RET is also rigorously scientific—meaning that it is based on and consistently uses the principles of empirical validation and logical analysis rather than the principles of magic, mysticism, arbitrary definition, religiosity, and circular thinking. It shows the individual that whenever he upsets himself at point C (the emotional consequence), it is not (as he almost always thinks is the case) because of what is happening to him at point A (the activating event).

Rather, it is because of his own irrational and unvalidatable suppositions at point B (his belief system). More precisely, when a person feels terribly depressed at point C, it is not because he has been rejected by someone or has lost a job at point A, but because he is convincing himself, at point B, of both a rational and an irrational hypothesis.

His rational belief (rB) is usually of the order: "I don't like being rejected, because it has real disadvantages. I wish, instead, that I were being accepted. But because I am being rejected, that is unfortunate, unbeneficial, and frustrating." If asked to sustain or verify this rational hypothesis or belief, the individual can easily present empirical, observation-backed data to prove that it *is* unfortunate that he is being rejected. Thus, he can show that rejection leads to (1) lack of love and approval; (2) loss of companionship, sex fulfillment, or job advancement; (3) knowledge by others that he has been rejected and their consequently being influenced to reject him, too; and (4) various other kinds of real inconveniences. He can also show that if these inconvenient consequences of rejection occur (and it is highly likely, though not necessary, that they will), it is inappropriate for him to feel delighted and joyous, while it is most appropriate for him to feel sorrowful, regretful, frustrated, and annoyed. His feelings of sorrow and frustration are appropriate because (1) it is hardly appropriate for him to feel unfrustrated and joyous when he is truly rejected and inconvenienced, and (2) feelings of sorrow and annoyance usually encourage him to work at *changing* the conditions that occur at point A (that is, rejection), so that in the future he is more likely to be accepted.

The individual's irrational belief (iB) is usually of the order: "I can't *stand* being rejected! It is awful, horrible, and catastrophic for me not to be accepted! I *should* have been approved rather than rejected, and the fact that I was not proves *(a)* that I am a worthless individual and/or *(b)* that my rejector is a rotter and a bastard!"

This irrational belief (iB) is really a magical, empirically unverifiable hypothesis because there is no possible way of proving or disproving it. Thus (1) he cannot prove that he can't *stand* being rejected, since this is a tautological assumption and consists of circular thinking. He cannot stand being rejected because he *thinks* he cannot stand it; he thinks he cannot stand it because he *decides* not to stand it; and when he thinks and decides that he cannot stand being rejected, he *feels* that he cannot stand it. (2) It is awful, horrible, and catastrophic for him not to be accepted only because, once again, he *thinks* it is awful, horrible, and catastrophic. The words "awful," "horrible," and "catastrophic" have surplus bombastic meaning and cannot truly be defined. They mean, first, that it is inconvenient for him to be unaccepted (which he already proved and accounted for in the course of his rational belief [rB] about nonacceptance); and they mean, second, that he *should* not, *ought* not, *must* not be inconvenienced. But why should, ought, or must anything not exist? Only because, by arbitrary fiat, he *thinks* and *declares* that it must not exist! Only because he absolutistically, definitionally believes "What I *want* to exist, *ought* exist!" Only because his wish is father to his thought. Only because he grandiosely, Jehovahistically ordains: "When I prefer to be accepted, I should be!" (3) He is a *worthless person* when he is rejected because he insanely decides or dictates that he is worthless under those circumstances. (a) As indicated a few paragraphs back, he doesn't have to rate or measure his *personhood*, his entire being, his total self at all; and he could merely decide to fully accept rather than to crassly rate himself. (b) When he dogmatically asserts that he is a worthless person because some of his main traits or characteristics are rejected by another individual, he is obviously illogically overgeneralizing. Just because someone else finds some of his aspects rejectable is hardly evidence that he, totally, is of no value. (c) Even if his rejection by another indicates that this other person finds him completely valueless, he would still be wrong if he concluded, "Because I am totally worthless to this *other*, I have to consider myself totally worthless to *me*." (4) If he concludes that the person who rejects him is a rotter and a bastard, he is making the same illogical overgeneralization about this individual as he makes when he puts himself, as a person, down when he experiences rejection; for his rejector has numerous—probably hundreds— of traits, many of which are desirable or efficient and many of which are undesirable or inefficient. At most, therefore, he can justifiably conclude that his rejector has some important traits or characteristics that are rotten, but not that he, as a total human being, is rotten.

For many reasons, such as those listed in the previous paragraph, the individual who feels (at point C) anxious, depressed, ashamed, or hostile when he is rejected by another (at point A) is creating these upsetting feelings by his own highly irrational beliefs at point B. In addition to sane beliefs, he has a number of interlocking insane beliefs, all of which are really tautological and definitional, and are not truly related to reality. But as long as he devoutly holds on to these irrational beliefs, he will strongly tend (1) to feel depressed and/or angry; (2) to be obsessed with his own circular thinking; (3) to mull his thoughts around, sometimes for hours or days on end, in his own inappropriate emotional juices; (4) usually to behave in such a manner that he enhances his chances for continued rejection; (5) to conclude after a while that he is hopelessly upsettable; and (6) to bring on various other unfortunate symptoms, disturbances, and psychosomatic reactions.

In the course of rational-emotive psychotherapy, many emotive, experiential, and behavioristic methods of psychotherapy are employed—but they are not used in a hit-and-miss eclectic manner. They are consciously utilized in order, in many vigorous and clear-cut ways, to interrupt the individual's irrational belief system and to teach him how to keep attacking it himself, not merely for the duration of therapy but for the rest of his life. Most uniquely, as will be shown in the verbatim therapy transcripts included in this book, cognitive and didactic methods of therapeutic intervention are employed. Although these are only a part of the RET armamentarium, they are in some ways its most distinctive and effective part.

After the therapist has shown the client the A-B-C's of how he has been and still is disturbing himself, he then goes on to point—disputing the irrational beliefs that the client devoutly holds at point B. Thus, in the case we are examining, where the individual is horrified because he may be or actually is rejected, he is shown how to dispute as follows: "Why can't I stand being rejected? Where is the evidence that it is awful, horrible, and catastrophic for me not to be accepted? Why should I have been approved rather than rejected? How does my rejection prove that I am a worthless individual or that my rejector is a rotter and a bastard?" At the same time that he is shown how to dispute his irrational beliefs, the client is shown why his rational beliefs are legitimate, how he can learn from them, and what he can do about using them to effectively change some of the noxious conditions—like rejection—that keep occurring at point A.

If the client actively starts to dispute his irrational beliefs and to substantiate his rational ones, he normally arrives at point E—the effect of his disputing. First, he achieves a cognitive effect (cE), or a revised philosophy about A. Thus, he will tend to conclude: "There is no reason why I can't stand being rejected, though I may well never like it. It is clearly *not* awful, horrible and catastrophic, although it may be highly inconvenient, for me not to be accepted. The only reason I absolutely *should* have been approved is because I foolishly *think* I should; it is *better*, but hardly *necessary*, for me to be approved. My rejection does not in the least prove that I am a worthless individual, but merely indicates that I may well have some ineffective traits and that some people may wrongly consider me worthless for having them. My rejector may be acting unfairly or stupidly in rejecting me, but he is entitled to his disagreeable behavior and is not a total rotter for displaying it."

Finally, if the client persists in this new cognitive effect or philosophy, he will tend to develop, according to RET theory and practice, a new behavioral effect (bE), which consists of a radically changed emotion or symptom. Thus, instead of feeling depressed, anxious, or hostile, as he originally did at point C, he will now tend to feel only disappointed, sad, and frustrated. He may still be highly emotional—since it is appropriate that he feel emotional when an important rejection occurs in his life—but he will not be truly disturbed, upset, or destroyed.

Through the cognitive aspect of RET, then (as well as through its experiential, emotive, and behavioristic aspects), the client is specifically taught how to be *discriminatingly* emotional—or to control his own emotional destiny and truly to run his own life. This kind of cognitive-emotional discrimination (which has often been inaccurately labeled "emotional insight") is, of course, produced in other types of therapy, too. But it is my hypothesis that it is learned much more readily and thoroughly by active teaching, as is usually done in RET, than by less cognitively-oriented kinds of therapeutic encounters. In fact, I would hypothesize that so far no one has invented any method of helping troubled individuals to make some of the finer distinctions and utilize some of the more elegant solutions to their problems than the RET method of very specifically and concretely teaching them rational sensitivity and emotional discrimination.

RET can even be more briefly (though not entirely adequately) explained by noting that, according to its formulations, virtually all human disturbance is self-created by the human individual because he pig-headedly and devoutly believes in two nonsensical words and their equivalents: "It's terrible!" The person who is easily and consistently upsettable more specifically believes that (1) "*It's terrible* when I fail to do some important task well or when significant others do not approve of me; and I am a pretty *worthless person* when these kinds of failures or rejections occur!" (2) "*It's awful* when you fail to treat me fairly or to give me the kind of favors I strongly desire you to give me; and you are a *rotten individual,* a *louse,* when you deal with me in that fashion!" (3) "*It's horrible* when the world is rough and things around me are quite difficult; and *I can't stand it* when life is that hard!"

As long as he maintains these magical, unscientific, definitional beliefs, it is virtually impossible for the individual not to be frequently emotionally disturbed. If he wants to be minimally disturbable and maximally sane, he'd better substitute for all his absolutistic *It's terrible*'s two other words which he does not parrot or give lip-service to but which he incisively thinks through and accepts—namely, "Too bad!" or "Tough shit!" Or, more precisely, in terms of the three basic "terrors," "awfulnesses," and "horrors" listed in the previous paragraph: (1) "*Too bad* that I fail to do some important tasks well or that significant others do not always approve of me! But that's the way I am and will in all probability always be: fallible and partially unlovable." (2) "*Tough shit* when you fail to treat me fairly or to give me the kind of favors I strongly desire from you! But that's the way you are: often unfair and ungiving." (3) "*Tough luck* when the world is rough and things around me are quite difficult! But even though I may never like it, that's the way it is, and I can definitely stand it if I can't change it for the better."

Will this rather simplistic, utterly realistic, and fully grown-up philosophy of life really eliminate all serious emotional disturbances to which humans always seem to have been and still very much are heir? Possibly not; but I would somewhat conservatively guess that it would minimize at least 90 percent of them. I could, of course, be wrong about this. But so far, in the clinic and in the research laboratory, seem to have been surprisingly right.

As for the clinic, conclusive results are by no means in yet and probably will not be until a large-scale study comparing the effectiveness of rational-emotive therapy with various other major forms of psychotherapy is completed. Unfortunately, although I would be delighted to conduct such a study, it is not at the moment feasible, because it would require at least a million dollars to execute, and no research fund or agency has been ready to grant me and my associates at the Institute for Advanced Study in Rational Psychotherapy even a small part of such funds to carry on this kind of an experiment.

Meanwhile, however, a number of smaller studies have been done that indicate that RET is quite effective when used with disturbed individuals, and particularly when it is used with clients who have had a considerable amount of psychoanalytic or client-centered therapy and made little or no improvement until their therapist switched to RET techniques. Thus, clinical papers showing the effectiveness of rational-emotive methods with various types of clients have been published by many therapists, including Ard (1966, 1967a, 1967b, 1968, 1969); Bedford (1969), Breen (1970), Callahan (1967), Diamond (1967a, 1967b), Geis (1970), Glicken (1967), Grossack (1965), Gullo (1966a, 1966b, 1968), Harper (1960a, 1960b, 1967), Hartman (1967), Hauck (1966, 1967a, 1967b, 1968, 1969), Hudson (1967), Konietzko (1968), Maultsby (1968, 1969d), and Wagner (1963, 1966).

Experimental studies of RET, showing that it is clinically effective when used with control groups or procedures, have also been done by a good many researchers, including Bard (1965), Burkhead (1970), Conner (1970), DiLoreto (1968), Ellis (1957), Gustav (1968), Hartman (1968), Karst and Trexler (1970), Krippner (1964), Lafferty (1962), Maes and Heimann (1970),

Maultsby (1969a, 1969b, 1969c), O'Connell (1970), Raskin (1965, 1966), Shapiro, Neufield, and Post (1962), Shapiro and Ravenette (1959), Sharma (1970), Taft (1965), and Zingle (1965).

Many independent researchers, most of whom were not even particularly aware of RET hypotheses and procedures, have published findings that confirm some of the major assumptions and principles of rational-emotive therapy. This is particularly true of the basic RET theory that emotions are largely caused, not by the stimuli or activating events that occur to people at point A, but by the cognitive evaluations, mediating processes, or belief systems that they engage in at point B. There is now a huge mass of experimental evidence to support this hypothesis, including studies by Beck (1967), Beck and Hurvich (1959), Beck and Stein (1967), Becker (1960), Becker, Spielberger, and Parker (1963), Brainerd (1970), Breznitz (1967), Carlson, Travers, and Schwab (1969), Cassidy, Flanagan, and Spellman (1957), Davison (1967), Davison and Valins (1969), Davitz (1969), Deane (1966), Folkins (1970), Frank (1968), Friedman, Cowitz, Cohen, and Granick (1963), Fritz and Marks (1954), Garfield et al. (1967), Geer, Davison, and Gatchel (1970), Geis (1966), Glass, Singer, and Friedman (1969), Gliedman et al. (1958), Gordon (1967), Grossack, Armstrong, and Lussiev (1966), Jordan and Kempler (1970), Kamiya (1968), Kilty (1968, 1969, 1970), Lange, Sproufe, and Hastings (1967), Lazarus (1966), Loeb, Beck, Diggory, and Tuthill (1967), Marcia, Rubin, and Efran (1969), McConaghy (1967), Miller (1969), Mowrer (1938), Nisbett and Shachter (1966), Nomikos et al. (1968), Pastore (1950, 1952), Paul (1966), Salzinger and Pisoni (1960), Schacter and Singer (1962), Steffy, Meichenbaum, and Best (1970), Sullivan (1969), Valins (1966, 1967, 1970), Valins and Ray (1967), Wenger, Averill, and Smith (1968), and White, Fichtenbaum, and Dollard (1969).

A great many other studies have also been done that more specifically show that when individuals are given concrete suggestions regarding emotional and behavioral changes, either with or without hypnosis, they significantly modify their behavior. Included among scores of studies of this kind are those by Barber (1966), Barber and Calverley (1965, 1966), Hampson, Rosenthal, and Frank (1954), Jellinek (1946), Levitt, Den Breeijen, and Persky (1960), Levitt, Persky, and Brady (1964), Meath (1954), Roper (1967), Rosenthal and Frank (1956), Sparks (1962), Wolf (1950), and Wolf and Pinsky (1954).

Still another group of experiments have been performed that present impressive evidence that when human beings have emotional disturbances, they have specific irrational ideas, especially those which I have been hypothesizing since I gave my first talk on rational-emotive therapy in 1956.

These include studies by Appleton (1969), Argabrite and Nidorf (1968), Beck (1967), Conklin (1965), Dua (1970), Jones (1968), Kemp (1961), Lidz et al. (1958), Meehl (1966), Overall and Gorham (1961), Payne and Hirst (1957), Rimm and Litvak (1969), Rokeach (1964), Spielberger, Parker, and Becker (1963), Tosi and Carlson (1970), and Velten (1968).

Further evidence favoring some of the basic principles and practices of RET has been presented in several studies that show that the kind of live, active-directive homework assignments that are an integral part of rational-emotive procedures are not only quite effective in aiding personality change but are usually more effective than more passive kinds of desensitization, such as those frequently employed by Wolpe (1958) and his followers. The efficacy of in vivo homework procedures has been experimentally validated by a good many researchers, including Cooke (1966), Davison (1965), Garfield et al. (1967), Jones (1924), Litvak (1969a, 1969b), Rimm and Medeiros (1970), Ritter (1968), and Zajonc (1968).

I could present a great deal more evidence that cognitive-behavior therapy, in general, and rational-emotive therapy, in particular, not only works but is probably more effective than any other major system of therapy thus far devised. Let me, however, conclude this introduction by making the important point that although RET procedures were originally invented to help individuals who had already become afflicted with serious emotional problems, they are so allied to the field of education that they have enormous implications for emotional prophylaxis as well as treatment. A number of clinicians and other professionals have now shown how rational-emotive psychology can be applied to "normal" or little disturbed individuals, especially to young children, in order to help prevent them from ever becoming as seriously upsettable as they presumably would otherwise become in the course of modern living. Articles and books vouching for the effectiveness of what I call emotional education using RET principles have been published by a number of writers, including Austin (1964), Ellis (1969d, in press c, in press d), Ellis, Wolfe, and Moseley (1966), Glicken (1966, 1968), Hauck (1967a), Lafferty, Dennerll, and Rettich (1964), McGrory (1967), Pollaczek (1967), Rand (1970), Wagner (1966), and Wolfe et al. (1970).

As a result of the good results so far obtained with using rational-emotive psychology in educational settings, the Institute for Advanced Study in Rational Psychotherapy in New York City has established the Living School, a private school for nondisturbed children, where a concerted effort is being made to teach all the pupils, in the course of their regular academic program, some of the main principles of rational living. By giving this kind of emotional education to the youngsters and their parents, it is hoped that methods will be worked out by which any public or private school in the world can eventually employ rational-emotive psychology to enhance the personal growth and enjoyment, as well as the academic performance, of its pupils.

To return to this casebook (refers to the original casebook: eds), the cases herewith presented are all fairly typical of RET procedures and are included to show what the rational-emotive therapist does to help his clients think more clearly and sanely about themselves, about others, and about the universe, and to indicate how they can thereby help themselves "emotionally." These cases by no means display all the many techniques that are frequently employed in RET; but they do highlight some of its main or most unique aspects. They also show what can be done by an effective rational-emotive practitioner to help some people in a relatively brief period of time, in spite of the fact that they have a number of serious emotional difficulties.

CHAPTER 7

SELF-ACTUALIZATION

EDITOR'S COMMENTARY:

In this selection, Ellis discussed some of the major tenets of the self-actualization theories presented by Maslow, Rogers, and others, comparing them to the REBT perspective. In particular, he discussed one of the key aspects of self-actualization, the notion of peak experiences which are often equated with transcendental experiences. Ellis contended that instead of peak experiences being self-actualizing, they may actually be the antithesis, arguing whether transcendental experiences actually exist.

Ellis also discussed Crawford's notion of self-actualization which stresses the importance of choosing to become fully functioning. Ellis argued that people need to work to achieve this by examining their likes and dislikes and acting on their preferences instead of escalating them to dogmatic demands on themselves. Furthermore, Ellis stressed that when people think to themselves that they must achieve self-actualization they may unintentionally sabotage themselves as they will when they condemn themselves and others.

The major focus of this selection described the REBT view on self-actualization which shares characteristics espoused by Maslow and Rogers, as well as by Korzybski and Hayakawa whose work on general semantics had a strong influence on REBT. In describing these 15 characteristics, Ellis emphasized in particular the REBT viewpoint that people rate only their behaviors, not their total being, and that they accept themselves regardless of performance or approval from others. This key theoretical construct is in sharp contrast to other theories that posit that self-esteem is contingent on performance.

Thus, while there are similarities between other therapeutic perspectives on self-actualization, REBT places more emphasis on self-acceptance versus self-esteem, which Ellis explained in this selection.

Excerpted from *The Albert Ellis Reader,*
Citadel Press, 1998

Achieving emotional health and self-actualization are goals that overlap but are not quite the same. As REBT shows, when you are anxious, depressed, enraged, and self-hating, you strive for certain healthy goals, such as unconditional self-acceptance, unconditional other-acceptance, and high frustration tolerance. But even if you achieve these aims and are hardly ever miserable, you still may be far from happy or self-actualizing. So REBT usually helps you, first, to be less disturbed, and second, to discover what you really enjoy in life. It then helps you to get more of that and to discover what you really dislike, and helps you to get less of that. Seems simple, but it has, as this paper points out, its complications. Other authorities on self-actualization—including Abe Maslow, Carl Rogers, S. I. Hayakawa, and Ted Crawford—have given imperfect answers to solving this problem. So here is the imperfect REBT answer!

Critique of Self-Actualization Theories

The self-actualization theories of Abraham Maslow, Carl Rogers, and other authorities have been seriously questioned by a number of critics. I shall now consider some of their major objections to see how Rational Emotive Behavior Therapy theory and practice deals with them.

Is self-actualization too individualistic, self-seeking, and indulgent? Maslow's concept of self-actualization has often been attacked for these reasons. This is partly true, but the REBT theory includes both self-interest *and* social interest. Because humans choose to live with others, their morality, emotional health, and self-actualization had better always include their being quite concerned about the present and future welfare of others *and* their entire social group. Their very survival—especially in a nuclear age—seems to require a great deal of social interest.

M. Daniels questions whether deciding to pick self-actualizing goals defeats people's spontaneous ways of living in a more fully-functioning manner. No, says REBT, not if people adopt an and/also and not merely an either/or approach. One of the main goals of actualizing can be to seek *more* spontaneous ways of living, and one main by-product of spontaneously (and risk-takingly) trying new pursuits is to discover new enjoyments and then to make re-achieving them a future *goal.* Experimentation partly *is* goal-seeking, and goal-seeking partly *is* spontaneously experimenting with new endeavors. They can both be spontaneous and planned. I once planned to unspontaneously force myself to speak in public in order to overcome my public speaking phobia, and as I did so, I began to spontaneously enjoy what I was doing. As a teenager, I spontaneously had my first orgasm without realizing that I was about to bring it on, and thereafter I plotted and schemed to bring on more and more of them!

Do people have an essential "real self" which they can discover and actualize? Maslow, Karen Horney, and to some extent Carl Rogers hold that people have an underlying biological or transpersonal "real" or "true" self that they can discover and actualize. But, as Daniels points out, their biological real self is somewhat restrictive, and REBT holds that it is quite different for all individuals and that, with experimentation and hard work, it can even be significantly changed. Thus, people with strong biological tendencies to be weak-willed, undisciplined, or irrational can learn and work hard to overcome their unfulfilling handicaps.

REBT holds that several human aspirations and goals—such as sex, love, gustatory, and meaning-oriented desires—are at least party (and individualistically) motivated but that they are also strongly socially and environmentally influenced; and, they can also be distinctly—and consciously—self-developed and modified. REBT is highly skeptical that humans have any "true" transpersonal, transcendental, or mystical selves, though they are certainly often born and reared with strong propensities to think or experience that they do. REBT acknowledges that a belief in religion, God, mysticism, pollyannaism, and irrationality may help people at times. But it also points out that such beliefs often do much more harm than good and block a more fully functioning life.

Daniels rightly observes that the biological "real" self of Horney, Maslow, and Rogers is supposed to be "truer" and "better" than a socially acquired conforming self, but that this idea "leads to the denial of constructive social involvement, to existential isolation and individualism." REBT upholds both individualism *and* social involvement—*not* either/or. It says that because people *choose* to live in a social group (family, community, nation) and not to be asocial hermits, they need to learn to care for themselves *and* for others, and preserve—and help actualize—themselves *as well as* their sociality. They can choose—or not choose—to put themselves first in some respects, but preferably should put others—particularly some selected other—a close second.

Maslow held that self-actualizing people are biologically and personally motivated (have a "real" self), and, somewhat contradictorily, held that they are also motivated by nonpersonal, objective, and universal "values of being." He also saw self-transcendence as altruistic and socially interested, and devoted to mystical pathways that transcend human consciousness and have a nonbodily, "spiritual" aspect. REBT holds that people can be biologically-inclined to be self-interested *and also* biologically and sociologically inclined to be altruistic and socially involved. So it unites or integrates Maslow's and Rogers's individualistic and socialized goals.

REBT, however, sees no evidence that humans ever truly transcend their humanity and develop a transpersonal, transcendental, or superhuman "self" that achieves "higher, miraculous states of consciousness." They frequently aspire to such mystical states, and devoutly believe that they experience them. But they are probably self-deluded and do not really achieve Absolute Truth, godliness, or completely nonhuman consciousness. So, however much human mystics experience Nirvana, selflessness, unity with the Universe, or similar "transpersonal" states, it is unlikely (though not impossible) that they really have superhuman powers and very unlikely that their special state of altered consciousness is "better" than the usual state of consciousness. In some ways it appears to be a deficient, pollyannaish, unauthentic state!

A. McIntyre partly concurs with L. Geller that moral consensus and agreed-upon self-actualization are based on conflicting premises that are mainly emotive and include assertions of personal preference or imply some more arbitrary ideal that should be achieved but is never really agreed upon. Again, this seems to be true, but mainly means that no single "ideal" set of characteristics will suffice for all people at all times, but that they can still select "ideal" (or "nonideal") traits and then experiment (which is almost the REBT essence of health and actualization) to determine whether they are suitable.

McIntyre says that because self-actualization involves a goal, as we search for progress in achieving it we discover more about it and change it. Daniels agrees that "a theory of self-actualization…can therefore only be particularly accurate; it is forever vague and incomplete." REBT adds that not only the theory but also the *practice* of self-fulfillment is almost by necessity experimental, changing, and incomplete.

Geller holds that it is meaningless to speak of general self-actualization, because it is highly multidimensional and involves the pursuit of excellence or enjoyment in whatever ways each individual chooses to desire and emphasize. This argument has much truth to it, since both "healthy" and "enjoyable," not to mention "maximally enjoyable" pursuits, differ from culture to culture and from individual to individual in each culture. "*Self*-actualizing," in fact, implies to some degree being chosen and actualized by each individual self. However, because almost all humans have many similar biological tendencies (e.g., to like to perform well and be approved of by others) and because most cultures abet many of these tendencies (though, of course, in different ways), the REBT hypothesis is that much of the time most contemporary people will lead both a "healthier" and "more enjoyable" life if they achieve several of the "self-actualizing" characteristics listed in this chapter.

Does self-actualization mean "peak experiences" and "altered states of consciousness"? Maslow sometimes implied that maximum self-actualization is achieved by what he called "peak experiences," though at other times he said that they "can come at any time in life to any person." Other writers have identified self-actualization with "altered states of consciousness." Both "peak experiences" and "altered states of consciousness," however, have several different meanings, and none seem to be intrinsically involved with self-actualization, as I shall now indicate.

Both Maslow and S. R. Wilson identify "peak experiences" and "altered states of consciousness" with the "real self" and its somatic-experiential element. They hold that people can learn to minimize their rational, symbolic interactional, or judging selves and become aware of somatic states and feelings that they otherwise ignore, and thereby achieve "peak" or "altered" experiences and become more self-actualizing. I (and REBT) hold that this is partly true, but that most humans only occasionally achieve this "unconscious" state; that they usually achieve it by consciously, philosophically striving for, interpreting, and defining it; that they almost always achieve it very briefly and keep flitting back to regular evaluative consciousness; and that "peak experiences" are both cognitive and somatic-experiential, as Maslow also said. Seymour Epstein, a well-known psychologist, has a view of the experiential part of our personality as being both cognitive and emotional that is illuminating in this respect.

Some authorities, such as the Zen Buddhists, identify "peak experiences" and "altered states of consciousness" with nonego, allegedly nonjudgmental, pure contemplative states (which, paradoxically, are judged to be "better" than ordinary states of consciousness). Such states probably can be—again, occasionally and briefly—achieved. REBT partly goes along with this view, since it encourages people to never judge nor measure their selves, essence, totality, or being, for that will lead them to overgeneralize and self-defeatingly deify or devilify themselves. But REBT favors people still rating their deeds, acts, and performances as "good" or "bad" for certain chosen values and goals, and I think that humans would not survive if they did none of this kind of rating.

Moreover, even if people could often achieve pure egolessness, zero judging, and a Zen state of no-mind, and even if that state helped them (at least temporarily) give up feelings of depression, panic, and damnation, they would then throw away the baby with the bath water, probably achieve little or no pleasure, and therefore be dubiously self-actualized. They could *define* egolessness (and its concomitant, desirelessness) as self-actualization. But in any usual sense of the word, would it really be that?

Psychologist Sid Wilson identifies people's "real," "somatic" self and "altered states of consciousness" with what Mihali Csikszentmihalyi calls flow experiences—that is, activities in which people become so intensely or flowingly involved that they derive unusual fun or joy because, as Wilson puts it, their "self-sustaining, self-protective thought processes that characterize ordinary consciousness are minimized." This "flow experience" is similar to what REBT calls a "vital absorbing interest" and indeed often adds to people's enjoyment.

However, as Wilson notes, most flow activities include rational thought and also include people's evaluating their performances but only minimally evaluating their selves or personhoods. I would call them a somewhat different but hardly an altered state of consciousness. Flow activities are definitely encouraged in REBT, but REBT also encourages and teaches people how to nondamn and nondeify their selves in innumerable nonflow, as well as in flow, activities. Flow may well lead to reduced self-judgment, but conscious, philosophic use of REBT will lead to even less self-judgment. What is more, flow is almost always temporary, and flowing individuals then return to self-evaluation—unless they use REBT or some other highly conscious thinking to permanently minimize it.

Maslow, Charles Tart (a transcendental psychologist), and others identify "peak experiences" and "altered states of consciousness" with mystical, transcendental experiences. This may well be an illegitimate connection, as it can easily be argued whether transcendental experience really exists. Thus, I can *believe and feel* that I am God, the Center of the Universe, the Devil, an Eternal Force, or what I will. But *am* I truly what I say and feel I am? Or am I deluded? Even if we call mystical, transcendental experiences "real" (and in one sense we may because my belief that I am God or the Center of the Universe itself is some kind of experience), is it good, is it enjoyable, is it self-actualizing for me to have this mystical feeling? Only if I (and my fellow mystical-minded individuals) think it is, for I could feel terrified by my believing myself to be the Devil—or God! And I could be delighted to be my all-too-human self who has no transcendental experiences. So mystical "altered states of consciousness," or "peak experiences," can be anti- instead of self-actualizing.

Rational Emotive Behavior Therapy, like most other therapies, has a dual goal: first, to help people overcome their emotional blocks and disturbances; and second, to help them become more fully functioning, self-actualizing, and happier than they otherwise would be. I have elsewhere outlined the REBT goals of nondisturbance, so let me now describe some of the goals that presumably would be desirable for a more fully functioning or self-actualizing person.

I take my main outlook in this respect from my friend Ted Crawford, who has been working on a theory of the fully functioning person and finds that most people are split or fragmented and think, feel, and act in terms of either/or rather than and/also. They need to go beyond the acceptance of an integrated wholeness that helps them accept and cope with meaning that has logic and consistency but that also acknowledges ambiguity, paradox, inconsistent "truths," and other troublesome cognitions that seem to block individuals from becoming fully functioning. To achieve this integrated wholeness, they can choose to accept the principles and practice of and/also many, many times "until the skills and attitudes that enable one to successfully go beyond 'and/also' are a stable habit."

Actively Choosing Self-Actualization

I have worked with Ted Crawford for a number of years on his theory of self-actualization and its linkage with Rational Emotive Behavior Therapy, so let me now state his latest, succinct version and then expand on it. To make a stable habit fully functioning, Ted states that one had better "consciously choose the goal or purpose of becoming fully functioning."

Yes, REBT holds that people are born as well as reared with strong tendencies both to defeat themselves, and to ignore their capacity to function more fully *and* to change their self-destructive thoughts, feelings, and behaviors to achieve fuller functioning. To a large degree, they *choose* emotional-behavioral disturbance (or health) and *choose* restricted (or fuller) functioning. Therefore, to more fully actualize themselves, they had better *choose* to work at achieving more growth, development, and happiness.

More specifically, to make themselves more fully functioning, people need to ask themselves, "What do I really like and dislike?" "How can I experiment and discover what I truly prefer and prefer not to feel and do?" "Which of my likes (e.g., smoking) and dislikes (e.g., exercising) will probably be self-harming as well as enjoyable?" "What am I likely to prefer and abhor in the future?" "What do I do to enhance my preferences and decrease my dislikes?" "How can I align my opinions more closely to the data of my experiences?"

By discovering the answers to relevant questions like these, and then by *acting on* this information, most people can push themselves toward greater self-actualization.

Ted Crawford advises that people who want to achieve greater self-actualization had better "dispute or otherwise let go of shoulds and musts." This is a cardinal theory and practice of REBT. More specifically, REBT holds that people usually make themselves needlessly anxious, depressed, self-hating, and self-pityingly and needlessly dysfunctional when they take their healthy preferences for achievement, approval, and comfort and change them into dogmatic, extreme musts, demands, and commands on themselves, others, and the environment. In so doing, they almost always sabotage their self-fulfilling urges and potentials. Therefore, as Crawford advises, they had better dispute or otherwise let go of their shoulds and musts.

How? By using a number of REBT cognitive, emotive, and behavioral methods. Thus, they can cognitively question and challenge their own absolutist demands and commands, reframe them, convince themselves of rational coping statements, read and listen to REBT materials, talk others out of *their* musts, use problem-solving methods, and otherwise acquire a basic philosophy of tolerance, self-acceptance, and long-range hedonism. Emotively, people can surrender their self-sabotaging musts by using strong coping statements, rational emotive imagery, shame-attacking exercises, role-playing, and other REBT dramatic evocative techniques. Behaviorally, nonactualizing people can act against and dispel their musts by making themselves use the REBT (and other cognitive-behavioral) methods of in vivo desensitization, forceful homework assignments, reinforcement and penalizing procedures, and skill-training techniques.

As Crawford points out, self-actualizing solutions can be better achieved if people "join the problem without the requirement of a solution or the promise of a solution. The requirement that a solution should and must be available blocks the development toward self-actualization." When people join a self-actualizing problem in an and/also way, they flexibly observe, guess, invent a theory, revise their guesses, and grow an emergent "solution" or new possibilities.

More concretely, people don't absolutely have to find a solution to the problem of actualizing themselves. If they tell themselves, "I *must* actualize myself! I *must* not fail to achieve perfect self-actualization!" that is akin to saying, "I *must not* think of a pink elephant!" Then they most probably *will* think of a pink elephant—and will block their actualizing themselves. The thought that it is necessary to achieve actualization will interfere with their asking and answering the kinds of questions mentioned above that will lead to their individually discovering what it is, how to achieve it, and how to work at achieving it.

Crawford notes that people who want to actualize themselves had better "explore the problem as a system without blaming anyone for the status quo or for resisting the 'solution' one has, and thereby redesign the system. When there is a problem, all participants contribute to the situation (or system) that creates the problem—even when they are innocent of wrongdoing. They are responsible for what they do but not blameworthy or damnable as *persons*." In more concrete REBT terms this means:

Don't blame *anyone*, including yourself, for *anything*. Acknowledge that you (and others) may behave ineffectually and thereby defeat yourself and others about many important goals and values. But only negatively rate or assess what you and they *do,* and actively refrain from measuring your *self*— or their *selves*—for poor performances. Work at unconditionally accepting your self, your *you*ness, your humanity, *whether or not* you perform well or are approved of by others.

At the same time, measure or rate what your problem in actualizing yourself is; how well you are working at "solving" it; how good your "solutions" probably are; and how you can keep working to improve them. But don't evaluate, nor especially damn, yourself (or other people) for the poor "solutions" you or they devise. You (and others) may act badly about your (and their) self-actualization, and you may use your "bad" solutions to work for "better" ones—but not if you denigrate yourself and them for both of your responsibility for low-level self-actualization.

Because you refrain from condemning *people,* your self-actualizing plans and accomplishments will very likely remain perpetually open-ended and revisable—which is one of the main characteristics (one might almost say requisites) of a more fully-functioning person. According to REBT, rational people consider and utilize alternate, nonrigid paths to happiness, and are therefore open to endless *re*actualization.

Ted Crawford notes that fully-functioning individuals "meet the challenge of a situation as soon as feasible in contrast to procrastination. Procrastination delays, usually significantly, the development of such a stable habit." More specifically, REBT adds to his antiprocrastination stance:

You additionally sabotage your emotional health and maximum fulfillment, after doing so by damning yourself and others, by indulging in low frustration tolerance (LFT). When you keep believing that life is too hard, that it *must not* be that hard, and that you can't stand the hassles and efforts required to enjoy it, you add discomfort, anxiety, and depression to ego disturbance, and thereby increase your frustrations and annoyances.

Procrastination and low frustration tolerance not only make you dysfunctional and miserable, but also enormously block your ability to learn and use REBT and other effective therapies. Catch-22: whining about life's unniceties creates LFT and then LFT augments whining and sabotages self-actualizing change!

Characteristics of Self-Actualizing Persons

The REBT view of self-actualization overlaps with views from other schools of thought, such as those of Carl Rogers and Abraham Maslow, which at times differ significantly from REBT. But the REBT view also mirrors the ideas of Alfred Korzybski, the founder, and S. I. Hayakawa, the promulgator, of general semantics, a school of thought that it is close to and which has significantly influenced REBT. As Hayakawa points out, some of the characteristics of the more fully-functioning individual that are endorsed by Maslow, Rogers, and general semantics, and with which REBT agrees, are these:

Nonconformity and individuality. Fully-functioning persons (FFPs) are not "fully adjusted" to nor outrightly rebellious against the social group. "The semantically well-oriented person is primarily concerned with the territory and not with the map, with the social reality rather than the social facade." REBT has always endorsed sensible nonconformity and individuality in sex, love, marital, vocational, recreational, and other aspects of life. It has, from its start, also been a highly unconventional form of psychotherapy and has only recently been accepted as a leader in the more conventional cognitive-behavioral movement.

Self-awareness. FFPs are aware of their own feelings, do not try to repress them, often act upon them, and even when they do not act upon them are able to admit them to awareness. In REBT terms, they *acknowledge* their negative feelings (e.g., anxiety and rage) but do not necessarily *act out* on them. They often make efforts to *change* their feelings when they are unhealthy and self-defeating. They "know themselves" but also know how little they know about themselves.

Acceptance of ambiguity and uncertainty. FFPs accept ambiguity, uncertainty, the unknown, approximateness, and some amount of disorder. "Emotionally mature individuals accept the fact that, as far as has yet been discovered, we live in a world of probability and chance, where there are not, nor probably ever will be, absolute necessities nor complete certainties. Living in such a world is not only tolerable but, in terms of adventure, learning, and striving, can even be very exciting and pleasurable."

Tolerance. FFPs are extensional—responding to similarities *and differences*, rather than intensional—tending to ignore differences among things that have some name. They do not see all trees as green, all education as good, nor all modern art as silly. The REBT version: "Emotionally sound people are intellectually flexible, tend to be open to change at all times and are prone to take an unbigoted (or, at least, less bigoted) view of the infinitely varied people, ideas, and things in the world around them."

Acceptance of human animality. FFPs accept their and others' physical and "animal" nature, and rarely disgust themselves about body products, odors, or functions. In REBT terms, they may not like various sensations and feelings but refrain from "awfulizing" about them.

Commitment and intrinsic enjoyment. FFPs tend to enjoy work and sports as ends or pleasures in themselves and not merely as means toward ends (e.g., working for money or playing sports to achieve good health). As REBT puts it, commitment to people, things, and ideas, mainly because people *want* to be absorbed and committed, is one of the main aspects of emotional health and happiness. Robert Harper and I have particularly endorsed people's throwing themselves into a long-term vital and absorbing interest in order to achieve maximum fulfillment and happiness.

Creativity and originality. Maslow, Rogers, and Hayakawa, as well as many other authorities, show that fully-functioning personalities are usually innovative, creative, and original about artistic as well as commonplace problems. In REBT terms, they tend to be self-directed rather than other-directed, original rather than conformist, flexible rather than rigid, and "seem to lead better lives when they have at least one major creative interest."

Social interest and ethical trust. S. I. Hayakawa, endorsing Alfred Korzybski, Abraham Maslow, and Carl Rogers, holds that FFPs are deeply ethical, trustworthy, constructive, and socialized. REBT, following Alfred Adler, puts the same point of view this way: "Emotionally and mentally healthy people tend to be considerate and fair to others; to engage in collaborative and cooperative endeavors; at times to be somewhat altruistic; and to distinctly enjoy some measure of interpersonal and group relationships.

Enlightened self-interest. Healthy and enjoying people are true to themselves as well as to others, often put themselves first, usually put a few selected others a close second, and the rest of the world not too far behind. Their self-interest is mainly directed toward *enjoying*, and not to *proving*, themselves.

Self-direction, FFPs, while interdependent and supporting, and at times asking support from others, largely plan and plot their own destiny (albeit within a social context) and do not overwhelmingly *need* outside support for their effectiveness and well-being.

Flexibility and scientific outlook. Science not only uses empiricism and logic, but as Karl Popper, Bertrand Russell, Ludwig Wittgenstein, and other philosophers of science have shown, it is intrinsically open-minded and flexible. As REBT emphasizes, people largely neuroticize themselves with rigid, imperative musts and shoulds, and, conversely, are significantly less neurotic and self-actualizing when they scientifically dispute their dogmatic, unconditional musts and change them to preferences and alternative-seeking desires.

Unconditional self-acceptance. Carl Rogers and Paul Tillich emphasized unconditional self-acceptance, and from the start REBT has held that humans will rarely be undisturbed and self-fulfilling unless they rate *only* their deeds and performances and *not* their global "selves." Instead, they can choose to accept "themselves" *whether or not* they perform well, are approved by significant others, or have deficits and handicaps. Many other psychotherapies, for example, that of Nathaniel Branden, encourage people to strive for self-esteem or self-efficacy, accepting themselves *because* they perform well and predict that they will continue to do so. But REBT tries to help them not rate their selves, their totality, at all, but rate only their behaviors, or, less elegantly, rate themselves as "good" or "worthy" just because they exist, because they *choose* to do so. Using REBT, self-actualizing people can reframe their "failures" as feedback rather than as self-damnation. This feedback provides important information about what does not work, and therefore calls for a change in approach to a situation rather than giving up on it.

Risk-taking and experimenting. Self-actualization without risk-taking and experimenting is almost unthinkable. People had better experiment with many tasks, preferences, and projects in order to discover what they really want and don't want, and to keep risking new defeats and failures in order to achieve better enjoyments.

Long-range hedonism. As REBT has noted since its inception in 1955, short-range hedonism—"Eat, drink, and be merry, for tomorrow you may die!"—has its distinct limitations, for tomorrow you will probably be alive with a hangover! Therefore, maximum self-actualization can largely be achieved by aiming for intensive and extensive pleasures today *and* tomorrow, and where the former (as in many addictions) sabotage the latter, immediate gratification had often better be avoided and long-range hedonism sought out and abetted.

Work and practice. As noted above, the three major insights of REBT are: (1), take responsibility for disturbing yourself and do not cop out by blaming others; (2), face the fact that your early disturbances do not automatically *make* you disturbed today; (3), understand that no magical forces will change you, but only your own strong and persistent work and practice—yes, *work and practice*. Similarly with self-actualization: Only by working at planning, plotting, scheming, and steadily acting at it are you likely to become a fully-functioning person.

Conclusion

The REBT view of human nondisturbance and self-actualization agrees with other therapeutic outlooks in many respects. Thus, a study of 610 clinical psychologists showed that all five major groups—psychoanalytic, behavioral, humanist-existential, eclectic, and cognitive—reported substantial agreement on the importance of self-system development, self-examination, and exploratory activities in personal change.

The self-actualizing characteristics that REBT emphasizes perhaps more than many other leading psychotherapies are flexibility and a scientific outlook, self-acceptance instead of self-esteem, and long-range hedonism.

In regard to achieving, and not merely endorsing, a more fully functioning personality, it advocates the points that Ted Crawford and I outlined at the beginning of this paper:

1. Actively choosing self-actualization
2. Disputing absolutist shoulds and musts that block its achievement
3. Preferring, but not requiring, the solving of self-actualizing problems
4. Tolerance of oneself and others
5. Overcoming procrastination and low frustration tolerance
6. Framing the problem as a systemic problem to be redesigned
7. Moving from either/ors toward and/also—including ambiguity, paradox, inconsistency, and confusion and then working toward an integrated wholeness

In this manner, Rational Emotive Behavior Therapy not only strongly endorses a self-actualizing, action-oriented philosophy, but also actively encourages some important ways in which it may be achieved. Above all, it stresses that the views outlined in this paper are its *current* formulations that had better be experimentally tried, and, when and if falsified, be quickly revised or abandoned.

CHAPTER 8

EXPLANATION OF REBT USING THE ABCs

EDITOR'S COMMENTARY:

In this selection, Ellis presented further explication of what he had intended to be a statement of personality theory. As well, he extended the argument that A (activating event), B (evaluation or attribution, either irrational or rational), and C (emotional consequence, usually a feeling or description such as feeling less anxious, or calm in the sense that psychiatrists who prescribed tranquilizers used the term and the way the consuming public understood it within the medical model) were interconnected. Seldom, he argued, was there a pure thought or pure emotion: thoughts were influenced and connected to feelings and descriptions of feelings, and feelings were influenced by thoughts that summarized one's perceptions or memories. These last have been referred to as referents in the REBT literature. By introducing D (disputation, or challenging and replacing irrational thoughts), Ellis judged that the formula showed the then RET to be active-directive. E (effective alternatives to irrational beliefs) represented for Ellis a radically different way of viewing oneself and the world. Other theorists including Maultsby, a psychiatrist, argued elsewhere for a parallel or paripassu presentation of ABC, one example being irrational and the second being rational, and both with the same "A". In this selection, Ellis especially emphasized the distinctions between a rational B and irrational B (rB and iB), with examples. He concluded this selection by comparing it to Zen Buddhism in terms of personal acceptance, although he did not make a distinction between secondary or symptom change and the elegant change that today distinguishes REBT from other forms of CBT.

Evolution of a Revolution

Excerpted from *Humanistic Psychotherapy,*
McGraw-Hill, 1973

Rational-emotive psychotherapy is a comprehensive approach to psychological treatment and to education that not only employs emotive and behavioristic methods but also significantly stresses and undermines the cognitive element in self-defeating behavior. Humans are exceptionally complex, so that there is no simple way in which they become "emotionally disturbed," and no single manner in which they can be helped to overcome their disturbances. Their psychological problems arise from their misperceptions and mistaken cognitions about what they perceive; from their emotional underreactions or overreactions to normal and to unusual stimuli; and from their habitually dysfunctional behavior patterns, which encourage them to keep repeating nonadjustive responses even when they know they are behaving poorly. Consequently, a three-way, rational-emotive-behavioristic approach to their problems is desirable; and rational-emotive therapy provides this multifaceted attack.

Primarily, RET employs a highly active cognitive approach. It is based on the assumption that what we label our "emotional" reactions are mainly caused by our conscious and unconscious evaluations, interpretations, and philosophies. Thus, we feel anxious or depressed because we strongly convince ourselves that it is not only unfortunate and inconvenient but that *it is terrible and catastrophic* when we fail at a major task or are rejected by a significant person. And we feel hostile because we vigorously believe that people who behave unfairly not only *would better not* but *absolutely should not* act the way they indubitably do and that it is *utterly insufferable* when they frustrate us.

Like stoicism, a school of philosophy which originated some twenty-five hundred years ago, RET holds that there are virtually no legitimate reasons for people to make themselves terribly upset, hysterical, or emotionally disturbed, no matter what kind of psychological or verbal stimuli are impinging on them. It encourages them to feel strong *appropriate* emotions—such as sorrow, regret, displeasure, annoyance, rebellion, and determination to change unpleasant social conditions. But it holds that when they experience certain self-defeating and *inappropriate* emotions—such as guilt, depression, rage, or feelings of worthlessness—they are adding an unverifiable, magical hypothesis (that things *ought* or *must* be different) to their empirically based view (that certain things and acts are reprehensible or inefficient and that something *would better* be done about changing them).

Because the rational-emotive therapist has a highly structured and workable theory, he can almost always see the few central irrational philosophies which a client is vehemently propounding to himself and through which he is foolishly upsetting himself. He can show the client how these cause his problems and his symptoms; can demonstrate exactly how the client can forthrightly question and challenge these ideas; and can often induce him to work to uproot them and to replace them with scientifically testable hypotheses about himself and the world which are not likely to get him into future emotional difficulties.

The cognitive part of the theory and practice of RET may be briefly stated in A-B-C form as follows:

At point A there is an ACTIVITY, ACTION, or AGENT that the individual becomes disturbed about. Example: He goes for an important job interview; or he has a fight with his mate, who unfairly screams at him.

At point rB the individual has a RATIONAL BELIEF (or a REASONABLE BELIEF or a REALISTIC BELIEF) about the ACTIVITY, ACTION, or AGENT that occurs at point A. Example: He believes, "It would be unfortunate if I were rejected at the job interview." Or, "How annoying it is to have my mate unfairly scream at me!"

At point iB the individual has an IRRATIONAL BELIEF (or an INAPPROPRIATE BELIEF) about the ACTIVITY, ACTION, or AGENT that occurs at point A. Example: He believes, "It would be catastrophic if I were rejected at the job interview." Or, "My mate is a horrible person for screaming at me!"

Point rB, the RATIONAL BELIEF, can be supported by empirical data and is appropriate to the reality that is occurring, or that may occur, at point A. For it normally *is* unfortunate if the individual is rejected at an interview for an important job; and it *is* annoying if his mate unfairly screams at him. It would hardly be rational or realistic if he thought; "How great it will be if I am rejected at the job interview!" Or: "It is wonderful to have my mate scream at me! Her screaming shows what a lovely person she is!"

Point iB, the IRRATIONAL BELIEF, cannot be supported by any empirical evidence and is inappropriate to the reality that is occurring, or that may occur, at Point A. For it hardly would be truly catastrophic, but only (at worst) highly inconvenient, if the individual were rejected for an important job. It is unlikely that he would never get another job, that he would literally starve to death, or that he would have to be utterly miserable at any other job he could get. And his mate is not a horrible person for screaming at him; she is merely a person who behaves (at some times) horribly and who (at other times) has various unhorrible traits.

His iB's, or IRRATIONAL BELIEFS, moreover, state or imply a *should, ought,* or *must*—an absolutistic *demand* or *dictate* that the individual obtain what he wants; for, by believing that it is catastrophic if he is rejected for an important job, he explicitly or implicitly believes that he *should* or *must* be accepted at that interview. And by believing that his mate is a horrible person for screaming at him, he overtly or tacitly believes that she *ought* or *must* be nonscreaming. There is, of course, no law of the universe (except in his muddled head!) which says that he *should* do well at an important job interview, or that his mate *must* not scream at him.

At point rC the individual experiences or feels RATIONAL CONSEQUENCES or REASONABLE CONSEQUENCES of his rB's (RATIONAL BELIEFS). Thus, if he rigorously and discriminately believes, "It would be unfortunate if I were rejected at the job interview," he feels concerned and thoughtful about the interview; he plans in a determined manner how to succeed at it; and if by chance he fails to get the job he wants, he feels disappointed, displeased, sorrowful, and frustrated. His actions and his feelings are *appropriate* to the situation that is occurring or may occur at point A; and they tend to help him succeed in his goals or feel suitably regretful if he does not achieve these goals.

At point iC the individual experiences IRRATIONAL CONSEQUENCES or INAPPROPRIATE CONSEQUENCES of his iB's (IRRATIONAL BELIEFS). Thus, if he childishly and dictatorially believes, "It would be catastrophic if I were rejected at the job interview. I couldn't stand it! What a worm I would then prove to be! I *should* do well at this important interview!" he tends to feel anxious, self-hating, self-pitying, depressed, and enraged. He gets dysfunctional psychosomatic reactions, such as high blood pressure and ulcers. He becomes defensive, fails to see his own mistakes in this interview, and by rationalization blames his failure on external factors. He becomes preoccupied with how hopeless his situation is, and refuses to do much about changing it by going for other interviews. And he generally experiences what we call "disturbed," "neurotic," or "overreactive" symptoms. His actions and feelings at point iC are *inappropriate* to the situation that is occurring or may occur at point B, because they are based on magical demands regarding the way he and the universe presumably *ought to be*. And they tend to help him fail at his goals or feel horribly upset if he does not achieve them.

These are the A-B-C's of emotional disturbance or self-defeating attitudes and behavior, according to the RET theory. Therapeutically, these A-B-C's can be extended to D-E's, which constitute the cognitive core of the RET methodology.

At point D, the individual can be taught (or can teach himself) to DISPUTE his iB's (IRRATIONAL BELIEFS). Thus, he can ask himself, *"Why* is it catastrophic if I am rejected in this forthcoming job interview? How would such a rejection *destroy* me? Why couldn't I *stand* losing this particular job? Where is the evidence that I would be a *worm* if I were rejected? Why *should* I have to do well at this important interview?" If he persistently, vigorously DISPUTES (or *questions* and *challenges*) his own iB's (IRRATIONAL BELIEFS) which are creating his iC's (INAPPROPRIATE CONSEQUENCES), he will sooner or later come to see, in most instances, that they are unverifiable, unempirically based, and superstitious; and he will be able to change and reject them.

At point cE the individual is likely to obtain the COGNITIVE EFFECT of his DISPUTING his iB's (IRRATIONAL BELIEFS). Thus, if he asks himself, "Why is it catastrophic if I am rejected in this forthcoming job interview?" he will tend to answer: "It is not; it will merely be inconvenient." If he asks, "How would such a rejection destroy me?" he will reply, "It won't; it will only frustrate me." If he asks: "Why couldn't I stand losing this particular job?" he will tell himself: "I can! I won't like it; but I can gracefully lump it!" If he asks: "Where is the evidence that I would be a worm if I were rejected?" he will respond: "There isn't any! I will only feel like a worm if I *define myself as* and *think of myself as* a worm!" If he asks, "Why *should* I have to do well at this important interview?" he will tell himself: "There's no reason why I should *have* to do well. There are several reasons why *it would be nice. It would be very fortunate* if I succeeded at this job interview. But they never add up to: "Therefore I must!"

At point bE the individual will most likely obtain the BEHAVIORAL EFFECT of his DISPUTING his iB's (IRRATIONAL BELIEFS). Thus, he will tend to be much less anxious about his forthcoming job interview. He will become less self-hating, self-pitying, and enraged. He will reduce his psychosomatic reactions. He will be able to become less defensive. He will become less un-constructively preoccupied with the possibility or the actuality of his failing at the job interview and will more constructively devote himself to succeeding at it or taking other measures to improve his vocational condition if he fails at it. He will become significantly less "upset," "disturbed," "overreactive," or "neurotic."

On the cognitive level, then, rational-emotive therapy largely employs direct philosophic confrontation. The therapist actively demonstrates to the client how, every time he experiences a dysfunctional emotion or behavior or CONSEQUENCE, at point C, it only indirectly stems from some ACTIVITY or AGENT that may be occurring (or about to occur) in his life at point A, and it much more directly results from his interpretations, philosophies, attitudes, or BELIEFS, at point B. The therapist then teaches the client how to scientifically (empirically and logically) DISPUTE these beliefs, at point D, and to persist at this DISPUTING until he consistently comes up, at point E, with a set of sensible COGNITIVE EFFECTS, cE's, and appropriate BEHAVIORAL EFFECTS, bE's. When he has remained, for some period of time, at point E, the individual has a radically changed philosophic attitude toward himself, toward others, and toward the world, and he is thereafter much less likely to keep convincing himself of iB's (IRRATIONAL BELIEFS) and thereby creating iC's (INAPPROPRIATE CONSEQUENCES) or emotional disturbances.

In addition to its cognitive methods, RET has exceptionally important behavioristic techniques that it consistently uses. It especially uses activity homework assignments, which the therapist or the client's therapy group assign to him during various sessions, and later check to see whether he is doing them. Such assignments may consist of the client's being asked to initiate contacts with three new people during a week's period, to visit his nagging mother-in-law instead of trying to avoid her, or to make a list of his job-hunting assets and of several means of his looking for a better job. These assignments are given in order to help the client take risks, gain new experiences, interrupt his dysfunctional habituations, and change his philosophies regarding certain activities.

A third major emphasis in RET is on emotive release. Thus, the rational-emotive therapist usually takes a no-nonsense-about-it direct confrontation approach to the client and his problems. He forces or persuades the client to express himself openly and to bring out his real feelings, no matter how painful it may at first be for him to do so. Frequently, he ruthlessly reveals and attacks the client's defenses—while simultaneously showing him how he can live without these defenses and how he can unconditionally accept himself whether or not others highly approve of him. The therapist does not hesitate to reveal his own feelings, to answer direct questions about himself, and to participate as an individual in rational marathon encounters. He does his best to give the client unconditional rather than conditional positive regard and to teach him the essence of rational-emotive philosophy; namely, that no human is to be condemned for anything, no matter how execrable his acts may be. His *deeds* may be measureable and heinous, but he is never to be rated or given a report card *as a person*. Because of the therapist's full acceptance of him as a human being, the client is able to express his feelings much more openly than in his everyday life and to accept *himself* even when he is acknowledging the inefficiency or immorality of some of his *acts*.

In many important ways, then, RET uses expressive-experiential methods and behavioral techniques. It is not, however, primarily interested in helping the client *feel* better, but in showing him how he can *get* better. In its approach to marathon group therapy, for example, RET allows the participants plenty of opportunity to encounter each other on a gut level, to force themselves to stay in the here and now, to face their own emotional and sensory reactions to themselves and to other members of the group, and to be ruthlessly honest with themselves and others. Instead, however, of beginning and ending on a purely basic encounter or sensitivity training level—and thereby risk opening up many people without showing them how to put themselves together again—the rational-oriented marathon also shows the participants exactly what they are telling themselves to create their negative feelings toward themselves and others. They are further told how they can change their internalized and uncritically accepted iB's (IRRATIONAL BELIEFS) so that ultimately they can feel and behave spontaneously in a less self-defeating manner and can actualize their potential for happy, nondefeating lives.

Basically, RET is an extension of the scientific method to human affairs. People, for biological as well as environmental reasons, tend to think superstitiously, unrealistically, and unscientifically about themselves and the world around them. In science, we teach them to set up hypotheses about external reality and then to vigorously question and challenge these hypotheses—to look for empirical evidence for and against them, before they are cavalierly accepted as truths. In rational-emotive therapy, the therapist teaches his client to question scientifically and to dispute all self-defeating hypotheses about himself and others. Thus, if he believes—as, alas, millions of people tend to believe—that he is a worthless person because he performs certain acts badly, he is not taught merely to ask: "What is truly bad about my acts? Where is the evidence that they are wrong or unethical?" More important, he is shown how to ask himself: "Granted that some of my acts may be mistaken, why am I a totally bad *person* for performing them? Where is the evidence that I must always (or mainly) be right in order to consider myself worthy? Assuming that it is *preferable* for me to act well or efficiently rather than badly or inefficiently, why do I *have* to do what is preferable?"

Similarly, when an individual perceives—and let us suppose that he correctly perceives—the erroneous and unjust acts of others, and when he makes himself (as he all too frequently does) enraged at these others and tries to hurt or annihilate them, he is taught by the rational-emotive therapist to stop and ask himself: "Why is my hypothesis true that these error-prone people are absolutely no good? Granted that *it would be better* if they acted more competently or fairly, why *should* they have to do what would be better? Where is the evidence that people who commit a number of mistaken or unethical acts are doomed to be forever wrong? Why, even if they persistently behave poorly, should they be totally damned, excommunicated, and consigned to some kind of hell?"

Rational-emotive therapy teaches the individual to generalize adequately but to watch his *over*-generalizing; to discriminate his desires, wants, and preferences from his assumed needs, necessities, or dictates; to be less suggestible and more thinking; to be a long-range hedonist, who enjoys himself in the here and now *and* the future, rather than merely a short-range hedonist, who thinks mainly of immediate gratification; to feel the appropriate emotions of sorrow, regret, annoyance, and determination to change unpleasant aspects of his life, while minimizing the inappropriate emotions of worthlessness, self-pity, severe anxiety, and rage. RET, like the science of psychology itself and like the discipline of general semantics, as set forth by Alfred Korzybski, particularly teaches the client how to *discriminate* more clearly between sense and nonsense, fiction and reality, superstition and science. While using many behavioristic and teaching methods, it is far from being dogmatic and authoritarian. Rather, it is one of the most humanistically oriented kinds of therapy, in that it emphasizes that man can fully accept himself just because he is alive, just because he exists; that he does not have to prove his worth in any way; that he can have real happiness whether or not he performs well and whether or not he impresses others; that he is able to create his own meaningful purposes; and that he needs neither magic nor gods on whom to rely. The humanistic-existentialist approach to life is therefore as much a part of rational-emotive psychotherapy as is its rational, logical, and scientific methodology.

RET, like many other modern forms of psychotherapy, is backed by a good many years of clinical experience by the present author and various other rational-emotive therapists. It is supported by several studies demonstrating its clinical effectiveness under controlled experimental conditions.

Rational-emotive psychotherapy has a great many therapeutic applications, some of which are unavailable to various other modes of psychotherapy. For one thing, it is relevant and useful to a far wider range of client disabilities than are many other therapies. Robert Harper, Cecil H. Patterson, and others have shown that many techniques, such as classical psychoanalysis, can only be effectively employed with a relatively small number of clients and are actually contraindicated with other individuals (such as with schizophrenics). Rational-emotive therapy, however, can be employed with almost any type of person the therapist is likely to see, including those who are conventionally labeled as psychotic, borderline psychotic, psychopathic, and mentally retarded. This is not to say that equally good results are obtained when it is employed with these most difficult individuals as are obtained with less difficult neurotics. But the main principles of RET can be so simply and efficiently stated that even individuals with very serious problems, some of whom have not been reached by years of previous intensive therapy, can often find significant improvement through RET.

Prophylactically, rational-emotive principles can be used with many kinds of individuals, to help prevent them from eventually becoming emotionally disturbed. At a school for normal children operated on the principles of rationality, the pupils from the first grade onward are taught a rational-emotive philosophy by their regular teachers, in the course of classroom activities, recreational affairs, therapy groups, and other games and exercises. They are taught, for example, not to catastrophize when they do not achieve perfectly, not to enrage themselves against others when these others act badly, and not to demand that the world be nicer and easier than it usually is. As a result of this teaching, they seem to be becoming remarkably less anxious, depressed, self-hating, and hostile than other children of equivalent age.

Rational-emotive ideas also have application to politics, to problems of the generation gap, to the treatment and prevention of violence and murder, and to various other areas of life. Because it is deeply philosophic, because it realistically accepts individuals as they are and shows them how they can obtain their fuller potentials, and because it is not only oriented toward individuals with emotional disturbances but toward all types of people everywhere, RET is likely to be increasingly applied to the solution of many kinds of human problems.

Is RET really more effective than other forms of psychotherapy? The evidence is not in that will answer this question. Clinical findings would seem to indicate that it benefits more people than do most other methods; that it can obtain beneficial results in surprisingly short order in many instances; and that the level of improvement or cure that is effected through its use is more permanent and deep-seated than that obtained through other methods. But this clinical evidence has been haphazardly collected and is now being substantiated through controlled studies of therapeutic outcome. My hypothesis is that RET is a more effective procedure for clients and therapists because it is active-directive, it is comprehensive, it is unusually clear and precise, and it is hardheaded and down to earth.

More important, rational-emotive therapy is philosophically unambiguous, logical, and empirically oriented. This can be especially seen in its viewpoint on the most important of therapeutic problems: that of human worth. Nearly all systems of psychotherapy hold that the individual is worthwhile and can esteem himself because he discovers how to relate well to others and win the love he needs and/or learns how to perform adequately and to achieve his potentials for functioning. Thus, Sigmund Freud held that man solves his basic problems through work and love. Alfred Adler emphasized the necessity of his finding himself through social interest. Harry Stack Sullivan stressed his achieving adequate interpersonal relations. William Glasser insisted that he needs both love and achievement. Nathaniel Branden demanded competence and extreme rationality. Even Carl Rogers, who presumably emphasized unconditional positive regard, actually has held that the individual can truly accept himself only when someone else, such as a therapist, accepts him or loves him unconditionally; so that his self-concept is still dependent on some important element outside himself.

RET, on the contrary, seems to be almost the only major kind of psychotherapy (aside, perhaps, from Zen Buddhism, if this is conceptualized as psychotherapy and not exclusively as a philosophy) that holds that the individual does not need *any* trait, characteristic, achievement, purpose, or social approval in order to accept himself. In fact, he does not have to rate himself, esteem himself, or have any self-measurement or self-concept whatever.

It is not only undesirable but it is impossible for the individual to have a self-image, and it is enormously harmful if he attempts to construct one. Ego ratings depend on the summation of the ratings of the individual's separate traits (such as his competence, honesty, and talents, for example), and it is not legitimate to add and average these traits any more than it is legitimate to add apples and pears. Moreover, if one finally arrives, by some devious means, at a global rating of the individual (or of his "self"), one thereby invents a magical heaven (his "worth," his "value," his "goodness") or a mystical hell (his "worthlessness," his "valuelessness," his "badness"). This deification or devil-ification (note that this word is devil-ification, not de-vilification) of the individual is arrived at tautologically, by definition. It has no relation to objective reality; it is based on the false assumption that he *should* or *must* be a certain way and that the universe truly *cares* if he is not what he *ought* to be; it refuses to acknowledge the fact that all humans are, and probably always will be, incredibly *fallible;* and it almost always results in the self-rating individual's harshly condemning and punishing himself or defensively pretending that he is "worthy" and "good" in order to minimize his anxiety and self-deprecation. Finally, since self-ratings invariably involve ego games wherein the individual compares his self-esteem to that of others, they inevitably result in his deifying and damning other humans in addition to himself; and the feelings of intense anxiety and hostility that thereby occur constitute the very core of what we usually call "emotional disturbance."

Rational-emotive therapy, by solidly teaching the individual to avoid *any* kind of self-rating (and only, instead, to measure his characteristics and performances, so that he may help correct them and increase his enjoyment), gets to the deepest levels of personality change. It offers no panacea for the termination of human unhappiness, sorrow, frustration, and annoyance. But it importantly reveals, attacks, and radically uproots the major sources of needless self-defeating and socially destructive behavior.

CHAPTER 9

CONQUERING ANXIETY

EDITOR'S COMMENTARY:

In this selection, Ellis made a firm and well-argued distinction between fear and anxiety. Fear was likened to a physical reaction due to a real threat such as a fast-moving car aimed toward you, or a raging-bull type yelling threats at another person. He defined anxiety carefully, using examples that included overreaction and exaggeration about something that had not yet happened. Concerning fear, the person had his or her behavior interrupted by the unexpected, whereas anxiety was more a psychological habit that could translate from slight exaggeration to overwhelming physical dysfunction from having dwelled on a maladaptive thought pattern. This selection illustrated the case of a woman who was mistreated as a child by her father and who married a husband with similar behaviors. She attributed her misfortune as an adult to some combination of genetics and bad luck. Contrarily, she was shown that as a child she did not have much choice but to believe what was told to her about her inadequacy and that she was being punished because of it. As an adult, however, if she continued to believe in that myth, she was paying off today for the past. At this point, Ellis also talked freely about the inner person, something he had written about ambiguously. Here, he agreed with examples from Skinner that psychologists or personal scientists needed to be guided by the facts. However, he argued that Skinner had not gone far enough, that, indeed, covert behavior could be analyzed and systematized—and the then RET inter alia had the theory and techniques to do so. While the woman in the case made substantial progress by not personalizing anything that her husband said that was negative, she began to feel better about herself when she accepted herself without question. She was able to achieve that status by working vigorously at some sentences that Ellis had asked her to apply, the gist of which were that she disputed irrationalities while she emphasized her self-worth (and not her self-esteem at some role). This selection did not make careful distinctions that might be made today between anxiety and stress (too much to do in too little time to do it, that mind-set resulting in habituation or "burn out"); however, it offered in just a few pages the full application and explanation of the then RET theory as it made way for the "behavior" that would be added later in the name change to REBT.

Excerpted from *New Guide to Rational Living,*
Wilshire Books, 1961 & 1975

Our clients and associates often try to confound us on one special point, where they feel that our technique of rational-emotive therapy comes a cropper and sadly begins to bog down. "You may rightly insist," they say, "that most difficulties arise from irrational beliefs we feed ourselves and that we can overcome our difficulties by changing these beliefs. But what about anxiety? How can we possibly control or change that by challenging and disputing our own assumptions? You'll never change that trait very much, no matter how rationally you approach it."

Rot! We can approach and control anxiety by straight thinking. For anxiety, basically, consists of Irrational Idea No. 6: *The idea that if something seems dangerous or fearsome, you must preoccupy yourself with and make yourself anxious about it.*

We don't claim that real or rational fears do not exist. They certainly do. When you prepare to cross a busy intersection, you'd better fear the possibility of getting hit by a moving vehicle and therefore feel *concerned* about your safety. Fear of this sort not only seems a natural human tendency, but also a necessity for self-preservation. Without your having appropriate fear or concern about your safety, your days on this earth would not continue very long!

Nonetheless, fear and anxiety differ. Anxiety (as we employ the term in this book) consists of *over-* concern, of *exaggerated* or *needless* fear. And it most frequently doesn't relate to physical injury or illness but to mental "injury" or "harm." In fact, probably 98 percent of what we call anxiety crops up as *overconcern for what someone thinks about you.* And this kind of anxiety, as well as exaggerated fear of bodily injury, appear needlessly self-defeating on several counts:

Selections from the Writings of Albert Ellis Ph.D.

1. If something truly seems dangerous or fearsome, you may take two intelligent approaches: (a) determine whether this thing *actually* involves danger and (b) if so, either do something practical to alleviate the existing danger; or (if you can do nothing) resign yourself to the fact of its existence. Bellyaching about it or continually reiterating to yourself the holy horror of a potentially or actually fearsome situation will not change it or better prepare you to cope with it. On the contrary, the more you upset yourself the less able you will prove, in almost all instances, to accurately assess and cope with this danger.

2. Although certain accidents and illnesses (such as airplane accidents or the onset of cancer) *may* befall you one day, and it will prove unfortunate if one of these misfortunes *does* occur once you have taken reasonable precautions to ward off such possible mishap you can usually do nothing else about it. Worry, believe it or not, has no magical quality of staving off bad luck. On the contrary, it frequently increases the probability of disease or accident by unnerving the vulnerable individual. Thus, the more you worry about getting into an automobile crack-up, the more likelihood exists that you will get yourself into just such a crack-up.

3. You exaggerate the assumed catastrophic quality of many potentially unpleasant events. Death emerges as the worst thing that can happen to you—and sooner or later you will die anyway. If you suffer from dire physical pain for a long period of time as when you have an incurable cancerous condition and cannot find relief in drugs, you can always commit suicide. Virtually all misfortunes which might occur—such as loss of a loved one or loneliness—turn out, when they actually occur, far less dreadful than you might have worriedly fantasized. The worst thing about almost any "disaster" proceeds from your exaggerated belief about its horror rather than its intrinsic terribleness.

Life holds innumerable pains in the neck for all of us; but true catastrophies (such as experiencing torture or witnessing a major disaster in which scores of people suffer or perish) rarely happen. And "terrors," "horrors," and "awfulnesses" arise from fictional demons—which we foolishly make up in our heads and cannot really define or validate. A "horror" doesn't mean something *very* unfortunate or *exceptionally* disadvantageous. It means (if you look honestly at your feelings) something that you think *more* than unfortunate and *beyond the realm* of human disadvantage. Clearly, nothing of this kind exists; and your most devoted belief in its existence will still not make it true.

Something "horrible" or "awful," moreover, really means something that you see as (a) unusually obnoxious and (b) absolutely should or must not exist *because* you find it obnoxious. Although you can fairly easily prove the first part of this belief—that you find the thing or act uncommonly obnoxious—you cannot prove the second part: that it *therefore* must not exist. Indeed, if a law of the universe held that Activating Events (at point A) that you find extremely unpleasant (at point B) *must not exist* (at point C), A and C could not possibly coexist. So when you dogmatically contend (a) that such events must not prevail and (b) that they distinctly (and horribly!) *do,* you patently believe in the impossible. If you accept reality—and stop making up immutable laws of the universe in your silly head—you can accept the obvious fact that whatever exists exists—no matter how unpleasant and inconvenient you find its existence. Consequently, nothing truly winds up as "awful," "horrible," or "terrible."

4. Worry itself develops into one of the most painful conditions. And most of us would remain better off dead than "living" in its continual throes. If you unavoidably encounter the real dangers of blackmail, injury, or death, you'd better frankly face such problems and accept whatever penalties may accrue from them rather than continue to live in panic. You may well prefer a life in jail or even no life whatever to spending the rest of your days running, hiding, and panting with intense anxiety.

5. Aside from the possibility of physical harm, or acute deprivation, what can you *really* ever fear? So people may disapprove or dislike you. So some of them may boycott you or say nasty things about you. So they may besmirch your reputation. Tough, disadvantageous; rough! As long, as you do not *literally* starve, go to jail, or suffer bodily harm as a result of their censure, why give yourself a super-hard time about the wheels that turn in their heads? If you stop worrying and *do* something about their possible disapproval, you will probably counteract it. If you can do nothing to help yourself; tough again. So the cards fall that way! Why make the game of life more difficult by fretting and whining about its inequities? Do—don't stew!

6. Although many things seem terribly fearful to a young child, who has little or no control over his destiny, as an adult, you usually *have* more control and can change truly fearful circumstances or, if you cannot, can philosophically learn to live without making yourself panicky about them. Adults do not *have* to keep reactivating fears that may once have had but no longer have validity.

Mrs. Jane Borengrad provides us with an illustration of the foolish perpetuation of childhood fears. As a child, she unprotestingly accepted her sadistic father, who would severely punish her for the slightest questioning of his authority. Then (because she believed she deserved no better treatment) she married an equally sadistic man and remained with him for ten years until he turned openly psychotic and got committed to a mental hospital.

During both her childhood and her first marriage, then, she lived under truly, fearful circumstances. But not during her second marriage to Mr. Borengrad. For she could scarcely have found a meeker, nicer partner. Nonetheless, she felt exceptionally disturbed and came to therapy in a veritable state of panic. Having majored in psychology in college, she stated her symptoms to me (A.E.) in somewhat sophisticated terms:

"It looks like I keep behaving exactly like Pavlov's dogs. I apparently conditioned myself to react to anyone close to me with fear and trembling, with submission and underlying resentment, and I keep going through the old conditioned-response business over and over. Even though my husband acts like the kindest man in the world, and my teen-age daughters behave like lovely dolls, I live in constant, generalized fear. Ring the bell just before presenting the steak, and pretty soon the dog slobbers for the food he knows he will get. Well, ring the bell with me, and I immediately cringe with terror—even though the sadistic treatment I used to receive from my father and my first husband no longer follows its ringing. When simply in the presence of any member of my family, bell or no bell, I quickly start cringing."

"Maybe it looks like conditioning to you," I said, "but I feel that the very word 'conditioning' seems so vague and general that it actually masks the detailed processes that go on. Now let's look much more closely at these so-called conditioning processes. First, let's see what used to go on with your father and your first husband."

"They would get so angry at some little thing that I did or didn't do that I noticed their anger, and also saw how they followed it up—by punishing me severely in some manner. Then, naturally, whenever I began to see them growing angry, I immediately felt very fearful of the punishment that would follow. And I either ran away, went into a panic state, or asked them to beat me quickly and get the horrible thing over with."

"All right; that sounds like a good description. But you left out a very important part of the process."

"What?"

"Well, you said that they got angry? and you knew they would punish you; and then you went into a panic state. But the second part of the process—the part where you knew that they would punish you—you gloss over that too easily. You probably mean, don't you, that you perceived their anger and then, in a split second, you told yourself something like: 'Oh, my heavens! There he goes again, getting angry at me for practically nothing Oh, how terrible!

Oh, how unfair! What a poor miserable, helpless creature I remain, having an unfair father (or husband) who takes advantage of me like this and against whom I feel too weak to protect myself!' Didn't you say this, or something like this, to yourself once you perceived your father's or your first husband's anger?"

"Yes, I think I did. Particularly with my father, I would tell myself how awful that I had a father like that, while Minerva Scanlan, my best girl friend, had such a nice, easygoing father who never yelled at her and never hit her or punished her. I felt so *ashamed* to have a father like mine. And I thought I came from such a terrible family—so bad, in fact, that I wouldn't even want Minerva or anyone else to know just *how* badly they treated me."

"And with your first husband?"

"There, too. Only this time I didn't feel so ashamed of *him* but of my *having married* him. I kept saying, whenever he got angry and I knew he would pounce on me, 'Oh, how could I ever prove so stupid as to marry anyone like him? After I saw so much of this kind of thing at home, too! And then I went right out and repeated this horrible mistake, voluntarily. And now I keep staying with him, when I should have the guts to leave, even if I have to work my hands to the bone to take care of the children myself. How could I act so stupidly!'"

"All right, then. Note how we not only have the stimulus, the anger of your father and your first husband, and the conditioned response, your great fear of punishment, but we also and more importantly have your self-blaming *interpretations* of the horror of the stimulus. You theoretically could have told yourself, 'There goes crazy old Dad getting angry again, and about to punish me unjustly. Well, too bad; but I can survive his punishment and eventually, as I grow up, get away from him and live in a nonpunishing environment.' You actually largely said to yourself, however, 'I feel blameworthy for coming from such a crazy family and for having such weakness as to let the old buzzard take advantage of me.' And, with your first husband, you could have said to yourself, 'Too bad: I made a mistake in marrying this individual who acts sadistically, but I feel strong enough to get away from him and leave him to his own crazy ways.' But you again said: 'I see myself as no good for making the terrible mistake of marrying this bastard; and now I remain too weak and idiotic to get away from him.'"

"You seem to say then, that neither my father's nor my husband's actions—their anger followed by their punishment—actually conditioned me to down myself, but my own unjustified interpretations of their actions really did the job."

"Yes, your own *partly* unjustified interpretations. For you existed, of course, especially when you lived with your father, as a little girl who appropriately could have suffered from your father's physical assaults; and no matter what you might have told yourself philosophically, you experienced some *real* danger, and you would have emoted inappropriately if you did not feel frightened at all."

"But things proceeded differently when I married my first husband."

"Yes. Again, with him, you might have had some reason for fear, since he behaved psychotically and could literally have killed you when he got angry. But as you yourself pointed out before you also could have left him—which you couldn't do when you lived as a girl in your father's home. So most of the so-called conditioned fear with your husband you taught yourself: By falsely telling yourself that you couldn't cope with the situation, shouldn't have married him in the first place, and turned into a slob for staying with him. If you had told yourself other and more sensible things, you would soon have left him—or might even have stayed and felt unterrified of him."

"'Conditioning,' then, represents something of a cover-up word for what we largely do to ourselves?"

"Yes, very often. In Pavlov's case, don't forget that he, Pavlov, conditioned the dogs from the outside: he completely controlled whether they would or would not get their piece of steak when the bell rang. And in the case of your father, a much bigger and stronger person than you, he also largely controlled whether or not you would get beaten once he got angry. But not entirely! For had you had a better and different philosophical outlook when you lived with your father—which not very many young girls manage to acquire—you could have (unlike Pavlov's dogs) changed the situation considerably. Thus, you could have somehow influenced your father and induced him to punish one of your brothers or sisters, rather than you. Or you could have managed literally to run out of the house most of the time you knew he might punish you. Or you could have accepted your punishment more stoically and not bothered yourself too much about it. Or you could have tried many other gambits to change or ameliorate the effects of your father's behavior. But because of your poor philosophy of life at the time—which, admittedly, your father helped you acquire—you passively submitted to his blows, and also blamed yourself for having such a father and for having to submit. Although your situation had fear-inspiring elements, you helped make it positively *terrifying*."

"I can see what you mean. And with my first husband, I guess, I did even worse. There, I didn't have to submit at all; but I just about forced myself—with what you again would call my poor philosophy of life—to do so, and again made myself terrified."

"Exactly. Although you brought about only some of your so-called conditioning in your relations with your father, you probably created the far greater part of it with your first husband. Where you could have nicely *un*conditioned yourself—by telling yourself how ridiculous it proved to suffer the punishments of such a palpably disturbed man—you did the reverse and worked very hard to condition yourself still more."

"And what about my present state, with my second husband?"

"Your present state proves, even more solidly, the thesis we have discussed. For you will remember, again, that in the case of Pavlov's dogs, when he kept presenting the bell without steak, the dogs soon got unconditioned and stopped salivating, since they soon realized, or somehow signaled themselves, that the steak and the bell did not go together any longer. Accordingly, therefore, if you had gotten classically conditioned by the experiences with your father and first husband, both tyrants, you would have gradually got unconditioned by your several years of experience with your second husband, who acts practically angelically when compared with the first two."

"He does. Unbelievably nice and unpunishing."

"But your merely staying in his or your daughters' presence, you say, causes you to go into a state of panic?"

"Yes, I can't understand it. But it just happens."

"I think you really *can* understand it, if you look a little more closely, and stop convincing yourself that you got 'automatically' conditioned by your past experiences. For if your husband's behavior obviously did not reinforce your previously learned fear, and this fear still actively persists, then *you* keep doing something to reinforce it, to keep it alive, yourself."

"You really think so?"

"Yes—unless we believe in some kind of magic. If you, as we just noted, at least partly set up the original terrible fear of your father and your husband, even though they certainly also contributed to the context of the fear, and if your present husband doesn't contribute to that context to any serious degree, who else but you *does* keep the fear alive?"

Hmmm. I see what you mean. And what do you think I keep telling myself to keep my fear alive?"

"What do *you* think? If you start asking yourself, you will soon start to see."

"I probably tell myself what you pointed out before: that I always exuded weakness and inadequacy and that I still do. And that therefore I *do* have something to remain afraid of—my own weakness."

"A good point. These things usually develop circularly, just as you indicated. First, your father abuses you, then you tell yourself you can't do anything to stop his abuse, then you get terribly anxious. But, once you get anxious, and you only half-heartedly try to overcome anxiety, you start telling yourself that you can't do anything about *that*. So you get anxious of getting, and of not feeling able to do anything about getting, anxious. Quite a pickle!"

"Precisely. I used to fear my father and my first husband—though, really, myself, my weakness. And now I fear *remaining* anxious—remaining weak. And even though my present husband and daughters do *not* abuse me, I feel afraid that I couldn't handle the situation if they *did*. I stay afraid of inadequacy—and so afraid of feeling afraid—that I make myself panicky most of the time."

"Precisely. Then, to take it one step further, you actually do get so frightened, and act so badly because of your fright, that you then get convinced of your original hypothesis—that because you have such weakness and inadequacy, no one could ever possibly love you, including, especially, your own present husband and daughters."

"So I really start with a great need for love and a fear that because I remain so worthless, I won't get this need fulfilled. Then because of my fear I behave badly. Then I note that I behave badly and say to myself: 'That proves my worthlessness! Then, because I have doubly proved this 'worthlessness,' I get even more afraid that I won't deserve love the next time. And so on, and on."

"Right. And then, going one step further, you hate yourself for staying so weak and for having such a dire need for love; and you resent your present husband and daughters for not fulfilling your dire need to the exact extent you demand that they fill it—and for not making up for all the anger and punishment that your father and your first husband foisted on you. So that amounts to a goodly degree of resentment—which only tends to make you still more upset."

"As you said before: Quite a pickle! But what do I do now to get out of it?"

"What do you think you do? If you tell yourself sentences. One, Two, Three, and Four to get result Number Five, and result Number Five seems highly undesirable, how do you manage not to get it again?"

"By untelling yourself sentences One, Two, Three, and Four."

"Yes. And also, 'Why, if I do happen to get anxious because I remind myself of some past threat that really doesn't exist anymore, can't I then *see* what I've done and calm myself down pretty quickly?'"

"And if I try this kind of disputing and challenging and persist at it, I can see no reason why I have to continue to live in this kind of panic state I've forced myself into for such a long time?"

"No, no reason at all. Try it and see. And if it works, as I think it will, that will prove great. And if it doesn't then we'll quickly discover what *other* nonsense you tell yourself to stop it from working."

"I mainly better believe that no matter what seems upsetting or frightening, I now do it myself. I may not have done it in the past. But now I do!"

"In the main, yes. Occasionally, you may have a truly fearful circumstance in your life—as when you navigate a sinking boat or a defective car. But these kinds of realistic fears occur rarely in modern life; and the great majority of the things we now get panicked about constitute self-created 'dangers' that exist almost entirely in our own imaginations. *These* we do ourselves. And these we can undo by looking at our crooked thinking and straightening it out."

"OK. What you say sounds reasonable. Let me do a little trying."

Mrs. Borengrad did try. Within the next several weeks she not only ceased feeling terrified when in the presence of her daughters and present husband, but felt able to do several other things, including making a public speech at her community center, a thing which she had never felt capable of doing before. She learned, and as the years go by she still continues to learn, that unlike Pavlov's dogs she can recondition or uncondition her feelings and her responses *from the inside* and that she does not *have* to respond to actual or possible anger with woeful feelings of fright.

Pavlov, as not generally realized by many of those who quote him, thought that although rats and dogs and guinea pigs largely get conditioned by mere contiguity of stimuli (for example, a bell) and unconditioned responses (for example, salivation when smelling and tasting food), humans respond more complicatedly and get symbolically conditioned by what he called their secondary signaling system, their thinking. B. F. Skinner also talks about verbal as well as nonverbal behavior and states and implies that humans get conditioned—or self-conditioned—by things that they tell themselves about their environment, as well as by purely external changes in their contingencies of reinforcement. Skinner, *Beyond Freedom and Dignity,* states:

Methodological behaviorism limits itself to what [we can observe] publicly; mental processes may exist, but their nature rules them out of scientific consideration. The "behaviorists" in political science and many logical positivists in philosophy have followed a similar line. But we can study self-observation, and we must include it in any reasonably complete account of human behavior. Rather than ignore consciousness, an experimental analysis of behavior has put much emphasis on certain critical issues.

Right! But Skinner does not go far enough. As I (A.E.) have noted in a special review of his book in the journal *Behavior Therapy*, he does not sufficiently emphasize self-reinforcement:

Ironically enough, Skinner himself has rarely gotten reinforced for his views on freedom and dignity; nor have I often gotten reinforced for my opposing views that man can largely control his own emotional destiny in spite of many of the environmental influences that impinge on him. Yet both Skinner and I pigheadedly stick to our largely unreinforced views. Why? ... [Skinner] leaves out some salient information about humans: (1) Pure free will does not exist, but this hardly means that individuals can make no choices. (2) Behavior gets shaped and maintained by its consequences partly because the "inner man" (or the individual) feels and perceives the consequences of behavior, and, at least to some degree, decides to change. (3) The *"inner man" defines some consequences as "desirable" or "undesirable." As noted above, Skinner gains the opposition of the majority of psychologists for his views,* defines *his own conclusions as "good" and "reinforcing," and* chooses *to see their opposition (social disapproval) as not particularly penalizing. Another thinker, with Skinner's views, might well choose to construe his peers' disagreement as too negatively reinforcing to buck; and he might consequently change his views, stop expressing them, depress himself about social disapproval, or commit suicide. (4) Although Skinner's "orneriness" has some prior environment determinants, he probably also exercises some elements of "free choice." He himself mentions "the interaction between organism and environment," implying that the former significantly interprets and manipulates the latter, as well as the latter shaping and maintaining the former. A comprehensive, therapeutic view of humans gives some degree of strength and autonomy to both the organism and the environment—as, I think, Skinner does, too, but as some of his extreme statements appear to belie.*

In general, you may wage the most effective kinds of counterattacks against your needless and inappropriate anxieties along the following lines:

1. Track your worries and anxieties back to the specific beliefs of which they consist. Usually, you will find that you keep explicitly or implicitly telling yourself: "Doesn't it emerge as terrible that—?" and "Wouldn't it seem awful if—". Forcefully ask yourself: *"Why* would it emerge as so terrible that!—?" and *"Would* it really seem so awful if—?" Certainly, if this or that happened it might well prove inconvenient, annoying, or unfortunate. But can you, really, ever find empirical evidence that anything that might happen to you turns *terrible* or *awful?* For, honestly, you don't mean (*do* you?) by these terms that if something happened it would seem *very* bad or even *100 percent* bad. You mean that it would prove *more* than bad—and how, ever, can *that* happen?

2. When a situation actually involves danger—as when you start to fly in a rickety old airplane—you can sensibly (a) change the situation (for example, don't take the trip) or (b) accept the danger as one of the unfortunate facts of life (thus, accept the fact that you may die in the rickety plane; that this would prove most unfortunate if you did; and that life, to have full satisfaction, may have to include considerable risk-taking). If you can minimize a danger, act to reduce it. If you cannot, or you would find it more disadvantageous to avoid it than to risk it, then you have less choice and you'd *just better* accept it. No matter how you slice it, the inevitable remains inevitable; and no amount of worrying will make it less so.

3. If a dire event may occur, and you can do no more to ward it off, then *realistically* weigh the chances of its occurring and *realistically* assess the calamity that will befall you if it actually does occur. Although another world war *may* occur tomorrow, will it *likely* come about? If it does occur, will you probably get maimed or killed? If you die, will it *really* prove much more catastrophic than your peacefully dying in bed ten or twenty years later?

4. You'd better use both verbal *and* active depropagandization to overcome a specific anxiety. First realize that *you* created the anxiety by your internal sentences and challenge and dispute them. Also, push yourself to *do* the thing you senselessly fear and keep repeatedly (and promptly and vigorously!) *acting* against this fear.

Thus, if you avoid riding on buses, realize that your overconcern has roots in your own negative propaganda: in your telling yourself that buses prove dangerous, that horrible things will happen to you in a bus, that if anything dreadful did happen on a bus you couldn't stand it, and so on. And contradict this nonsense by showing yourself that buses provide unusual safety; that very few people get injured while riding on them; that if an unpleasant event occurs on a bus, you can handle it. Preferably, force yourself, over and over again, to keep riding on buses and to keep showing yourself, while riding, rational beliefs about bus-riding. The more you do the things you senselessly fear *while* contradicting your self-imposed anxiety, the quicker and more thoroughly your needless panics will vanish.

5. Most anxieties related to the dread of making public mistakes or antagonizing others, of losing love. Always suspect that some dire fear of disapproval lies behind your seemingly more objective fears, and continually and powerfully challenge and fight this fear by showing yourself that disapproval may bring disadvantages—but only self-defined "horror."

6. Convince yourself that worrying about many situations will aggravate rather than improve them. If, instead of telling yourself what "awfulness" would reign if something obnoxious happened, you tell yourself how silly, senseless, and self-defeating you will act if you *keep worrying* about this "awful" thing, you will have a much better chance of short-circuiting your irrational anxieties. Don't, however, blame or condemn yourself *for* your senseless worrying.

7. Try not to exaggerate the importance or significance of things. Your favorite cup, as Epictetus noted many centuries ago, merely represents a cup which you like. Your wife and children, however delightful, remain mortals. You need not take a negativistic, defensive "so-what" attitude and falsely tell yourself: "So what if I break my cup or my wife and children die? Who cares?" For you'd better care for your cup and your wife and children, in order to lead a more zestful and absorbing life. But if you exaggeratedly convince yourself that this remains the *only* cup in the world or that your life would turn out completely useless without your wife and children, you will falsely overestimate their value and make yourself needlessly vulnerable to their possible loss.

Remember, in this connection, that to enjoy an event wholeheartedly does *not* mean that you must catastrophize its absence. You may enjoy your cup, your wife, and your children wholeheartedly and truly care for them. But their sudden removal, although certainly a distinct loss and something that you may considerably *regret,* need not prove *calamitous.* This loss, however difficult, merely removes *something* that you ardently desire and love—it does not remove *you.* Unless, of course, you *insist on* identifying *yourself* with the people and things you love; and that kind of identification goes with emotional disturbance.

8. Distraction, as we noted in the last chapter, may temporarily dissipate groundless fear. If you worry about a plane's falling, forcing yourself to concentrate on a magazine or a book may give you some respite. If you

fear that you speak poorly, vigorous focusing on the content of your talk rather than on the reactions of your audience will often calm your fears. For deeper and more lasting removal of anxieties, however, a thoroughgoing philosophic approach, along the lines previously noted in this chapter, will prove much more effective.

9. Tracking your present fears to their earlier origins, and seeing how though they *once* seemed fairly appropriate they no *longer* hold water, often serves as a useful anxiety-reducing technique. As a child, you normally feared many things, such as staying in the dark or fighting with an adult. But you now have grown up. Keep showing yourself this and demonstrating that you can easily take certain chances now that you might have wisely avoided some years ago.

10. Don't make yourself ashamed of still existing anxieties, no matter how senseless they may seem. Certainly it seems wrong, meaning *mistaken,* for a grown person like you to retain childish fears. But *wrong* or *mistaken* does not mean *criminal* or *damnable.* And if people dislike you because you show anxiety, too bad—but hardly devastating! Admit, by all means, that you feel needlessly fearful; forthrightly tackle your silly worries; but don't waste a minute beating yourself over the head for making yourself anxious. You have much better things to do with your time and energies!

11. No matter how effectively you combat your anxieties, and temporarily eradicate them, don't feel surprised if they return from time to time. Humans fear again what they have once feared, even though they generally no longer remain afraid of this thing. If you once had a fear of high places and you conquered it by deliberately frequenting such places, you may still, on occasion, feel afraid when looking down from heights. In these circumstances, merely accept the returned fear, actively work against it again, and you will quickly see, in most instances, that it returns to limbo.

Always remember, in this connection, that you remain mortal; that humans have innate limitations; that they don't *completely* overcome groundless fears and anxieties; and that life continues as a ceaseless battle against irrational worries. If you fight this battle intelligently and unremittingly, however, you can *almost* always feel free from *almost* all your needless concerns. What more can you ask?

CHAPTER 10

COPING WITH DISABILITY

EDITOR'S COMMENTARY:

In this selection, Albert Ellis recounts the history of his personal disabilities and how he has efficiently coped with them. In a text that he wrote about fatal illness, he explained much more of this history in detail. Yet, this selection is terse and lucid in that Ellis covers his childhood hospitalizations, his diabetes, and his advancing age—including what was probably BPH or benign prostate hypertrophy (he coped with it by sitting rather than standing during urination so that he could do productive work). Ellis intentionally sought to act as a model for some clients who suffered disability (some who often suffered them poorly). While advanced age itself is not disabling, some limitations that came with it during Ellis's advanced years were managed by him with equanimity, efficiency, acceptance—and sometimes humor.

Excerpted from *The Albert Ellis Reader,*
Citadel Press, 1998

At the age of forty, I was diagnosed as having full-blown diabetes, so that has added to my disabilities. Diabetes, of course, does not cause much direct pain and anguish, but it clearly does lead to severe restrictions. I was quickly put on insulin injections twice a day and on a seriously restricted diet. I, who used to take four spoons of sugar in my coffee in my prediabetic days, plus half cream, was suddenly deprived of both. Moreover, when I stuck with my insulin injections and dietary restrictions, I at first kept my blood sugar regularly low but actually lost ten pounds off my already all-too-thin body. After my first year of insulin taking, I became a near-skeleton!

I soon figured out that by eating twelve small meals a day, literally around the clock, I could keep my blood sugar low, ward off insulin shock reactions, and maintain a healthy weight. So for over forty years I have been doing this and managing to survive pretty well. But what a bother! I am continually, day and night, making myself peanut butter sandwiches, pricking my fingers for blood samples, using my blood metering machines, carefully watching my diet, exercising regularly, and doing many other things that insulin-dependent diabetics have to do to keep their bodies and minds in good order.

When I fail to follow this annoying regimen, which I rarely do, I naturally suffer. Over the many years that I have been diabetic, I have ended up with a number of hypoglycemic reactions, including being carried off three times in an ambulance to hospital emergency wards. In spite of my keeping my blood sugar and blood pressure healthfully low over these many years, I have suffered from various sequelae of diabetes and have to keep regularly checking with my physicians to make sure that they do not get worse or that new complications do not develop. So, although I manage to keep my health rather good, I have several physicians whom I regularly see, including a diabetologist, an internist, an ear, nose, and throat specialist, a urologist, an orthopedist, and a dermatologist. Who knows what will be next? Oh, yes: Because diabetes affects the mouth and the feet, my visits to the dentist and podiatrist every year are a hell of a lot more often than I enjoy making them. But whether I like it or not, I go.

Finally, as a result of my advancing age, perhaps my diabetic condition, and who knows what else, I have suffered for the last few years from a bladder that is easily filled and slow to empty. So I run to the toilet more than I used to do, which I do not particularly mind. But I do mind the fact that it often takes me much longer to urinate than it did in my youth and early adulthood. That is really annoying!

Why? Because for as long as I can remember I have been something of a time watcher. I figured out when I was still in my teens and was writing away like a demon, even though I had a full schedule of courses and other events at college, that the most important thing in my life, and perhaps in almost everyone else's life, is time. Money, of course, has its distinct value; so does love. But if you lose money or get rejected in your sex-love affairs, you always have other chances to make up for your losses, as long as you are alive and energetic. If you are poor, you can focus on getting a better income; if you are unloved and unmated, you can theoretically get a new partner up until your dying day. Not so with time. Once you lose a few seconds, hours, or years, there is no manner in which you can get them back. You cannot retrieve them. *Tempus fugit*—and time lost, wasted, or ignored is distinctly irretrievable.

Ever since my teens, then, I have made myself allergic to procrastination and to hundreds of other ways of wasting time and letting it idly and unthinkingly go by. I assume that my days on earth are numbered and that I will not live a second more than I actually do live. So, unless I am really sick or otherwise out of commission, I do my best to make the most of my sixteen daily hours, and I frequently manage to accomplish this by doing two or more things at a time. For example, I very frequently listen to music while reading and have an interesting conversation with people while preparing a meal or eating.

This is all to the good, and I am delighted to be able to do two things at once, to stop my procrastinating and my occasional daydreaming and, instead, do something that I would much rather get done in the limited time that I have to be active each day and the all too few years I will have in my entire lifetime. Consequently, when I was afflicted by the problem of slow urination in my late seventies, I distinctly regretted the five to ten minutes of extra time it began to take me to go to the toilet several times each day and night. What a waste! What could I effectively do about saving this time?

Well, I soon worked out that problem. Instead of standing up to urinate as I had normally done for all my earlier life, I began to do so sitting down, making sure I had some interesting reading for the several minutes that it took me to finish. But then I soon figured out that I could do other kinds of things as well to use this time.

For example, when I am alone in the apartment I share with my mate, Janet Wolfe, I usually take a few minutes to heat up my regular hot meal in our microwave oven. While it is cooking, I often prepare my next hot meal and put it in a microwave dish in the refrigerator, so that when I come up from my office to our apartment again, I can pop it in the oven. Therefore I am usually cooking and preparing two meals at a time. As the old saying goes, two meals for the price of one!

Once the microwave oven rings its bell and tells me that my meal is finished, I take it out of the oven, and instead of putting it on our kitchen table to eat, I take it into the bathroom and put in on a shelf by the side of the toilet, together with my eating utensils. Then, while I spend the next five or ten minutes urinating, I simultaneously eat my meal out of the microwave dish and thereby accomplish my eating and urinating at the same time. Now some of you may find this is inelegant or even boorish. My main goal is to get two important things—eating and urinating—done promptly, to polish them off as it were, and then to get back to the rest of my interesting life. As you may well imagine, I am delighted with this arrangement and am highly pleased with having efficiently worked it out!

Sometimes I actually arrange to do tasks while I am also doing therapy. My clients, for example, know that I am diabetic and that I have to eat regularly, especially when my blood sugar is low. So, with their permission, I usually eat my peanut butter and sugarless jelly sandwiches while I am conducting my individual and group sessions, and everyone seems to be comfortable with it.

However, I still have to spend a considerable amount of time taking care of my physical needs and dealing with my diabetes and other disabilities. I hate doing this, but I accept the fact that I have little other choice. So I use REBT to overcome any tendencies toward low frustration tolerance that I may still have. Whenever I feel that I am getting impatient or angry, I tell myself about my various limitations, "Too damned bad! I really do not like taking all this time and effort to deal with my impairments and wish to hell that I didn't have to do so. But, alas, I do. It is hard doing so many things to keep myself in a relatively healthy condition, but it is much harder, and in the long run much more painful and deadly, if I do not keep doing this. There is no reason whatsoever why I absolutely must have it easier than I do. Yes, it is unfair for me to be more afflicted than many other people are, but, damn it, I should be just as afflicted as I am! Unfairness *should* exist in the world—to me, and to whomever else it does exist—because it exists! Too bad that it does—but it does!"

So, using my REBT training, I work on my low frustration tolerance and accept what I cannot change. Of course, barring a medical miracle, I cannot change any of my major disabilities, but I can live with them, and I do. I can even reduce them to some extent, but I still cannot get rid of them. Tough! But it is not awful.

REBT posits that there are two main instigators of human neurosis: first, low frustration tolerance (I *absolutely must* have what I want when I want it and must never, never be deprived of anything that I really, really desire); second, self-denigration (when I do not perform well and win others' approval, as at all times I *should, ought,* and *must,* I am an inadequate person, a retard, a no-goodnik!).

In addition to suffering from the first of these disturbances, many disabled people in our culture suffer even more seriously from the second.

People with serious disabilities often have more performance limitations in many areas (at school, work, and sports) than those who have no disabilities. To make matters worse, they are frequently criticized, scorned, and put down by others for having their deficiencies. From early childhood to old age, they may be ridiculed and reviled, and shown that they really are not as capable or as "good" as others are. So they not only suffer from decreased competence in various areas but also from much less approval than more proficient members of our society often receive. For both these reasons—because they notice their own ineptness and because many of their relatives and associates ignore or condemn them for it—they falsely tend to conclude, "My deficiencies make me a deficient; inadequate individual."

I largely taught myself to forgo this kind of self-deprecation long before I developed most of my present disabilities. From my early interest in philosophy during my teens, I saw that I did not have to rate myself as a person when I rated my efficacy and my lovability. I began to teach myself, before I reached my mid-twenties, that I could give up most of my feelings of shame and unconditionally accept myself as a human even when I did poorly, especially at sports. As I grew older, I increasingly worked at accepting myself unconditionally. While I use my REBT-oriented high frustration tolerance to stop myself from whining about disabilities, and rarely inwardly or outwardly complain about this, I also use my self-accepting philosophy to refrain from ever putting myself down about these handicaps. In REBT, one of the most important things we do is to teach most of our clients to rate or evaluate only their thoughts, feelings, and actions and not rate their self, essence, or being. So for many years I have followed this principle and fully acknowledged that many of my behaviors are unfortunate, bad, and inadequate because they do not fulfill my goals and desires. But of course, I strongly philosophize that I am not a bad or inadequate person for having these flaws and failings.

I must admit that I really hate growing old. Because, in addition to my diabetes, easily tired eyes, and poor hearing, old age definitely increases my list of disabilities. Every year that goes by I creak more in my joints, have extra physical pains to deal with, slow down in my pace, and otherwise am able to do somewhat less than previously So old age is hardly a blessing!

However, as I approach the age of eighty-five, I am damned glad to be alive and to be quite active, productive, and enjoying. My brother and sister, who were a few years younger than I, both died almost a decade ago, and just about all my close relatives are also fairly long gone. A great many of my psychological friends and associates, most of whom were younger than I, unfortunately have died, too. I grieve for some of them, especially for my brother Paul, who was my best friend. But I also remind myself that it is great that I am still very much alive, as is my beloved mate Janet, after more than thirty years of our living together. So, I really am very lucky!

Do my own physical disabilities actually add to my therapeutic effectiveness? I would say, yes—definitely. In fact, they do in several ways, including the following. With my regular clients, most of whom have only minor disabilities or none at all, I often use myself as a model and show them that, in spite of my eighty-five years and my physical problems, I fully accept myself with these impediments and give myself the same unconditional self-acceptance that I try to help these clients achieve. I also often show them, directly and indirectly, that I rarely whine about my physical defects but have taught myself to have high frustration tolerance (HFT) about them. This kind of modeling helps teach many of my clients that they, too, can face real adversities and achieve USA and HFT.

I particularly work at teaching my disabled clients to have unconditional self-acceptance by fully acknowledging that their deficiencies are unfortunate, bad, and sometimes very noxious, but that they are never, except by their own self-sabotaging definition, shameful, disgraceful, or contemptible. Yes, other people may often view them as horrid, hateful people because our culture and many other cultures often encourage such unfair prejudice. But I show my clients that they never have to agree with this kind of bigotry and can actively fight against it in their own lives as well as help other people with disabilities to be fully self-accepting.

I often get this point across to my own clients by using self-disclosure and other kinds of modeling. Thus, I saw Michael, a forty-five-year-old man with brittle diabetes. He had great trouble maintaining a healthy blood sugar level, as his own diabetic brother and sister were able to do. He incessantly put himself down for his inability to work steadily, maintain a firm erection, participate in sports, and achieve a good relationship with an attractive woman who would mate with him in spite of his severe disabilities.

When I revealed to Michael several of my own physical defects and limitations, such as those previously mentioned, and when I showed him how I felt sad and disappointed about them but stubbornly refused to feel at all ashamed or embarrassed for having them he strongly worked at full self-acceptance, stopped denigrating himself for his inefficacies, shamelessly informed prospective partners about his disabilities, and was able to mate with a woman who cared for him deeply in spite of them.

In this case, I also used REBT skill training. It shows people with physical problems how to stop needlessly upsetting themselves about their drawbacks.

But it also teaches them various social, professional, and other skills to help them minimize and compensate for their hindrances. In Michael's case, in addition to teaching him unconditional self-acceptance, I showed him how to socialize more effectively; how to satisfy female partners without having perfect erections; and how to participate in some sports, such as swimming, despite his physical limitations. So although still disabled, he was able to feel better and perform better as a result of his REBT sessions. This is the two-sided, or duplex, kind of therapy that I try to arrange with many of my clients with disabilities.

Partly as a result of my own physical restrictions, I am also able to help clients with their low frustration tolerance (LFT) whether or not they have disabilities. As I noted earlier, people with physical restrictions and pains usually are more frustrated than those without such impediments. Consequently, they may well develop a high degree of LFT. Consider Denise, for example. A psychologist, she became insulin dependent at the age of thirty and felt horrified about her newly acquired restrictions. According to her physicians, she now had to take two injections of insulin and several blood tests every day, give up most of her favorite fat-loaded and salt-saturated foods, spend a half hour a day exercising, and take several other health-related precautions. She viewed all of these chores and limitations as "revolting and horrible," and became phobic about regularly carrying them out. She especially kept up her life-long gourmet diet and gained twenty extra pounds within a year of becoming diabetic. Her doctors' and her husband's severe criticism helped her feel guilty, but it hardly stopped her in her foolish self-indulgence.

I first worked with Denise on her LFT and did my best to convince her, as REBT practitioners often do, that she did not need the eating and other pleasures that she wanted. It was indeed hard for her to impose the restrictions her physical condition now required, but it was much harder, I pointed out, if she did not follow them. Her increased limitations were indeed unfortunate, but they were hardly revolting and horrible; I insisted that she could stand them, though never necessarily like them.

At first I had little success in helping Denise raise her LFT because, as a bright psychologist, she irrationally but quite cleverly parried my rational arguments. However, using my own case as an example, I was able to show her how, at my older age and with disabilities greater than hers, I had little choice but to give up my former indulgences or die. So, rather than die, I gave up putting four spoons of sugar and half cream in my coffee, threw away my salt shaker, stopped frying my vegetables in sugar and butter, surrendered my allergy to exercise, and started tapping my fingers seven or eight times a day for blood tests. When Denise heard how I forced my frustration tolerance up as my pancreatic secretion of insulin went down, and how for over forty years I have thereby staved off the serious complications of diabetes that probably would have followed from my previous habits, and from her present ones, she worked on her own LFT and considerably reduced it.

Simultaneously, I also helped Denise with her secondary symptoms of neurosis. As a bright person and as a psychologist who often helped her clients with their self-sabotaging thoughts, feelings, and behaviors, she knew how destructive her own indulgences were, and she self-lambasted and made herself feel very ashamed of them, thereby creating a symptom about a symptom: self-downing about her LFT. So I used general REBT with her to help her give herself unconditional self-acceptance in spite of her indulging in her LFT. I also specifically showed her how, when I personally slip back to my predisability ways and fail to continue my antidiabetic exercise and other prophylactic routines, I only castigate my behavior and not my self or personhood. I therefore see myself as a goodnik who can change my no-goodnik actions, and this attitude helps me correct those actions. By forcefully showing this to Denise, and using myself and my handling of my disabilities as notable examples, I was able to help her give up her secondary symptom, self-deprecation, and go back to working more effectively to decrease her primary symptom—low frustration tolerance.

In this article, I have mainly tried to show how I have personally coped with some of my major disabilities for over sixty years. But let me say that I have found it relatively easy to do so because, first, I seem to be a natural born survivor and coper, which many disabled (and nondisabled) people are not. This may well be my innate predisposition, but also may have been aided by my having to cope with nephritis from my fifth to my eighth year and my consequent training of myself to live with physical adversity. Second, as noted earlier, I derived an epicurean and stoic philosophy from reading and reasoning about many philosophers' and writers' views from my sixteenth year onward. Third, I originated REBT in January 1955 and have spent over forty years, the great majority of my professional life, teaching it to clients, therapists, and members of the public.

For these and other reasons, I fairly easily and naturally use REBT methods in my own life and am not the kind of difficult customer (DC) that I often find my clients to be. With them, and especially with DCs who have disabilities and who keep complaining about them and not working too hard to overcome and cope with them, I often use a number of cognitive, emotive, and behavioral techniques for which REBT is famous and which I have described in my book, *How to Cope With a Fatal Illness,* and in many of my other writings.

Several other writers have also applied REBT and cognitive behavior therapy (CBT) to people with disabilities, including Rochelle Baiter, Warren Johnson, Rose Oliver, Fran Bock, and J. Sweetland. Louis Calabro has written a particularly helpful article showing how the antiawfulizing philosophy of REBT can be used with individuals suffering from severe disabilities, such as those following a stroke, and Gerald Gandy has published an unusual book, *Mental Health Rehabilitation: Disputing Irrational Beliefs.*

The aforementioned writings include a great many cognitive, emotive, and behavioral therapy techniques that are particularly useful with people who have disabilities. Because, as REBT theorizes, human thinking, feeling, and acting significantly interact with each other, and because emotional disturbance affects one's body as well as one's physical condition affects one's kind and degree of disturbance, people who are upset about their disabilities often require a multifaceted therapy to deal with their upset state. REBT, like Arnold Lazarus's multimodal therapy, provides this kind of approach and therefore is often helpful to people with disability-related problems.

Let me briefly describe a few of the cognitive REBT methods that I frequently use with my clients who have disabilities and who are quite anxious, depressed, and self-pitying about having these handicaps. I bring out and help them dispute their irrational beliefs (IBs). Thus, I show these clients that there is no reason why they must not be disabled, although that would be distinctly desirable. No matter how ineffectual some of their behaviors are, they are never inadequate persons for having a disability. They can always accept themselves while acknowledging and deploring some of their physical and mental deficiencies. When other people treat them unkindly and unfairly because of their disabilities, they can deplore this unfairness but not damn their detractors. When the conditions under which they live are unfortunate and unfair, they can acknowledge this unfairness while not unduly focusing on and indulging in self-pity and horror about it.

Preferably, I try to show my disabled clients how to make a profound philosophical change, and thereby not only minimize their anxiety, depression, rage, and self-pity for being disadvantaged, but become considerably less disturbed by future adversities. I try to teach them that they have the ability to consistently and strongly convince themselves that nothing is absolutely awful, that no human is worthless, and that they can practically always find some real enjoyment in living. I also try to help them accept the challenge of being productive, self-actualizing, and happy in spite of the unusual handicaps with which they may unfortunately be innately endowed or may have acquired during their lifetimes. I also point out the desirability of their creating for themselves a vital absorbing interest, that is, a long-range devotion to some cause, project, or other interest that will give them a real meaning and purpose in life, distract them from their disability, and give them ongoing value and pleasure.

To aid these goals of REBT, I use a number of other cognitive methods as well as many emotive and behavioral methods with my disabled clients. I have described them in many articles and books, so I shall not repeat them here. Details can be found in *How to Cope With a Fatal Illness*.

Do I use myself and my own ways of coping with my handicaps to help my clients cope with theirs? I often do. I first show them that I can unconditionally accept them with their disabilities even when they have partly caused these handicaps themselves. I accept them with their self-imposed emphysema from smoking or their one hundred extra pounds of fat from indulging in ice cream and candy. I show them how I bear up quite well with my various physical difficulties and still manage to be energetic and relatively healthy. I reveal some of the time-saving, self-management, and other discipline methods I frequently use in my own life. I indicate that I have not only devised some sensible philosophies for people with disabilities, but that I actually apply them in my own work and play, and I show them how. I have survived my handicaps for many years and damned well intend to keep doing so for perhaps a good number of years to come.

I might never have been that interested in rational or sensible ways of coping with emotional problems had I not had to cope with a number of fairly serious physical problems from the age of five onward. But rather than plague myself about my physical restrictions, I devoted myself to the philosophy of remaining happy in spite of my disabilities, and out of this philosophy I ultimately originated REBT, in January 1955. As I was developing REBT, I used some of its main principles on myself, and I have often used them with other people with disabilities. When I and these others have worked to acquire an antiawfulizing, unconditional, self-accepting philosophy, we have often been able to lead considerably happier and more productive lives than many other handicapped individuals. This hardly proves that REBT is a panacea for all physical and mental ills. It is not. But it is a form of psychotherapy and self-therapy especially designed for people who suffer from uncommon adversities. It points out to clients in general, and to physically disadvantaged ones in particular, that however much they dislike the harsh realities of their lives, they can manage to make themselves feel the healthy negative emotions of sorrow, regret, frustration, and grief while stubbornly refusing to create and dwell on the unhealthy emotions of panic, depression, despair, rage, self-pity, and personal worthlessness. To help in this respect, it uses a number of cognitive, emotive-evocative, and behavioral methods. Its results with disabled individuals has not yet been well researched with controlled studies. Having used it successfully on myself and with many other individuals, however, I am strongly prejudiced in its favor. But controlled investigations of its effectiveness are an important next step.

CHAPTER 11

THERAPY WITH PSYCHOTICS
AND
BORDERLINE PSYCHOTICS

EDITOR'S COMMENTARY:

Ellis often quipped to people who knew him well (such folks usually being professional psychotherapists) that he had treated more psychotic and borderline patients than anyone else in New York! What he meant had limitations, but he tried to make his point concerning patients with the diagnosis of borderline personality in his debates with Otto Kernberg MD, the great psychoanalyst who championed object-relations psychotherapy. Ellis maintained that a core issue for most personality disorders was the refusal by the patient to be uncomfortable, and that phenomenon was variously referred to by Ellis as low frustration tolerance (LFT) or discomfort anxiety (DA). As a made-up term, he also called it "I can'tstandit-itis." What he meant was that the borderline personality (referred to in DSM I and II as pseudo-neurotic schizophrenia or really schizophrenia masked by neurosis) was biologically predisposed to go to extremes in perception; namely, that other people were seldom OK but were either good or bad. This is the black-white phenomenon often described by writers about borderline personality. Ellis argued that people could be trained to be less extreme if they would tolerate the fact that other people had quirks, idiosyncratic, neurotic, and self-defeating behavior. That said, if the patient tolerated those quirks about other people, they could learn to tolerate them in themselves and then to identify with and build a stronger definition of self-worth. Thus, for that diagnostic group of character disorders, Ellis argued somewhat differently than did proponents of DBT or dialectical behavior therapy (i.e., Marsha Linehan)—although some of what Ellis had to say can be found not only in Linehan's theory and work but in the work of Kernberg, Masterson, Freeman & Beck, and Jeffrey Younge). Concerning psychotic patients, Ellis worked with them to take their prescribed medications. Compliance or tolerating expert judgment from others was a goal of Ellis's intervention. Often, both borderline and psychotic patients were neurotic, so standard REBT could be used to help people with those problems. However, working with an individual to follow medication regimens faithfully and not to use the medication in ways other than it was prescribed was important during the course of REBT intervention. Discontinuing medication capriciously was another issue regarding LFT/DA to be overcome by learning HFT or high frustration tolerance in REBT. Lastly, Ellis would comment in training programs that intervention with character disorders or in the management of psychosis was not short term as it was so often with management of neurotic behaviors. Ellis's work anticipated later interventions with psychotic patients using CBT written about by Daniel David PhD, Tulio Scrimali MD, and Viorel Lupu MD which did not buy into the theoretical issues of Silvano Arietti MD but which used RE&CBT to try to extinguish or partially extinguish hallucinations and delusions with and without medication.

Excerpted from *Humanistic Psychotherapy,*
McGraw-Hill, 1973

Rational-emotive psychotherapy was originally devised largely for use in the treatment of so-called "neurotics." However, most of these clients, it appears, can be more accurately labeled borderline psychotics or outright psychotics, and the classification of them as neurotics may have been a gross underestimation of the gravity of their condition.

It will be recalled that several years ago an article appeared in the *American Journal of Psychiatry* that pointed out that Freud had misdiagnosed most of his early analysands, since he referred to them as "hysterics" or "neurotics" when actually, in the light of our modern diagnostic methods, they would be labeled as schizophrenic. This Freudian type of misdiagnosis may still be prevalent. Particularly if a psychotherapist is in private practice, he will soon find that because he charges a rather high fee per session, and because his clients (partly because of their severe sickness) tend not to be wealthy individuals, he is largely seeing people who are practically *driven* to seek help, rather than those who would merely benefit if they did receive it. These clients, who think they *need* steady and often prolonged support from a therapist, are the ones most likely to be overt or borderline psychotics.

A great many regular psychotherapy clients, in the experience of numerous therapists, including myself, have had histories of prior institutionalization. Some of them are seen when they are temporarily on leave from a mental hospital; and many more after they have been discharged. Many of those who have never been hospitalized come for treatment because they feel they are on the verge of cracking up or because they are suicidal. Obviously, these are very "sick" people.

It was once widely believed that almost all highly disturbed individuals, including those who are basically psychotic, are made the way they are by their early environment—especially by traumatic occurrences during their first few years of life. There is increasing, and in fact overwhelming, evidence for abandonment of this view, and for the belief that probably all human beings are born with rather distinct "holes in their head." Psychotics, then, are born with a much bigger hole than the rest of us inherit.

By this is meant that the human animal is biologically predisposed to think crookedly on many occasions, to defeat his own ends, to be oversuggestible and overgeneralizing, to become both anxious and hostile with very little or no objective provocation, and to continue to reinfect himself with anxiety and hostility no matter what kind of upbringing he has, nor in what kind of society he has been reared. The belief that men and women are *first* genetically predisposed to emotional disturbance, and that they then *later* are the victims of environmental traumata that help actualize these predispositions, and that induce them to become perhaps four or five times as disturbed as they might biologically tend to be, has been forced on a growing body of psychotherapists, including myself, by clinical observation during recent years.

The resistance of seriously disturbed clients to treatment can often be traced to the innate inherited tendencies of these people. In some cases, it has become clear that they resist because they are telling themselves that they *cannot* help themselves; or because they resent having to *work* at therapy; or because they want to spite the therapist; or for some other ideological reason. In many other instances, however, it eventually becomes evident that the clients very much *do* want to improve and *are* working hard at doing so; but they just have great *difficulty* helping themselves, and it is highly probable that this difficulty is inborn, has plagued them all their lives, and is an essential component of their disturbance. In other words, whereas many neurotic individuals, for various perverse reasons, simply *will* not think clearly and logically about themselves, it appears that these particular clients who resist getting better on non-ideological grounds are usually psychotic or borderline psychotic individuals who *cannot* think straight, or who can do so only with great difficulty.

Observation of these clients over a long period of time has convinced me that they seemed to have severe focusing difficulties. Either they did not focus adequately on solving their life difficulties, and instead were unusually diffuse, discursive, and disorganized in their thinking; or else, in many instances, they overfocused, in a highly rigid manner, on some specific aspect of their life, usually some negativistic or catastrophic aspect, and therefore were unable to focus adequately on other aspects of any problem-solving situation. The more of this behavior one observes, the more apparent it becomes that these clients are not in the neurotic range, even though their behavior is often typical of that of so-called neurotics, but that they are basically psychotic. They have a true thinking disorder—as Eugen Bleuler insisted is fundamentally true of schizophrenics. It is also interesting to note that Shakow has summed up his thirty years of studying schizophrenics with this observation: "If we were to try to epitomize the schizophrenic person's system in the most simple language, we might say that he has two major difficulties: first, he reacts to old situations as if they were new ones (he fails to habituate), and to new situations as if they we recently past ones (he perseverates); and second, he overresponds when the stimulus is relatively small, and he does not respond enough when the stimulus is great." In both these two major difficulties that Shakow notes, it is obvious that the schizophrenic is, at one time or another, under- *and* over-focusing.

Clinical observations by Aaron T. Beck confirm that seriously disturbed people have a fundamental, and probably innate focusing or thinking disorder. Beck notes that "the present study indicates that, even in mild phases of depression, systematic deviations from realistic and logical thinking occur. . . . The thinking-disorder typology outlined in this paper is similar to that described in studies of schizophrenia. . . . These findings suggest that a thinking disorder may be common to all types of psychopathology."

Beck also notes that "*magnification* and *minimization* refer to errors in evaluation which are so gross as to constitute distortions. These processes were manifested by underestimation of the individual's performance, achievement or ability, and inflation of the magnitude of his problems and tasks. Other examples were the exaggeration of the intensity or significance of a traumatic event. It was frequently observed that the patients' initial reaction to an unpleasant event was to regard it as a catastrophe. It was generally found on further inquiry that the perceived disaster was often a relatively minor problem."

Beck's statement has two most important implications. It implies, first, that the Freudian theory of the great importance of childhood trauma is untenable, since individuals who are thus "traumatized" may very well *invent* their "traumas" by exaggerating the significance of the usual life difficulties that occur to them. And it implies, second, that these patients have a basic thinking disorder, probably with innate as well as socially determined roots, that causes them to be qualitatively different from other so-called neurotics, who are unduly upset about life's problems, but who can fairly easily be taught to cope with and live with such problems.

There is considerable other evidence that indicates many cavalierly diagnosed "neurotics" are really fundamentally psychotic, that they *cannot* (and not just *will* not) easily think straight about themselves and others, and that they are therefore most difficult to help when they come for psychotherapy. A few illustrations will show that even the most normal human beings are born with serious thinking deficiencies, and that in consequence they usually tend to have some kind of emotional disturbances and to act in self-defeating ways.

Take, for example, scientists, who in their own fields of endeavor are supposed to think scientifically, which means that they are supposed to be among the most objective and dispassionate observers and experimentalists. Actually, as a writer showed in an article in *Science,* some of the greatest scientists, such as Charles Darwin, had great difficulty in changing their ideas, and frequently refused to do so when clear-cut factual evidence indicated that it would be wise if they did. When data presented to them showed that something they believed in wholeheartedly was untrue, they by no means enthusiastically changed their views. Men of science are known to cavil with the evidence, ignore it, sometimes refuse to accept it; and it may be only ten or twenty years later that they finally reluctantly accept it and give up their original fallacious hypotheses. And these, remember, are often great minds, and great scientific minds at that, who are thinking in this irrational manner.

It is a human failing to resist accepting new information, even when it would be to our best interests to do so. Moreover, we humans tend, because of the principle of inertia, to fail to make use of much valuable information and insight that we theoretically accept. Because we are in a well-oiled groove of behavior, riding in reasonable comfort in what can be called Groove A, we find it exceptionally difficult, on many occasions, to pull ourselves out of that Groove, and to start swinging in Groove B—even though we know that it would be much wiser if we got ourselves to do so. When, for example, we are dully watching television, and know that it would be much better if we got up and started to work on some task that we have to do, we resist getting up, and stubbornly keep giving ourselves silly rationalizations why we should still watch the television screen. Then, when we finally manage to get to the required task, and we somehow start swinging easily and pleasantly in *that* Groove, which we may call Groove B, we refuse, with surprising frequency, to get out of it, when it comes time for us to go on, sensibly, to Groove C—which may consist of going to bed, playing with our children, eating, or even returning to Groove A again (because, perhaps, there is then a special show on television which it really would be wise for us to see).

Human beings—and in fact, in my belief *all* human beings—are perversely like this. They don't merely occasionally but *continually* behave stupidly and sabotage their own best interests, no matter how bright or educated they may be. How serious this self-defeating, utterly irrational tendency of the human animal can be struck me with great force when I picked up a medical magazine and saw a photo of a very brilliant young female physician who had won a prize for her valuable researches. Lo and behold!—it was obvious from her picture that she weighed at least two hundred pounds.

Now this set me to thinking. For I know at least fifty or sixty physicians intimately. All of them, of course, have four years' training at medical school, one year of internship, and years of medical experience. In addition, some of them have three or more years of residency in some medical specialty and a good deal of unusual clinical or research experience. Most of them are internists and general practitioners who spend a good deal of their time advising their patients to stop overeating, give up smoking, refrain from drinking too much, and get enough sleep.

Suppose we ask, now: What percentage of these physicians follow to a reasonable degree the simple laws of physical hygiene which are taught to practically all school children? Probably no more than 5 percent; for practically all these physicians whom I personally know are overeating, smoking, drinking too heavily, or sleeping too little, and some of them are doing all these self-defeating things. Which means that 95 percent of a highly intelligent, well-educated population is clearly destroying itself!

One of my own clients, a highly competent physician, came in to see me a while ago and said: "Doctor Ellis, you may think that I'm disturbed, but you really should be seeing everybody on the staff of my hospital, because they're all at least as crazy as I am! Especially one man, who has his M.D. and is also a Ph.D. in physiology. He's under thirty-five years of age, and is undoubtedly one of the outstanding authorities on obesity in the country. Well, you wouldn't believe it. He weighs at least three hundred pounds!"

Don't take my word for any of this, but open-mindedly look around you. Observe the scores of really self-destructive people whom you personally know—including (naturally!) most of the psychiatrists, psychologists, and psychiatric social workers with whom you are intimately acquainted. And look also, if you will, at the scores of other individuals you know who have had years of psychoanalysis and other forms of therapy, and who may possibly be getting along better now than they were when they first entered treatment, but who mentally are still far from well balanced. Does not the ubiquity and the incidence of neurosis and psychosis among your closest relatives and associates indicate something highly significant about the human, all-too-human, *tendency* of modern men and women, not to mention adolescents, to be severely disturbed?

If one honestly looks at the facts of moderate and serious emotional disturbance in this nation (as well as in virtually all other parts of the contemporary world), one will soberly ask: How come that 95 to 99 percent of the population is acting in such a childish, irrational, self-destructive manner? Is this kind of behavior *truly* the result of early childhood rearing?

The evidence would appear to enlist a negative answer to this last question. My own clients, for example, come from many different parts of the world, and have been reared in a hundred different ways by radically different kinds of parents. Some of them were brought up most permissively, some with exceptionally rigid, moralistic codes of behavior. Some of them were adored and pampered by their parents; others were constantly hated and punished. Some were members of large families; some were only children; and still others were raised in orphanages. It is almost impossible to describe the large variety of different kinds of upbringings that these clients had. Yet, particularly when they are schizophrenic, it is amazing how similar are their ways of thinking in many instances, and how incredibly alike their symptoms often are.

An alcoholic schizophrenic male, forty years of age, was having much trouble in his marriage but was afraid to leave his highly dominating (and also schizophrenic) wife because she took all the main responsibilities in their relationship and let him avoid making any major life decisions. I was then doing psychoanalytically oriented psychotherapy and largely showed this client how his passivity and avoidance of decision making was related to the passive role that he had been raised to play with his highly dominating and negativistic mother, and that he was perpetuating, in his relations with his wife (and with others), the same kind of "safe" symbiotic relationship he had engaged in with his mother. The client clearly saw this lifetime pattern of passivity and agreed that he was behaving as if his wife were his mother, and as if he still had to be dependent on the former as he had previously been (and still to some extent was) on the latter. In consequence, he was presumably able to acquire some additional ego strength and to get a divorce from his wife. He seemed to be significantly improved, was very grateful for the help he had presumably received in therapy, and quit treatment about eight months after he had first entered it.

Unfortunately, however, the client still kept drinking heavily; got into trouble on a succession of jobs because of his drinking; and within the next few years made two more poor marriages, in both of which he played a somewhat less passive role than before, but both of which were to exceptionally weak, gutless women whom he continually had to support and father. These marriages ended in divorces; and the client was unable to make and maintain any solid heterosexual relationships. He returned for occasional sessions of therapy during this time, but only to agree verbally that he was still messing himself up and that he needed much more self-discipline and less of a dire love need if he truly was to get better and become nonalcoholic.

Several years later, this client returned for regular psychotherapy; and was seen for twenty-seven individual sessions and forty-five group sessions during the year. This time, he was systematically treated with rational-emotive psychotherapy. His past history with his mother, and his other passive-dependent relationships, were hardly mentioned; instead, a concerted effort was made to get him to define, most precisely and concretely, his present philosophic assumptions that lay behind his self-destructive behavior.

It was quickly ascertained that he was strongly saying several self-defeating assumptions to himself, namely: (1) "It would be absolutely terrible if I made all my decisions and frequently made the ones that later turned out to be wrong. For then I would be utterly incompetent and could not possibly respect myself." (2) "Since it is awful if I make mistakes on major decisions, I had better maintain intimate relations with a woman (such as my mother or my first wife) who dominates me and is glad to make all the decisions herself; then, at least, I can't be blamed for making any serious blunders. Or, if I find it inconvenient living with such a woman, I then would better become intimately associated with one who is weaker than I and who will therefore accept me and still love me *even* if I make such errors. For if I am loved in spite of my mistake making, then I am not totally worthless." (3) "Because, one way or the other, I am bound to wind up with a dominating woman or one who is quite weak, and because I really would *like* to be intimately related to one who is strong in her own right and who would *still* accept me without dominating me, I am really utterly inadequate for remaining the weak way I have always been. My alcoholism and my poor relationships with women over the years clearly prove that I am a jellyfish in spite of my years of psychotherapy and my attempts at joining Alcoholics Anonymous groups; so how can a jellyfish like me *ever* expect to get any better?" (4) "Other people, such as my mother and first wife, on the one hand, and my second and third wives, on the other hand, really don't appreciate me, and *want* me to remain weak and unmanly; so they are no damned good, too, and I hate their guts!"

In the course of his year of rational-emotive psychotherapy, this schizophrenic client was clearly shown that he had had these negative evaluations of himself and others for many years, and that he still kept reindoctrinating himself with them on many occasions. He was then shown *why* these were irrational philosophies:

1. How, he was asked, would making wrong decisions for himself make him *utterly* incompetent? How could he possibly expect *always,* or even *usually,* to make correct decisions when he, like all the rest of us, was definitely a fallible human? Suppose, in fact, he were truly incompetent at decision making. That would certainly be inconvenient and unpleasant; but how would his incompetence in that respect make him a thoroughly worthless individual, who could not possibly respect himself? Could not a truly incompetent person—such as a mentally deficient individual—*still* accept himself as incompetent, refrain from belaboring himself, and thereby manage to find *some* life enjoyments? Why, then, could not the client—if he *were* quite inadequate?

2. Why, in his relations with women, would it be awful if he kept making mistakes in regard to major life decisions? It is true that if he had a dominating wife who made his decisions for him, he would then make fewer grave errors. But then *she* might very well make the same kind of errors that he was avoiding making—and what good would *that* do him or her? Even, indeed, if she made fewer errors than he would make, would giving up his independence to her truly be worth it? Then, again, if he married a weaker wife, made more than his share of errors, but was forgiven by her for making them just because she *was* a weakling, would that really make his errors any the less inconvenient? *Why* did he need the love of such a weaker woman? And *how* would his getting her approval make him only a kind of half-shit? Would not his opinion of himself, both when he related to a stronger woman who took over decision making for him and when he related to a weaker woman who would not blame him for his errors, actually be purely definitional?

3. Assuming that he did wind up with either a dominating woman or a very weak one, how did *that* prove that he was thoroughly inadequate and that he could *never* gain any true measure of self-sufficiency? Similarly, assuming that

he was still alcoholic after years of A.A. meetings and of psychotherapy, how did *this* behavior show that he was a *hopelessly* disturbed person? Obviously, it was undesirable for him to be still dependent and alcoholic after many years of suffering—but why was it *horrible* for him to have such symptoms? Why was he thoroughly worthless for still remaining sick? Would, moreover, severely castigating himself for his disturbance be likely to help him, in any way, *rid* himself of this disturbance? Or would it not be much more likely, this self-blaming, to help him remain disturbed indefinitely? Could he not manage first to accept and forgive himself for having serious behavioral symptoms—and then work concertedly at ridding himself of these symptoms by comprehending and reevaluating the philosophic assumptions that were causing them?

4. Assuming that other people, such as his dominating mother and first wife and his weak second and third wives, didn't really appreciate him and did want him to remain weak and unmanly, why was *that* terrible? Wasn't it only to be *expected* that these individuals would behave toward him in the way that they had behaved? And even if their behavior was unhelpful, why did *he* have to take it seriously and go along with it? Why, especially, did he have to *give in* to the domination of his first wife or to *father*, in his turn, his second and third wives? They had no real control over him; so why should he blame *them* for being the way they were?

During the original sessions of psychotherapy, he had mainly concentrated on learning how to live comfortably with his basic self-destroying philosophies, rather than to root them out and destroy them. He had consequently divorced his first wife—who really was *so* dominating and irritating that it was hardly worth staying with her, in spite of her taking over his decision making—and then managed to find other women who were even weaker emotionally than he and with whom he could *afford* to assume responsibilities and make mistakes, since they would hardly ever criticize him for doing so. Thus, he had never really questioned, challenged, and surrendered his fundamental view that "It is terrible for me to make mistakes, especially when some significant figure in my life is around to criticize me for making them." He had merely arranged to be intimately related to significant figures who did not berate him when he erred.

In his second major round of psychotherapy, this client was induced to admit that he *must* change this basic self-defeating philosophy if he was to get better, and he was pushed by me and his therapy group to work determinedly against this world view. Whenever he failed to speak up adequately and take the risk of being wrong in individual or group sessions, he was forced to keep doing so, and was continually asked what *was* so terrible about his failing, if he did fail to do remarkably well, in that respect. He was given specific homework assignments—which are usually an integral part of rational-emotive psychotherapy—to look for female companions who were neither overly dominating or terribly weak and to keep going with them even when they were critical of his behavior. He was shown, time and again, by the therapist and the group, that he still *did* have a notable fear of failing, even when he sometimes claimed that he had pretty well gotten over it; and that he simply *had* to keep working and practicing, and especially working at taking significant risks, before he could expect to minimize this fear.

An interesting aspect of this case is that whereas during the first round of therapy, the therapist emphasized the transference relationship between him and the client, made sure that a highly positive transference was obtained, and often showed the client that he was trying to use the therapist as a father-figure who would make his decisions for him, during the second round of therapy there was a minimal utilization or interpretation of the transference relationship. The therapist was much firmer than he had previously been; kept indicating that he would definitely *not* give him reassurance or love; and instead kept prodding and pushing him to stand on his *own* feet, and to examine his *own* internalized attitudes. And the therapy group was, if anything, even firmer and harsher with the client, and would not let him get away with almost anything, especially when he endeavored to give rationalizations for his lack of risk taking. On one occasion, when he complained to the group that he could not easily look for a new job, since he had such a bad employment record in the past and could hardly expect to get a decent position now, the group vigorously tore apart his rationalizations, and gave him the homework assignment of writing up a brand-new resumé, made to order for the kind of job he said he wanted. As a result of their taking this no-nonsense attitude, he immediately wrote up the kind of resumé they insisted that he write, and within two weeks he had obtained a much better job than he had held in years.

In the second round of therapy, again, no attention whatever was given to the client's dreams (which had been intensively analyzed on several occasions during the first series of sessions). Only current rather than past material from his life was dealt with; and he was directly taught, on many occasions, many principles of rational living. The client was also induced to read books and other material on sane living and on several occasions reported that he had benefitted more from this kind of reading than he had from some of the therapy sessions.

As a result of this highly active-directive treatment, the client began to improve in a much more significant manner than he had previously done. For the first time in his life, he began going with the kind of females who were really on his educational and social level. He started to talk out at public meetings, such as at Alcoholics Anonymous, where he had previously kept quite silent; and with personal friends, he began to express feelings and attitudes he had been previously afraid to express, for fear of being criticized. After he had been in the second series of therapy sessions for two weeks, he stopped drinking entirely.

The client's exceptionally low estimation of himself notably began to improve as the weeks went by; and even when he tried to do something and clearly failed, he was able to accept his failure philosophically and refrain from excoriating himself. He still retained some underlying perfectionistic tendencies, but he was able to reduce them to a level far below that which he had previously demanded of himself and to live fairly successfully with those tendencies that remained. At times, he reverted to the negativistic kind of thinking about himself and others that is so characteristic of schizophrenics; but he did so far less frequently than before. Finally, it appeared that his hostility to others almost entirely disappeared, even though his self-denigrating tendencies were by no means as significantly reduced.

This, incidentally, is a common finding among schizophrenic clients treated with rational therapy. At first, they tend to like themselves better—but at the expense of becoming more hostile to others. Then, when the philosophic sources of this hostility are attacked, they often are able to accept others remarkably well, even when these others are behaving in a frustrating, unjust fashion. At the close of therapy, they may well be considerably less hostile than self-hating, although their self-depreciative propensities have also significantly decreased. The reason for this greater improvement in hostility than in self-criticism may stem from the human propensity—which many not too severely disturbed persons show as well—for an individual to find it easier to forgive others than himself, and to hold these others up to less rigid standards of behavior than he insists on holding himself up to.

In any event, this client ended the second round of therapy with a remarkable lack of hostility to others; and at the same time he also became much less self-deprecatory and more self-expressive and risk taking. He had not been completely cured, and one may wonder whether true schizophrenics are *ever* shriven of their basic tendency to think in an imprecise, out-of-focus manner. But he is now getting along unusually well in his vocational, amative, and social life, and it appears as if he will continue to do so indefinitely. For all practical purposes, he is behaving, at worst, in a moderately neurotic way, and is not acting psychotically.

The basic incurability of severe emotional disturbance is awesome to behold. Although I know many significantly improved and ostensibly cured schizophrenics walking the streets today (former and present clients of mine and other therapists), I have never seen a former schizophrenic who has been truly cured. Many of my own ex-clients, diagnosed as pyschotics and borderline psychotics, are getting along rather well in life, keep their heads above water, refrain from getting into any serious difficulties, and manage to make their way in the world without being dependent on others. But whether they are my own clients or those treated by others, one cannot conclude that they are mentally well, that they are in good mental-emotional health. Among other problems, they still have a significant degree of what Paul Meehl calls "cognitive slippage," and they never exactly think in the same well-focused, clear-headed way about themselves and others as do nonschizophrenics. They are doing wonderfully well, in many instances, with their underlying psychological deficits; but they are still basically psychotic, and can fairly easily be detected as such by an experienced clinician.

Nonetheless, rational-emotive psychotherapy with schizophrenics does not depend for its efficacy on the acceptance of the fact that psychosis is largely inborn and that it is by no means entirely the result of early upbringing. In fact, practitioners of this therapy would find it most convenient to hold that all emotional disturbance is the result of social conditioning, since it has a more precise explanation of just how negative conditioning comes about than do virtually all other therapeutic systems. The Freudians, for example, vaguely talk of the child's superego being constructed by his listening to the moralistic views of his parents; while the rational therapist talks in terms of the precise philosophies which the parents are teaching the child and the exact sentences into which the child translates these philosophies, and then uses to reindoctrinate himself continually in a neurotic or psychotic manner.

It would be very convenient to acknowledge the all-important influence of early childhood conditioning on the child—if it actually *were* that important. The hard facts seem to show, however, that the child becomes emotionally aberrated not *merely* because his parents blame him for his mistakes and shortcomings (which they all too often quite harmfully do), but because he *is born* the kind of individual who is *easily* harmed by such blaming.

To be more specific: parents or other early teachers usually help a child plummet down the toboggan slide toward disturbed feelings and behavior by doing two things when he does something that displeases them: (*a*) they tell him that he is wrong for acting in this displeasing manner, and (*b*) they strongly indicate to him that he is a worthless individual for being wrong, and that he therefore deserves to be severely punished for his wrongdoing. Now, the fact that parents in just about every part of the world tend to behave in this same manner, and at one and the same time to show the child that (*a*) he is wrong, and (*b*) he is a good-for-nothing when he is wrong, indicates that there is something essentially *biologically* based about their own slippery thinking and silly behavior in this connection. For if they were really sensible about bringing up their children, they would obviously show the child that: (*a*) he is wrong when he engages in activities that displease them and other members of their social group; and that (*b*) he is still a highly worthwhile individual who will merely, if he wants to get along well in his community, eventually have to discipline himself and learn to do less wrong in the future.

Perfectly sane and intelligent parents in other words, would be much more concerned about the child's *future* rather than with his *present* behavior when he makes mistakes, and would calmly and persistently educate him so that he stopped focusing on his *past* mistakes, and concentrated instead on the possibility of his not making them again in the *future*. Consequently, they would practically never blame or vindictively punish the child for his misdeeds, and thereby induce him to devalue himself *as a person*; but instead they would objectively evaluate his wrongdoings, at times penalize him *without* blame (just as we objectively penalize rats in mazes when they go into the wrong passageways), and slowly teach him to be less error-prone while still letting him know that, just *because* he is human, he will always be distinctly fallible and imperfect. Stated once again, then: if parents were truly straight thinkers themselves, they would unperfectionistically correct but never moralistically castigate a child when he was patently wrong or annoying or antisocial. The fact that practically no group of parents in any part of the world has ever raised children in this manner is another bit of evidence that leads me to believe that man is born to be a blaming, emotionally disturbed, and hence self-defeating animal.

A human child is not easily able objectively to assess himself and his surroundings. Instead, he almost invariably accepts the castigating attitudes of his parents, internalizes them, and makes them his own for the rest of his life. Even, in fact, where his parents do not happen to be exceptionally critical individuals, he usually manages to pick up negative, perfectionistic attitudes toward himself from his teachers, peers, reading material, TV dramas, motion pictures, and other sources and media, and almost invariably begins to become guilty, or to hate himself, for his blunders, instead of thinking about them in a reasonable manner, calmly accepting the fact that he is and will always be fallible, and concentrating on how he is going to make fewer errors in the future instead of on how he should severely punish himself for his present mistakes. Once again, therefore, it would appear that the human child is programmed, at birth, so that he *easily* accepts a philosophy of perfectionism and self-blame, and so that it is quite difficult for him to live with a minimum of guilt, even though he is often able to rationalize away some of his conscious self-blaming. Underneath, he almost invariably still *feels* worthless, because he remains unable to distinguish clearly between wrongdoing and blaming—or between his doing a misdeed and his being a valueless person for committing this misdeed.

Once humans are born the way they are, and once they are raised in a society—such as our own—where they are encouraged to keep blaming themselves for their wrongs, they not only easily acquire negative philosophies early in their lives, but thereafter keep reindoctrinating themselves with these same self-sabotaging philosophies; and it is their continual reindoctrinations, rather than the early views themselves, that keep their disturbances going. More concretely, they take others' disapproval of their behavior, and instead of saying to themselves (*a*) "I don't like this disapproval," and (*b*) "Now, how do I get them to approve of me in the future, or else how do I get myself to live happily *in spite of* their disapproval," they say (*a*) "I don't like this disapproval," and (*b*) "Because others disapprove of me, I can't *stand* it. It is absolutely terrible that they disapprove of me; and this proves that I am worthless!"

Emotional illness is, at bottom, metaphysically founded: since the disturbed person unempirically and unvalidatably is convinced that because he *now* may be little valued by *others*, he is forever doomed to be worthless to himself *and* to all signifcant others. Or else, in the case of exceptionally hostile rather than self-hating sick people, the disturbed individual bigotedly and antiscientifically assumes that because *he* does not like others' behavior *they* must be absolutely valueless to themselves and everyone else and that they deserve to be everlastingly punished or killed. This is particularly true of the schizophrenic individual, who more than most other disturbed persons rigidly and ruthlessly believes in his own utter worthlessness and/or that of other significant people in his life.

By the same token, emotional disturbance is *definitional* in nature. The seriously disturbed person takes an annoyance, an irritant, or a frustration and he *defines* it as a horror or a terror. Or he takes a mistake, or an inefficiency, or a human handicap and he *defines* it as an unforgivable atrocity or sin. He mightily *exaggerates the significance* of his own fallible behavior and that of others; he perfectionistically *demands* instead of sanely *preferring* minimal errors from himself and others. He unrealistically translates his *wants* into *dire needs,* thereby expects the impractical or impossible, and concretely *creates* his own continual misery and hostility.

More specifically, disturbed humans, and schizophrenics in particular, invariably dogmatically believe in several highly irrational philosophic assumptions, which they never or rarely question or challenge, and which they keep insisting, unconsciously or consciously, are absolutely true. These irrational ideas are briefly mentioned below:

Irrational Idea No. 1: The idea that it is a dire necessity for an adult human being to be loved or approved by virtually every significant other person in his community.

Irrational Idea No. 2: The idea that one should be thoroughly competent, adequate, and achieving in all possible respects if one is to consider oneself worthwhile.

Irrational Idea No. 3: The idea that certain people are bad, wicked, or villainous and that they should be severely blamed and punished for their villainy.

Irrational Idea No. 4: The idea that it is awful and catastrophic when things are not the way one would very much like them to be.

Irrational Idea No. 5: The idea that human unhappiness is externally caused and that people have little or no ability to control their sorrows and disturbances.

Irrational Idea No. 6: The idea that if something is or may be dangerous or fearsome one should be terribly concerned about it and should keep dwelling on the possibility of its occurring.

Irrational Idea No. 7: The idea that it is easier to avoid than to face certain life difficulties and self-responsibilities.

Irrational Idea No. 8: The idea that one should be dependent on others and need someone stronger than oneself on whom to rely.

Irrational Idea No. 9: The idea that one's past history is an all-important determiner of one's present behavior and that because something once strongly affected one's life, it should indefinitely have a similar effect.

Irrational Idea No. 10: The idea that there is invariably a right, precise, and perfect solution to human problems and that it is catastrophic if this perfect solution is not found.

These basic unreasonable premises, and innumerable variations on them, underlie, I contend, just about all so-called emotional disturbance. Moreover, these ideas are not subscribed to in mystical, symbolic, or pictorial form by the vast majority of human beings; but are thought of in simple declarative or exclamatory sentences for the most part. Thus, when a disturbed person believes Irrational Idea No. 2, that he should be thoroughly competent, adequate, and achieving in all possible respects if he is to consider himself worthwhile, he tells himself, when he is not or may not be competent in some area that he defines as being important (*a*) "I am not very good at this job (or sport, or game, or artistic field)" and (*b*) "Therefore, I am a thoroughly inadequate person, who cannot possibly live a happy existence, and who might just as well kill myself unless I somehow manage to be much better at this performance."

The disturbed individual, of course, may not *consciously* realize that he devalues himself as a person because he demands that he be thoroughly competent in some area or areas; but, at the very least, he *un*consciously believes this nonsense in innumerable instances when he feels worthless. Moreover, his unconscious, irrational beliefs and value systems are *not*, as the Freudians erroneously contend, so deeply buried in the individual's unconscious mind that it necessarily takes years of psychoanalysis to dig them up and make them conscious. On the contrary, almost all of them are just below the top level of consciousness, and can quite easily and quickly be revealed by an active rational therapist (and often by the individual himself).

The schizophrenic or other emotionally disturbed person is sick not only because something happened to traumatize him and help him think distortedly about himself and others in the past, but also because—*being human*—he is still, in the present, reindoctrinating himself with all kinds of false beliefs about himself and the world; and that therefore his present-day value system, or set of philosophic assumptions, not only is to be shown to him very clearly, but is to be systematically and vigorously attacked, by the therapist and then by the client himself, before he can be expected to change his world view and to make himself better. This is exactly what is done in rational-emotive psychotherapy.

In rational psychotherapy the schizophrenic, as well as the nonschizophrenic, client is consistently shown that it is practically never the stimulus that upsets him and makes him respond in an abnormal manner; rather, it is what he tells himself or interpretatively and evaluatively signals to himself about the stimulus. This exceptionally important aspect of human behavior was first clearly and fully expounded by the Roman Stoic philosopher, Epictetus, some two thousand years ago, and was later reformulated by his disciple Marcus Aurelius. It has been repeated over the centuries by a great many other philosophers and psychologists, notably by Robert S. Woodworth, who insisted that the stimulus-response, or S-R, formula did not sufficiently explain human behavior, but that it had to be replaced by a stimulus-organism-response (S-O-R) formula, which was truer to the facts of human existence.

It is the Epictetus-Woodworth explanation of behavior that I teach my schizophrenic clients. That is to say, I show them precisely how, in every instance that they become anxious, guilty, depressed, angry, or otherwise self-defeatingly overemotional, they have consciously or unconsciously, immediately preceding their negative emotion, told themselves a declarative or exclamatory sentence (or signaled themselves in some other communicative manner in a few instances), and how this sentence *caused* their dysfunctional emoting. Then I show them how to parse their own disturbance-creating phrases and sentences, logically rather than grammatically, to see exactly why they *are* irrational or illogical. Finally, I teach them to contradict and challenge their own irrationalities, until they replace them with sane, nondisturbing philosophies of life.

Stated a little differently: schizophrenic individuals usually have absolute needs for certainty and order (as well as perfection); and a good many of their paranoid and other delusions represent a desperate attempt to create certainty where none, in fact, exists. If I can rationally get them to admit that there isn't, as far as we know, any absolute order in the universe, and that they can live happily in this world of probability and chance, they frequently surrender their delusionary symptoms, conquer their overweening anxiety, and live much more fulfillingly.

CHAPTER 12

WORKING WITH CHILDREN WITH CONDUCT DISORDERS

EDITOR'S COMMENTARY:

In this selection focusing on children, Ellis addresses issues such as lying, stealing, bullying, and delinquency. He makes some reference to why deviations represent problems and provides examples. This selection was written about four years before the Living School was established at the Institute, with the goal being to incorporate rational thinking into the curriculum. In the chapter summary, Ellis argued that one could try to change a child's environment or one could try to change his or her perceptions of the environment. No matter how difficult it might be, Ellis argued that it would be worth trying to change a child's perception of his or her world whenever possible. This often proved to be difficult as children regressed to behavior that had been well learned, even though that behavior might have produced results that often were at odds with the powers that be.

Excerpted from *How to Raise an Emotionally Healthy, Happy Child,*
Wilshire Books, 1966

Most of the neurotic symptoms that we have been discussing in this book are defeating to the child himself but not necessarily to those with whom he associates. Thus, if the child is anxious, has severe problems of achievement, is undisciplined, and is sexually aberrated, he is likely to suffer severely; but it is quite possible that those around him will not suffer equally and may not even be aware of his disturbances. There are, however, a number of problems which the child inflicts not merely on himself, but on others, and these are notably dysfunctional in many instances.

If, for example, a child is emotionally disturbed and resorts to stealing because of his disturbance, he immediately impinges on the rights of others—and these others almost invariably take an exceptionally dim view of his problem. Instead of seeing him as an emotionally upset child, they concentrate mainly on his symptom; and since this symptom is unpleasant and antisocial, they tend to condemn him roundly for displaying it.

In truth, what parents automatically construe to be maliciously antisocial behavior more often than not is the child's natural tendency to selfishness—and, resultantly, to thoughtlessness. Nowhere is this more the case than in the area of destructiveness. When two boys tear up a sheet, their sole thought often is that it would make a super sail for their toy boat. Not taking the time to put herself into her children's frame of reference, a mother sees only wanton destruction of property and vents her anger in genuinely hostile shouts and blows. And a bewildered child concludes that it is wrong to play, create, and be inventive.

In either case, whether poor conduct is volitional or unwitting, parents rarely take the time to understand why the child acts as he does because of their indignation over the fact that he does. Driven by the censure of those around him to condemn himself enormously for behaving poorly (especially if his original impetus for being antisocial was some degree of self-depreciation), he will become increasingly self-blaming, and hence emotionally aberrated.

Let us examine some of the specific problems that these children often display, to see how you can understand and counter them if they should ever arise in connection with your own child.

Lying

Practically all children (as well as all adults) lie at one time or another, and most of them engage in a good deal of prevarication. Why? For several fairly obvious reasons: They are frequently punished if they tell the truth; they can get away with things they don't want to do by lying; they can make themselves "superior" to others by boasting of deeds that they have not performed; they wish so heartily that certain things would occur that they actually see them, in their mind's eye, as occurring; they are afraid to admit their mistakes, for fear that they would be despicable if they did; etc. None of these reasons for lying are exceptionally good, in that there invariably are, at least in theory, better ways of dealing with the situations about which the lies are manufactured. But the fact remains that children are not too capable of finding the best solutions to various difficulties, and the lies which they tell are one form or another of second-best solutions in many instances.

There are, moreover, occasions in which it is actually wise and sane for a child to lie. If he would be unduly and unjustly penalized for truth-telling—for example, thoroughly thrashed because he has unwittingly spilled a jar of jam—it is highly rational of him to pretend that he has not spilled it, and even to manufacture conditions which tend to show that someone else is responsible for his misdeed. Or if he knows that his parents or some other child would be completely shocked and hurt by his telling them his true feelings about them, it would be perfectly proper for him to tell a white lie, and to keep some of his feelings to himself.

Many times, too, a child appearing to relate a most far-fetched tale, may actually be telling the pure truth, only to be punished for it by an overly suspicious parent who is underconfident in her child. Thus, when Danny brings home a miniature puzzle and boasts he has won it in a gym contest, Mother, going by his poor past athletic performances, accuses him of having taken it from a friend. Be sure of your own facts before accusing your offspring of lying.

Nonetheless, there are many occasions when children self-defeatingly or pathologically lie. If Jimmy, for example, tells how well he did in an essay contest at school, when there actually was no such contest, or when he submitted one of the worst papers in the contest, he is palpably avoiding facing reality, and is showing that he has a dire need to impress people with his nonexistent prowess. If Sandi tells her parents that she is doing her homework regularly, when actually she practically never does it, and is falling further and further behind in class, she is not merely cleverly avoiding some onerous work, but is probably seriously avoiding activity that simply has to be done, and that she will soon be severely penalized for not doing.

Lies such as these, which are falsely ego-boosting on the one hand, or which are techniques for getting away with murder on the other hand, are pathological not merely because they are untruths, but because they are prevarications which simply do not work. For Jimmy, in all probability, will be found out in his lies about the essay contest or about similar things which he boasts about having done when he clearly has not done them; and then he will actually sink *lower* in other people's eyes, when his whole intent, through lying, is to have them think *better* of him. And Sandi will probably not be able to get away with her maneuvering, and will either have to catch up on her homework all at once, or be forced to take the subjects she is avoiding all over again and then have to do more work than she would have to do if she had stopped her nonsense and buckled down to the work.

The first thing to note, therefore, if your child is engaged in pathological lying, is that his behavior is aberrant just because it is self-defeating and not because it is simply dishonest. Since this form of lying is already handicapping your child, it is foolish for you to take a moralistic attitude toward it and attempt to penalize the child even more. It is far wiser, in most instances, if you try to understand the source of the lying—the philosophic assumptions which the child holds that drive him to lie. And again—search yourself and determine to what extent you may have been responsible for implicitly planting those philosophies.

These sources, as usual, are the same as those behind other kinds of emotional disturbances, namely, the two basic irrational ideas: (1) that the child must do things perfectly well and be acclaimed for his performances; and (2) that he simply cannot tolerate frustrating situations or difficult tasks, and should not have to put up with them. If, instead of attacking the child and his lying, you forthrightly but kindly attempt to tackle the irrational ideas that impel him to lie, you will have a good chance of helping him.

Thus, you can show Jimmy that even though you know that there was no essay contest in school, or that he did poorly in the one that was held, you still like him as a person, and would like to help him do better when the next contest is held, you will be on the road to convincing him that he does not have to be the best essayist alive in order to win yours and others' approval. And if you show him that you can respect and help him even though you know that he is lying, you may particularly persuade him that he does not have to be perfect to get along in the world, and that imperfect creatures such as he are still lovable. On the other hand, if you show Jimmy that you know darned well that there was no essay contest and that he's a little rotter for pretending that there was and that he won it, his basic insecurity will probably be even more enhanced, and he will quite possibly have a greater need to make up exaggerated stories about himself the next time.

In Sandi's case, if you kindly but firmly show her that it is quite understandable why she should lie about doing her homework, and why she should not do it in the first place, but that nonetheless this kind of irresponsible behavior will get her nowhere in life, and will inevitably bring her more disbenefits than gains, she will see that you are really on her side, rather than against her; that she certainly is not getting away with anything; and that the chances are that you are right, and that she'd better do her homework in the future when it is due, not because *you* think she should but because *she* will be severely penalized if she doesn't. On the other hand, if you point the finger of guilt at Sandi and condemn her thoroughly for lying about the homework, she may become angry, rebellious, and highly defensive, never admit to herself that she is goofing, and use her resentment against you as a beautiful alibi to keep goofing.

Calmly accept, then, your child's lying. Determine whether it is done for sane or crazy reasons. If the former is true, ignore it. If the latter is true, you may still be wise to ignore the lies themselves, but to get, instead, at the irrational philosophies that underlie and cause them. Or you can bring the lies to the attention of the child, but show him that you are only doing so in a helpful, corrective manner, and not because you think that he is a hopeless child who has to lie, and who should be punished severely for doing so. In any event, remember that the lie is not the issue; it is the *reason* for it that must be sought out by you and intelligently handled and uprooted.

A highly effective breeding ground for lies is a climate of hypocrisy. Much of society is concerned with irrational rules of etiquette whereby men doff their hats to women they don't respect (or even know) and tell relatives how nice it is to see them when their visit is really a bore. There is no need to go to another extreme and encourage your child to tell his hostess, "I think your party was stinky"; on the other hand, he should not be forced into paying completely unfelt obeisances. Rare is the child, as any parent knows, who does not with fair regularity blurt out, with complete ingenuousness, some rather blunt remark. Yet what is more natural than a curious child, spying a lady getting onto his bus, asking loudly, "Why is her stomach so fat?" What chance has a child, dragged off the bus by a red-faced mother, or slapped for similar questions, of becoming anything but a liar himself? "The best way to make a child a liar for life," says A. S. Neill, "is to insist that he speak the truth and nothing but the truth."

Tattling

Like lying, tattling may sometimes be fairly healthy. A child who has a great deal of confidence in his mother and believes that she is on his side, no matter what he does, may routinely confide in her all sorts of things about his peers that they would just as soon not have her know; but he may not in the least be malicious in this kind of tattling. Or a child who is exceptionally talkative may unwittingly, in the course of many things that he expresses, give out information that would better be left concealed; and, again, he may have no hostility when he does so and may be considered to be reasonably normal in this respect.

Much tattling, however, is of a negative nature. Mary tattles on Susie and Janie because she moralistically feels that they have done the wrong thing, that she would never do anything similar, that they therefore deserve to be punished, and that she should be seen as the fair-haired girl of the neighborhood for not doing what they did. This kind of tattling, although Mary may not in the least realize it, is part of the power struggle that she much of the time engages in; and, as the authors of a noted United States Department of Health, Education, and Welfare booklet on "Behavior Problems and Fears" indicate, "it suggests that the tattler is weak, and has to come to an adult for support."

If your child tattles and does so in a manner that shows his jealousy of and hostility to others, do not chide him for being a tattler, for that (as usual) will tend to make him still less secure, and hence potentially more hostile. Try the following approach:

(1) Let him see that you are not shocked by his description of the nasty behavior of the people on whom he is tattling but that you rather expect them to be the way they are. Not that you necessarily condone their behavior; but that you are not horrified by it either, and that you certainly are not going to condemn them for it. Tell him something along these lines: "Yes, dear, I see that Lionel lied when he told his mother that he was going to be with you and actually he went to the movies. And it would have been better if he had told the truth. But children like Lionel do lie every once in a while, and we cannot expect them to be little angels and never lie. Now, are you really so surprised that Lionel acted that way? And can't you see that his behavior is rather common? This doesn't mean that you should lie the way that Lionel did. But if you did lie to me, the way he did to his mother, I'm sure I'd understand it and think little of it. We often do undesirable things like lying; but that's the way we are—humans who easily make mistakes."

(2) If your child persists at tattling, gently but firmly show him that his is not the best kind of behavior and that it has distinct disadvantages. For example: "Well, I can see that Bob was wrong in bullying that other child; and I'm glad that you see that he was wrong and that you are determined not to do that kind of thing yourself. However, dear, if Bob finds out that you told me about this, when he specifically asked you not to say anything to anyone about it, he's going to be very displeased—and you may be the one whom he starts bullying next. For you wouldn't want anyone to tattle on you like this,

would you, even when you had definitely done something wrong? No, I'm sure you wouldn't. So don't you think it would be better if you merely tried to persuade Bob not to do any more bullying, rather than go off and tell everyone, the way you're telling me now, what a big bully he is?"

(3) See if you can't do something to tackle your child's basic insecurity, so that he will not feel impelled to tattle on others in the future. Show him, if you can, that he is not a better individual if he makes himself superior to others by proving that they have done worse things than he has done; but that, instead, he is a valuable person to himself, and even to others, if he accepts the fact that he is not flawless and other children are not ogres and if he makes few comparisons between himself and these others. If he wants to do fine deeds—not in order to prove how worthwhile he is, but because of other satisfactions that often go with doing them—that is fine. But if he has to knock others down, that is not fine, and does not increase his stature one bit. If he really wants to be a strong individual, he will gracefully accept the good deeds of others—and for the most part forget about their weaknesses.

(4) Be a good model to your child by looking into your own heart and stopping some of your own backbiting of others before it even gets started. If your child continually hears you putting other people down, thereby showing how "great" you are, he will tend to imitate your behavior; and much of his tattling may stem from this kind of imitativeness.

Stealing

As we noted in the illustration that was used at the beginning of this chapter, stealing is sometimes done as a method of false ego-boosting by children. They feel great, as they "get away with" the stolen goods, thus proving how clever they are; or they impress their friends with their prowess at thievery; or they buy the love of their peers with stolen goods, thus proving how "nice" they are; or, rather than depreciate themselves for their various lacks and misdeeds, they preoccupy themselves with the diverting action of stealing, which distracts them from some of the other serious problems they have to face.

This does not mean, again, that all stealing by children is necessarily pathological. A child may truly be deprived, even hungry, and may steal to make up for this deprivation. Or he may hobnob with a neighborhood gang for whom stealing is the norm and where he would be left out if he did not engage in theft. Or he may have a mother who is incredibly careless about leaving money around the house, and who continually tempts him to take some of it because he knows perfectly well that she would never notice that any part of it was missing.

A young child, especially, is quite apt to see a shiny red truck at a playmate's house or in a store and quite cheerfully (to a mother's later horror) take it home with him. The child's thought is solely that the object is pretty and should be fun to play with; the fact that it belongs to someone else never entered his mind. "They are not immoral," says Bettelheim, "since they have yet to learn what morals are. They proceed from the simple premise that what they want is justified by the fact that they want it, and the only problem is that adults so often have different ideas."

As usual, however, when a child's stealing is fairly persistent, and when it covers up some other negative feeling about himself, it is truly pathological, and should be duly brought to his attention and checked. And the first step in this regard, as we noted previously, is to point out to the child that his behavior is wrong—meaning that it needlessly harms other human beings and helps create the kind of a disordered world in which he would not particularly like to live himself—but that he is not to be condemned for performing this wrong behavior. He is a person who has the power to change his behavior and to desist from stealing in the future.

Try to determine whether your child has a terrible feeling of injustice, and whether that is encouraging him to steal. Even if he is treated well by you and his associates, he may have an idea that he should be treated still better, and that consequently the world is unjust. If so, try to show him that it would be very lovely if things were made easier for him, and that perhaps you even will try to arrange this to some extent, but the fact still remains that he can put up with deprivation and even injustice, and (since the world is the way it is) he will just have to do so if he is to live happily. Teach him, in other words, not to overfocus on the horror of being frustrated or deprived; that in an imperfect world we cannot, by simply willing it, have everything we desire; that in the very act of doing one thing we like (such as going to the circus), we must give up another (such as watching a TV program scheduled for that time). Reassure him that he is not the only person in the world who must see his wants unfulfilled; we all are deprived daily.

If your child's stealing symbolizes his wanting something other than the actual objects he is taking—denotes, for example, that he really wants more attention than he is getting or that he wants to excel at something—try to get at the basic source of his thievery rather than at the act itself. For if you manage to stop him from stealing—by, for example, taking him away from tempting situations or penalizing him so severely that he sees that the game is not worth the candle—and you still have not done anything about his underlying reason for stealing, it is most probable that he will use some other form of negative behavior as a compensatory device. Thus, instead of stealing to gain attention, he might bully other children, make a spectacle of himself in class, resort to other unsavory devices. So, the symptom of stealing may sometimes be eradicated fairly easily; but the cause may perniciously go marching on unless you make an honest attempt to understand and do something about it.

Bullying

When a child engages in a certain amount of intimidation of others, this is not to be thought of as necessarily being disturbed behavior, since most of us are born as well as raised with a strong tendency to want to be king of the hill, and it is very difficult to be king unless we somehow convince others that they should kowtow to us. A healthy, leading type of child, therefore, does practice some amount of browbeating when he is with other children (or even adults), and it would probably be a shame if you tried to beat all of this trait out of him.

Constant and vicious bullying by your child of his playmates and schoolmates is another thing entirely. As with many other seemingly "strong" and "assertive" acts, this kind of bullying is actually a form of weakness; it signifies that the child apparently cannot stand to be with equals but insists on forcing others to act more weakly than he and often resorts to brute force or dire threats to get them to act this way. Such bullying may stem from the fact that the child is bullied, in his turn, by others; from his way of seeing life only or mainly as a dog-eat-dog kind of existence; from his being overly deprived in various ways; from his grandiosely thinking that he has to run everything his way; and from other pressures caused by his external and internal environment.

The correct counter-bullying procedure? Not, certainly, greater bullying itself. For if you threaten your child with physical punishment and otherwise coercively harass him because he is intimidating other children, the chances are that he will become even more malcontent and intolerant. He may actually stop his bullying; but he will take out his disturbance in some other manner. Moreover, he may only become a more subtle kind of bully, one who makes sure that other children do not report his activities to their own parents or to you.

As ever, you should try to find out exactly why the child resorts to threatening tactics. If he threatens others out of his own underlying feelings of weakness and anxiety, then you should attempt to show him that he does not have to have these feelings. Teach him to discriminate, if you can, between physical and mental strength so that he will realize that a truly strong child does not have to be the mightiest one on the block, and that real emotional strength often consists of living comfortably with one's physical weakness, instead of impressing others with how muscular one is. Show him how some of the biggest and brawniest individuals have turned out to be mentally weak-kneed, in that they were ultrasensitive to what others thought of them, while some of the puniest individuals have proven themselves to be unusually tough, in that they bucked the world with their views and were not intimidated by others. Teach him that it is no disgrace—although it may well be disadvantageous—to be physically weak or even to be cowardly, in the sense of avoiding fistfights with bellicose members of his peer group. Teach him that it is even more disadvantageous—though, again, not disgraceful—for him to be intellectually namby-pamby and not to have a pronounced mind of his own.

Although it is well, in our society, to teach your child, if he is a male, that boys are different from girls, and that in some respects masculinity is a trait to be desired, make sure that you do not overemphasize this trait and make him feel that it is the most desirable of all characteristics to have. For masculinity usually connotes physical prowess and (oddly enough) supersensitivity to insult—both of which often make an individual mentally vulnerable and hence far from strong. Females, moreover, can well be powerful individuals, in the sense that they know what they want in life and have no intention of being diverted by the negative opinions of others; and it is silly to call all such females "masculine," since they may be highly "feminine" in various other ways.

For both sexes, the ideal that should be taught is not one of outward "masculine" or "feminine" characteristics, but of inner or characterological strength. A girl may be large-breasted and highly emotional, but she can still be shown how to stand on her own feet and to say "yes" when she means yes and "no" when she means no. A boy may be small and frail and still learn how to think for himself even when most of his peers are conforming in unthinking ways. Where one's physical characteristics are largely inborn and difficult to change, one's attitudes and ideas are much less subject to heredity and can be significantly modified over the years. It is therefore pernicious—as I show in *The American Sexual Tragedy*—to overemphasize physique and other external manifestations of "manliness" or "womanliness"; and if we must designate certain human traits as desirable, then it would be far wiser if we selected those that can be worked upon and changed, such as standing one's own ground in spite of what other people think, than if we choose anatomical attributes which are largely beyond our own control.

If your child is bullying others mainly because he has low frustration tolerance and cannot stand—or thinks he cannot stand—not to have things his own way, then this is the idea that you should counterattack. Try to show him that it would be nice for him to have others continually do his bidding, but that this is hardly necessary; and that if other children do not kowtow to him, he can easily stand their doing what they want rather than what he wants. Teach him, again, that being overly annoyed at being frustrated is not being strong—as the movies, unfortunately, would often have us believe, as they show gangsters punching others in the jaw when they are thwarted—but that it is actually weak. A truly strong individual is tough-*minded* rather than just tough-knuckled. He does not like the rebuffs and unniceties of the world; but, at the same time, he does not whine about them and think that they must immediately be righted by his making things rough for others.

Your main technique, then, in trying to overcome your child's bullying should be corrective rather than punitive, educational rather than restrictive. You have to try to teach him (or her) the proper kinds of attitudes, ones that will tend to prevent him from having bullying tendencies in the first place, rather than ones that will induce him to stop himself after he has already started to intimidate others. This takes some time to do in most cases, since children can mainly first correct themselves after the fact—after they have already made mistakes. It is only after they have uncondemningly corrected themselves for a fairly long period of time that they then start, as it were, correcting themselves prophylactically, beforehand. And although—as in learning to tie their own shoelaces—this process at first has to be well thought out and carefully worked upon, it later becomes semiautomatic and requires little effort. At first, therefore if you use the right teachings with him, you may expect your bullying child to become more adept at squelching his threatening tendencies. But ultimately he may lose the tendencies almost completely, and just not think of intimidating others to get his own way.

Destructiveness

If your child is destructive, and particularly if he resorts to vandalism and other kinds of public sabotage, you may well have a real problem to handle. Not that a certain amount of this kind of behavior is not healthy, for it is. Most children at times chalk up sidewalks or fences, take light bulbs out of public buildings, damage other children's possessions, and engage in many other kinds of minor vandalism. Largely, they do it to show off or to save face with their peers; but sometimes they do it quite on their own because they are in a bad mood or because they want to see how much they can get away with.

Some types of seemingly destructive behavior on the part of children, as Shirley Camper points out, are even constructive. Thus, a child may take apart a watch because he is curious to see what makes it tick; and he may thereby destroy it without having any intention of so doing. Or a child may enjoy working with a hammer and saw on old pieces of wood; but having no such pieces about, may start to rip up the living-room furniture. In these cases, you may simply solve the "destructiveness" problem by seeing that a sufficient number of old watches, or hunks of wood, or even old pieces of furniture are around to provide the child with materials that he can less destructively take apart.

Another cause of destructiveness in a child is his ignorance of societal attitudes toward property rights. It takes a long time for him to learn, even though his baby sister's toy dog may be great fun to throw against the wall, that (a) she, too, has a right to enjoy playing with it; that (b) she owns it; and that (c) she is likely to become very upset if its stuffing starts pouring out and it loses a leg. Frequently the parent, in lieu of teaching the child that he must not impinge on others' rights, violates the child's *own* rights by failing to respect his toys or the inviolability of his playroom.

The fact remains, however, that some children, and often those who are old enough to know better, are really wreckers of many things in their environment and that they demolish for disturbed reasons: (a) They are hostile and want to wreak vengeance on other people and their possessions. (b) They feel weak and want to compensate for these feelings by showing how "powerful" they can be. (c) They are overly frustrated because they cannot compete well in some fair and aboveboard manner, so they sometimes resort to underhanded or sneaky kinds of destructiveness in order to "win." (d) They are terribly unhappy about something and find that they can divert themselves from their unhappiness, at least temporarily, by being destructive.

(e) They want to show off before others and can think of no better way of doing so than by breaking windows, ripping up furniture, or indulging in some other dramatic form of sabotage.

The best way to deal with this kind of behavior on the part of your child is, as ever, first to get at its philosophic roots. The destructive child believes that he is stronger, or more worthwhile, or somehow greater if he gives vent to physical force against material objects. Actually, of course, he isn't, since he doesn't change himself one iota even when he radically modifies, by destroying, the objects around him. He therefore has to be disabused of the notion that physical violence against the world will enhance him, release him, or make up for his inner frustration.

As in the case of the angry and temper-tantrum-ridden individual, the destructive child generally sees only two major possibilities of life: (a) feeling upset inwardly and taking out this feeling on his surroundings; or (b) feeling upset and suffocating his feelings until he believes that he is going to burst at the seams. Of these two possible modes of behavior, he finds that the first is better than the second—and often he is quite right about this, because it is the lesser of these two evils.

There is a third path, which you should try to teach a destructive child. Attempt to show him that he is angry and hence destructive because of *what he tells himself* about a given situation, and not because of *the situation itself*. Thus, he becomes angry at school restrictions not because they are restrictive, but because he convinces himself, over and over, that these restrictions are unfair and that he cannot stand unfairness of this sort. After convincing himself of these things—all of which are highly questionable and essentially false—he then feels "irresistibly" impelled to break the school's windows, or take out its light bulbs, or carve up its desks, or to do other destructive acts against its "unfair" and "intolerable" system.

If, therefore, you can show the child that restrictions are not necessarily unfair; that he can stand unfairness even when it does exist; and that he is making a situation really intolerable by lashing out against it, when it will palpably do him no good to do so—there is then a good chance that he will be much less destructive. But not only do you have to convince the child of these points—more importantly, you must finally induce him to *convince himself* of them. For, if you merely brainwash him of his original brainwashing, he can easily reinstitute it and sink back to the old morass. Depropagandization itself, therefore, is not enough; you have to persuade him to keep thinking, to keep depropagandizing himself—practically forever.

At the same time, of course, you can show him the advantages of constructive courses of action. You can show him that not being vandalistic, but instead being cooperative with authorities (even when these authorities are not wholly fair to him) is much more likely to get them on his side, and to induce them to do away with some of the restrictions he deplores. And you can show him that if he makes a concerted, but still creative and unhostile attack on the things that bother him in life, such as unfair restrictions that are placed on him, he is much more likely to correct these bothersome things than if he negativistically and hatefully tries to assail them or the people who are instituting them. By being caught up in constructive efforts, he is likely to have little energy left to expend in fruitless retaliations against the situation.

Don't, in other words, try to prevent the destructive child from taking action against whatever he considers annoying, for that is a healthy, vigorous way of meeting the vicissitudes of life. Try to prevent him, instead, from taking ineffective, unproductive action—the kind that will only get him what he doesn't want out of life, and that will quite possibly help make the world even less fair for him and others than it now is. Sane destructiveness can be a good thing—as when we have to knock down an old, useless building to construct a new, more useful edifice in its place. But insane, wild, shotgun-type destructiveness is the issue; and that is the kind that you should try to win him away from. If this is your goal, then you can truthfully show him, in most instances, that you are out for his own good, and not merely for your own of for that of society; and that by considering others, too, he is most likely to help himself.

Cheating

Cheating, like most other forms of antisocial behavior, is not all to the bad, and is sometimes logical. If all your child's classmates are cheating on an exam, and he refuses to do so but also does not inform on the others, then he will, at least on a short-range basis, be severely handicapped. Or if some crotchety old lady refuses to let your child and his peers play anywhere near her house, and he and the others try to see how near they can play and get away without her noticing them, this kind of cheating is perfectly healthy, and it is probably best to ignore it. Encouraging it is sometimes risky—since the child may then overgeneralize and think that you are condoning all kinds of cheating. But if you make a great issue of minor cheating activities on his part, you will probably also do more harm than good.

Other forms of cheating may by no means be so harmless. If your child routinely cheats on examinations at school, this may well be a sign of his having no confidence that he can pass such exams honestly and may mean that he has an exceptionally low estimation of himself. If he cheats in his transactions with the other boys, or in keeping score in the ball game, or in claiming to have done more of the household chores than he has actually accomplished, this may mean that he is a perennial goofer who thinks that the world is too rough for him, and who is determined to get away with everything he possibly can get away with in life.

These more serious forms of cheating—just like the other kinds of conduct problems that we have been examining in this chapter—have philosophic as well as psychological roots. The youngster who always cheats on examinations usually believes (a) that it is terrible for him to fail on an exam; (b) that he would be a perfect fool if he did fail; (c) that he cannot risk being imperfect and therefore has to succeed beautifully on the exam; and (d) that because he has cheated before and has managed to pass that way, the chances are that he could never succeed without cheating and therefore must resort to this pattern of examination-taking forever. These are all value systems or philosophic hypotheses which the cheater strongly holds—and holds without any confirming evidence. They are essentially definitions that hold water only because the child thinks that they do. But they are very powerful values and motivate human behavior; they literally compel him to keep cheating and therefore never to discover what his true examination-taking ability is.

By the same token, the child who chronically cheats on doing his chores may easily hold certain other values: (a) that it is horrible for him to carry out certain moderately onerous tasks; (b) that it is wise for him to spend more time and energy avoiding than doing such tasks; (c) that life is entirely unfair to him if it forces him to do the same kind of work that others generally do; (d) that he is too weak and inferior to survive in a world of difficulties; and (e) that he is a great person if he outwits his parents and others and successfully goofs. These, again, are all values which he strongly tends to hold, but for which there is, of course, no empirical confirmatory evidence. And they are values which, if he believes in them, will normally get him into much more trouble than they seem, on the surface, to be worth.

These kinds of values, which underlie most serious cheating by children, can be calmly attacked and undermined. You can, for instance, steadily point out to your child, in an objective and dispassionate way, that it is not terrible, though it may be quite inconvenient, for him to fail exams; that even if he does consistently fail, he is still not worthless, but can be a valuable human being to himself (and sometimes to the world as well); that he can risk being imperfect, and be on the same level as the rest of us fallible human beings; and that even if he has cheated many times in the past, there is no evidence that he could not do well on tests if he stopped cheating and buckled down to some active studying. You can also point out to the child who cheats for goofing reasons that it may be onerous but it is hardly horrible for him to carry out various chores; that it is hardly wise for him to exert as much or more energy avoiding life's difficulties as he would have to do in successfully facing them, for failure to acquire tools (such as proper study habits, the ability to solve math problems) may handicap him in the *future* and impel *further* cheating to cover his deficiencies; that things are hardly exceptionally unfair to him when he has to perform certain onerous duties; that he is not too weak to survive in a world of difficulties; and that he is hardly a great person if he does manage to outwit the authorities and to "successfully" goof.

By your own noncheating, nonperfectionistic, and nongoofing actions, as well as by highly verbal attacks on his philosophic assumptions, you can often break the ideological back of your child's cheating propensities.

You can also, if you wish, use penalization techniques, to see that he does not get away with his cheating. But by penalization, I mean just that—and not punishment; for the latter, as we have been showing in this book, include degrading the individual while also penalizing him; and there is no point in your degrading your child if you discover him cheating. One of the main reasons why he does cheat, in fact, is because he would consider himself degraded if he did poorly and if he did not cheat. If, therefore, you depreciate him for cheating, you are only thereby tending to enhance, rather than to alleviate, his deep-seated feelings of inadequacy. So if you want to penalize him for his cheating, you may do so in those cases where he is most persistent in this form of behavior, and where other persuasive methods do not seem to be working. But penalize him in an effort to help rid him of his cheating-creating philosophy and not to get him to live with it, thereby merely squelching the tendencies that he still very much keeps alive underneath the surface of his personality.

Should you inform on your child if he is cheating? Usually, no. In the first place, if you tell the authorities that he is cheating on tests or something of that sort, they may not be as permissive and unpunishing as you are. Secondly, behavior such as cheating should normally be dealt with directly by you, as his parents, and not by other authorities. Thirdly, if you do inform on him, he may well consider you an enemy, and may completely stop confiding in you in the future. Fourthly, there are usually better ways in which you can deal with his cheating other than by "ratting" on him.

Whatever you do about his cheating, the main thing is to try to discover its philosophic core and then to try to make him aware of it. If you and he can discover why he is cheating consistently, then there is a good chance that something can be done about it. The knowledge of the cause itself will not necessarily do away with the symptom, but it may mean that half the battle is won.

Delinquency

About the most antisocial thing your child can do is to be truly delinquent, which usually means to participate in a variety of acts, such as truancy, vandalism, stealing, gang warfare, and even more serious acts such as murder. More often than not, he would be engaging in these acts with several other children, rather than alone; but it is also possible for him to be a loner and still a delinquent.

Is delinquency ever within the normal range? Yes, at least in a few cases. A number of years ago, when I was Chief Psychologist of the New Jersey Department of Institutions and Agencies, I did psychotherapy once a week with the delinquent girls who were incarcerated in the State Home for Girls in Trenton. Most of these girls—and particularly, of course, those that were referred to me—were exceptionally neurotic or psychotic individuals who had first committed delinquent acts and were later caught and convicted mainly because they were seriously disturbed. Thus, they would openly lie, steal, stay home from school, or have promiscuous sex relations, even after they had already been in some amount of difficulty for their previous similar escapades; and it was almost inevitable that they would be caught and apprehended.

I discovered, however, that at least a few of these incarcerated delinquents were in the normal range of both intelligence and emotional stability, and that they were largely victims of circumstances. Thus, there were girls who came from poor neighborhoods, who were often Negro, and who had exceptionally rigid, moralistic parents. When they joined in with other boys and girls and engaged in slightly rowdy activities, they were either quickly pounced upon by the authorities or were actually reported to them by their parents. Where other children, from white middle-class homes, would have been stoutly defended by their parents and protected from being taken to court or adjudged juvenile delinquents, these youngsters were sometimes literally helped into the reformatory by their own families. Ironically, some of them became genuine delinquents after they were incarcerated—since, as everyone seems to know, reformatories and prisons are excellent places for learning better methods of lawbreaking.

The fact remains, however, that most adjudged delinquents are highly disturbed individuals; many of them are outrightly psychotic rather than neurotic. Children who consistently commit armed robbery, or who seriously hurt others, or who go to real extremes and commit murder, are almost always at least in the borderline psychotic range of behavior; and therefore they compulsively rather than volitionally perform their delinquent acts. They are not even, in a psychological sense, responsible for much of their behavior, since they are not very well able to control it; and they certainly should not be condemned for performing their misdeeds. They often have to be put into protective custody—preferably in a mental hospital rather than a reformatory—in order to stop them from committing further antisocial acts; but they should not be excoriated for being institutionalized.

More concretely, juvenile delinquents usually have exceptionally low estimations of themselves and are thoroughly convinced that they cannot compete successfully with others if they stick to normal pursuits. They believe that they are worthless; they feel that they will never be truly accepted by members of respectable society; they frequently view themselves as physically ugly or undesirable; they tend to do poorly in school and to drop out when they are still on a low educational level; and they have serious doubts about their manliness or womanliness. Sometimes they are exceptionally defensive, so that they are not conscious of their underlying feelings of inferiority, and pretend and "feel" that they are actually superior. But very often they are fully conscious of their inadequacies and imagine enormous handicaps to go with the ones that they actually do possess.

Like other disturbed individuals, delinquents are more often than not severe goofers. They find routine tasks, such as attending school or working steadily on a job, monotonous and boring; they shy away from any work that is difficult or requires persistence; and they get great joy out of making a "soft" living. They are consequently, once again, literally driven to occupational pursuits, such as gambling or stealing or strong-arm tactics, which are antisocial and criminal in our society.

Delinquents are also, in many instances, arrant excitement-seekers. They crave momentary thrills and rousing "good times" and therefore they constantly drink, smoke marijuana, take goof-balls, or even resort to heroin. Their crimes themselves may seem highly exciting to them; or they may have to resort to crime in order to pay for their excitement-seeking. Similarly, because they rarely are able to attain good, steady heterosexual relationships, they often pay for their sex, in one form or another, if they are males, or resort to prostitution, directly or indirectly, if they are females.

As can again be seen from this description of their character, delinquents are usually as emotionally disturbed as they can possibly be; and it is folly to talk about dealing with delinquency, on either an individual or a social basis, unless we take into account the depth of the disturbance that is present. So if your child happens to be involved in delinquent acts, you would do well to assume that he is probably emotionally unstable, and that his acts are part and parcel of this kind of instability. This means that you'd better look for the philosophic roots of his disturbance: the anxiety and hostility-creating ideas which encourage and practically drive him to behave in a seriously antisocial way.

Melvin D. was a fifteen-year-old boy who came from an upper-middle-class home and who had been presumably given all the advantages of a respectable upbringing. He had a good allowance; was given a great amount of personal freedom; went to an excellent private school; and had parents who continually went to bat for him whenever he got into trouble—which he had been doing regularly, from the age of eight onward. When I saw him for psychotherapy, he was on probation for two years, mainly because he and one of his older chums had broken into a nearby gas station late one night and robbed it of thirty dollars in cash and whatever else they could lay their hands on.

Melvin's main gripe against the world was that he was very small for his age and looked two or three years younger than he actually was. Because of his height, he could not make any of the school teams, was not popular with the girls in his school or around his neighborhood, and was sometimes considered to be a sissy. He also felt unfairly dealt with by life because although his parents were kind and permissive, they, too, were ridiculously small-statured in his eyes, and he thought that they looked silly, and that the whole family group made an asinine appearance.

When I saw Melvin for treatment, I attempted to show him that he may, indeed, have been somewhat handicapped by his small stature, but that he was really much more handicapped by his own denigrating ideas about himself and his family and by his exaggerated fears of what others might do to him. Even if others did not despise him or overpower him, as he oversuspiciously thought that they might, his own self-deprecatory attitudes were sufficiently overpowering to undermine him; and if he wanted to get along in life, and live up to the potential which he seemed to possess, he would have to give up his inadequacy feelings and try to make it in the world *in spite of* his real, but actually rather minor, handicaps.

At first, Melvin would have none of my arguments. He had already obtained some notoriety in his school for his delinquency; and although he was somewhat ashamed of the fact that he had not got away with the crime he and his associate had attempted, he was rather pleased by the fact that everyone knew about it, and presumably thought him daring. As a tactical measure, I first worked with him on his shame, trying to show him that he had nothing to be ashamed of, either in having tried to rob the store in the first place or in failing in his robbery attempt in the second place. I contended that even if both these things were wrong and stupid—which I, for one, thought that they were—he'd better accept himself as a bright human being who from time to time did very stupid deeds. That was the way of the world, I insisted: the Einsteins and the Oppenheimers, the Leonardos and the Michelangelos, no matter how brilliant and talented they were, all behaved quite moronically at times—because they were human, because they were inevitably fallible.

Moreover, I said to Melvin at one point, "even if you were *generally* idiotic and *kept* doing more crazy than sane things, you still would not have to blame or depreciate yourself; you still wouldn't be a bum."

"Why wouldn't I be?" he asked. "What would be good about me then?"

"*You* would be good about you," I answered. "Your goodness as a person is your you-ness, your aliveness, and not the things that you do."

"But if I don't do anything very well, and nobody thinks I am any good, how could what you call my you-ness be anything but bad?"

"Because what I call your you-ness is not your performances and not what others think about you. These constitute your external value, or your worth to the world. And, under the circumstances that you state, your external value would be low; and that would be sad, since it is nice to know that others value you highly and will give you certain benefits, such as love or money, because they do. But your external value, or your worth to others, is not the same thing as your internal value, or your worth to yourself. You could *still* have a high self-worth, or like yourself distinctly, even when others did not like you and thus awarded you a low external value."

"How *could* I? That sounds like thinking that I'm Napoleon, when everybody else knows that I am not!"

"No, not exactly. Being Napoleon is still an external thing; and if everyone thought that you were Melvin and not Napoleon, you would be Melvin—no matter what you thought. But having self-worth is not an external thing, but is quite within your own control, and does not depend on what others think of you. Isn't it possible, for example, for everyone to think that you're really a great guy and a scholar and for you to think that you're just not great or scholarly enough, and that therefore you're no darned good?"

"Yes, I suppose it is, though that would be rare."

"Would it be? Look at the actual situation of your life, right now. Most people think you are fairly short and so do you—so both you and they are measuring your external measurements fairly accurately. But you think you are *too* short and that you are not a very good person for being so short; while most other people seem to ignore how short you are and think you are all right in spite of your height. So, obviously, your estimation of yourself—how awful you are for being short—is different from theirs."

"But I could be right and they could be wrong—isn't that possible?"

"Yes, it certainly is. But that isn't the point. The point is that *evaluations* of yourself as a person, as a living individual, are never really right or wrong—they just *are*. You are entitled to think that you are inferior for being short and others are entitled to think that you are all right for being short—although you and they would both have to admit, if a measuring rod were used on you and on other people, that you would definitely be shorter than most of the other boys of your age."

"You seem to mean that everyone would have to agree that they are tall or short, in relation to the measurement of others; but my measurement or evaluation of myself can't really be evaluated in the same kind of objective way."

"That's just what I do mean: that measurements of external things, such as height, weight, and even intelligence are fairly objective and can be legitimately assessed; but that internal values, such as how good or worthwhile you are *as a person* cannot really be measured in the same way. Values like these are not objective but subjective, and there is no way of scientifically proving them. You cannot decide whether you are short or tall—for your own height and that of other people decides that for you. But you can decide whether you are good or bad for being short—that is your own decision, the personal and subjective value that you place on your measurements."

"But I could decide, couldn't I, that it is good for me to be short or tall?"

"Yes, in some degree you could objectively decide—and so could other people decide for you—that it is beneficial for you to be tall, for then you could make the basketball team, see better when you were in a crowd, push smaller people around, etc. But because it is good—meaning, advantageous—

for you to be tall does not mean that you are good for so being. You, and only you, would still have to decide whether you value yourself for being tall or whether you think you are a bum for being that way."

"Then how, or on what basis, should I evaluate myself? The whole thing seems very slippery!"

"It certainly does! I would say that either you should not evaluate what you call your *self* at all—but merely *accept* this process of your being, just because you are alive and therefore have some kind of a self. Or else, if you must measure this *self*, I'd say that you would be much better off if you arbitrarily defined it as good rather than as bad—and let it go at that!"

"Why? Because it just works out better that way?"

"Yes, that's exactly why. If you measure your self-worth or your internal value to yourself at all, and you define this self as bad, rotten, or no good, then you will get into serious trouble; while if you define it as good or worthwhile, you will not get into that kind of trouble."

"So if I say, 'I am no good because I am short or because I am anything else,' I will feel terrible and will tend to act badly; while if I say, 'I am good, whether or not I am short,' I will feel better and will tend to act well. Seems odd, and yet I think I'm beginning to get it. But it *is* slippery!"

"It certainly is!"

Melvin continued to get it, and he could soon distinguish quite accurately between himself, or his self-concept, and his traits and his deeds. In this respect he did much better than many of my adult patients do; and it should be understood that I was able to talk to him on this high philosophic level only because he was very bright and sophisticated. If he had been younger or less intelligent, I would have used a much simpler approach. It is surprising, however, how many sharp children of Melvin's age, or even a few years younger, can be approached in this philosophic fashion, in spite of the fact that they are highly disturbed. Using other methods of psychotherapy with them—such as ventilation of feeling or play therapy—often helps them to *feel* considerably better but not necessarily to *get* better; while if the rational-emotive philosophic approach works, it achieves much deeper and more lasting results.

In any event, after a good many more talks with Melvin along the foregoing lines, he was able to accept the fact that even if he was somewhat handicapped because of his small stature, he certainly didn't have to reject himself entirely because of it. When he began to understand this, he began to lose his defensiveness, became much less hostile to others, saw that he didn't need to gain their attention in a boasting, delinquent manner, and buckled down to much more constructive aspects of living. He went on to college and was even able to use his shortness and his slightness to become coxswain of his school's boat-racing team. His conduct became exemplary, and he relinquished, even in his fantasies, his delinquent tendencies.

Similarly, many other delinquents can be handled by showing them that they philosophically believe that they must do perfectly well in their school, sports, social, or other activities, and because, not being able to achieve these high levels, and irrationally hating themselves unless they do, they compensatorily turn to delinquent modes of behavior. They can also often be shown that their hostility toward others is unjustified, even when these others are treating them badly, because they are falsely convincing themselves that the world should be immensely kind and giving to them, when it normally isn't. If these irrational ideas, which underlie their delinquent thoughts and actions are calmly, persistently shown to them, and then dispassionately demolished, many of these delinquents can become self-respecting, unhostile individuals who, at least, keep their delinquency within normal ranges.

Summary

Children who have conduct problems are not merely acting in relation to some outside stimuli, which can then be changed. Sometimes this is true, for most children tend to act badly when they are sufficiently abused or deprived; and we might say that it is their "normal" tendency to do this. Consequently, some problems of conduct may be resolved by your determining what unfortunate factors exist in the child's life, and by your seeing that these are minimized or eliminated. Thus, you can stop being overly critical of a child who has delinquent tendencies; see that he is not unnecessarily put upon by others; do away with exceptional deprivations or frustrations that he now has to bear; and otherwise change his environment to reduce undue pressures on him. Similarly, if you believe that his companions have any unusual influence on him—as when he is delinquent partly or largely because he lives in a neighborhood where delinquency is prestigeful—you may sometimes be able to remove him from these influences by moving to another neighborhood, by sending him to a different school, or by forbidding him to associate with certain children. Along somewhat similar lines, you can also use diversion tactics, so that when the child's environment is too pressuring, you can try to interest him in constructive sports, plan a family program to keep him occupied, praise him for doing what he does do reasonably well, and otherwise try to take his mind off the fact that conditions around him are deplorable.

Changing the child's external environment and diverting him from the unfortunate conditions around him are therapeutic methods, however, that have limited scope and effectiveness. In the main, children are problems to themselves and others largely because they interpret their surroundings poorly and because they view themselves and others in a jaundiced, negativistic light. For a more depth-centered cure of their poor conduct, therefore, you have to try to persuade them to question and challenge their destructive views, both in theory and in practice, until they finally realize that they are self-defeating and then give them up. Moreover, to do a thorough job in this respect, you have to teach these children to acquire a perennial habit of stopping and thinking, when things go wrong in their lives, and of questioning their own philosophies and assumptions about the world and themselves.

Is it easy to rear children, and especially those who have already shown antisocial behavior, in this manner? Indeed it is not! After all, they are children; they do have low mental ages, even when they are intelligent; they have difficulty in stopping to think and find it much easier to let themselves go suggestibly and uncritically through life. So don't expect any miracles in regard to teaching them thoughtful, rational attitudes. Don't, in fact, expect anything—but still try, as hard as you can, for a better solution to the problem than now exists. To some degree, and sometimes to a surprising degree, you will be rewarded. But you can no more be a perfect teacher than a child can be an infallible learner. Human beings, both yourself and others, are invariably error prone. Always, as you do your best to help malfunctioning children, remember *that!*

CHAPTER 13

AN REBT ARGUMENT FOR SELF-WORTH

EDITOR'S COMMENTARY:

In this selection, Ellis—probably more than in any writing before or perhaps since— went to the heart of REBT by asserting that one's worth as a human being is not a marketplace term. He argued that self was a matter of definition or pragmatism, and that he had erroneously believed at one time that defining oneself as "good" would lead to feelings of worth and that defining oneself as "bad" would culminate in morose or depressed feelings. Without proof on theoretical grounds, Ellis argued that clinically it would be better for a person to define him- or herself as good rather than bad. He argued a fortiori against rating the self because that evaluation or comparison was impossible to make in any case and that line of thinking would lead to generalization. To rate a role or activity, however, was something he countenanced. However, to leap from rating a role to rating the self (which implied all past, present, and future roles) made no sense. What Ellis urged readers to do was to accept self. Today, that might be considered an ontological or existential starting point enabling a person to separate who she is from what she does. On this score, Ellis surely was influenced by both Rogers and Tillich. Today, researchers in cognitive science would challenge Ellis asserting that self is solely a matter of definition. In fact, good double blind studies repeated from place to place tend to show that the mechanisms for what neuropsychologists call executive self are part and parcel of the human condition. Further, neuroscience and neuropsychology (see especially recent academic and popular writing from Mario Beauregard) argue that self as a concept is in part genetic. That leads to the possibility of definition, as Ellis called it, within cultural contexts coupled with the genetics. Of course, the moment Ellis argued for self as definition, he was using language which he intended to be understood by readers anywhere at any time. He extrapolated from this line of argument that a person could think about thinking. Indeed, that capacity seems to help to define the unique status of homo sapiens compared to all other species: they differ in kind, not just in type from their mammalian relatives. Lastly, Ellis made a judgment that it would be wise for a person to accept him- or herself unconditionally but not to accept unproductive or antisocial behavior. He believed this argument helped to distinguish his theory-therapy from that of Rogers—whether nondirective or existential. He also thought that the idea of dread and being thrown into life (borrowed by Tillich from Heidegger) were needlessly coupled. Being thrown into life was existential for Ellis, whereas dread could be worked against— as could self rating—to achieve greater individual happiness.

Excerpted from *Humanistic Psychotherapy,*
McGraw-Hill, 1973

A basic tenet for rational living is that people not rate themselves in terms of any of their performances, but instead fully accept themselves in terms of their being, their existence. Otherwise, they tend to be severely self-deprecating and insecure, and as a consequence they function ineffectively.

Why should this be so? To value oneself in terms of any deeds or acts will work only as long as one is performing rather well. Even if such deeds or acts are excellent at the moment, it will probably be only a matter of time when they will become less praiseworthy. Among other things, the individual grows older with the passing years—and consequently does worse eventually at various feats at which he may do well in his youth. Besides, no one is perfect, and being fallible, all of us will sooner or later fail in many respects. Where will they be, then, who insist on rating themselves by performances?

Knowing, moreover, that the chances of ultimately failing at some prized goal are normally high, people tend to work overtime at worrying about the possibility of such failure; and in the process will frequently interfere with their chances of success. For worrying is distracting and time consuming and hardly enables one to cope with any kind of problem solving; on the contrary, it almost always sabotages.

The investment of personal value, or worth as a human being, in any performance, makes it very "dangerous" to attempt to do that thing. A man would be loath to risk the game at all, if he is prepared to define himself as a failure should his performance fail. He therefore tends to make up excuses and avoids trying; or if he pushes himself ahead and compels himself to make an effort, he does so while worrying, "Will I do well?" or "Is it going to be good enough?" Frequently he enjoys the action so little, and finds such difficulty in keeping at it, that he finally concludes with something like, "Hell! It's not really worth all this trouble. Who wants to do *that* sort of thing, anyway?" The result is often a withdrawal from the activity, a conviction that, in spite of a dearth of objective evidence to judge by, it is not really worth doing.

Thus, the artist who *wanted* to be a painter of fine murals would have a delightful goal to strive for, and would probably have a very fine time trying for it. But if he absolutely *had* to be a great muralist, and was convinced that he must be a marvelous painter, or else he is a person without worth, a non-person, an inhuman, he would then soon find it too risky to paint—for who wants to prove what a worthless being he is? And rather than take that risk, the would-be artist will probably end up with excuses or rationalizations: "I don't have the time or money for painting," or "The lumbago in my arm is too painful for me to do any amount of painting," or "Nobody wants murals these days, anyway, so what's the use of trying to paint any?"

If a person must rate his self, his "personal worth," or "self esteem," he had better do it in terms of some quite safe standard, such as his aliveness or his being. He can then, in accordance with this standard, quite justifiably conclude, "I am good, not because I do very well at anything, and not because certain people tend to approve of me, but just because I am alive, because I exist." For when he accepts his goodness as a human being in terms of being or aliveness, he obviously can accept himself under virtually all conditions that he may possibly face during a lifetime. By this standard, he would only fail to have goodness when dead.

Valuing oneself in relation to being or existence is the logical solution to the problem of self-worth. It is derived from the works of Paul Tillich, of Robert S. Hartman, and various other existentialist philosophers. Hartman has had a profound influence on the development of rational-emotive psychotherapy; for psychotherapy, as Perry London and various other practicing therapists have shown, is really largely concerned with morals and values, even when the therapist does not fully consciously recognize this fact. And the effective therapist would better have a good philosophy of life himself and be well prepared to discuss deeply philosophic questions with his clients if he wants to get very far with many of them.

Unfortunately, the more I used a modification of the Tillich-Hartman approach with my clients, and the more I tried to show them that they never really had to denigrate themselves as human beings no matter how poor their performances might be and no matter how little certain significant others cared for them, the more I began to encounter some very bright individuals who would not quite buy this line or who at least had serious philosophic objections to it. For these clients would object; "You say that the individual is good just because he's alive, and that he needs no other requisites for self-worth. I can see how this may work. If someone really believes this idea, he cannot very well devalue himself in any serious way, even though he may fully admit that many of his actions are less than good or are even reprehensible. But how can you positively state that a person *is* good merely because he exists? How can you *prove* this hypothesis? He's alive, all right; you can definitely, empirically prove that. But what makes him good *because* he's alive? You might just as sensibly say, 'He's *bad* because he's alive.' For both these statements, that he's good or that he's bad because he exists, are definitions or tautologies, and neither of them is really provable."

"Well," I could only agree, when I listened to the arguments of these clients, "they're right! How *can* I prove that the individual's aliveness equals his worthiness? I can, of course, disprove any client's assumption that because he exists and because he behaves poorly, he is indubitably worthless (that is, of no value to himself and deserving of being dead). For his assumption, too, is tautological, and there is no empirical data by which he can uphold it. But how can I prove to him that he really *is* intrinsically worthwhile?"

There really *is* no answer to the question, "What am I worth?" or "How do I prove that I am a good person?" since the question is rather meaningless and foolish in the first place. If I ask myself, "What do I do?" "What are my traits?" or "What is the value of this performance of mine?" such a question is meaningful, since it inquires about a trait, characteristic, or performance which (1) can be observed and (2) can to some degree be measured or rated. Thus, I play tennis, I possess a good backhand swing in this game, and my particular performance at tennis today was good, since I won all the matches I engaged in with competitors. But if I ask myself, "Who am I?" how am I going to answer this question *except* in the light of my traits, characteristics, and performances? How am I to give a meaningful answer to such a vague, undefinable, rather meaningless question?

I *am,* as David Bourland has noted, nothing very observable or measurable. For whenever we use any form of the verb *to be,* we tend to overgeneralize about ourselves. Thus, I really am not, although I may erroneously label myself as, "a tennis player." Instead, I am a person, an individual, who among many other things *sometimes plays tennis.* Nor am I a "good backhander at tennis." For I am an organism, a human who has several usual (and some unusual) tennis characteristics—including the one that I often hit the ball back at my opponent with a good backhand stroke *and* I often also do several other things while playing tennis, such as usually serve badly and retrieve the ball quickly, or hit it with a mean twist. Nor am I a great tennis player because my game today was particularly good. Rather, I am a man, a creature who today played very well, and who tomorrow may play very badly, the next day well again, and so on. If I *am* anything, then, I am very complex; and it is rather foolish and false to refer to me as simplistically *being* a tennis player, a psychologist, a writer, or almost anything else. I am, much more accurately, a *person who* does various kinds of things. So "Who am I?" is a silly question to ask about me. "What are my traits and how, at various times, do I perform them?" is much more sensible to ask.

Similarly, "What is my identity?" is a fairly meaningless question, despite the efforts of Erik Erikson to answer it. For the only conceivable answer to a question like this is, "I am a male," or "I am an American teenager," or "I am a writer of books on psychology." And all these are false overgeneralizations. I am really a human being, and I do innumerable things, some well and some badly. I cannot be legitimately characterized as a "leftwinger," a "rational emotive therapist," a "musician," or by any similar overinclusive or underinclusive term. When I use these kinds of appellations to describe myself, I am using shorthand—and very inaccurate shorthand at that—which probably far more obscures than reveals what *I and my traits* truly are.

When I ask, moreover, "What is my identity?" what I really mean, when I am honest, is, "How do I shape up against you? Am I not a member of a group (such as the group of liberal middle-aged Americans) which is at least equal to, and preferably superior to, the group of which you are a member? Isn't my identity, as compared to yours, real, honest, true, and good? Don't I, because of my identity, deserve to live and prosper, while you (for all I care) can easily shrivel up and die?" The questions, "Who am I?" and "What is my identity?" could technically mean, as Erikson sometimes seems to imply, that I merely want to know what my traits are and what my real thing is, so that I may, with the use of this knowledge, enjoy myself during my seventy-five years or so of existence. But they truly, for the most part, are one of the main ways in which I play ego games—by which I devoutly hope to "prove" that I am great and you are not, that the world will justly honor me and damn you, and that I shall sooner or later get to heaven while you ignobly fry in hell.

That, in fact, is the basic reason for what we call self-esteem, feelings of worthwhileness, or ego strength: to show that I am good and you (that is, the entire rest of the world) are not; that because I am good, I deserve to go on living and to enjoy myself; and that because I am good and deserve to go on living and enjoy myself, I shall ultimately attain some kind of salvation. When I have a good ego, I don't merely want to live and enjoy—I want to undevilify and to deify myself.

"Well," you may observe, "that may all be true. But as the sages have noted for centuries, isn't it also necessary that things be so? Can a human really live satisfactorily *without* ego, self-esteem, pride, feelings of worth, or whatever you want to call it?"

Why can he not? "Certainly," I started to tell a client when I saw that it would not be easy to convince him that he was good just because he was alive, "I can't prove to you that you're really worthwhile, just as you can't prove to me that you're really not. For whatever standards or measures we seem to use in these arguments, we're being tautological. I say, 'You're good just because you exist,' and you rightly show me that that's merely my *definition* of goodness or worth. And you say, 'I'm worthless because I perform badly,' and I rightly show you that that's merely your *definition* of badness. We both get nowhere with such arguments, because they don't have, nor can they ever have, any empirical referent. But why do we even have to think about or label your worth or value at all? Why do we *need* such a concept?"

"Well, *don't* we? I just can't even think of a human being not rating himself at all—not liking or hating himself."

"Why not? Why does he *have* to invent *any* kind or type of self-evaluation?"

"So that he can efficiently live, I guess."

"Efficiently?" I ask. "Nonsense! The more he evaluates or rates himself, the less efficient he is likely to be. First of all, he spends much, or even most, of his time and energy doing this evaluating. Secondly, he never comes up with a very accurate or consistent answer. Thirdly, he ultimately—because he is immensely error-prone and demandingly perfectionistic—evaluates himself rather negatively and thereby seriously *interferes* with many of his own performances. How does all *that* help?"

"I see what you mean. But I still can't see how he could avoid evaluating himself completely."

"Well, let me show you how he can," I confidently retort. Then I go on to show the client that all he really has to do is to keep entirely within the empirical realm and view his life in this manner:

1. He obviously exists or is alive—which can fairly easily be observably

determined (and checked with others' observations).

2. He can either choose to remain alive or to let himself die—another empirically observable choice.

3. He can, if he chooses to remain alive, either strive for more pleasure than pain or for more pain than pleasure—a third empirically determinable choice.

4. He can decide in favor of living and of pleasure on the basis of the hypothesis. *It* is good for me to live and to enjoy myself," or on the basis of the hypothesis, "*I* am good and therefore I deserve to live and enjoy myself." If he decides on the former basis, he avoids rating or evaluating himself, although he does rate or evaluate his performances (that is, living and enjoying). If he decides on the latter basis, he brings in ego and evaluates himself.

5. Without any self-evaluation and ego-rating, he can decide to continue to live and to have as much enjoyment in life as he can find. His major questions to himself then do not become, "Who am I?" "What is my identity?" or "What is my worth?" They become, rather: "What are my traits?" "What sort of things do I enjoy and not enjoy doing?" "How can I improve some of my traits and find more things to experience—so that I will continue to live and to have a maximally satisfying existence?"

This is the main line that I now take with my clients. "Look," I tell them. "If you *must* rate or value yourself, or wallow around in what is ordinarily called ego and ego games—and I strongly advise you against it—you have a simple solution to the problem of worth. Just define yourself as good, in terms of your existence, your aliveness. Dogmatically tell yourself, 'I am alive, and I am good because I am alive.' This simple formula, if you really believe it, will work, and will be virtually unassailable. For, believing it, you will never feel terribly anxious or self-deprecating as long as you are alive. And when you are dead, you still won't have much to worry about!

"But if you want a preferable solution to the problem of human worth—and I strongly suggest that you strive for this solution—then you'd better avoid rating yourself at all. You are not *good* and you are not *bad*—you are merely *you.* You possess many traits, most of which you may (and often would better) rate: your abilities to read, to talk, to write, to run, to jump, to drive, just to name a few. But you never have to jump, as if by magic, from rating these traits to rating *you.* You can, if you wish, give your various facets, your characteristics, your talents, a report card; but you'd better not give *you* a similar report card. Then, minus such a self-rating, and minus playing the ego game and the power struggle of vying for 'goodness' with other human beings, you can ask yourself 'What do I really want in life?' and can try to find those things and enjoy them."

No therapist will have an easy time inducing clients to give up rating themselves and to stick more rigorously, at most, to assessing, measuring, and evaluating their traits. Humans, unfortunately, seem to be almost universally born and reared to give themselves self-evaluations. They use, to be sure, different trait ratings for these self-rating standards. In the United States, for example, they rate themselves as "good" if they have lots of money, education, or artistic talent; while in many more primitive parts of the world they rate themselves as "good" if they have a considerable amount of physical strength, child-begetting ability, or perhaps head-hunting proclivity. But wherever they are, they are not prone merely to accept themselves, with whatever traits and talents they happen to have, and to look for enjoyments that *they* happen to like (rather than those other people think that they *should* like).

Is this self-rating tendency of human beings more or less inborn? I think so—for if people all over the world, no matter how they are raised, tend to deify themselves and denigrate others, or vice versa, and to depress themselves horribly when they do not succeed in whatever aspects of life their culture tells them that they *should,* there is some reason to suspect that they naturally and easily fall into a self-assessing and ultimately self-condemning pattern. Love, 'tis often, said, makes the world go round. Yes: self-love, mainly, or the frantic striving on the part of the great majority of humans to achieve such love.

Although man has unique powers of observation and logic, and is consequently the one animal primarily born to be a scientist, he also has unique tendencies toward religiosity, magical thinking, anti-intellectualism, and nonempiricism. Rollo May thinks that man is innately predisposed toward what he calls the daimonic. But while May gives up and thinks that man had better make peace with his demon-creating tendencies and deeply imbedded roots in irrationality, I take a much more optimistic view. I contend that man *can* think more rationally, even though he rarely does; that he *is* able to give up superstition and magic; and that he can teach himself and fairly consistently stick with the logico-empirical method of confronting not only the external world but also himself and his own functioning. Further, if he really does this much of the time, he can stop his absurd ego games and self-rating, and can tolerantly accept both himself and others and look for a much saner goal in life: to enjoy the experience of living.

So I say, again, to my clients: "All right, face it: you have screwed up very badly much of your existence. You failed to do as well as you could have done in your work; you married the wrong girl and then endlessly goofed on making the most of a bad deal or getting out of it as quickly and gracefully as possible; and you have been far worse a father to your children than you probably could have been, and have consequently helped them cause themselves a lot of needless trouble. O. K. So you did all this with your deadly little hatchet and there's no point in trying to excuse your acts or say that they were right. They weren't right: they were stupid and wrong. *Now,* why are you blaming yourself and denying your worth for acting in these execrable ways?"

"Well, *should* I have done those wrong things, and thereby hurt myself and others?"

"Of course you *should*—because you *did. It would have been desirable,* of course, had you not acted in those ways; but because a thing is desirable never means that it *should* exist. Only some unalterable, godlike law of the universe could ever say that you should, you must, do what is desirable. And where is there such a law? Can you demonstrate that that kind of law ever has existed, or ever will?"

"No, I see what you mean. And if there's no invariable law of the universe that says that I *should* not have done what I did, then I guess you also mean that there's no supplementary law which says that I should be punished for breaking that law."

"Right! You are intrinsically penalized, of course, for many of your wrong acts. If you fail to do as well as you could have done at work, you lose out on some of the rewards of succeeding. If you stay with a wife who is incompatible, and you make conditions of living with her even worse than they had to be, you then lead something of a miserable married life. So acting poorly or inefficiently usually (though not always) has its intrinsic penalties. But when you think that you're a rotter and that you *should* be punished, you really mean that some magical, overlooking superbeing in the universe is spying on you, is noting your errors, and is determining to punish you for them. Well—is it likely that there really is such an overlooking super being who is so sadistically inclined that he's going to deliberately add *extra* punishment to your lot, when you have already seriously penalized yourself by your stupid behavior?"

"No, I guess it doesn't look like that. I guess I really do believe in some kind of devil when I think that I *deserve* to be punished when I have acted badly."

"You certainly do. And how about the hereafter business? Do you really believe that if you lead an error-prone, screwed-up life on this earth, you will be reincarnated somewhere else and made to suffer there for your earthian inadequacies?"

"Well, hardly! But my actions, admittedly, imply that on some level I do believe that kind of drivel. For I certainly *often feel* as if I'm going to be eternally damned when I don't do the right thing in this terrestrial existence."

"Yes. So you do keep damning yourself in various ways, and you do feel that you should be temporarily or eternally punished. The point is: you, as a human, are not rateable in any way, though your deeds may well be. Now, every time you do feel like a louse or a worm, you'd better fully admit that you are rating yourself negatively and then vigorously dispute this rating. You will not thereby necessarily solve the practical problems that beset you—such as the problems of how to work better, how to get along with your wife, or how to be a good father to your children—but you will solve your emotional problem. You will continually, unconditionally accept *yourself,* even though you will continue to dislike and refuse to accept a good deal of your behavior. You will keep rating your *traits,* but stop rating *you.*"

"Can people really consistently do this?"

"Not perfectly, not always, not to the *n*th degree. But if they keep working at it, they can do it pretty well, and rarely have ego problems while otherwise remaining exceptionally human. In fact, to have an ego problem really means that you are striving to be *super*human and just will not fully accept your humanity, your fallibility. If you follow the rational-emotive procedure, which is one of the most humanistic methods of personal problem-solving ever invented, you will unconditionally accept yourself and others *as human.* This kind of tolerance is, I contend, the essence of emotional well-being. Why not try it and see for yourself?"

The rational-emotive approach to psychotherapy is not only unusually effective clinically, but is now backed by a considerable amount of experimental evidence which almost consistently supports its phenomenological tenets and indicates that human emotions and behavior are enormously influenced by cognitions. Besides being successfully practiced today by a number of clinicians who attest to its usefulness, it also has significant applications in education, in industry, and in other important aspects of human living. There is clinical, experimental, and other support for rational-emotive therapy.

All psychotherapy is, at bottom, a value system. The individual who is disturbed decides that he would rather be less anxious, depressed, hostile, or ineffective, and he thinks that he can be helped through talking with a therapist. On his part, the therapist agrees with the client that it is unnecessary for him to be so troubled and that he can somehow help him to feel and to behave better. Both the client and the therapist could agree, theoretically, that severe anxiety, depression, and hostility are beneficial—in which case the therapist could, as a social scientist, help the client to become more rather than less disturbed. But they both have similar prejudices or belief systems about what we tend to call emotional problems, and they agree to collaborate to minimize rather than to maximize such problems when the client feels that he is overafflicted with them.

It has been clinically observed that most of the time when the client is beset with anxiety, withdrawal, inhibition, and depression he values himself very poorly and thinks of himself as worthless, inadequate, or bad. As long as he has this picture of himself, or appraises his being in this manner, it seems almost impossible to help him very much with his basic emotional problems (although it may be possible palliatively to divert him from them in various ways). Consequently, the main goal of intensive, depth-centered psychotherapy usually becomes that of helping the client to stop devaluing himself and to gain what is usually called "self-confidence," "self-esteem," or "ego strength."

The rational-emotive approach to psychotherapy hypothesizes that there are two main approaches to helping the client gain self-acceptance, one inelegant and one elegant. The inelegant approach is to have him believe that he is "good" or "worthwhile" as a person, not because he does anything well or is approved by others, but simply because he exists. The more elegant approach is to show the individual that he does not have to rate, assess, or value himself at all; that he can merely accept the fact that he exists; that it is better for him to live and enjoy than for him to die or be in pain; and that he can take more delight in living by only measuring and valuing his traits, characteristics, and performances than by superfluously bothering to value his so called *self*. Once the client is helped to be fully tolerant of all humans, including himself, and to stop giving them any global report cards, he has a philosophic solution to the problem of personal worth and can truly be self-accepting rather than self-evaluating. He will then consider himself neither a good nor a bad human being, but a person with fortunate and unfortunate traits. He will truly accept his humanity and stop demanding superhumanness from anyone.

CHAPTER 14

AIMING FOR HAPPINESS
WITH REBT WHILE
OVERCOMING INERTIA

EDITOR'S COMMENTARY:

In this update and revision of his magnum opus, Ellis opens the selection by comparing his theory and therapy to the work of Rogers, Perls, Adler, and Jung, among others. Instead of working for amalgamation, Ellis opted to challenge them by arguing that we disturb ourselves with core dysfunctional irrational beliefs and emotional reactions and behaviors that we ourselves construct in reaction to activating events (the A in Ellis's ABC theory). He stated that a major goal of REBT was self-actualization, and he argued that he learned about it through one of his passions, reading philosophy. Without obsessing, he argued, human beings would be wise to search for and develop a philosophy of personal happiness. He then moved to clarify the arguments such as biological self (taught variously by Maslow and Horney) and his argument that even if self had biological roots it was different for each person. Of course, he had in mind and then combined genetic endowment with social construction by claiming that REBT was not either/or but both of them. Ellis then argued for various considerations of self-actualization (e.g., whether it was emotive, a distraction, etc.). He next visited the issue of REBT and its consideration of self-actualization. Differing from arguments for autopoeisis or biological unfolding of self, Ellis argued that he actively taught clients how to actualize themselves. He did so first by teaching them to overcome irrational blocks to progress, and then working in non-obsessive ways to achieve goals. He did not at all infer that self-actualization was an inevitability as Maslow did. He then outlined the characteristics of a self-actualizing person. Consistent with REBT, he argued for flexibility, the scientific method, and long-term hedonism. As was stated at the outset, repetitions and even some contradictions can be expected when a readers surveys over fifty years of Ellis publications. These irregularities have been treated as a tribute to Ellis's diversity and enormous writing-work ethic. This chapter to some extent, then, repeats some basic themes from Chapter 7 in this volume.

Excerpted from *Reason and Emotion in Psychotherapy,*
Carol Publishing, 1994

As I approach the end of this revised edition of *Reason and Emotion in Psychotherapy,* I can see with increasing clarity how complex the field of psychotherapy has become, especially compared to my view of it in 1955. At that time, I made a Herculean attempt to simplify and make more efficient some of the main aspects in the field. For where Freud and his followers were much too complicated, in both their theory and their practice, and were leading most of their clients into specious explanations of how they became disturbed and what they could do about it, and were doing (I thought) more harm than good, other therapists were often overly simple and one-sided and missed many important factors in alleviating psychological dysfunctioning.

Carl Rogers, for example, beautifully emphasized giving clients unconditional positive regard but obsessed about the client-therapist relationship being the *supreme essence* of personality change. Fritz Perls saw that some radical experiential methods had better be employed but was allergic to sensible thinking. Alfred Adler was great on persuading people to change some of their basic assumptions, but was not very emotive or behavioral. Carl Jung greatly encouraged individuation and self-actualization but was too mired in myths and in mysticism. B. F. Skinner was *too* solidly behavioral.

To some extent my early writings changed all this and pushed the idea that we humans profoundly affect, and often disturb, ourselves with (1) core dysfunctional Beliefs about, *and* (2) emotional reactions to, *and* (3) dysfunctional behaviors that we construct and maintain regarding the undesirable Activating Events (A's) that occur (or that we create) in our lives.

Because my original ideas about the ABC's of disturbance and the interactions of cognitions, emotions, and behaviors in both "causing" and alleviating this disturbance were clearer and more testable than many other therapists' views, they led from the 1960s onward to the creation of an enormous number of studies in the cognitive-behavioral movement. My own attempts to abet these studies were almost entirely thwarted by lack of research funds, because (to my surprise) I soon discovered that government and other grants are almost exclusively given to academic institutions and to researchers allied with such organizations. So the Institute for Rational-Emotive Therapy, which I founded and have always directed, has over the years been able to sponsor little important research of its own.

Fortunately, however, a number of other researchers in the REBT and CBT area have had regular academic positions and have done many notable studies in the realm of assessing and changing beliefs and the emotional and behavioral disorders that tend to accompany them; and they have encouraged a large number of their students to produce doctoral theses and other studies in these areas. Just to mention a few of these researchers, they include Albert Bandura, Aaron Beck, Howard Berlow, Gerald Davison, Raymond DiGiuseppe, Marvin Goldfried, Leslie Greenberg, Fred Kanfer, Howard Kassinove, Michael Mahoney, Alan Marlatt, Donald Meichenbaum, Neil Jacobson, Robert Schwartz, and Paul Woods.

As might be suspected, this research has not only made REBT and CBT probably the most studied of all the therapies but has led to many theories and systems that are now much more complicated than my original fairly simple one. This is good, because practically all psychological theories and practices become less monolithic and more pluralistic as they develop. This has certainly happened with REBT and CBT. In fact, there are now so many different models of cognitive emotive behavior therapy, many conflicting with each other, that it is hard to give them suitable names!

One of the most developed aspects of REBT and CBT in recent years has been that of self-fulfillment or self-actualization. As usual, philosophers gave rise to this aspect thousands of years ago, for several Asian thinkers, such as Confucius, Lao-Tsu, and Gautama Buddha were not only concerned with helping people overcome their disturbances but also with teaching them how to lead happier lives. Epicurus, Epictetus, Marcus Aurelius, and other Greco-Roman philosophers also did very well in this respect.

Because of my passion for philosophy, and especially for the philosophy of happiness, my early books on REBT not only told people how to ward off misery and neurosis but how to be self-fulfilled and more actualizing in their sex, love, marriage, and family affairs. So REBT has always tried to show clients and nonclients how to achieve two lifelong goals: (1) to stubbornly refuse to make themselves panicked, depressed, self-hating, and enraged when beset with real Adversities or unfortunate Activating Events; and (2) to also keep unfrantically looking for greater, deeper, and more lasting enjoyments. Like Epicurianism more than Stoicism, REBT is honestly hedonistic rather than ascetic. But it also endorses the Stoic principle of long-range rather than short-range hedonism: Minimize your needless pain and maximize your pleasures of today—and of tomorrow.

In modern times, self-actualization has been promulgated by a number of theorists and therapists, including Kurt Goldstein Abe Maslow, Wilhelm Reich, Fritz Perls, and Carl Rogers. REBT partly accepts their advocacies but tends to be more realistic than romantic and therefore modifies their views in several important ways.

Individualistic and social self-actualization Concepts of self-actualization have been attacked as being too individualistic, self-seeking, and indulgent. This is partly true, but the REBT theory includes both self-interest *and* social interest. Because humans *choose* to live with others, their morality, emotional health, and self-actualization had better always include their being quite concerned about the present and future welfare of specific others *and* their entire social group. Their very survival—especially in a nuclear age—seems to require a great deal of social interest. So REBT favors individualistic *and* social-oriented actualization. By themselves, both have severe limitations and inconsistencies. Together, they make more social *and* individual sense.

Is planned self-actualization "true" and practical? M. Daniels questions whether deciding to pick self-actualizing *goals* defeats people's spontaneous *ways* of living in a more fully-functioning manner. No, says REBT, not if people adopt an "and/also" and not merely an "either/or" approach. One of the main goals of people's actualizing themselves can be for them to seek for *more* spontaneous ways of living. And one main by-product of letting themselves spontaneously (and risk-takingly) *try* new pursuits will often be to discover new enjoyments and then to *make* reachieving them their planned future goals. Experimentation partly *is* goal-seeking; and goal-seeking partly *is* spontaneously experimenting with new endeavors. They can both be spontaneous *and* planned. I once planned to unspontaneously force myself to speak in public, in order to overcome my public speaking phobia. As I did so, I began to spontaneously enjoy what I was doing. As a teenager, I spontaneously had my first orgasm without realizing that I was about to bring it on. Thereafter I plotted and schemed to bring on more and more orgasms!

Do people have an essential "real self" that they can discover and actualize? Abe Maslow, Karen Horney, Frances Vaughan, and to some extent, Carl Rogers hold that people have an underlying biological or transpersonal "real" or "true" self that they can discover and actualize. But, as Daniels points out, their "biological" real self is somewhat restrictive; and REBT holds that it is quite different for different individuals and that, with experimentation and hard work, it can even be significantly changed. Thus, people with strong biological tendencies to be weak-muscled or undisciplined or irrational can learn and work hard to overcome their unfulfilling handicaps.

REBT holds that several human aspirations and goals—such as sex, love, gustatory- and meaning-oriented desires—are at least partly (and individualistically) motivated but that they *also* are strongly socially and environmentally influenced. They *also* can be distinctly—and consciously— self-developed and modified.

REBT is highly skeptical that humans have any "true" transpersonal, transcendental, or mystical selves, though they are certainly often born and reared with strong propensities to *think* or *experience* that they do have superhuman cores. REBT acknowledges that a *belief* in religion, God, mysticism, Pollyannaism, and irrationality may at times help people. But it also points out that such beliefs often do much more harm than good and block a more fully functioning life.

Daniels rightly observes that the biological "real" self of Horney, Maslow, and Rogers is supposed to be "truer" and "better" than a socially acquired conforming self, but he objects that this idea "leads to the denial of constructive social involvement to existential isolation and individualism." REBT upholds *both* individualism *and* social involvement—not *either/or*. It says that because people *choose* to live in a social group (family, community, nation, the earth) and *not* to be asocial hermits, they had better care for themselves *and* for others and preserve—and help actualize—themselves *as well as* their sociality. They can choose—or not choose—to put themselves first in some respects, but preferably should put others—particularly some selected others—a close second.

Is self-actualization self-transcendence? Maslow held that self-actualizing people are (1) biological and personally motivated, have a "real" self, and somewhat contradictorily held that (2) they are also motivated by nonpersonal, objective, and universal "Values of Being" (B-values). He also saw self-transcendence as (1) altruistic and socially interested and (2) devoted to mystical pathways that transcend human consciousness and have a nonbodily, "spiritual" aspect.

REBT holds that people can be biologically inclined to be self-interested *and also* biologically (and sociologically) inclined to be altruistic and socially involved. So it unites or integrates Maslow's (and Rogers's) individualistic and socialized goals.

REBT, however, sees no evidence that humans ever truly transcend their humanity and develop a transpersonal, transcendental, or superhuman "self" that achieves "higher miraculous states of consciousness." They frequently aspire to such mystical states, and devoutly *believe* that they experience them. But they are probably self-deluded—sometimes psychotic—and do not really achieve "Absolute Truth," godliness, or *completely* nonhuman consciousness. So, however much human mystics experience Nirvana, selflessness, unity with the universe, or similar "transpersonal" states, it is unlikely (though not impossible) that they really have superhuman powers and very unlikely that their special state of altered consciousness is "better" than the usual state of consciousness. In some ways it appears to be a deficient, Pollyannaish, unauthentic state!

Is self-actualization too ideal and emotive? A. McIntyre partly concurs with L. Geller that moral consensus and agreed-upon self-actualization are based on conflicting premises that are mainly *emotive,* and include assertions of personal *preference* or imply some more arbitrary *ideal* that *should* be achieved but is never *really* agreed upon. This again seems to be true, but mainly means that no single "ideal" set of characteristics will suffice for all people at all times, but that they can still *select* "ideal" (or "nonideal") traits and then *experiment* (which is almost the REBT *essence* of health and actualization) to *determine* whether they are suitable.

Can a theory of self-actualization be final and complete? McIntyre says that because self-actualization involves a goal, as we search for progress in achieving it we discover more about it and change it. Daniels agrees that "a theory of self-actualization ... can therefore only be partially accurate; it is forever vague and incomplete." REBT adds that not only the theory but also the *practice* of self-fulfillment is almost by necessity experimental, changing, and incomplete.

Is self-actualization too relative to be meaningful? Geller holds that it is meaningless to speak of *general* self-actualization, because it is highly multidimensional and involves the pursuit of excellence or enjoyment in whatever ways each individual chooses to desire and emphasize. This argument has much truth to it, since both "healthy" and "enjoyable," not to mention "maximally enjoyable," pursuits differ from culture to culture and from individual to individual in each culture. *"Self*-actualizing," in fact, implies that each individual "self" chooses to actualize herself or himself. However, because almost all humans have many similar biological tendencies (e.g., to like to perform well and be approved by others) and because most cultures abet many of these tendencies (though, of course, in different ways), the REBT hypothesis is that most contemporary people much of the time will lead both a "healthier" and "more enjoyable" life if they achieve . . . ."self-actualizing" characteristics. . . .

CHAPTER 15

MANAGING FEELINGS OF SHYNESS AND INADEQUACY

EDITOR'S COMMENTARY:

In many selections, Ellis makes his points about shyness and inadequacy with slim definitions but lots of case examples. In this selection he argued more on a Bandura-like imitation of desired outcomes by clients rather than the weight of argument he often employed in other selections over the course of his career. He judged shyness, for example, to be a drop-bucket term—a term that included an admixture of feelings. Often, REBT therapists look for a "pure" emotion doggedly when none exists. The examples Ellis gave in his sparse non-casework presentation in this chapter make this point. Ellis often taught, for example, that the opposite of anxiety or depression was not happiness and euphoria. Instead, he argued, the opposite was calmness or feeling "OK." However, some colleagues and students argued that calmness and self-acceptance were not emotions in the pure sense. Ellis countered that the search for purity itself could be irrational. The key point in this chapter is that assertion was a choice for Ellis, even if that choice involved working against one's biology to remain comfortable by not taking risks.

Evolution of a Revolution

Excerpted from *A Guide to Personal Happiness,*
Wilshire Books, 1982

This area could be called the common cold of psychology because so many of us are affected by it. The emotional problem is shyness, which goes under many other names, including lack of confidence, fear of asserting oneself, insecurity, and feelings of inadequacy. In looking at the case excerpts that follow, you will see how certain core beliefs create the feelings and actions that we label as shyness. You will also see how overcoming shyness relates to personal happiness and what you can do to become less shy and more assertive.

The client in the first case is a 22-year-old female secretary. Since this is the initial session, the therapist knows little about the client aside from what the client writes on a biographical information form. What follows is the transcript of most of the session, along with comments pointing out how the principles taught to the client can help you with similar problems in your own life. Let us join as the session is beginning.

T = Therapist   C = Client

T. Okay, this [client's form] says "lack of self-confidence, feelings of inadequacy and shyness in certain social situations, need for perfectionism in myself and others." The perfectionism, you see, is probably the main issue. Because as long as you're a perfectionist, how could you not be shy?

C. I don't see how that follows.

T. Well, shyness is a high-class name for feeling scared. That's mainly what it means. It's too bad we use the word *shy* because it covers up the real feeling. The only things a person can legitimately be afraid of are some kinds of real harm or damage, such as physical injury. But that is hardly the issue here. You're not afraid that a person whom you just met is going to punch you, are you?

C. No. Hardly that!

T. So you're afraid of doing something imperfectly.

C. Right! Exactly!

T. You're probably afraid that you're going to act stupidly, say the wrong thing, or something like that, and afraid I'm going to think "What a nut she is for acting that way!" And you're going to believe you're no good—because you're a perfectionist.

C. Exactly.

T. Now if you weren't a perfectionist, if you really said to yourself, "Oh, yes, I see that my act is stupid but that doesn't mean *I* am." Let's just suppose you believed that and suppose you also told yourself, "He's wrongly downing me as a person for my stupid behavior." Would you be shy?

C. I guess not. I do feel shy when I wear glasses, so I wear contacts.

T. But let's suppose you forgot your contacts, and you therefore felt shy. It's not just because you wear the glasses. It's because, one, you view that as an imperfection, which it might *not* be. I might like you better with the glasses. Some people do, some don't. And, two, you're saying, "It's horrible to have that imperfection. I *should* be perfect." Aren't you?

C. Yes, I am.

T. Well, why *should* you be perfect?

C. It's really terrible. It relates to everything I do. It's probably because I expect too much of others. They don't live up to my image of them and I guess I don't live up to my image of me.

T. Let's take your own image of yourself, which is the issue. Why must you have an image?

C. I don't know.

T. Well, the answer is because you're human and humans foolishly make up images of themselves. They don't have to, but they almost invariably do. Let's get back to the issue of glasses. You could say, "Since I look worse to most people with glasses, it is, therefore, a handicap to wear glasses." Right?

C. Yeah.

T. And if possible you could add, "So I'll get contacts, or not wear my glasses at times, or find a few people who like glasses." You see, that would be the way to overcome your handicap. But instead you jump from "I don't like *it*" to "I don't like *me*" for that dislikable behavior, wearing glasses. You start rating yourself as a human. Now that's nutty. And that's what we call an image. "Because my glasses don't make me look good, my image is no good." Or, "I am no good. My being, my essence, is worthless." Now, is your essence *really* no good because you have this bad defect—because you don't look well in glasses?

C. No.

T. But that's what you believe.

C. Yeah, I do believe it, but I don't know how to overcome it.

Shyness, and all the other names it goes under, really means being overly fearful of doing or saying the "wrong" thing and/or not looking as you "should." What is meant by "wrong" or "should" depends on your own definition. The most important thing to understand here is why you are overly fearful or anxious. The answer is that *others may criticize or not like you, and then you foolishly rate yourself as a rotten person.* You think that others *must* accept you and view you in a favorable light. This *irrational demand for perfection lies behind extreme shyness.* It is your *demanding* perfect behavior, looks, or some other trait that leads to self-downing. You have the idea, "If I have a lousy *trait,*" (which just about all of us do) "I am, therefore, a lousy *person.*" This is a false idea, as you will see as we return to the session.

T.   Ask yourself a simple question: "How does my defect, whatever it is, make me less of a person?" "How does a defect of any kind make me a rotten person?"

C.   Because it's a weakness.

T.   Well, how does a weakness make *you* weak? You, for example, might have a blackness on your skin, perhaps a mole or something like that. Does that make you black?

C.   Of course not.

T.   Well, then how does a weakness make *you* completely weak for all time? Because when you have a weakness you say, "I *am* a weakling," which is an overgeneralization. "I have a weakness right now and that means I'll *always* be a weakling." Well, how is it possible for you to predict that?

C.   I'm always condemning myself for doing certain things.

T.   But condemning yourself is what we're talking about, because it's another way of saying, "I am rotten if my act is rotten." Now give me a rotten act that you do, for example.

C.   I guess I'm passive at times.

T.   All right. "I would like to ask X for something but I'm afraid."

C.   Yeah, I'd like to be more aggressive but sometimes I don't know how to go about it.

T.   Well, aggressive might mean hostile, so I don't like the word. You mean, you'd like to be more assertive—"I'd like to express myself, to ask for what I want, tell people what I don't want to do." A guy asks you to go to bed with him, and you would like to say "No" or something like that. And "If I meet a guy and I want to go with him,

I'd like to ask him for his number, be assertive. And right now I'm less assertive than I'd like." Right?

C. Yeah, right.

T. So that's a handicap, that's a deficiency. Now how does that make *you* a deficient person?

The key lesson here is: *You do not equal your trait.* This is a simple yet profound key to reducing shyness. Most of us tend to overgeneralize and jump over the bounds of logic by believing that "If something about my *appearance* or my *performance* is defective, then *I* am defective." This implies that "I should (must) act or look perfectly, or else I can't accept myself."

C. I *should* be stronger.

T. Oh, wait a minute, wait a minute! Where'd you get the *should?*

C. I should accept myself as being the way that I am?

T. I'd *better,* not I *should.* Do you realize that *should* is almost always wrong? Because *should* means "I've *got* to, and if I don't do what I've got to, I'm no good!" Let me give you a simple illustration. It shows what human disturbance is, and it's a very good model. You go out of here in a half-hour and you say to yourself, "I'd like ten dollars in my purse, because I might want to take a cab, go to the movies, or eat something. I really *wish,* I *want* it, I *prefer* to have ten dollars." You then look in your purse and you have only nine. Now how do you feel? You'd prefer ten but you have nine. How would you feel?

C. That I'd like to have another dollar. Uh—disappointed.

T. Only disappointed?

C. Yeah, disappointed.

T. You wouldn't be happy?

C. No.

T. And you wouldn't be indifferent?

C. No, not at all.

T. You wouldn't be depressed or suicidal?

C. No, definitely not.

T. So you'd be *disappointed* and that's appropriate, "I'd like X, I have X minus 1, and I'm disappointed." Okay, suppose you are going out a second time and this time you devoutly believe, "I *must,* I *should,* I've *got* to have at least ten dollars. Not one hundred, not two hundred, but at least ten. I *must* have a guarantee of always having a minimum of ten." Again, you look in your purse and again you find nine. How would you then feel?

C. Terrible. Destroyed.

T. Yes, destroyed. "I don't have what I *must*, I don't have what I *should!*" You'd be anxious, destroyed, and maybe hostile. "The world's not giving me what I *must* have!" But mind you, it's the same nine dollars. It isn't the missing dollar that's upsetting you. One time you have nine and you're *disappointed.* The other time you have nine dollars and you're *destroyed* and *hostile.* Because of the *must.* As soon as you escalate a *preference* into a *must,* you make yourself anxious or depressed.

C. Yes, I can see that.

T. Now let's go one step further. You're still saying, "I *must,* I absolutely *must,* at all times have at least ten dollars"—the same hypothesis. And then you look in your pocket and you have eleven. Now how would you feel?

C. Great.

T. For how long? That's the right answer, but for how long?

C. Until I need the ten dollars again or until I use the eleven up.

T. No, even before that you would feel anxious. You still have the eleven dollars. You *have* to have at least ten and you have one more; but you're still anxious. Why?

C. After you spend it?

T. No, let's suppose you don't spend it. You're still anxious.

C. Why are you still anxious?

T. Because you're going to say to yourself, "Suppose I *spend* two, suppose I *lose* two, suppose I get *robbed?*" You see?

C. Yeah.

T. Because you know the world is such that you might *not* have ten dollars a minute from now. Right now you have eleven. That's great and you're happy. But how do you know you're going to keep it?

C. Yeah, I don't.

T. Whenever you set up a *must, a should,* an *ought,* or a *got to,* you're miserable when you *don't* have what you think you must and you will probably be miserable even when you *do.* Do you see that?

C. Yes.

T. A *should* equals a *must,* you see. "I should" means two things: One, "It would be better," and two, "Therefore, I *must!*" That's what the word means. Now that's what you're also saying about yourself. One, "It would be nice if I didn't have flaws, if I were perfect." And that's okay because that's not going to get you into trouble. But then you're saying; two, "And I *must* be perfect." Now how would you feel if you were not perfect?

C. Terrible.

T. Unless you arrange to be perfect. But is that likely?

C. No.

T. Suppose I wave a wand, a magic wand, and I wave it and you become perfect. You look gorgeous. Your body is exactly the way you want it. Your mind is brilliant. You're charming. Just like that, you're perfect! Now, for a while, you'll be happy. But what will you say to yourself after an hour or two? If you're perfect at this moment, what are you going to think a little later?

C. That I really couldn't be perfect.

T. No, let's suppose you know you're perfect.

C. How long will it last?

T. That's right. At this moment the therapist made me perfect with his magic wand. My breasts are the right size, my hips are marvelous, my height is great. But what is going to happen to me tomorrow? Do you know?

C. No.

T. Of course not. You're asking for two impossible things. First, "That I be perfect *right now*," which is not going to happen because you're fallible, you're human. And, second, "That I *always* remain perfect."

As the ten-dollar example illustrates, *when you demand perfection, you will down yourself and feel miserable when you spot an imperfection.* Even if you now feel you are perfect, which is unlikely, you will become anxious over the possibility that tomorrow you may not be. Your demanding, which RET calls *shoulditis* or *musturbation,* leads to a no-win situation. As an antidote, you can vigorously challenge your ideas that (1) "I *must* appear perfect to myself and others;" (2) "It is *awful* if I don't;" and (3) "I am a *rotten person* if I have flaws." *Question these beliefs* by asking for evidence to support them, and you will see how irrational and self-defeating they are. *Act against these beliefs* by pushing yourself to do whatever it is you are insecure about doing—such as meeting new people, asserting yourself, or going for an interview. You will then begin to accept yourself with your imperfections. Enormously fearing other peoples' opinions and thereby making yourself anxious and unassertive is quite the opposite of striving for personal happiness. Often people will not approve of your looks or behavior, but you don't *have to* take them too seriously. *You decide if there is some merit to their criticism, and act accordingly. Negatively rating yourself, your totality, is why you fear criticism and demand perfection.*

C. I try to accept myself for being the way that I am.

T. All right. But what's the hassle?

C. I'm not happy with myself the way I am.

T. Well, we don't want you to be happy with your negative traits. We want you to be dissatisfied with *them,* but not with *yourself.* Name one of your traits you really don't like.

C. How about lack of assertiveness. I mentioned it earlier.

T. All right, let's take lack of assertiveness. Unassertiveness means, "I'd like to ask people for things I want but if I do, they may disapprove of me and I *can't stand* that." Now why can't you stand disapproval? Suppose you asked a man you really liked for something. You said, "Will you go to the museum with me?" And he said, "No, I won't go! People who go to museums are stupid!" Now why must you take that seriously!

C. Because I feet that he wouldn't want to be with me.

T. Well, suppose he said, "No, let's not go to the museum, let's go home and screw." Then how would you feel? He refused to go to the museum with you but he would gladly screw you. How would you take that?

C. That he just wanted my body. I would feel *awful.*

T. You see, you're putting yourself down. Let's suppose that he really liked your body and he didn't even know you. All he wanted to do was screw you. He's a male, and males frequently will go for your body. They hardly know you at all, and they might not even like your traits, but they want to screw you. Now how does that make *you* a worm if they only want your body?

C. Because they should want more than that.

T. Notice the *should.* They *should* want you for your personality, your mind, but they don't. Maybe they're sexually indiscriminate. Maybe you have a marvelous personality and mind, but they're only interested in your genitals. So you conclude, "If they don't like my mind, I'm a rotten person," instead of, "That's their taste. They're obsessed with sex."

C. I'd think that there must be something wrong with me.

T. But why must there be? Why can't it be *their* taste that they only go for women's bodies and not give much of a damn for their minds or personality? Some men only want to screw; that's all they enjoy.

As soon as they see a woman, they don't care how stupid or bright she is. They only want to screw her. Now why does that mean there's something wrong with you?

C. It doesn't, I guess.

T. But you're saying, "If I were really noble, and great, and charming, they would want me for my mind."

C. Right.

T. But you're forgetting *them*. It's *their* taste. They may only pay attention to your mind *after* they screw you—which is true of many men. They're very excited. They look at your breasts and your ass, and right away they get an erection. And they say, "Oh boy, what a great piece she is!" And if you went to bed with them, some of them will really enjoy your mind and like you for it. But some won't. Now how does that prove *you're* no good?

C. It's their problem, I guess.

T. That's the point! You're not really facing that; that *they* have certain tastes. Suppose I meet you socially and I say to myself right away, "Oh damn, dark eyes. I really like blue!" and I completely reject you. Let's say I even say to you, "Oh, you have dark eyes. I only go for blue-eyed women." You're going to feel rejected, assuming that you like me. Right?

C. Yeah.

T. But does it really mean anything about *you*?

C. No, I don't think so.

T. Is it a flaw to have dark eyes? The next man you meet might mainly like you *because* you have dark eyes. He thrills to dark eyes, but I happen to like blue. Now how does my preference for blue eyes make you into a nothing?

C. No reason.

Some people, of either sex, might be interested in you only because of your body, eye color, or type of car. If so, don't jump to the false conclusion, "Something is wrong with me." Instead, recognize that people have individual tastes and may like you or not like you for a great variety of reasons. If you believe "People *must* like me as a 'person,' before being interested in me sexually," and then down yourself when they don't follow your rule, you ignore human nature and demand that people act differently from the way they often do. Holding on to your rule will only lead to self-downing and anger at others. Surely a miserable state of affairs!

T. Suppose you're going to a party with your male friend.

C. If I don't know anyone there, I get very nervous and I clam up.

T. Because, "If I say the wrong thing—"

C. They'll think I'm stupid.

T. Well, suppose they do.

C. Well, I don't want them to think that way.

T. Well, that's undesirable, but will it really *destroy* you?

C. Maybe.

T. How will it? Let's suppose you go to this party and you say exactly the wrong thing, and everybody there thinks, "What an idiot she is!" Now how will that *destroy* you?

C. Because I want to make a good impression.

T. Fine. But you're believing, "I've *got* to make a good impression."

C. Because I want people to think highly of me.

T. You mean, "I *need* it!" You see, you're not being honest with yourself. You're not admitting that you don't have *wants* about approval. If you want an ice cream cone, that's a want; and if you don't get it you say, Tough! So I'm not getting it." But your search for approval is a dire *need.* You're falsely saying "I *want*" when you really mean "I *need.*" Now unless you see that you have made this into a dire need and change it back to only a desire, you will continue to be anxious.

C. I see what you mean.

T. Most of the people you'll meet at the party are strangers whom you'll never see again. Right?

C. Yeah.

T. And the irony is as long as you have your *need* for approval, you're probably going to appear anxious; and they might say to themselves, "She's a weak, anxious person. How inadequate!" Some of them will. A lot of them will just say, "She doesn't talk well." But some of them will say, "She's a total slob because she doesn't talk well!"

C. I don't talk. I keep still.

T. Then some will believe, "She's dull, she's stupid, she can't talk." Which is not true, because you're talking very well to me. You're quite articulate right now because you're talking about your problem and you're not *focusing* on whether I like you. Isn't that true?

C. Yes. I want help from you but really don't care if you like me.

T. You obviously can do it. But as soon as you say to yourself, "The therapist *must* like me!" rather than "I *want* him to but he doesn't *have* to," you're going to go dumb even with me. So try to acknowledge your need rather than wrongly calling it a *desire*.

C. But why do I so easily escalate my desire for approval into a dire need or necessity?

T. Most people are born and reared with a strong tendency to create a dire need for approval. This is a natural, nutty, human condition. It has relatively little to do with upbringing, but upbringing makes it worse. This is the way you *easily* think and feel. Why do most people over 40 get fat? Because that's their biological tendency. Now they don't *have* to gain too much weight. Nobody *has* to overeat. But they *easily* do it. You are probably a natural perfectionist who normally *escalates your wants into needs.* And you'd better fight this tendency and keep fighting it because you're quite able to do so and to become a person who ultimately wants *without* needing.

C. Well, how do you go about doing that?

T. By first acknowledging your necessitizing. Don't say to yourself, "I'm not talking up at parties because I *want* people's approval." That's a lie. Admit the truth—"I *need*, or *think* I need, their approval." That's step number one. Look at your *got tos*, your *have tos*, your *musts*, your *shoulds*, your *oughts*, your *needs*. Then, as soon as you observe one, immediately ask yourself, "Why the hell do I *have* to win their approval?" Now what's the answer.

C. Well, in certain situations when I want something, I honestly feel that I do have to.

T. But you see! You just gave the *wrong* answer. "When I really *want* something, I *have* to have it." You're like a two-year-old. The two-year-old thinks she has to have a red lollipop and stubbornly rebels against accepting an orange one even if that's the only one available. Now does she really *have* to have the red lollipop?

C. No.

T. She *thinks* she does. Now aren't you in the same position?

C. I guess so.

T. And, incidentally, if she doesn't have the red lollipop and she thinks she *has* to have it, what happens?

C. She'll start crying.

T. She'll make herself terribly upset. But is it the lollipop; is it her desire for the lollipop which is upsetting her?

C. No.

T. It's her *dire need*. And you're not facing your needs, not trying to give them up. Even when I was questioning you, do you see how you were hanging on to them?

The demand, the need for approval, is the core-problem in shyness. Desiring approval is fine and will only lead to disappointment if approval is not attained. But when you escalate a desire or a wish into a *demand* or *need,* you will be anxious about doing something and depressed or angry when you haven't met your goal for approval. When you tell yourself you *must* be liked at a party, you ironically make yourself anxious and are thus *less* likely to succeed.

You often refrain from going after what you want for fear others will not think well of you. And you then take others' neglect as "proof" of your worthlessness. A key thing to remember is: *Be yourself, don't try to prove yourself.*

The client in the following case is a 31-year-old male teacher. He fears being dominated by those close to him, which is directly related (as you will see) to insecurity, lack of assertiveness, and feelings of inadequacy. This case shows how such negative feelings can affect one's social and family relationships, and what one can do to become less susceptible to being, or feeling, dominated.

T. (Reading from client's form) "Difficulty in dealing with my brother and mother, run from relationships." All right, which one do you want to start with?

C. Run from relationships.

T. All right, you've never been involved, or you have been involved?

C. I have not been involved.

T. What's the pattern of your dating normally?

C. I date a girl who is safe for me. One that is not very attractive, one that I can screw easily, so that it's almost a nonrelatable type of girl. Because I say, "Well, she's not for me, and I don't like her that much because of her looks, but she'll screw, and that's as far as I want to go." That's one type of relationship, sexual. The other type is with someone whom I just won't touch. It's a nonsexual involvement. In other words, I categorize my women into sexual and nonsexual.

T. Why won't you touch these others? What's stopping you from touching them?

C. I believe that they'll get to like me more, and I'll get into a relationship. This scares me.

T. What are you afraid will happen?

C. That my mother won't be happy. This happened when I almost got involved with a certain girl, which is the problem. I enter into an area that gets scary.

T. But we're trying to find out *why* it is scary. Is it mainly your mother, that your mother is going to object to practically every woman that you get involved with? Is that what you're saying? And, therefore, you don't want to see her upset and you withdraw? Is that the reason, or is it something else? Suppose this woman had been acceptable to your mother. Would you then have withdrawn from her?

C. Yeah.

T. Because? What would *then* have been dangerous? You're *inventing* some danger. What would it be?

C. The real thing is that I'm scared they'll like me.

T. And if they do?

C. If they do, that means I may get married.

T. So, "If I get married—" Let's just assume that you *do*.

C. Okay, if I get married I will lose my identity.

T. How will you lose your identity if you get married?

C. I will not have any say.

T. Why is that so? You'll hurt her by refusing what she wants? She'll dominate you? Is that it?

C. Well, the domination point is part of it. I feel kind of weak in my own opinions. Thus, if I get into a relationship, I feel that I will be just knocked right out. I just will be taken over. I will be dominated, and my feelings will just not be considered.

T. As you are by your mother, for example? Are you dominated by your mother?

C. Yeah, I am.

T. And by your brother?

C. Yeah.

T. Well, let's suppose they thought poorly of you. They disapprove of what you do. Why do you have to take their views so seriously?

C. Because it's a habit.

T. Because you don't *stop* this habit and say, "Screw it! I am going to accept myself no matter who thinks what of me." And you have the belief, "Other people are correct if they think I am a worm, and it's awful if they think I am!"—It's that *belief* that leads to your weakness, your willingness to let women dominate you. You see that?

C. I'm not sure.

T.   It's really your belief, "I need people's approval," that makes you so dominatable and as long as you have that belief, you will be afraid that women whom you care for will subject you and not consider your feelings.

C.   And I'd better not marry any woman except a weakling who won't dominate me. But then I'll get bored with her, so that won't work out.

T.   Yes. Your problem is to become firm. And the main way you're going to become stronger is by not giving *that much* of a damn what people, including women, think of you.

As the client has shown, when one has the problem of feeling weak and in danger of being dominated by others, this negatively affects many types of relationships. The core problem here, as in the previous case of shyness, is a *demand for approval.* The client is afraid that significant others will disapprove of his choices and will think badly of him; and that he, in turn, will then think badly of himself. He, therefore, will tend to do what *others* want him to and to please them rather than himself. This is what we generally mean by being "dominated" by others, and it is often opposed to choosing your personal happiness. The *thinking* part of challenging your fear of involvement includes *forcefully disputing* your irrational Beliefs (iBs) by asking for objective evidence to support them: These Beliefs usually are: 1) "I *must* have my partner's approval of what I do or say!" 2) "It is *awful* when, and I *can't stand* it if, I don't get that approval!" 3) "If my partner thinks badly of me, that proves that I am *a rotten person who does not really deserve to be happy.*"

Ask yourself the following questions: 1) "Although it is *nice* to have others' approval, where is the evidence that I *must* have what would be nice? After all, it would be nice to have a million dollars also but I hardly *need* it!" 2) "Although there are *disadvantages* to being disapproved of, why would it be *awful* or *horrible,* and where is the evidence that I *can't stand* it? Would I shrivel up and die?" 3) "How can someone's thinking badly of me ever prove that I am a *rotten person?*" Questions such as these, if asked with vigor, will help you see how irrational your beliefs are. The *behaving or acting part of disputing* your fear of involvement consists of practicing speaking your own mind and doing what you want to do even when your chosen partner may disapprove of you and reject you.

T.   Apparently all the therapy you had still hasn't helped you to look at your demand for approval, because I doubt whether it's been philosophic.

C. What do you mean?

T. It showed you all kinds of things about yourself, right?

C. Yeah.

T. But those things aren't why you're disturbed. They had practically nothing to do with your rating yourself as a person. Do you know why?

C. No.

T. Let's suppose you know all those things about yourself—your childhood, your past, and all the things you probably went through in life. Why would this knowledge do you little good? Suppose you now have insight and realize that when you were three, your mother looked at you cross-eyed and said, "You're terrible," and you hated her and loathed yourself. Why would that knowledge not change you?

C. Because I still have the habit of looking for approval.

T. Because you *still* have a three-year-old philosophy: "I *need* my mother's and other people's approval!" Until you give that up a thousand times—not merely understand that you have it but *attack* it and *give it up*—it'll always be around. You see, it's your *belief* that upsets you, *not* your experiences with your mother. And your strong tendency is to say, "I *need* people's approval, and if I stand firm, they won't approve of me" which is partially true. Some of them won't. But you go beyond that observation to the irrational Belief, "Wouldn't it be *horrible* if they didn't?" And you're not questioning that belief, are you?

C. No.

T. Well, you'd better! And the way to work against it is to get involved, especially with a "dominating" woman, and then to hold firm. How can she dominate you? How can she really rule you?

C. Yeah. It's amazing how I've stayed clear of those women.

T. Because you're convinced that they would *have to* dominate you. But let's suppose that a woman really was very dominating—most really aren't, but let's suppose she was. And suppose that if you got close to her, she would try to run you by the nose. You wouldn't have to *let* her, would you?

C. No, I wouldn't.

T. But how are you going to know that, unless you risk it?

C. Yeah. I see that.

T. And if you told me right now that you know a very dominating woman, that she's quite attractive to you, and that you're afraid she will make you do everything she wants, I'd say, "Try to get involved with her. Get some *practice* in relating to her and standing firm. For if you run away from a thing all your life, you're never going to get practice in coping."

Insight into your past, although it can be interesting, will do little to help you recognize and work against self-defeating beliefs. *These beliefs are behind your disturbed feelings and actions and lead to increased emotional pain* and decreased happiness. Doing what you fear, such as dating "dominating" partners, is a key way to work against irrational beliefs, because you begin to see that you don't *have* to be dominated, and that you *can* risk disapproval.

C. Regarding clothes—I want to buy my own and pick them out myself. I don't like my brother giving me a suit and won't wear it if he does. He's my same size and thinks I should love to wear his cast-offs.

T. That's okay to refuse, as long as you don't *overly* rebel and say to yourself "I'm not going to wear the suit *because* he gave it to me." "I'm not going to wear it because it's not my style," is very different. You see the difference? Suppose your brother just happened to buy a suit you like? Does he wear the same size as you?

C. Yeah.

T. Let's suppose, for some reason or another, his woman friend hates this fine suit so he won't wear it. It's just your size and you like it. Why would you refuse it, if that's so?

C. Well, he did give me one suit I really liked. But I had it in the closet for months and I fought him about it. "I don't want it, I don't want it!" Finally, one day I put it on and I wore it. At that time I think my head was in good shape.

T. Right. Because you were saying, "Do I *like* this suit?" And not, "Who gave it to me?" If he gives you a suit, there's no magic about his giving it that makes him run you by the nose.

C. He had a sexual problem once where he couldn't get a hard on. Okay, so he used to tell me this. So all of a sudden I couldn't get a hard on either.

T. Well, that's self-suggestion, probably. "If my brother can't get it up, maybe I won't be able to either." And then you don't because you're worried about it.

C. So that has set a rebellion in motion in my head, by my saying, "I don't want to know anything about you or do anything you want."

T. But that's *over*rebellion. You think—wrongly—that just by hearing about his doings, you will automatically become overinfluenced. So you make yourself afraid to hear anything about him.

As is the case with this client, when you feel that you are weak and that, therefore, others dominate you, you may compensate by swinging all the way over in the other direction. This leads to over- rebellion (frequently seen in adolescents), which means you're trying to do the *opposite* of what others want, even when what they ask you to do would be beneficial. This behavior is based upon the irrational idea, "If I do *anything* they want me to do, I will surely become hopelessly dominated by them."

C. With women, I feel the need for support before I can stand up to them.

T. But again you're saying, "I can't do it myself." But you *can* run your own life. You're quite able to take chances and risks, stand up to people, and go with so-called dominating females. And if things get rough, you can just calmly hold your ground. You don't have to rebel, but just hold your ground and do what you want to do. And if they don't like it, that's tough! So they don't like it! The point is not to do things because others do them, and not to *not* do them because others do them. Just find out "What do *I* want," and take a chance on that. And if it works out, great, and if it doesn't, too bad! "I'll do something else." You'd better take risks, and you're avoiding them—especially emotional risks.

C. But the big risk is that I came in here to see you, and I'm happy that I did.

T. Right! What's the worst thing that could have happened to you, seeing me?

C. You could have been a screamer who yelled at me.

T. But let's suppose I did yell at you. "You're a ninny! You've had all this therapy, and you're still kissing people's asses!" Suppose I yelled at you like that? Then what would have happened? Let's suppose that I was even right, that you were acting inadequately, and I said, "You're a dumb cluck! You *shouldn't* behave like that!" How could my yelling affect you?

C. Well, by my inside feeling that I'm a dumb cluck.

T. By your *agreeing* with me that you were. There's no other way I can affect you.

C. Yeah, by my agreeing.

T. That's right. Your *agreement,* which *you* control. You don't control me. I can call you every name under the sun, and you can't stop me. But you do control your agreeing with me. When a child, a two-year-old child, listens to his mother, the problem is not so much what she tells him: "You're no good! You're a louse! You *shouldn't* do this!" It's his nutty *agreeing* with her. And then he *continues* agreeing with her for the next 20 years. That's what's affecting him, *not* what she did or said.

C. His agreeing.

T. That's right. The same thing goes with your brother, your mother, and with other females, if you feel awful because they say you're no good, you're *agreeing* with them. They can say exactly the same thing, and you can tell yourself, "Well, maybe they're right about my behavior, but I'm not a worm for doing it. So I *acted* crummily. Now how am I going to *change* these acts?" You never have to put *yourself* down, no matter who says what. Suppose the whole world says you're a dummy. They'd all be wrong. Now do you know why they'd be wrong?

C. Because I don't have to agree with them.

T. And because there are no dummies. They may be right about your poor behavior, but to call *you* worthless labels you as a person who can *only* and *always* engage in dumb behavior. It also means that your *totality,* your *essence,* is damnable, contemptible. And that's a nutty idea. No human, including you, is contemptible. Your *behavior* may stink, but *you're* no *stinker.* Do you see the difference between those two views?

C. Yeah, I am not what I *do.*

T. Right! And some people will damn you, there's no doubt about that. They'll put *you* down when a few of your *acts* are incompetent. That's *their* craziness.

C. This is the basic meat of my problem. If a person says something bad about me, I agree.

T. Right. Instead of saying, "Well, he might be right about my deed or trait. I did that job foolishly, but I am never a rotten person. I'm a *person who did a rotten job.* What the hell am I going to do next time to do a better job? You can't rate *me*, I'm too complex, I'm an ongoing process." You can't rate *a process,* you can't rate a *human.* You can only rate his or her deeds, acts, performances. And you're spending your whole life rating *yourself* instead of rating your *behavior.*

C.   Yeah, I'm my own worst enemy.

T.   Right. You rate your traits, and you say, "That was good or that was bad," which is correct. Because you want to do better in life, do things more efficiently. But then you foolishly tell yourself, "If my traits stink then *I'm* no good. If my traits are good, *I* am a great person." They're both incorrect. You cannot really rate humans; you can only rate their acts. People are processes, like the process of evolution. *You can't rate a process.* Another way of saying this is: You can rate your acts, but you can't rate *that which acts*—you. Humans are born and reared with this nutty tendency to give themselves a report card; and you've indulged in this tendency all your life. It's hard not to do it because it is a strong tendency. When you meet a woman, you're not merely saying, "Would it be enjoyable to me to be with her?" You're saying, "Can I *succeed*? Suppose she dominates me! Suppose I fall on my face! That would be horrible! I'd be a slob!" So you make your relationship with her too "dangerous."

The previous dialogue represents a most important lesson in overcoming your shyness, insecurity, and fear of domination. Your *acts* can be legitimately rated but your *person,* your *self,* cannot be. Fear of disapproval stems from *agreeing* with the idea that you, the total person, can be rated on the basis of one or several of your many deeds and traits.

We wish to make it clear that we are not advocating a policy of not caring at all about people's opinions, since there are real advantages to having certain people like us. What we are advocating is a philosophy that leads to that golden mean between the extremes; namely that you *desire* rather than *demand* approval and that you attempt to please significant others *only at certain times* (such as when you love them or want to get something from them). We question your *compulsively* and *invariantly* striving to please them.

C.   Sometimes I feel it's dangerous to see a "strong" woman.

T.   The "danger" is that she might try to dominate you; and you'd better either hold your ground and refuse to be her slave—or else get away. That's all that would happen, if you weren't telling yourself, "Yes, she's right! I am a worm who should be dominated, and she's got my number! So I'll let her put a ring through my nose for the rest of my life." If we can get you to see your *agreement* with people who put you down, to listen to their name-calling but refuse to agree with it, you would then be undominatable. Your *agreement,* and not their putting you down, enslaves you.

C. Only now am I beginning to realize that I am allowed to have my own opinions.

T. Right. *You* allow yourself to. The universe doesn't care one way or the other whether you have your own opinions or kiss others' asses. But *you choose* to either kiss their asses and adopt their views or to stand on your own feet and hold your own opinions. If others don't like your views, tough! You can always find some people who do.

C. And there are a lot of people out there.

T. Right! And there are lots of women, some of whom won't see you for dust, especially if you're firm and strong. But others will think you're great that way. Why not go through enough of them until you find those who don't need to be dominating?

C. Yeah, it's my choice.

T. Right, your choice. That's what you'd better tell yourself a thousand times. *Your* decision, *your* choice. It's their choice to try to dominate you and your choice, which you can always take, to stand firm.

C. I guess I've chosen so far to stay and be dominated—and then make myself angry. Or to cravenly run away.

T. Yes, and even when you do run, you don't have to put yourself down. Instead of, "Suppose I let them dominate me. What a weakling I'd be!" you could tell yourself, "Suppose I let them dominate me, I'll then stand firm and go back to my own views." You always have a choice. Also: "If they won't stop being so dominating, I'll leave the relationship."

C. I see. But I had to flee from this last girl before I really gave the relationship a chance. The pain of being dominated was too much. The pressure started to build up.

T. But it was *your* pressure. You *let her* dominate you, which you didn't have to do. And then you told yourself, "I'm a weakling!" which you weren't. You were a human being who acted weakly some of the time. And you probably said to yourself, "If I let this relationship continue, I won't be able to escape!" Nonsense! Of course, you're able to escape. You can always escape, even if you are legally married to a would-be dominating woman!

The key point here is that you can choose to become assertive and to achieve personal freedom and happiness rather than to make yourself insecure, self-downing, and "dominatable." Ironically, most people will tend to have more respect for you when you stand firm; and *you have the right to seek out this type of person*. Assertiveness is a sort of middle ground between (1) always doing what others want to gain their "needed" approval, and (2) aggression, in which you believe that others have no rights and must behave as you wish. Assertiveness simply means seeking what you want and avoiding what you don't want, without downing yourself or others.

These two cases have demonstrated some of the problems associated with having a belief system based on the *need* for approval and the demand for perfection. This type of belief system, and the self-downing that goes with it, leads to the feelings and behaviors we call shyness, insecurity, fear of asserting oneself. If you suffer from those problems, your solution lies in (1) *forcefully attacking* the irrational beliefs we have mentioned and (2) *acting against* these beliefs by practicing contradictory behaviors. This will help you to a more secure (no self-rating) existence, and to achieving considerably more personal happiness.

CHAPTER 16

ACCEPTANCE OF PERSONAL UNCERTAINTY AND PROBABILITY

EDITOR'S COMMENTARY:

According to Ellis's theory, there are no certainties in the world. Despite that reality, argued Ellis, transpersonal psychotherapists try to convince clients that there is absolute certainty. Ellis argued that this was tantamount to teaching a client to function and believe in irrationalities. For example, Ellis stated that absolutist therapists might argue that fortune tellers were credible because what they said sometimes came true. What the person may not realize is that by the very act of belief what the person wishes to come true may come true because at some level she is working to make it so. This argument is akin to Ellis's strategy regarding imagery for stress reduction and for goal attainment (one technique shared with solution-focus therapists such as O'Hanlon). Ellis concluded this selection by showing how he helped clients accept uncertainty and be happy anyway. He doubted that many religionists could actually "let go" and unconditionally accept themselves because their beliefs tended to be extra-personal. Ellis was not confronted with the counter-arguments to his arguments that relied on rhetoric. For example, to say that there are no certainties in life is to invoke certainty to reach this conclusion: it inherently denies what it explicitly affirms. On pragmatic grounds, however, Ellis concluded that religion and some extra-self beliefs could be helpful for some people in order to overcome irrational disturbance and to accept themselves—more or less!

Evolution of a Revolution

Excerpted from *Why Some Therapies Don't Work,*
Prometheus Books, 1989

In order to reduce human neuroses, most schools of psychotherapy seek to help people increase their acceptance of life's probabilities and uncertainties. Thus, clients learn to accept that life is not, or need not be, totally predictable or "knowable." They learn to accept life's natural ambiguities and even the tentativeness of their own existence. Clients experience minimal anxiety by surrendering their demands for certitude. They abandon their "need" for guarantees in a life full of inexactitude. They thereby reduce their depression, rage, and horror.

Rational-emotive therapy holds that, as far as is known, there are no absolute certainties in the world (Ellis, 1973a, 1983b, 1988). On the contrary, RET views life through more realistic and objective lenses and sees it, instead, as replete with uncertainty. It is, therefore, only with high (or low) degrees of probability, and not with 100 percent assurance, that various things can be known or accomplished.

Despite the omnipresence of uncertainty, indeterminacy, and dubiosity, people, especially those with fanatical or mystical penchants, demand that they must have Absolute Knowledge and, contrary to a lack of supporting evidence, assert that it is, in fact, obtainable. Such individuals believe that they *need* complete certainty and that they especially need certain or absolute "meaning" in their lives. They refuse to accept that, as far as one can empirically, logically, or realistically determine, there is *no* cosmic or sacrosanct meaning. Yet, people continue dogmatically to embrace their unrealistic demands for certitude (Ellis, 1962, 1973a, 1983b, 1987b, 1987d, 1988). Rational-emotive therapy helps them to become secure by accepting insecurity and ambiguity and by giving up their irrational demands for total meaning and certainty.

While RET asserts that it is not only unrealistic but also dysfunctional to demand or command anything from life, transpersonal psychology insists that it is actually good for people to have incontrovertible faith and dogmatic conviction in unchangeable absolutes. To prove that certainty is attainable, and since they believe that it is functional to "know" it, transpersonal devotees often blindly convince themselves that, despite nonexistent and disconfirming data, phenomena such as ESP, ghosts, fortune-telling, psychic surgery, elves, fairies, goblins, astrology, voodoo, and other paranormal experiences exist (Agena, 1983; All Together, Now: Meditate, 1985; Asimov, 1984; Fichten,

1984; Gardner, 1986; Hansel, 1984; Harper, 1983, Kurtz, 1985a, 1986a).

Transpersonalists' dogmatic demand for certainty is also evident in many of their case scenarios. Consider a case cited by Fritz (1984). Desperate for certainty, two pregnant women at Fritz's workshop on creating the ideal birth stoutly claimed to have had telepathic contact with their unborn children. Most of the other workshop participants believed them!

The preponderance of the transpersonalists' need for certainty is also evident in more common, everyday examples. Witness, alas, the many astrologists, fortune-tellers, and tarot-card readers that one can find by merely thumbing through the *Yellow Pages*. Since advertising in the *Yellow Pages* and in local town newspapers is expensive, we may assume that these "sages" are making enough money to cover their carrying costs. This illustrates the demand for such services in our American population. If Nancy and Ronald Reagan take these seers seriously enough to let them influence political decisions (Regan, 1988), why should not all the rest of us indulge in this kind of certainty seeking?

Typically, "seers" seem to make reasonable incomes from ostensibly reading the futures of their clientele. Unbeknown to these clients, however, soothsayers typically offer them "Barnum" statements that can apply to anyone. These general statements are similar to those seen in newspaper horoscope columns. However, the naive believer sees that they "clearly" predict his or her personal life and, therefore, concludes that they are "indubitably" valid and accurate.

Other "evidence" used to support the "validity" of fortune-telling is that the predicted future sometimes actually comes true. While general predictions may often prove accurate for just about anyone (since they are in fact *general*), some others are realized by means of self-fulfilling prophesies. By merely believing that something will come true, we may unconsciously and inadvertently make it come true. As a result, fortune-tellers make a great deal of money by exploiting people's irrational beliefs that they *must* know their fates and that the uncertainty of *not* knowing is unbearable. Rather than helping their devotees to modify or restructure such irrationalities, many transpersonalists reinforce these fallacious notions of needing certainty to secure their own personal gains.

Individuals who demand intellectual certainty also tend to demand emotional certainty or the guarantee that they will always be in total control of their feelings. They avoid losing complete emotional control by using distraction strategies, such as compulsively reciting a mantra or by denying that they feel anxiety. Rather than teaching their clients how to minimize their self-defeating emotional reactions, transpersonal psychotherapists encourage emotional "control" that turns off emotions. As a result, clients fail to experience appropriate emotional highs and lows and, instead, often strive to feel "calmness" or "nothing." Please remember that *Nirvana* does not mean *bliss* (as many Americans wrongly believe) but *desirelessness*. And who can be happy in *that* state?!

Although some devout religionists, mystics, and true believers can superficially "let go" and "be themselves" (Ellis, 1972c), many of them believe that they must always have thorough control over themselves and the universe. They feel terrorized by any potential emotional looseness, opting for extreme stoic, asocial, and flat existences. They will not allow themselves to feel and express emotions freely and spontaneously because they cannot be absolutely sure of the outcome of these experiences. They often believe that they must always be completely controlled. Rational-emotive therapy, on the other hand, not only helps people minimize their emotional disturbances, but also helps them to become more emotionally alive. By encouraging people to develop vital and absorbing interests, as will be discussed later, it encourages them to achieve emotional heights, rather than extremes of disturbing affect or no affect (Ellis, 1985, 1988; Ellis & Becker, 1982).

Whereas RET helps clients accept an uncertain and often unpredictable world, transpersonal psychologists deny that the world is actually an uncertain place and that accepting this is valuable. Rather, they argue that certainty can be known and that such absolute knowledge is attainable through paranormal means. Rational-emotive therapists encourage clients to perceive, interpret, and evaluate the world logically and empirically. Transpersonalists abjure this kind of realism and practicality (Barron, 1987; Bhatty, 1987; Bufe, 1987; Ehrlich, 1986; Kinzer, 1987; Gusic, 1988).

Ironically, when transpersonalists accept uncertainty and probability, they try to prove that *anything* goes and that therefore mysticism is "true" and "valid" (Capra, 1983; Ferguson, 1980). As Wilczek and Devine (1988) indicate, linking Taoist mysticism and parapsychological mumbo-jumbo "is a pernicious idea, which has led many good minds wildly astray." Restivo (1983) also attacks Capra's (1983) claims that there are parallels between modern physics and ancient mysticism.

Selections from the Writings of Albert Ellis Ph.D.

Most major schools of psychotherapy emphasize some degree of free will and personal choice, though the idea of complete determinism has been practically abandoned in modern psychology. Although biological and genetic limits on human potential and personality exist, people are not necessarily totally governed by their physiology and are not programmed to be just one way or have one set destiny. Their lives, instead, are biased by both their genetic markers and environmental conditioning (Ellis, 1976a). They do, however, have some flexibility or choice of how they think, feel, and act (Ellis, 1962, 1972a, 1973a, 1977f, 1988).

Rational-emotive therapy holds that humans are limited by their biological natures and does not endorse the naive view of J. B. Watson (1919) that they are solely the product of their environments and learning histories. Such a view ignores research in genetics and the interaction between nature and nurture. Therefore, RET acknowledges this interaction and stresses that people had better work to change themselves and their disturbances as much as their biological tendencies will allow. For example, if people are limited by a biochemical brain disorder, such as mental deficiency or schizophrenia, that limits their potential for achieving high degrees of productivity and happiness, they *can* still work to maximize the extent to which they *are* capable of such achievements. Rational-emotive therapy, therefore, endorses a much more optimistic and humanistic stance than the more deterministically based schools of psychotherapy.

Rational-emotive therapy contends that humans have strong innate tendencies to think about their thinking and to be able to decide their own emotional destinies (Ellis, 1962, 1973a, 1984a, 1984b, 1987a, 1988; Ellis & Harper, 1975). Although it holds that humans do not have perfect free will, they are somewhat (not totally) able to change their thinking and to modify their emotional and behavioral responses to their environments. People *do* have some "will" and *can* exercise their options to change their thinking, their emoting, and their behaving.

Whereas the less cognitively oriented schools of psychotherapy consider past events or environmental stimuli primarily responsible for human neuroses, rational-emotive therapy tries to help clients accept responsibility for their part in making themselves disturbed and for strongly choosing to work at changing themselves. Because RET emphasizes the importance of cognition in human disturbance, clients learn to modify their thinking in more rational and realistic directions to minimize their self-defeating distresses and maximize their long-term productivity.

Transpersonal psychology differs from rational-emotive therapy in that although it sometimes favors will, personal choice, and self-change, it also frequently holds that we are ruled by inexorable karma or fate. Transpersonalists typically argue that even our thinking and our choices to change our behavior are fatalistically predetermined. This is another example of the transpersonal penchant for creating unfalsifiable hypotheses and dogmatically stating that these hypotheses are "known" to be undeniable facts.

The transpersonal position with respect to free will and personal choice is, therefore, highly equivocal and contradictory. Transpersonalists often assert that humans really cannot control or manage their own physical and mental destinies (Bhatty, 1983; Rama, 1982). Yet, they also teach their followers to turn off their emotional excesses so as to achieve "non-feeling" states. They apparently believe that such a choice is really not chosen! Transpersonalists, therefore, frequently include a deterministic philosophy that is pessimistic and that advocates helplessness.

Transpersonal psychology also differs from RET in that it tends to be ultraconservative and displays rigid allegiance to tradition and to the past (Levine, 1984; Neese, 1984). Rational-emotive therapy avers that because people are innately impressionable or gullible, their early experiences influence their goals and standards but have much less impact on their rigid and disturbed efforts to create absolute musts *about* these roles. Moreover, although life experiences may contribute to the development of people's personal beliefs or life philosophy, their persistent choosing, in the here-and-now, to *continue* to endorse and hold on to these beliefs primarily leads to their cognitive-emotive-behavioral disturbances. Rational-emotive therapy does not dismiss the past as irrelevant in contributing to personality or attitude development. It maintains that, for effective therapy, people had better focus on their current decisions to continue thinking crookedly and behaving inappropriately. As stated previously, the rational-emotive philosophy and approach is, therefore, significantly more optimistic than the transpersonal approach. It shows people how their current endorsement of irrational beliefs now serves to maintain their level of disturbances and how they can choose, in the here-and-now, to change their thinking and reduce their disturbances (Bard, 1987, 1988; Ellis, 1962, 1971, 1973a, 1977a, 1979c, 1981a, 1985, 1988; Ellis & Abrahms, 1978; Ellis & Harper, 1975; Grieger & Boyd, 1980; Grieger & Grieger, 1982; Walen, DiGiuseppe & Wessler, 1980; Wessler & Wessler, 1980).

The acceptance of one's limitations and innate human fallibility is a goal common to most therapeutic modalities. Acceptance of human fallibility leads to self-acceptance, which is achieved when people accept themselves and others unconditionally, *whether or not* they fail and *whether or not* significant others approve of them (Ellis, 1962, 1972b, 1973a, 1976c, 1985, 1988; Ellis & Dryden, 1987; Ellis & Harper, 1975; Lazarus, 1977).

Rational-emotive therapy teaches that all humans are exceptionally fallible by nature, and that realistically we had better expect them to err often and commit many undesirable acts. As we are not perfect in our biological, psychological, and emotional makeups, we may expect numerous flaws, limitations, sins, misdeeds, and blunders. Even Christian philosophy asserts that humans are not perfect and are yet forgivable.

Rational-emotive therapy, like some parts of Christian philosophy, teaches people to accept themselves and others fully *with* their fallibility. It shows them how to make the best of their imperfections. It encourages them not to denigrate themselves for their limitations (Ellis, 1962, 1973a, 1977a, 1988; Hauck, 1973, 1979) and to increase their tolerance of others. Thereby they can maximize individual happiness and social cooperation (Ellis, 1988; Ellis & Becker, 1982).

Many transpersonally oriented groups are demanding and intractable about human fallibility. Many devout political factions and religious sects are as intolerant of the flaws and mistakes of their own members as they are of the attitudes and policies of people in other organizations that hold different credos. Such intolerance is often at the core of both religious and political wars. Transpersonalists harbor absolutistic and unyielding notions about the ways that they themselves and others must think and behave; they are not only irrational but also dangerous to society.

Transpersonal psychology is often quite perfectionistic about the human condition. Many sects refer to the God within each individual and tell clients that "you are perfect the way you are" and that you *must* remain perfect. Transpersonal psychology frequently insists that people can be godlike and virtually eliminate all human ills and failings by accepting Absolute Truth (Amritu, 1982; Bhatty, 1984a; E. Brown, 1984; Fairfield, 1984; Ferguson, 1980; Stace, 1960; Rosicrucians, 1984). This demand for perfection leads not only to anxiety, depression, shame, and guilt when personal failure occurs, but also to anger, damnation, intolerance, and aggression when other people fail.

The dire need for perfection often fosters grandiosity. For example, a number of fundamentalist and transpersonal sects believe that only they know God's truths or the "secret of it all," and that the rest of us mere mortals will remain forever ignorant. They assert that, come Judgment Day, those without this "bounty" will be severely punished (Butterfield, 1984; Frick, 1982; Starr,

1984). What an extraordinary sense of entitlement!

Perfection is an almost undefinable and sometimes contradictory concept. Thus, some transcendentalists consider a human to be "perfect" but also see his or her traits as changeable for the "better." If so, how could he or she be "perfect" to begin with? Yet, despite the illogic of such a concept, transpersonal factions commonly endorsed it.

The goal of RET is to help people accept that they are, and most probably always will be, fallible, "sinning," and error making. It never encourages rational emotivists to become apathetic or unconcerned about their sins or limitations but actively helps them to remedy their failings so as to maximize their productivity and happiness. Rational-emotive therapy helps people accept the rational belief that just because they *do* bad things, *feel* bad emotionally, or *think* bad thoughts, this does not make them "bad *people.*"

To assume that one can and must become perfect is not only irrational, but also iatrogenic. It predisposes people to be dysfunctional in several ways, some of which we have already addressed. In addition to producing needless turmoil, increased lack of cooperation, and distancing from others, people who believe that they *need* to be perfect tend to be distraught about their current performances and status. The need for perfection, therefore, discourages them from enjoying themselves or their state of affairs in the here-and-now. It tends to bar them from seeing and learning from their mistakes and to push them to berate themselves globally for their inadequacies.

Transpersonal psychology often encourages "radical transformation." As Charlene Szymusiak (1985, p. 38) notes, "Radical transformation isn't just being adjusted or having a spiritual high. It reasons that, within a *few years* of doing this practice, you will open your eyes and gaze upon your original perfection. It reasons that your day-to-day conduct—how you relate to other human beings, temptations, and pressures—will begin to reflect that perfection. That's radical change."

Similar perfectionistic notions have been espoused by many other transpersonal leaders and groups (Bordewich, 1988; Ehrlich, 1986; Goleman, 1979; Hock, 1983; Lindsey, 1987; Morain, 1988; Schneider, 1987). The almost inevitable result? Much ultimate disillusionment and anguish!

Insight and awareness are concepts addressed by all major schools of psychotherapy, though divergent schools define them differently. We can view insight as understanding the original (or early) causes and/or as discerning the current causes of disorders. Insight may also include "getting in touch with one's feelings" or coming up with a problem-solving answer to difficulties. In terms of these concepts, rational-emotive therapy and transpersonal psychotherapy tend to differ significantly.

Transpersonal psychologists tend to espouse mystical, all-encompassing, and transcendental "insight." They often claim that the gaining of "higher consciousness," "heightened awareness," and "unified" insight will by itself produce miraculous personality changes (Capra, 1983; Deikman, 1972; Maharishi Mahesh Yogi, 1983; Mann, 1984; Shah, 1982; Tulku, 1977, 1978). This view is hardly that of RET!

Rational-emotive therapy emphasizes three types of insight that are important for clients to accept in order to facilitate personality change. These insights are more realistic, pragmatic, and concrete than those sought by transpersonal psychologists.

Rational-emotive therapy contends that it is important for people to realize, first, that they, themselves, largely create their own emotional disturbance by accepting or inventing absolutistic demands for themselves, for others, and for their environment. It asserts that individuals had better work to identify the unconditional shoulds and musts that they endorse and that help make them disturbed. The first type of RET insight, therefore, is to help people see and agree that, in RET terminology, A (an Activating Event) does not produce C (an emotional or behavioral Consequence). Rather, B (people's Belief system) creates C. Thus, sticks and stones may break your bones and directly cause you physical pain, but names, words, deeds, and other Activating Events do not hurt you *emotionally*. Your emotional pains are, instead, a function of the ways you perceive, interpret, and evaluate interpersonal and world conditions.

The second insight RET clients are encouraged to accept is that no matter how or where or when they originally made themselves disturbed, they now, in the present, are continuing to upset themselves. If the client's emotional upset stems directly from events that occurred in the past, since he/she cannot have them *un*occur, the client will *always* have to be disturbed. Yet, as experience shows, clients can get over past, unchangeable events. They undo the influence of these events because clients modify the ways they think, feel, and act about past occurrences. RET shows them how to discern what they *continue* to think and how they *maintain* their old disturbances.

The third insight or realization that RET encourages people to recognize is that there is no magical or passive way to eliminate or minimize their disturbances. Rather, they need to resort to *steady and consistent work and practice*. *Knowledge* of irrational beliefs and the acceptance of some degree of responsibility for individual disturbance will likely help the client. But only through his/her diligent *efforts* at restructuring beliefs, feelings, and behaviors is the client likely to achieve personality modification. Awareness and insight, in and of themselves, will be helpful; but *hard work* at *applying* RET's insights No. 1 and No. 2 is most important!

Let us consider the notion that insight alone can lead to desired therapeutic changes. Consider, for example, that a couple enters psychotherapy to correct a problem of low sex desire. What are their individual goals? Each can ask himself and his partner this very question. Do they want therapy merely to help themselves understand *why* they have this problem? Or, do they also want it to help themselves *get over* it? Obviously, the preference is toward the latter solution.

Too often, people believe that merely by knowing or having insight into the source(s) of their problems they will remove them. How unlikely! A person's mere knowledge that he/she became sexually uninterested because of an ultraconservative upbringing or because of being damned every time a sexual thought emerged will not automatically lead to sexual spontaneity. A more direct approach is needed to *change* thinking and behaving. The client may find it interesting to go back later and try to determine what caused his/her problems, but that knowledge alone (if it is found) will seldom solve anything. Also, people who get over their problems are rarely concerned with why they got them in the first place. Viable therapeutic solutions, therefore, require direct interventions beyond a mere understanding of how a client came to be the way he/she is.

Rational-emotive therapy and transpersonal psychotherapy dramatically differ with respect to their utilization and understanding of insight and awareness. Whereas the transpersonal perspective is bent toward more metaphysical and abstract notions of disturbance and is unlikely to lead to nondisturbance, RET stresses practical insights (Ellis, 1962, 1971, 1973a, 1988; Ellis & Dryden, 1987; Ellis & Harper, 1975). As a result, RET is more active, directive, and effort oriented than its transpersonal counterpart.

RET is much more integrative and systemic than is TP (Ellis, 1984e, 1985, 1987a, 1987e, 1988, 1989; Ellis and Dryden, 1987). Even in the area of cognition, it not only uses several kinds of insight, such as those described at the beginning of this chapter, but it also makes use of several other cognitive methods that transpersonal therapy ignores. These include:

1. *Referenting.* When people refuse to give up their harmful behaviors (such as procrastination or smoking) and when they push out of mind the disadvantages of their addictions, RET encourages them to make a list of all the self-defeating results of their compulsions and a list of the advantages of stopping them. They then reread and actively think about these lists several times a day to help themselves surrender their addictions and compulsions.

2. *Reframing.* Clients who seriously panic and depress themselves about the unfortunate events in their lives (such as failures and rejections) are shown how to focus on the *good* aspects of these bad things. Thus, if you get rejected by a potential sex or love partner, you can show yourself how beneficial it is that you quickly discovered that this person is not for you, and thereby saved yourself much wasted time and energy by not continuing to pursue this person.

    Rational-emotive therapy particularly shows people how to reframe their dysfunctional feelings and behaviors so that instead of horrifying themselves about them, they accept the challenge of dealing with them, changing them, and refusing to denigrate themselves for having them (Ellis, 1988).

3. *Cognitive distraction.* Rational-emotive therapy tries to help people change their disordered feelings by uprooting the philosophic sources of these disorders. It also palliatively uses various forms of cognitive distraction (such as thought stopping, progressive relaxation, and entertainment) to help people calm themselves down so that they can *then* employ more elegant disputing techniques. Unlike other forms of therapy (including TP), RET *first* employs cognitive distraction techniques but *also* goes on to more permanent disputing of people's irrational beliefs.

4. *Modeling.* As Bandura (1977) has shown, modeling is an effective mode of cognitive therapy. Whereas transpersonal therapists often model disturbed behavior (such as shamanistic rituals and trance states), RET practitioners model more rational and productive behaviors (such as undisturbedly accepting and coping with unfortunate events and problems).

5. *Uprooting secondary disturbances.* Rational-emotive therapy assumes that people often have both primary *and* secondary emotional disturbances. When they tell themselves, "I *must* not fail!" and "I *have*

to be approved by others!" they first make themselves anxious and/ or depressed. Then, noting that they feel upset, they frequently tell themselves, "I *must* not be anxious!" or "*I can't stand* being depressed!" and then make themselves panicked about their panic or depressed about their depression. Rational-emotive therapy therefore first shows them how to surrender their secondary disturbances (by accepting themselves *with* their primary feelings of anxiety and depression) and then deals with their primary disturbances and shows them how to think, feel, and act in order to dispel them.

6. *Coping statements.* Rational-emotive therapy shows people how to dispute their irrational beliefs (at point B in the ABCDEs of rational-emotive therapy), but it also shows them how to create and steadily employ (at point E, Effective New Philosophy) rational coping statements. Thus, clients and others who use RET write down and often repeat to themselves—and *think* through, instead of merely suggestively parroting—self-statements like "I do not *need* what I want. I *prefer* it but can also live happily without it." "I would very much *like* people to treat me fairly and considerately, but they never *have* to!" "A *hassle* is not a *horror.* It is highly inconvenient for me to be rejected, but it's not the end of the world!"

7. *Imagery and visualization.* Where transpersonalists often use unrealistic and pollyannaish positive imagery (such as visualizing one's "good" body cells devouring one's "bad" cancerous cells), RET uses practical imagery and behavioral rehearsal (such as visualizing oneself playing tennis satisfactorily or speaking well in public) to help people have increased confidence in their performances. It also uses rational-emotive imagery.

8. *Psychoeducational methods.* Rational-emotive therapy does not merely rely on individual and group therapy sessions to help people overcome their problems. With clients and members of the public, RET also uses many psychoeducational techniques such as pamphlets, books, charts, graphs, talks, courses, audio and video cassettes, films, workshops, marathons, and intensives. These educational resources can speed and intensify individual and group therapy and significantly help many individuals who never come for therapy. Thus, the regular Friday-night "Problems in Everyday Living" workshop that I (A.E.) give at the Institute for Rational-Emotive Therapy in New York City has, over the last quarter of a century, helped tens of thousands of people. Through experiencing me talking to volunteers about

their personal problems, people in the audience can see that they themselves have emotional difficulties and can deal with them by using the same techniques that I demonstrate to the volunteers.

9. *Recording of sessions.* Rational-emotive therapy clients are encouraged to record their own therapy sessions and listen to them one or more times, to hear various points that they may have missed during the live sessions. Clients frequently report that they get as much or more from listening to the recordings as they get from the original sessions.

10. *Problem solving.* As RET practitioners help their clients to see that their rational and irrational beliefs create in them appropriate and inappropriate feelings, they also encourage clients to replace their Jehovian demands and commands with their wishes and preferences. In addition, RET therapists help these clients to reconsider their practical problems and to figure out better solutions to them. In RET, we do not *only* or *mainly* resort to practical problem solving, but we use it *in addition to* the philosophic disputing of people's irrational beliefs.

11. *Semantic precision.* As Alfred Korzybski (1933) wisely said, people's overgeneralized and illogical thinking affects their language, and then their language encourages them to think even *more* illogically. So in RET we often question and correct the self-defeating language people use. Thus, if clients say, "I *must* perform well," we say, "No, not *must*—but *had better.*" If they say, "My mother *makes me* angry by yelling at me," we say, "No. You *anger yourself* about your mother's unfortunate yelling." If clients say, "I *can't* change my ways," we say, *"You find it difficult* to change, but there is no evidence that you *can't."*

Transpersonal psychotherapy, then, uses insight, awareness, and other cognitive methods in limited, inefficient, and often misleading ways. Rational-emotive therapy employs a wide armamentarium of insightful and other cognitive methods while discarding the mystical, religious, and supernatural "insights" that are so dear to the hearts of transpersonalists but whose good effects are often dubious and whose potential for harm is considerable.

Almost all forms of psychotherapy attempt to eliminate people's neurotic defenses. They attempt to help clients become free of their rationalization, intellectualization, denial, hypocrisy, dishonesty, avoidance, resistance, compensation, aggression, coercion, identification, and grandiosity. Defenses may consist of unconscious defense mechanisms or may be fairly conscious. Both kinds enable people to resist acknowledging and changing self-sabotaging attitudes and actions. Rational-emotive therapists attempt to help clients surrender their defenses as well as feelings of shame, guilt, and self-deprecation that spur them to become defensive (Bernard, 1986; Ellis, 1962, 1971, 1985, 1988),

Transpersonal psychology frequently serves to bolster people's neurotic defenses by encouraging them to think nonscientifically, to set up unfalsifiable hypotheses, and to blindly endorse and profess these hypotheses as if they are unquestionably true. When shown that no evidence exists to support their theories, transpersonalists desperately resort to rationalizations, lies, hypocrisy, and hoaxes to try to substantiate them. Rather than considering alternative hypotheses to explain "supernatural" phenomena, transpersonalists tend to hold onto their theories devoutly and unyieldingly, criticize the field of science for not being "advanced" enough to understand their mystical "phenomena," and infest their theories with a mixture of tautological reasoning and abstraction that prohibits any testing of their assumptions. For example, transpersonalists desperately try to prove the existence of magic and miracles despite a lack of substantial evidence, deny that highly dubious psychic phenomena are created by sleight of hand or optical illusion, abjure science's state-of-the-art as not capable of realistically addressing their issues, and tautologically argue that a miracle cannot be challenged. Their unwillingness to accept reality predisposes them to enlist these typical defensive postures (Kurtz, 1985a, 1986a).

Much of the core of transpersonal psychology constitutes a set of neurotic defenses against people's unwillingness to accept reality. For example, the grim reality that humans are distinctly fallible and highly limited creatures who live in a difficult and often hostile world and who are definitely, at least in this century, going to die and become nonliving and nonexistent (Ellis, 1981b, 1983b, 1986a, 1986b; Sobel, 1981) is completely dismissed by most transpersonalists. Rather, they insist that human life is eternal, thereby denying reality. They also rationalize that since this claim is not factually supportable, science has not yet advanced enough to observe immortal life. Such excuses are taught to transpersonal devotees to counter any and all arguments opposing their implausible constructs.

Besides utilizing neurotic defenses to propagate their theories, transpersonalists often soft-soap reality in a highly polyannaish manner. They assert, for example, that through prayer and spiritual enlightenment, all people can achieve "absolute peace" (Komaki, 1984, p. 3), "all wisdom and intelligence" (Dowlatashahi, 1983, p. 27), "solve the problems of any government regardless of the nature of the problem—political, economic, social, or religious" (Maharishi Mahesh Yogi, 1983a, p. A14), "bring utopia to all mankind" and perfect health and longevity to the individual and the nation (Maharishi Mahesh Yogi, 1983b, p. B20), and postpone the aging process (Silva Mind Control, 1984). They thus offer quite a kettle of grandeur! This illustrates transpersonalists' abysmally low tolerance for frustration, since it is easier for people to fabricate eternal bliss than to actually work for it!

Rational-emotive therapists directly confront people's defenses and strive to help them see the world through realistic lenses. Rather than merely distracting themselves into prayer or creating utopian pictures, RET clients learn to accept the world the way it is—and then, often, to improve it. Transpersonalists generally refuse to accept such a reality since they believe they absolutely *need* cosmic or supernatural meaning in life and *need* perfect solutions to life's problems. Such demandingness predisposes them to develop defensive views to prevent them from realizing that they will *not* likely get what they believe they need. Their defenses also help them to maintain their theories dogmatically instead of opening up and challenging them. Facts that fit their theories are accepted; those that do not are either discarded or forced to fit.

CHAPTER 17

PERSONALITY AND
CHARACTER FORMATION

EDITOR'S COMMENTARY:

In this selection, Ellis argued that RET has a distinct personality theory that is considerably different from other personality theories. In typical Ellis fashion, he went so far as to point out the "crooked thinking" of theorists such as Adler, Freud, Jung, Reich, and Rogers and attacked their positions on several points, stressing their illogical thinking about how environment influences personality, the overemphasis on the past, the overgeneralizations about the influence of heredity on personality, and the focus on self-worth and self-esteem. He also characterized other personality theorists of being defensive and resistant to change, even though evidence may have existed that was contrary to their viewpoints.

Contending that many personality theories were inadequate, Ellis outlined the A-B-C theory of personality, noting that there was considerable validity for this theory. He included a rather thorough discussion about how heredity influences personality, emphasizing biological predispositions but acknowledging environmental influence as well. He acknowledged that personality is influenced by such factors as interpersonal relations, rewards and penalties, self-rating, gullibility, innate tendencies, the media, and so forth. He concluded that because of these multiple influences that may conflict with each other, humans are both consistent and inconsistent.

The remainder of this selection includes a detailed discussion by Ellis on ten major dimensions of personality that Coan and Corsini developed, including his position on whether RET is objective or subjective, elementaristic or holistic, apersonal or personal, quantitative or qualitative, static or dynamic, endogenistic or exogenistic, deterministic or indeterministic, past or future oriented, cognitive or affective, or unconscious or conscious.

Ellis's theory, which is actually based on personality disturbance and evolved out of practice of the theory, provides more detail than previous writings. In this chapter, Ellis also urged personality theorists to test the hypotheses he outlined in this article in order to have a concrete idea regarding the nature of people. That said, this reading will also illustrate that Ellis did not specifically call for research concerning developmental issues related to his theory. Aspects of personality development do exist and have been researched or commented upon by other writers-researchers (e.g., Michael Bernard and Ann Vernon).

Excerpted from *The Essential Albert Ellis,*
Barricade Books 1990

Windy Dryden, Ph.D., wrote: "Ellis's view is that, originally, infants have rational behaviors (e.g., sucking and crying out when pained), but these seem to be largely instinctive and have few rational ideas to spark them. As they become older and their cerebral cortex develops, they create more rational predictions, checks, and conclusions about their pleasant and unpleasant feelings; and from the age of 5 or 6 onward they probably develop a great many rational ideas—for example, "Pleasure is good, and I want more of it; pain is bad, and I want less of it. Therefore, let me try to seek out pleasure and avoid pain."

According to Ellis, the main irrational belief that young children probably first develop is that leading to discomfort disturbance, or low frustration tolerance (LFT)—for example, "Because pain and discomfort are so bad, I can't stand these feelings. They must not exist, and it's awful when they do!" LFT may therefore be the first major irrationality of young children.

The second major irrationality of children is their self-downing—for example, the idea "Because I must do better than I am doing, I am a bad child who often deserves to be deprived or punished." As children develop their sense of self (ego), perhaps a year or two after they develop their sense of comfort and discomfort, and particularly as they develop language (with the help of their parents), they begin to see themselves, not merely their actions, as "good" and "bad," as "deserving" and "undeserving."

Ellis holds that even the child's original irrational idea, "I must be loved and approved, and it's awful if I'm not!" is probably at first a dire need for comfort—for being taken care of, soothed, and given goodies. Later, probably, the child adds the ego, self-downing irrationality, "If I'm not loved and catered to, as I must be, there must be something wrong with me, and therefore I am no good!"

These are only some tentative hypotheses about the development of children's rationality and irrationality that Ellis has put forward, and research should be done to test their plausibility. Ellis notes that RET developmental theory is still in its infancy, but he believes that it could well lead to some fascinating growth and development."

REFERENCES

Coan, R. W. (1968). Dimensions of psychological theory. *American Psychologist, 23,* 715–722.

Corsini, R. J. (Ed.). (1978). *Readings in current personality theories.* Itasca, IL: Peacock.

Ellis, A. (1962). *Reason and emotion in psychotherapy.* New York: Lyle Stuart.

Ellis, A. (1977). RET as a personality theory, therapy approach, and philosophy of life. In J. L. Wolfe & E. Brand (Eds.), *Twenty years of rational therapy* (pp. 16–30). New York: Institute for Rational-Emotive Therapy.

During the past several years, I have begun to develop a theory of personality that significantly disagrees with the views of other personality theorists who have also originated schools of psychotherapy—such as Adler, Freud, Jung, Reich, and Rogers. In this paper I shall first state why virtually all existent personality theorists make wrong conclusions about how humans function; then I shall outline and defend my own theory, which is developing out of the practice of rational-emotive therapy (Ellis, 1962, 1973a, 1973b, 1977a; Ellis & Grieger, 1977; Morris & Kanitz, 1975).

WHY PERSONALITY THEORISTS OFTEN GO WRONG

Personality theorists almost invariably go wrong because, like most humans, they think crookedly. Their tendency to cognize irrationally leads them astray in various respects. They consequently come up with highly brilliant views of "human nature" which often include almost incredible errors of logic and antiempiricism. Examples of crooked thinking in personality theories include the following.

1, *Attribution of special reasons to events and behaviors.* Humans tend to attribute special (transpersonal) reasons to various nonhuman events. Because they then feel comfortable (in the Gestalt psychology sense of effecting "closure") with these "explanations," they then wrongly believe they have "proved" the validity of their assertions. Thus, primitives pray for rain; it eventually does rain, and they see their prayers as an explanation for the downpour. Sailors observe a certain kind of cloud formation before it rains, and they loosely see this formation "causing" a storm. The primitives clearly believe in magic, for their prayers have no connection whatever with the rain. But sailors also think crookedly; for cloud formations only constitute part of a worldwide pressure system of events, ranging from conditions at the North Pole to those at the Equator, all of which contribute to the downpour. Meteorologists know about these causes but often fail to explain them to laypeople when they talk about the "causation" of rain; and we laypeople buy the simple explanation of the rain clouds causing storms and do not bother with other complications that go with these causal connections.

And so with personality theories. If I murder someone, and you want to "explain" the "cause" of my act, you will likely focus upon some outstanding "influences"—for example, my mother taught me that hostility pays off, or my early religious teachings led me to embrace an eye-for-an-eye philosophy. Certainly, these influences *may* have affected me. But of a hundred children whose mothers or whose early religious teachings favored hostility, very few, if any, would murder someone later in life! Literally hundreds of influences may have contributed to my act, such as (*a*) my tendency to demand that things go my way, (*b*) my rebellion against social teachings, (*c*) my low frustration tolerance, (*d*) my vulnerability to feeling hurt, (*e*) my happening to have a gun when I experienced extreme hostility, and so on. Considering all these possible "causes," your simplistic, unitary "explanation" of my murderous act hardly seems accurate, even though it may show some mild degree of causality.

Rational-emotive therapy (RET) holds that any special, exclusive reason for a behavioral act or personality pattern rarely, if ever, exists. If I murder regularly (and thus have the "trait" of a murderer), I may do so for many reasons, none of which probably has exclusive importance. If I regularly kill people, probably simultaneously (*a*) I have a strong innate predisposition toward feeling hostile at "injustices," (*b*) *I* think murder is justified under certain conditions, (*c*) I believe I can get away with homicide, (*d*) I have somehow developed a low frustration tolerance, (*e*) I have problems, perhaps connected with my early interpersonal experiences, in relating to others, (*f*) I think in absolutistic, *must*urbatory ways, and so on. Any one of these tendencies or conditions could make me a confirmed murderer; and a combination of several of them would increase the probability of my turning into one. Your selecting one primary "cause" of my homicidal character merely shows that almost all humans frequently attribute "special," determining causes to the origin or development of personality traits, when the "real" causes probably arise out of multifaceted, often obscure, partly accidental conditions.

2. *Illogical thinking about special reasons for personality behaviors.* Once we attribute special causative reasons for personality behaviors, we usually tend to feel so convinced of their truth that we ignore evidence that contradicts our hypotheses. Such reasons seem to "fit" the observed facts of human functioning, and in perceiving this good fit we convince ourselves of their indubitable "truth." Even when we finally surrender these "explanations" for another set, we may do so because they jibe better with our preconceived aesthetic notions of good fit. They have greater "elegance." They "feel" better than the old ones. So we decide that (for now and for all time to come) they *are* better.

We can easily, then, convince ourselves of the validity of an elegant theory—by (*a*) ignoring data that do not fit, (*b*) falsifying data that fit poorly, or (*c*) failing to seek better theories that fit the data more accurately. When the "true" explanations for a given behavior remain truly multifaceted and complex, we have more temptation than usual to settle for special reasons for this behavior—simply because a simple explanation fits better and feels better.

3. *Environmentalist prejudices.* The great majority of psychologists remain do-gooders, hoping not merely to understand but also to help change dysfunctional behaviors. They believe that the basic way to do this consists of relearning, or behavior modification. They also know that some behaviors (e.g., obsessions and phobias) have such strong instinctive or overlearned factors that people have great difficulty in changing them.

Because of their essential altruism and hopefulness, some personality theorists who begin with the assumption, "We must help people change their disordered traits," go on to the empirical observation, "Humans find it very difficult to change solidly rooted inherited predispositions," and wind up with the illogical conclusion, "Therefore, such traits must have arisen from learning rather than hereditary tendencies."

Other forms of illogical thinking about environmental influences on personality include the following:

a. Because people have great difficulty in making certain personality changes, they find it impossible to change.
b. Because a behavior has learned elements, it has virtually no innate component, and one can fairly easily unlearn it.
c. If a personality trait involves a hereditary predisposition, one cannot change it.

d. Because one has learned to behave badly, one has no responsibility for continuing this behavior, or environmental conditions have to change before one can modify this behavior.

e. Because others have conditioned one to behave in a defeating manner, helpers must recondition one to behave differently.

f. Because the environment significantly contributes to dysfunctioning, only through someone's significantly changing the environment will one have the ability to act less dysfunctionally.

g. Because virtually all human behavior includes learning, learning constitutes the main element in this behavior, and one must use external forces to modify it.

Due to do-goodism and cognitive slippage, the importance of environmental factors in the formation and changing of personality tends to get enormously exaggerated; almost all systematic views of psychotherapy fall victim to this kind of exaggeration.

4. *Overemphasis on dramatic incidents from the past.* We humans tend to dramatize so-called traumatic incidents and to remember them vividly. Thus, you may vividly recall how you wet yourself at age four and made a fool of yourself in class at age six. Because these remembrances leave dramatic effects, people make erroneous conclusions such as

a. The original occurrence *caused* negative self-ratings.

b. Having no memory or bad feelings about them results from the mechanism of repression.

c. Recalling such "traumatic" memories and the accompanying feelings has curative effects.

d. That particular happening and one's original reaction to it invariably "caused" one's present lifestyle and tells the therapist a great deal about one's personality.

e. If one reacted dysfunctionally to an early remembered incident, one must react the same way in similar circumstances today and for the rest of one's life.

Dramatic early events in people's lives may well tell us something about them personality-wise. But theorists tend to overemphasize this phenomenon and to make all-encompassing, and often false, conclusions about it. Just as people make false "observations" and conclusions about contemporary dramatic events (e.g., accidents), so too do they and their psychological observers easily make misleading "observations" and conclusions about past dramatic events. Such events probably had *some* importance, but we tend to make them *all*-important. Since most people experience satisfaction in reviewing their past histories, they foolishly expend much time and energy talking to therapists about their past when they would do themselves more good by thinking about their present and future. For this reason, woefully inefficient psychotherapies, such as psychoanalysis, continue to have immense popularity (Ellis, 1962; Ellis & Harper, 1975).

5. *Overgeneralization.* People have an exceptionally strong tendency to overgeneralization, as Aaron Beck (1976), Albert Ellis (1962, 1977a), George Kelly (1955), and Alfred Korzybski (1933) have pointed out. Because of this tendency, personality theorists seem to make certain valid observations about human personality and then go on to make certain overgeneralized, hence partly false, conclusions about these observations. Here are some examples:

a. Because humans desire certain things—such as approval and success—they *must* have them to achieve any significant degree of happiness.
b. Because dreams to some degree show people's underlying wishes and anxieties, virtually all dreams consist of wish fulfillments or indicate deep-seated fears.
c. Because dreams and free associations sometimes reveal material of which the individual has little awareness, they constitute the royal road to the unconscious and give highly accurate information.
d. Because people sometimes symbolize sex organs in their dreams by objects such as guns or keyholes, every time they dream about such objects they really mean sex organs.
e. Because some individuals feel inferior due to physical or other deficiencies, such deficiencies always lead to feelings of inferiority.
f. Because feelings of love frequently enhance happiness, every one requires a fine one-to-one relationship to exist in a "normal" or "healthy" manner.

Hundreds of such overgeneralizations contribute to false views of personality. The human tendency to jump from "Some people do this some of the time" to "Virtually everyone does this all of the time" and from "A minority of individuals under certain conditions act this way" to "The majority of people always act this way" leads to misleading, and virtually pandemic, views of personality.

6. *Hereditarian biases.* Many psychologists have hereditarian biases and consequently overemphasize the importance of innate influences on

personality (Pastore, 1949). Cyril Burt, for example, for many years seems to have faked data to support his theories about the importance of genetic factors in intelligence (Evans, 1976). Typical hereditarian mistakes include such conclusions as the following:

a. Because heredity represents a strong element in virtually all behavior, it almost exclusively determines that behavior.

b. If certain individuals have an innate tendency to act in a certain way, virtually all the members of their groups act that way because of their genetic differences from other groups.

c. If a personality trait has strong hereditarian influences, people with that trait find it virtually impossible to change it significantly.

d. If one personality trait has strong heredity determinants, other traits must have equally strong innate determinants.

Hereditarian overgeneralizations lead to many false conclusions about personality. Proenvironmentalist theorists overemphasize the significance of learned factors, while prohereditarians overemphasize innate factors. Environmentalists tend to forget that social learning rests on an inherited tendency to learn or to adopt social "conditioning" (Ellis, 1976). Hereditarians tend to forget that no matter what their genetic background, humans start learning immediately after birth. Both sets of theorists, failing to look at the other side of the fence, overlook the fact that all behaviors include a combination of learned and innate factors, and both tend to present a one-sided view of personality.

7. *Human autism and grandiosity.* Humans often take an autistic, grandiose, cosmological view. They conceptualize that the universe revolves around them and runs in accordance with their wishes and goals. They will not accept that the world seems to have no intrinsic purpose and that it has no interest, concern, or love for them. They exist and it exists; and their existence, of course, depends on an outside world in which they live. But individuals and the world have no necessary connection. The universe existed without humans probably for billions of years and may well do so for billions of future years. We have no evidence that it exists *just* for us.

People seem loath to accept the great influence of accident, purposelessness, and unintentionality in cosmology. They consequently tend to invent special reasons for personality behaviors, and they frequently come up with semimystical, transpersonal, religiously oriented views that have nothing to do with reality.

8.   *Self-rating influences.* Humans value life and happiness and, reasonably enough, rate their performances with how well these permit them to enjoy life. But then they jump to rating their total selves, and this has no sensible basis (Ellis, 1962, 1972, 1975; Ellis & Harper, 1975). That doesn't stop humans from continuing to rate their essences as well as their deeds!

Personality theorists tend to make the same error. They talk in favor of self-esteem, self-confidence, and self-regard, not realizing that even if we do achieve self-esteem we harm ourselves thereby if we remain preoccupied with our own ratings rather than simply changing our dysfunctional behaviors. If we rate ourselves as "good," we imply that we can also be rated as "bad"— and as a consequence we live on the verge of anxiety, due to these self-determined "report cards."

Personality theory includes an enormous "self-worth" literature—most of it quite misleading! For humans, as such, do not actually have differential worth. They merely have aliveness. Intrinsic worth or value differs little from other mythical entities, such as "spirit" and "soul" (Ellis, 1972).

9.   *Absolutistic and musturbatory thinking.* People tend to take proper probabilistic views (e.g., "I like others' approval") and then escalate them into absolutes and musts (e.g., "I must have others' approval"). This kind of thinking also leads personality theorists astray, who promulgate *musts* by the dozen instead of more realistic it-would-seem-better-ifs (Ellis, 1973a, 1973b, 1977a; Ellis & Grieger, 1977). Some of the *musts* that theorists uphold include

a.   You must have a happy, secure childhood to achieve a happy adult life.

b.   If you have an emotional problem, you must have prolonged intensive therapy.

c.   To change your behavior, you must have specific reinforces, such as money or love.

d.   Self-defeating behavior must result from irrational ideas.

e.   You must feel terribly anxious about the possibility of eventually dying.

f.   When people treat you unfairly, you must feel real hostility toward them.

10. *Defensiveness and resistance to change.* Personality theorists generally tend to resist change in their thinking, and they construct defenses against acknowledging defects in their theories. They consequently ignore evidence that contradicts their views. They claim their theories explain practically all

aspects of personality. They give specious answers to the objections of critics. They avoid probing new areas that might uncover evidence that confutes their hypotheses. They neglect to even read other personality theorists. They come to conclusions that do not jibe with the evidence they themselves turn up. They cling to views that have long outlived their usefulness. They see flaws in their own theories but refuse to acknowledge these flaws publicly.

Possibly for ego-bolstering and grandiose reasons, personality scientists hold to and promulgate views that never had, or at least no longer have, a high degree of validity. Let me see, therefore, if I can do at least a little better!

TOWARD A NEW THEORY OF PERSONALITY

Assuming, as claimed above, that many contemporary theories of personality have woeful inadequacies and little likelihood of verification, can a more valid theory arise out of clinical data?

The A-B-C Theory of Personality

Rational-emotive therapy has implied from its very beginning a theory of personality, stemming from its theory of personality change. Scores of clinical reports have given evidence for the validity of this A-B-C theory by citing case histories of people who came for RET in a state of near despair and, after consultation, usually soon thereafter emerged as significantly improved—with their symptoms gone, with new understanding of how they created their problems, and with a readiness to face the world and make for themselves a better, more joyous existence (Ellis, 1977b; Murphy & Ellis, 1977). In addition to clinical evidence, the A-B-C theory has considerable experimental backing. DiGiuseppe, Miller, and Trexler (1977) and Murphy (Murphy & Ellis, 1977) have comprehensively reviewed clinical outcome studies in which some subjects experienced RET and others experienced no therapy or other forms of psychotherapy. When the researchers made statistical comparisons between experimental (RET) and control groups, in almost all these studies subjects given RET changed their behavior significantly better than did non-RET subjects (Ellis, 1977b).

We can state the essence of RET theory in this way: When people feel upset at point C (emotional Consequence), after they have undergone some unpleasant Activating Event (at point A), they almost always conclude that A caused C. They say, "No wonder I feel depressed; my mate has just left me," or "Of course I feel anxious in view of this exam that I may fail." For most people—including clients and personality theorists—the connection between A (Activating Experience) and C (emotional Consequence) seems evident and obvious.

RET rejects this "evident" explanation, and RET therapists have taught thousands of clients to reject it over the past two decades. The stimulus does not explain the reaction; S-R theorizing does not work. RET conceptualization, following Woodworth (Woodworth & Schlosberg, 1954) constitutes an S-O-R theory. RET makes B, the individual's Belief System, the crucial issue. A does not determine C—B does! Consequently, if two people get labeled "stupid," and one laughs at the statement and the other feels depressed, we cannot explain these radically different Consequences by A (the Activating Event) but rather by B (the Belief System) *about* A.

The salient points of RET have appeared in much detail elsewhere (Ellis, 1962, 1971, 1973a, 1973b, 1977a; Ellis & Grieger, 1977; Ellis & Harper, 1975; Maultsby, 1975). Now, the crucial issue arises: How do people obtain their Belief Systems—rational Beliefs (rBs) and irrational Beliefs (iBs)? Why does Johanna have such a healthy attitude and behave so sanely while her brother, John, has such an unhealthy view of life and acts so unsuccessfully?

Hereditarian Influences on Personality

Although almost all formal views of modern personality formation say otherwise, it seems probable that the main influence on human personality comes from heredity. It seems almost impossible to deny this, since if we humans do exhibit different personality traits as we react to environmental conditions, we obviously inherit this kind of teachability or conditionability. Thus, we seem unusually teachable compared to "lower" animals. Our teachability, mediated through our unusually large and specially wired cerebral cortex, comprises one of the main essences of our humanity. Subhuman animals remain much more driven by instincts, while humans largely have what Maslow (1954) called "instinctoid" tendencies—strong predispositions to act in certain ways that nonetheless can get radically modified by environmental and educational influences.

RET-oriented personality theory hypothesizes that probably 80% of the variance of human behavior rests on biological bases and about 20% on environmental training (Ellis, 1976). We find a good example of this in the iB's (irrational Beliefs) which spark people's disturbances. At first blush, these beliefs seem to stem primarily from cultural learning: from absorbing the standards that parents, schools, churches, and other institutions teach. Almost all of us largely subscribe to these standards, in spite of the fact that many of them appear insane and inane. Do not our personalities, then, get mainly set by culture?

Yes—and no! Our "normal" standards do seem to follow cultural prescriptions and proscriptions—so that most of us wear considerable clothing even when temperatures soar, permit ourselves to love intensely only one member of the other sex at a time, and try to win the approval of many people whom we hate or in whom we have little interest. We do these silly things to follow cultural conventions. But in addition, because we innately tend to elevate *preferences* into *musts,* we frequently convince ourselves that we *have to* do these preferable things; that we must find it awful and horrible (rather than merely damned annoying) if we do not; and that we rate as thoroughly *rotten persons* if we fall below cultural standards.

Just as we often take stupid cultural norms and make them into absolutistic *shoulds,* we do much the same thing with sensible rules. Thus, our culture teaches us that we had better wear warm clothes in winter—but we tend to add that we *must* wear the most fashionable clothes, no matter how uncomfortable or expensive we personally find them. Our culture tells us the advantages of falling in love; so we often insist that we *have to* love and gain the love of the most special person in the world, who will madly love us forever! Our culture informs us that we will benefit by having others approve of us (so that they will give us jobs, act companionably, do us favors, and so on). And then we demand that virtually everyone we meet, including perfect strangers we will rarely encounter again, *must* like us!

This kind of *must*urbation—admittedly encouraged but not demanded by our society—seems largely innate. Just about all humans in all cultures frequently *must*urbate—even though they soon note its pernicious results. We demand guarantees; we insist that we have to do well, others must treat us considerately, and world conditions have to arrange themselves so that we get almost everything we want immediately, easily. Just about all children frequently think this way, and virtually no adults fully surrender this kink of crazy thinking.

Personality consists not merely of our silly demandingness but perhaps even more of our wishing, wanting, and desiring. Wants give purpose to life. If we had no desires (as extreme Zen Buddhism strives for, in a state called Nirvana), we would hardly survive; and if we did, who would really want to? Desiring, seeking, striving, yearning seem the main essence of living.

But where do most of our desires originally come from? Almost certainly, from biological predispositions. We naturally enjoy eating. We innately enjoy and prefer certain odors, sights, and sounds. We fundamentally like to play, to build, to create. In all these pursuits, we learn cultural standards and generally follow them. In our society, for example, we eat beef but not grasshoppers; we copulate in private rather than in public; and we play tennis and golf more than we perform archery. But just about all our culturally taught pursuits rest on a pronounced biological basis; as Karl Buehler (1965) stated, we inherently have a "function pleasure."

The RET emphasis on the importance of the biological bases of human behavior attempts to balance the environmentalist position, which has dominated personality and therapy theory for the last half century. Freud (1965) had strong biological leanings, but virtually all his main followers, including Fromm (1941, 1975), Horney (1965), Sullivan (1953), and Berne (1964) have overemphasized so-called cultural and early childhood conditioning. Many good reasons exist for suspecting that self-defeating behavior basically has innate (as well as acquired) causes. Since I have elsewhere (Ellis, 1976) reviewed these reasons in detail, I shall not repeat them here.

Multiplicity of Origins and Maintainers of Personality

The RET theory of personality posits a multiplicity of origins and maintainers of personality, often environmental as well as biologically based, such as (1) interpersonal relations with other humans; (2) specific teachings by others; (3) teachings through impersonal communications, such as books and other forms of mass media; (4) group influences; (5) reinforcers or rewards, such as money, social approval, honors, medals, or compliments; (6) penalizers, such as disapproval, failures, fines, imprisonment, or threats; (7) self-ratings— evaluations of the self as "good" or "bad"; (8) self-observation—noting how one behaves and comprehending the usual consequences of such behavior; (9) modeling after others, particularly after outstanding individuals; (10) identifying with certain people or groups and going along with their behavior; (11) formulating goals, purposes, and ideals and striving to achieve them; (12) magical and mystical notions, such as belief in perfection, in Utopia, or in rewarding or punishing deities; (13) gullibility and suggestibility to the teachings and persuasions of others; (14) urges favoring freedom and individuality; (15) innate tendencies to seek love, pleasure, and self-actualization; (16) emotional consequences of behavior considered "beneficial" by the individual: feeling "good" about operating according to the "correct" norms of self or others, achieving success, and so on; feeling "bad" about violations of laws, ethics, customs, traditions, or mores, and specifically feeling anxious, guilty, and depressed about such violations.

Because people have so many internal and external influences and because these significantly conflict with each other in many ways, human behavior displays both consistencies and inconsistencies. Consistencies ("personality traits") probably arise out of the strength and statistical prevalence of one influence over another. But no matter how much "evidence" we find for our "explanations" of personality, we never have all the facts; we can always think of an alternative "reason" that also connects with the known data; we can easily find five or more "answers" for the existence of the same trait; and we have no sure way of knowing which one, two, or all of these answers truly account for the personality factors we seek to explain. In view of this, a truly dynamic psychology had better include not only "vertical" factors—relate to past and future—but also "horizontal" considerations and concern itself with the organism's selection calculus relative to a decision for action considering the importance of all these and other influences of past and present, of near and far, of inner and outer factors.

Does theorizing about personality, then, seem a rather hopeless pursuit? To some extent, yes. For the present, and perhaps never, we probably will not arrive at precise, certain hypotheses that cover all or most of the observed data. Nonetheless, if we watch the kinds of errors outlined in the first part of this article, we can at least come up with some tentative (and I hope highly tentative!) conclusions.

RET's Stand on 10 Major Dimensions of Personality

Many personality analysts have come up with major dimensions of personality on which various theorists can take a stand. Coan (1968) outlined six dimensions, and Corsini (1977) has added four more. On these factors (as described in Corsini, 1977), RET makes the following choices:

1. *Objective–subjective.* Objective theories of personality feature explicit, observable, unequivocal behavior that one can count and number; subjective theories concern themselves with the inner personal life of an individual. In this respect, RET favors observing and counting behavior for research purposes. But it largely deals with inner personal life, with the ineffable individual, and sees the person as having *some* degree of choice or "free will"

and a significant ability to change his or her traits (behavior patterns). Thus, RET mainly remains in the subjective camp.

2. *Elementaristic–holistic.* Elementaristic theory sees the person as composed of parts: organs, units, elements put together to make a whole. Holistic theories see the person as having a central unity and the parts as aspects of the total entity. While RET sees people as having units or elements (e.g., high sexuality or low energy) that influence their whole lives, it also sees them as having interacting parts (including cognitions, emotions, and behaviors) that cannot really be separated, and it primarily sees them as having a holistic or central "consciousness" or "will" that tends to direct these various parts.

3. *Apersonal–personal.* Apersonal theories have impersonal, statistically based outlooks and consider generalities rather than individualities. Largely based on group norms, they differ from personal theories, which deal with the single individual in an idiographic manner. RET distinctly uses general laws of behavior, statistically based—e.g., the probability law that behind virtually every "emotional" disturbance lies an irrational idea, and this idea takes the form of some *should* or *must.* It claims unusual efficiency as a theory of personality and of personality change precisely because it has inducted these general laws from observations of many people and has clinically and experimentally tested them often. It therefore claims a scientific, partly nomothetic basis. But it also deals, especially in therapy, with individuals in their own right, emphasizes their uniqueness and their changeability, accords them personal responsibility for their own disturbance and change, and sees them idiographically. We can label RET as largely being a personal theory of personality.

4. *Quantitative–qualitative.* A quantitative theory makes it possible to measure units of behavior. A qualitative theory does not see behavior as exactly measurable, viewing it as too complex for such dealings. RET stresses quality rather than quantity, since (as noted in this article) personality seems infinitely complex in its origins and development, so that we can only partially and inaccurately quantify it. RET hypothesizes, however, that quantity frequently metamorphoses into quality in behavioral change. Forcing oneself *many times* to think and act differently finally helps one to "naturally" enjoy something one previously disliked—or vice versa.

5. *Static–dynamic.* Static theory sees the individual as a reactor, not a learner; filled with instincts, and based on generalizations presented by heredity. Dynamic theory concerns itself with the individual as a learner, with interactions between behavior and consciousness and between consciousness and unconsciousness. RET sees people as having instinctoid tendencies rather

than fixed instincts—and as having, for example, the tendency to see their own behaviors (including their own disturbances) and to change these. In this sense, in spite of its strong emphasis on heredity, RET has an unusually powerful dynamic quality.

6. *Endogenistic–exogenistic.* Endogenous theories view the person as biologically based. Exogenistic theories consist of social learning theories. RET supports both endogenistic *and* exogenistic views. It sees the person as biologically based, but it also strongly holds that people have the innate capacity to make themselves less conditionable, less suggestible, and more self-directing. RET also sees humans as inheriting strong tendencies toward gregariousness and social learning, so that they always remain highly affectable by both their heredity and their social environment.

7. *Deterministic–indeterministic.* Deterministic theories see individuals as not responsible for their behavior, as the pawns of society, heredity, or both. Indeterministic theories put emphasis on self-direction and place control within the person. RET stands mainly in the indeterministic camp. But it sees choice as *limited*. It hypothesizes that the more rationally people think and behave, the less deterministically they act. But rationality itself has its limits and hardly leads to completely free, healthy, or Utopian existences!

8. *Past–future.* Some theories see the individual in terms of past influences, biological or social, and others see the person as explained by his or her anticipation of future goals. RET takes a two-headed-arrow stand in this respect, for it definitely sees people in terms of what they have inherited and learned in the past, but it also strongly sees them as able to think for themselves, make some free choices, and, by hard work and effort, carry out their goals. RET techniques emphasize the present and future and waste little time with the past.

9. *Cognitive–affective.* Cognitive theories include the so-called ego theories, which see people as essentially rational, with the emotions subserving the intellect. Conversely, affective theories of personality see them as operating on an emotional basis, with the intellect at the service of the emotions. Although RET has a reputation for cognitive therapy, its personality theory contains strong affective elements as well. It says that humans inextricably intertwine and cannot really separate their emotions and cognitions, and that what we call "emotion" largely consists of and results from powerful evaluations or cognitions. Secondly, RET places cognition or "intellect" squarely in the service of "affect" or emotion. It hypothesizes that people get born with a tendency to "value" or "feel" or "desire" in order to survive and to survive

reasonably happily; and that the term "rational," as used in RET, only applies to thoughts, emotions, and acts that abet these basic affective goals. Although RET uses cognitive, emotive, and behavioral methods of treatment, and uses them on theoretical grounds and not merely because they work, its aim and philosophy remain exceptionally hedonistic.

10. *Unconsciousness–consciousness.* Theories that stress the unconscious see the person as having considerable investment below the level of awareness. Consciousness refers to awareness, and consciousness theories see the individual as basically rational. In this personality dimension RET leans toward the consciousness side, but it heavily emphasizes the role of "unconscious" automaticity and habituation in the formation of disturbance. It therefore advocates a great deal of behavior therapy, forced practice, throwing oneself into doing "risky" things whether one likes to do so or not, and *in vivo* homework assignments designed to bring about "nonthinking" habituation or dehabituation.

Other RET Hypotheses about Personality

RET posits many concepts about personality, some of them unique and some held by other systems, especially by other cognitive-behavior therapeutic formulations. Some of the main RET personality hypotheses that now have a large amount of clinical and experimental research data behind them (Ellis, 1977b) include the following:

1. Human thinking and emotion do not constitute two disparate or different processes, but significantly overlap. Cognition represents a mediating operation between stimuli and responses. Emotions and behaviors stem not merely from people's reactions to their environment but also from their thoughts, beliefs, and attitudes about that environment.

2. People self-reflexively "talk" to themselves, and the kinds of things they say, as well as the form in which they say them, significantly affect their emotions and behaviors and sometimes lead to emotional disturbance.

3. Humans have the ability not only to think (and generalize) but to think about their thinking and to think about thinking about their thinking. When disturbed, they often tend to think about their disturbances and thereby create additional anxiety or depression.

4. People cognize, emote, and behave interrelatedly. Cognition contributes to emotion and to action; emotion to cognition and to action; and action to

cognition and to emotion. When people change one of these three modalities they concomitantly tend to change the other two.

5. When people expect something to happen they act significantly differently than when they have no such expectancies. Their cognitive expectancy influences both their emotions and their behaviors.

6. Humans have powerful innate and/or acquired tendencies to construct basic values and to think and act rationally (to abet) and irrationally (to sabotage) such values. They frequently have irrational or absolutistic ideas that interfere with healthy thoughts, emotions, and behaviors.

7. People have strong tendencies not only to rate their acts, behaviors, performances, and traits as "good" or "bad" but to rate their *selves* or *essences* similarly, and these self-ratings constitute one of the main sources of their disturbances.

8. People have a strong tendency to do things that seem easier in the short run even though they may bring poor future results.

SUMMARY AND CONCLUSION

While a full theory of human personality would go beyond the here and now and would look backwards into history to seek out biological and environmental causes and forward into the anticipated future, a multiplicity of factors makes all theories partly fanciful. These factors include poor reporting, the crucial element of how theorists construe and misconstrue the facts of biology and social influence, and the existence of so many elements in personality that no theory can put them all together properly. This explains why we have so many competing theories, all plausible, none satisfactory. While theory making seems an interesting but harmless occupation, it would appear more useful if theorists and experimenters concentrated on (1) the here-and-now aspects of behavior rather than its "origins" or "development," and (2) effective methods of modifying dysfunctional behaviors more than the "whys" of how they arose.

With such a practical emphasis, social scientists would not only come to better conclusions about how people change, they would also tend to discover which elements of therapy prove most effective and elegant, would hasten their discarding of the many useless and iatrogenic therapies now prevalent, and would help more people live increasingly satisfying lives. As a model, RET has helped researchers in their efforts to discover efficient ways of helping humans overcome intractable pain, to discover some basic facts of the nervous system which have led to theories about the biological and sociological origins and development of pain (Cherry, 1977).

In psychotherapy, research on therapy procedures by Bandura (1971), Beck (1976), Goldfried (Goldfried & Davison, 1976), Kanfer (1970), Mahoney (1974), Meichenbaum (1977), Mischel (1976), and many other experimenters has led to significant advances in personality theory. If this kind of research continues, we have a good prospect of looking more closely at the origins of human personality and disentangling (if possible) hereditarian from environmental influences. Without such research and the basic solid knowledge of behavior which it tends to give, the present confusing situation in which almost 100 separate theories of personality and personality change keep competing for attention (and the situation grows worse annually) will continue, and we may never come to any definitive conclusions.

As a basic issue, there is the question of whether personality theory shall be viewed as religion or science. If religion, then anyone can have a revelation and state that boys universally crave sexual intercourse with their mothers— or similar garbage. Given a beard and a doctoral degree, one can make any assertion without any proof, and obtain many devout listeners. If we read the 100 or so personality theories in existence, from the completely biological theory of William Sheldon (1942) to the almost completely psychological theories of George Kelly (1955), we can find literally tens of thousands of assertions made in good faith by honest people, few of which have any proven validity and, worse, many of which seem completely unprovable. Thus, we can have evidence that the moon does not consist of green cheese, but we seem to have no way of proving the existence or nonexistence of archetypes.

Personality theorists might do well to take some of the hypotheses in this article as the beginning of a truly scientific inquiry into personality. In this way we might finally determine the nature of people in the here and now, in their interactions in life and in therapy, and do so under controlled clinical and experimental conditions. Wouldn't this seem preferable to the continual creation of fanciful and intellectually *mus*turbatory conceptionalizations that lead nowhere—as a reading of the latest issues of many journals devoted to personality theory will show?

REFERENCES

Bandura, A. (1971). *Psychological modeling: Conflicting theories.* Chicago: Aldine.

Beck, A. T. (1976). *Cognitive therapy and the emotional disorders.* New York: International Universities Press.

Berne, E. (1964). *Games people play.* New York: Grove Press.

Buehler, K. (1965). *Die krise der psychologie.* Stuttgart: Gustave Fisher.

Cherry, L. (1977, January 30). Solving the mysteries of pain. *New York Times Magazine,* pp. 12–13, 50–53.

Coan, R. W. (1968). *The optimal personality.* New York: Wiley.

Corsini, R. (1977). *Current personality theories.* Itasca, IL: F. E. Peacock.

DiGiuseppe, R., Miller, N., & Trexler, L. (1977). A review of rational-emotive psychotherapy outcome studies. *The Counseling Psychologist,* 7(1), 64–72.

Ellis, A. (1962). *Reason and emotion in psychotherapy.* New York: Lyle Stuart.

Ellis, A. (1971). *Growth through reason.* Palo Alto, CA: Science and Behavior Books; Hollywood, CA: Wilshire Books.

Ellis, A. (1972). Psychotherapy and the value of a human being. In J. W. Davis (Ed.), *Value and valuation* (pp. 117–139). Knoxville: University of Tennessee Press.

Ellis, A. (1973a). *Humanistic psychotherapy: The rational-emotive approach.* New York: Julian Press and McGraw-Hill Paperbacks.

Ellis, A. (1973b). Rational-emotive therapy. In R. J. Corsini (Ed.), *Current psychotherapies.* Itasca, IL: F E. Peacock.

Ellis, A. (1975). *How to live with a "neurotic"* (rev. ed.). New York: Crown.

Ellis, A. (1976). The biological basis of human irrationality. *Journal of Individual Psychology, 32,* 145–168.

Ellis, A. (1977a). *How to live with—and without—anger.* New York: Reader's Digest Press.

Ellis, A. (1977b). Rational-emotive therapy: Research data that supports the clinical and personality hyotheses of RET and other modes of cognitive behavior therapy. *Counseling Psychologist, 7* (1), 2–42.

Ellis, A., & Grieger, R. (Eds.). (1977). *Handbook of rational-emotive therapy* (vol. 1). New York: Springer Publishing Co.

Ellis, A., & Harper, R. A. (1975). *A new guide to rational living.* Englewood Cliffs, NJ: Prentice-Hall; Hollywood, CA: Wilshire Books.

Evans, P. (1976). The Burt Affair . . . sleuthing in science. *APA Monitor, 1,* 4.

Freud, S. (1965). *Standard edition of the works of Sigmund Freud.* London: Hogarth Press.

Fromm, E. (1941). *Escape from freedom.* New York: Rinehart.

Fromm, E. (1975). *The anatomy of human destructiveness.* Greenwich, CT: Fawcett.

Goldfried, M. R., & Davison, G. C. (1976). *Clinical behavior therapy.* New York: Holt, Rinehart & Winston.

Horney, K. (1965). *Collected Writings.* New York: Norton.

Kanfer, F. (1970). Self-regulation: Research, issues and speculations. In C.

Neuringer & J. L. Michael (Eds.), *Behavior modification in clinical psychology*. New York: Appleton-Century-Crofts.

Kelly, G. (1955). *The psychology of personal constructs*. New York: Norton.

Korzybski, A. (1933). *Science and sanity*. Lancaster, PA: Lancaster Press.

Mahoney, M. (1974). *Cognition and behavior modification*. Cambridge, MA: Ballinger.

Maslow, A. H. (1954). The instinctoid nature of basic needs. *Journal of Personality, 22,* 326–347.

Maultsby, M. C. Jr. (1975). *Help yourself to happiness*. New York: Institute for Rational Living.

Meichenbaum, D. H. (1977). *Cognitive behavior therapy*. New York: Plenum.

Mischel, W. (1976). The self as the person. In A. Wandersman (Ed.), *Behavioristic and humanistic approaches to personality change*. New York: Pergamon.

Morris, K. T., & Kanitz, J. M. (1975). *Rational-emotive therapy*. Boston: Houghton Mifflin.

Murphy, R., & Ellis, A. (1977). *A comprehensive bibliography of rational-emotive therapy and cognitive-behavior therapy*. New York: Institute for Rational Living.

Pastore, N. (1949). *The nature-nurture controversy*. New York: King's Crown Press.

Sheldon, W. (1942). *Varieties of human temperament*. New York: Harper.

Sullivan, H. S. (1953). *Conceptions of modern psychiatry*. New York: Norton.

Woodworth, R. S., & Schlosberg, H. (1954). *Experimental psychology*. New York: Holt.

CHAPTER 18

LFT: EGO ANXIETY, AND DISCOMFORT ANXIETY

EDITOR'S COMMENTARY:

With 20/20 hindsight, it appears that Ellis described several forms of anxiety over the years. Among the several were ego anxiety or the ultimate fear that one's aliveness would be not only lessened (as in self-downing) but destroyed as in "awful" or "terrible" or "horrible" statements that implied catastrophe or personal doom and nonexistence, and the new discomfort anxiety (DA). Concerning the latter, Ellis made a distinction between it and low frustration tolerance (LFT). He referred to the latter sometimes as discomfort disturbance (DD). Included in this selection is a brief introduction by Windy Dryden in which he briefly explains the historical and developmental arguments for the distinction between DA and LFT, discomfort disturbance, and how LFT and DA overlap, as well as how elements of ego anxiety and the others overlap.

Excerpted from *The Essential Albert Ellis,*
Springer, 1990

INTRODUCTION

By 1978 Ellis was showing his clients and the therapists he supervised how important low frustration tolerance (LFT) was in creating and maintaining human disturbance. But till then he had not quite seen that LFT was often a form of anxiety than can be fairly clearly differentiated from ego anxiety.

The 28-year-old client whose case is presented in the following paper had, as a result of

RET *and previous therapy, overcome a great deal of self-downing but still often referred to his being "very anxious." Ellis concluded that the client had a classic case of "discomfort anxiety." He discovered that as soon as he brought "discomfort anxiety" to the attention of his supervisees and other therapists, they found this construct very useful in their attempts to help clients.*

Ironically, Ellis was somewhat hasty in labeling LFT "ego anxiety," even though the two disturbances clearly overlap and are basically the same. Ellis now holds that LFT not only creates some forms of anxiety but also some forms of depression and self-pity, and these feelings, although they have something in common with anxiety (especially common irrational beliefs), are not exactly the same. LFT, therefore, may more appropriately be named discomfort disturbance because it is often involved in depression, self-pity, love slobbism, extreme jealousy, addiction, compulsion, and other disorders, as well as in anxiety.

Nonetheless, the strength of the following paper is that it clearly distinguishes between two exceptionally common elements in emotional disturbance: ego-oriented and discomfort-oriented processes. As Ellis shows, these elements are not entirely different. Discomfort disturbance goes with a thought like "I, special me, must get exactly what I want when I want it!" and therefore includes ego grandiosity. Ego disturbance stems from thoughts like "I cannot stand failing and being rejected because I'll then get less goodies in life (which I must not get. If I cannot acquire these goodies, there must be something radically wrong with me.!")

Similarly, ego disturbance often includes the thought "I am such a worthless slob that therefore I need to be taken care of and catered to, or else I will be unable to get what I really want." Discomfort disturbance often includes the idea "Since I must have exactly what I want and frequently cannot get it, I am an incompetent and inadequate individual!"

Ego and discomfort disturbance often overlap or coalesce. Ellis has found that many people, however, have severe ego disturbance and little discomfort disturbance; and many others have much of the latter and little of the former. The most disturbed people, he has usually found, have high degrees of both.

There are two major forms of discomfort disturbance, or LFT: (1) anger at other people (e.g., "I absolutely need you to care for me and do my bidding, and you are a real turd if you don't!") and (2) anger at world conditions (e.g., "I absolutely need conditions to be arranged so that I am cared for and get everything I want, and the world is a horrible place if I am deprived!").

Because these two forms of LFT are closely related, Ellis says that humans almost invariably disturb themselves in only two major ways: by thinking in absolutist terms that produce ego disturbance and discomfort disturbance. He encourages his supervisees to look for both of these processes in anxious, depressed, self-hating, enraged, and self-

pitying people, and he argues that in doing so they will soon be able to zero in on the key source of their clients' emotional-behavioral disturbance.

This chapter amalgamates two papers first published in *Rational Living* the forerunner of the *Journal of Rational-Emotive & Cognitive Behavior Therapy:* Discomfort anxiety: A new cognitive-behavioral construct (parts 1 and 2), *14* (1979) and *15* (1980), respectively.

DISCOMFORT ANXIETY VERSUS EGO ANXIETY

For the past several years, largely on the basis of clinical evidence derived from my practice of rational-emotive therapy (RET), I have been distinguishing between two major forms of anxiety: discomfort anxiety (DA) and ego anxiety (EA). *Discomfort anxiety* I define as emotional tension that results when people feel (1) that their comfort (or life) is threatened, (2) that they *should* or *must* get what they want (and *should not* or *must not* get what they don't want), and (3) that it is *awful* or *catastrophic* (rather than merely inconvenient or disadvantageous) when they don't get what they supposedly *must.* *Ego anxiety* I define as emotional tension that results when people feel (1) that their self or personal worth is threatened; (2) that they *should* or *must* perform well and/or be approved by others; and (3) that it is *awful* or *catastrophic* when they don't perform well and/or are not approved by others as they supposedly *should* or *must* be.

Ego anxiety is a dramatic, powerful feeling that usually seems overwhelming; is often accompanied by feelings of severe depression, shame, guilt, and inadequacy and frequently drives people to therapy (or to suicide!). Discomfort anxiety is often less dramatic but perhaps more common. It tends to be specific to certain "uncomfortable" or "dangerous" situations, and consequently shows up in such phobias as fear of heights, open spaces, elevators, and trains. But it can also easily generalize to uncomfortable *feelings* themselves, such as feelings of anxiety, depression, and shame. Thus, DA may be a primary symptom (e.g., anxiety about elevators) or a secondary symptom (e.g., anxiety about feeling anxious about elevators).

As a secondary symptom, DA may generalize to almost *any* kind of anxiety. Thus, people may first feel anxious about feeling anxious about elevators; but they may later worry about whether they are *also* going to feel anxious about trains or escalators; and they may therefore actually make themselves exceptionally uncomfortable (anxious) about *many* forms of anxiety (discomfort) and may thereby become pandemically anxious. Or they may at first feel anxious about a specific event (e.g., about entering an elevator) and later, realizing that they may well become anxious about that event, they may also make themselves anxious about any symbol of that event (e.g., a picture of an elevator) or about any thought of that event (e.g., the thought "Suppose I have to take an elevator when I visit my friend. Wouldn't that possibility be awful?").

Because it is often less dramatic than ego anxiety (or self-downing) and because it may be a secondary rather than a primary symptom, discomfort anxiety may easily be unrecognized and may be somewhat wrongly labeled as general or free-floating anxiety. Thus, if people are anxious about going in elevators, they may clearly recognize their anxiety or phobia and label it "elevator phobia." But if they are anxious about being anxious (that is, fearful of the uncomfortable sensations they will probably feel if they enter an elevator or if they even think about entering an elevator), they may feel very anxious but may not see clearly *what* they are anxious about. Nor may their therapists!

The construct of discomfort anxiety helps to explain several phenomena relating to emotional disturbance in clearer and more therapeutic ways. Thus, if clients tell me they are so terrified of snakes that they feel extremely upset whenever they see even a picture of a snake, I can pretty well guess that they hardly think the *picture* will bite them. I can quickly surmise that they are not only afraid of snakes but also of their anxiety itself—of the uncomfortable *feelings* they will predictably have when they think about (or view a picture of) a snake.

My problem with these clients, therefore, is to get them first to stop awfulizing about their feelings of anxiety; to help them accept their discomfort (or potential discomfort) as a damned bother (and not as a holy honor!). Then, when they truly see that it's not awful to *feel* anxious, they can stop obsessing about this feeling and work on anti-awfulizing about the original feared object, the snakes. Their discomfort anxiety about their feelings helps keep them from confronting these feelings and working through them.

A research study that possibly shows the explanatory and therapeutic value of the construct of discomfort anxiety is that of Sutton-Simon (1979), who found some seemingly contradictory results that may be explained by the use of this construct. She noted that, in a study of subjects with fears of heights, subjects with social anxiety, and subjects with fears of heights plus social anxieties, those with fears of heights did not display significant irrationality on the Jones (1968) Irrational Beliefs Test (IBT); while those with social anxiety did show significant irrationality on the IBT.

This would be expected, according to the construct posited in this chapter, since fear of heights would presumably largely involve discomfort anxiety, while social anxiety would largely involve ego anxiety. Sutton-Simon (1979) observes that ego anxiety may be cross-situational, while discomfort anxiety may be specific to situations, although one person may experience discomfort anxiety in many situations. DA may be "hooked up" to the particular cues of the situation, while EA may be more of a quality of a person.

Although the construct of discomfort anxiety presented here seems to have some new and useful elements, it overlaps with several previous hypotheses about emotional disturbance and its treatment. Thus, Low (1952) pointed out that disturbed individuals often get upset about their symptoms of anxiety and panic, and that they may be helped by defining these symptoms as uncomfortable but not dangerous. Ellis (1962, 1979) emphasized secondary symptoms of disturbance, such as anxiety about anxiety, and stressed the role of low frustration tolerance and short-range hedonism in disturbed behavior and in clients' resistance to changing this behavior. Weekes (1969, 1972, 1977) highlighted the importance of anxiety about anxiety, especially in agoraphobia. Rehm (1977) offered a self-control model of depression that stresses hedonic as well as ego factors in this disturbance. The present formulations go somewhat beyond these other theories in developing a construct of discomfort anxiety and in distinguishing it more clearly from ego anxiety.

DISCOMFORT ANXIETY AND DEPRESSION

The concept of discomfort anxiety also tends to give a better explanation of the origins and treatment of depression than many of the other explanations. Abramson and Sackheim (1977) point out a seeming paradox in depression. On the one hand, depressed individuals—as Beck (1976) emphasizes—blame themselves and look upon themselves as unable to help themselves; they are distinct self-downers. But on the other hand, they insist, in a somewhat grandiose manner, that they must have certainty and must control the outcome of the events in their lives; and they depress themselves when they don't actually have that kind of full control. They are therefore both self-denigrating and self-deifying, which seems to be something of a paradox.

In RET terms, and in terms of ego anxiety and discomfort anxiety, this paradox seems quite resolvable. In RET, it is hypothesized that the individual tends to have three basic irrational Beliefs (iB's) about himself or herself and the universe: (1) "I *must* succeed at the important things that I do in life and win the approval of significant people in my life, and it is *awful* when I don't. I am therefore not as good as I *should* be, and I am therefore worthless." (2) "You *must* treat me kindly, fairly, and considerately, and it is *horrible* when you don't. You are therefore a crumb or a louse." (3) "The conditions under which I live *must* be easy, or at least not too difficult, and *must* give me all the things I really want quickly and without too much of a hassle; and it is *terrible* when they aren't that way. The world is a really rotten place in which to live and *should* not be the way it indubitably is."

Very often, depressed people have two of these basic ideas—the first and the third—and sometimes they have the second as well. There is no reason, of course, why they should not have two or three; and I also do not see why the first and the third, when they are strongly held, necessarily conflict with each other. The first one, "I *must* succeed at the important things that I do in life and win the approval of significant people in my life; and it is *awful* when I don't!" seems to be essentially self-downing. But its perfectionism is essentially grandiose, since the implication is that "I *must* be outstanding, perfect, and godlike; and if I am not what I must be in these respects, *then* it is *awful* and I am a worthless or rotten person." This same kind of grandiosity is also implied in the third irrationality; namely, "Because I am (or *should* be) a great person for whom everything goes easily and well in life, *therefore* the conditions under which I live must not be too difficult, and therefore it is *terrible* and the world is a horrible place if they are that difficult."

Implicit grandiosity, therefore, underlies virtually all emotional disturbance; namely, the unspoken (or spoken!) demand and command that "*I* must succeed and be universally approved; *you* must treat me kindly and fairly; and the *world conditions* must be easy and immediately gratifying for me." When these demands and commands are not met—as, of course, in reality, they usually are not—then I "logically" make myself anxious, despairing, depressed, or angry. Without these omnipotent insistences, I would only tend to make myself sorry, regretful, annoyed, and irritated.

Discomfort anxiety is particularly important in anxiety and depression, as I think will be shown in the following case illustration. Several years ago I saw a man of 28, who was severely anxious or panicked, as well as angry and depressed, virtually every day of the year, and had been so for 10 years prior to that time. He had been in intensive psychotherapy since the age of 15; and had improved moderately during this time, so that he at least had been able to go through college and work steadily as a bookkeeper. But he had been institutionalized twice, for a period of a year at a time; had not been able to achieve any intimate relations with women; and had led a very restricted and highly routinized existence. He frequently became so depressed that he seriously considered suicide.

On the surface, this man's problem was ego anxiety, since he insisted that he had to do things well and win others' approval, and he put himself down severely whenever he failed to do so. He said that he hated himself, had no self-confidence, and had an enormous fear of failure; and he was afraid to make any major decisions, for fear that he might make a mistake and would then have to castigate himself for this mistake.

Actually, however, this client had benefited somewhat from previous therapy, particularly from reading Ellis and Harper's (1975) book, *A New Guide to Rational Living*, which he used virtually as his bible. In many respects, he felt relatively little shame or guilt as, for example, when he dressed sloppily and was criticized for not socializing, and when he acted quite selfishly, even with friends and relatives whom he most loved and respected. So I began to suspect that his main problem was discomfort anxiety, rather than ego anxiety, although he also had aspects of the latter (as perhaps almost every human does). In a typical fit of anxiety, depression, and anger, he would think and act in the following ways:

1. He would become exceptionally "anxious" or "panicked" when he had to wait in line at a store or wait to be served at a bar. Here, he seemed to be demanding that conditions be easier and that he be served immediately; he had fairly clear-cut low frustration tolerance or discomfort anxiety.

2. Once he became "panicked," he would tell himself, "I *must* not overreact in this manner; what a worm I am!" and would experience ego anxiety. But, often much more strongly, he would insist to himself, "I *must* not be panicked and feel such horrible discomfort at being panicked!" and would experience secondary symptoms of discomfort anxiety.

3. He would then notice that he was continually panicked over hassles and difficulties; and when he saw that this was so (largely as a result of the RET he was undergoing), he would then insist that life was *too* hard and that it *was* awful that he kept being set upon in these horrible ways. He would naively ask me, "Don't *you* feel terrible when people force you to do what you really don't want to do, such as wait on line for a long time at a store?" When I answered that I certainly did not like that kind of thing but that I accepted it and thereby was able to edit out almost entirely some of the inconvenience I was caused, he simply could not understand how I could accept it. He

considered it intrinsically horrible to be balked in any desire, even relatively little ones like wanting to be waited on quickly at a store, and thought that everyone in the universe thought it equally horrible.

4. As he kept upsetting himself in these ways, he realized that he was, at least in the degree of his upsetness, different from other people. So he again put himself down for that and went back, once more, to ego anxiety. Then he also felt horrified about the uncomfortableness of continually feeling panicked and reverted, once more, to discomfort anxiety about this continual discomfort; that is, he would not accept it and viewed it as being a virtually unlivable state. Again, he felt suicidal (though not actively so) because of these continued feelings; and again he wondered about his suicidalness and whether he was a rotten person, much different from and worse than others, for having such feelings. At times, however, he merely accepted such feelings and thought that he was quite justified in thinking about killing himself because of the "horrible" discomforts of living.

5. Because this client defined almost all of his strong wants or desires as absolute needs—which is the philosophical essence of discomfort anxiety— he reemphasized his irrational belief, "I *must* do well!" For he devoutly believed that only by doing well would he get more of the things that he absolutely "needed." When he did not perform beautifully, therefore, he not only downed himself for his inadequacy but also felt that his performance was below his "need" level, and he thereby experienced discomfort anxiety as well as ego anxiety.

All in all, this client's DA continually intermingled with and helped reinforce his EA, and vice versa. Like many severely disturbed people, he probably would have functioned poorly with only EA, for he often seriously downed himself for his errors and for experiencing others' disapproval. But it is unlikely that he would have been as critically disturbed as he was without his suffering from both ego anxiety and discomfort anxiety. From observing him and many other clients like him, I hypothesize that some individuals suffer emotionally because of their ego anxiety and some because of their discomfort anxiety, and that those who have a combination of severe EA and DA are even more disturbed than those who have one or the other and are also less likely to change themselves or to benefit from any form of psychotherapy.

Another often-noted phenomenon that can be explained nicely by the hypothesis of discomfort anxiety is the observation that people who suffer severe depression frequently have lost their parents or other significant persons early in their lives; that this kind of depression is also related to job loss, to serious economic reversal, or to retirement from a satisfactory position; and that, as Levitt and Lubin (1975) show, depression proneness is not related to such traditional demographic variables as age, sex, and race, but instead increases as educational background, annual income, and ability to improve one's financial situation decrease. If these observations are true, we can easily conclude that people who are deprived of parental or economic satisfactions early or later in their lives suffer loss of status and consequent ego anxiety, and that they therefore are more prone to having severe feelings of depression. But we can perhaps more logically conclude that people who are deprived in these affectional and economic ways often (though not, of course, always) have low frustration tolerance or discomfort anxiety, and that a combination of actual frustration plus their discomfort anxiety *about* this frustration often drives them over the brink into the arms of severe depressive reactions. Frustration, Dollard, Doob, Miller, Mowrer, and Sears (1939) once wrongly claimed, leads to aggression. In itself, it doesn't. Nor does it lead to depression. But frustration *of people with abysmal discomfort anxiety* (for which there may exist a biological proneness or vulnerability, as well as a reinforcement or escalation resulting from unusually frustrating events) may lead to almost any kind of disturbed reaction, including aggression and depression.

As Beck (1967, 1976) and Ellis (1962) point out, depression is usually linked with ego anxiety, with people deprecating themselves for their poor performances and believing that, therefore, because *they* are worthless or hopelessly incompetent, they cannot handle life situations and particularly difficult situations that are occurring or may occur. But even in this ego anxiety aspect of depression, discomfort anxiety is probably also a factor, for depressed individuals are not merely telling themselves that they are so incompetent that they cannot master normal life situations and prove how "worthwhile" or "great" they are. They are also probably telling themselves that they are so hopelessly inept that they cannot ward off present and future *inconveniences* and *discomforts,* and that therefore their lives are, and will continue to be, terrible and horrible.

Depression also involves another and perhaps more common element of discomfort anxiety. For depressed people frequently have such abysmally low frustration tolerance that they refuse to accept ordinary or mild hassles, let alone unusual ones, and they can easily whine and wail when they don't have *good enough* events in their lives, or when they once had it easy and comfortable, but now that they have lost their jobs or lost money they don't any longer have it *that* good.

Years ago, before I realized how important a factor discomfort anxiety usually is in the case of severe feelings of depression, I mainly showed my depressed clients that they did *not* have to rate themselves for doing poorly in life (or for doing less well than others were doing) and that they could accept themselves unconditionally, *whether or not* they performed well and *whether or not* significant others approved of them. This helped them immensely in many instances, but in others I found that it was hardly sufficient.

I now *also* look for their discomfort anxiety, and I practically always seem to find it. If I am able to help them, as I often am, to give up their demanding and commanding that conditions be easier and more immediately gratifying, and their insisting that they get what they want quickly and effortlessly, I find not only that they get over their profound depressions, sometimes in fairly short order, but that they also have much less of a tendency to return to a depressed state when something unfortunate occurs in their lives at a later date.

TREATING DISCOMFORT ANXIETY

I do not find it easy to help people raise their level of frustration tolerance and thereby reduce or eliminate their discomfort anxiety. I am fairly convinced that virtually all human beings have a strong biological tendency to defeat themselves by being short-range hedonists and going for immediate rather than long-range gain (Ellis, 1976). That is why so many of them refuse to give up addictions such as smoking, overeating, alcohol abuse, and procrastination, which they "know" are harmful and which they keep resolving to overcome. But when they are induced by various kinds of therapy, including RET, to stay with discomfort, to see that it is *only* inconvenient and *not* unbearable, they often increase their frustration tolerance, overcome their discomfort anxiety, and make significant changes in their dysfunctional feelings and behaviors.

One reason for this lack of change in clients who have significant elements of both ego anxiety and discomfort anxiety is that they often bring up these two elements as if they were *one* problem. Consequently, their therapists mistakenly shuttle back and forth trying to help them with this supposedly *single* problem and end up trying, in a sense, to solve a quadratic equation with two unknowns—which is impossible to do! Thus, in the case of the client mentioned earlier, he could be said to have had two somewhat distinct problems, both of which started from the same premise. The premise would be, "I must get a good result at the things I do, especially a good result at producing my own feelings." This premise would lead to two rather different conclusions: (1) "When I do the wrong things and produce the wrong kind of feelings, I can't stand the *discomfort* I create. Under these conditions, the world is too hard for me to live in happily and I might just as well be dead!" (2) "When I do the wrong things and produce the wrong kind of feelings, I can't stand *myself* for acting so foolishly. Under these conditions, I am hopelessly inept, will always fail to get what I want, and hardly deserve to go on living!"

If clients with discomfort anxiety present material that shows these two irrational ideas, the therapist may get "hooked" into their system by trying to show them how to accept gracefully the discomfort that the world brings them and that they themselves produce. If the therapist fails to zero in on the client's problems *one at a time,* then the two will get confused with each other and the disputing of the client's irrational ideas will be so confounded that a satisfactory solution is unlikely.

It is important, therefore, for the therapist to recognize these two *different* (though perhaps overlapping) points clearly, and to deal first with one and then with the other, so that clients finally see that they have two disparate irrational ideas and that both of them produce dysfunctional emotional and behavioral results. Thus, if the therapist initially focuses on clients' discomfort anxiety, the clients may give up the idea that they *must* not experience "wrong" feelings because the discomfort of experiencing them is *too* difficult and *should not* be that difficult. After doing this, the therapist then probably has a better chance of zeroing in on clients' ego anxiety and helping them give up the idea that they *must not* experience "wrong" feelings because they are *lousy people* for acting ineptly. Either one of the irrational beliefs may be clearly seen and uprooted if the therapist considers them *independently.* But if they are tackled together, or if the therapist and client keep shuttling back and forth from one to the other, then there is a good chance that neither will be seen clearly nor given up.

If I am correct about the existence of discomfort anxiety (DA) and ego anxiety (EA) and their tendency to reinforce each other when they coexist in an individual, then these concepts serve to explain some other aspects of human disturbance and psychotherapy that have long been noted in the literature. For one thing, many indulgent forms of psychotherapy have often produced good, albeit temporary, results. Thus, large numbers of malfunctioning individuals have felt better for awhile and achieved transient symptom removal as a result of hypnosis, suggestion, reassurance, approval, and catharsis. I believe that most of these clients actually start to *feel* better rather than to *get* better in any permanent sense, but they definitely often do improve (Ellis, 1968, 1970, 1974). I would speculate that they do so largely because these indulgent techniques of therapy temporarily allay their discomfort anxiety. Even though it returns fairly soon—because their basic notion that they *must not* suffer frustration and deprivation has not been surrendered and may even be augmented—they at least feel significantly better and relatively symptom-free for a short period of time.

Another interesting phenomenon that can be partially explained by the concept of discomfort anxiety is the case of individuals who are converted to some highly implausible and probably irrational idea, such as the idea that God or Jesus has a personal interest in them and will save them from harm. Such people consequently achieve a distinct personality change, such as becoming recovered alcoholics. I hypothesize that these people, through their devout belief in some kind of magical cure, become highly motivated to work at their discomfort anxiety and to go through present pain to reap the rewards of future gain. Perhaps, for reasons that might be called wrong, they do the right thing: discipline themselves to give up alcohol, drugs, overeating, smoking, or gambling. They then see that they *can* control their own destiny, whereas previously they incorrectly thought that they could not. They may even acquire some sensible ideas along with the irrational ones that initially led them to discipline themselves and ameliorate their low frustration tolerance.

Still another aspect of therapy that can be explained by the concept of discomfort anxiety is the phenomenon of therapists leading many clients to believe in false or scientifically groundless ideas and thereby inadvertently helping these clients to become less disturbed. Thus, orthodox Freudians show people that their parents treated them cruelly when they were children and that this past cruelty makes them neurotic today (Freud, 1965); primal therapists go even further than this and teach their clients that they all suffered from intense primal pain as a result of their parents' iniquity and that if they now scream, yell, and release this pain, they will significantly improve their ability to function (Janov, 1970). Both of these concepts are probably false, for they are largely stimulus-response rather than stimulus-organism-response theories, and they posit early childhood stimuli that were most likely nonexistent.

Interestingly enough, however, when a Freudian analyst or a primal therapist induces clients to mull over their past histories and biological tendency of humans and of certain other animals (e.g., rats or guinea pigs); that organisms of this sort innately strive to predict what is going on around them, to control their environments so that they get more of what they want and less of what they don't want, and thereby to survive satisfactorily or "happily." When they perceive that there is a high degree of probability that they will be able to do this, they persist in their adjustive reactions and therefore are "healthy" or "non-neurotic." When they perceive (rightly or wrongly) that they probably cannot control their life situations and get what they want, they either gracefully live with their continued frustrations (developing a philosophy of accepting the inevitable) or they refuse to accept this grim reality (whimpering and whining and developing a philosophy of desperate nonacceptance, a neurotic or nonadjustive outlook that frequently results in depression and withdrawal).

I am also hypothesizing that human phobias are particularly related to discomfort anxiety. When people have, for example, a phobia of airplanes, they usually have some element of ego anxiety; that is, they devoutly believe that *they,* now that they are alive, should live practically forever and *must* not die before their time; and they also frequently believe that it is shameful for them to display their fear of airplanes in front of others (e.g., flight personnel and plane passengers), and consequently they have to stay out of planes to avoid this "shameful" activity.

More important, however, they seem to have enormous discomfort anxiety about the supposed unpredictability of the plane's falling ("Yes, I know there is little chance of its falling, but suppose it does!"), and they also have discomfort anxiety about their own initial anxiety reactions (which are often exceptionally uncomfortable). They therefore avoid plane flights, often to their own disadvantage.

In desensitizing these individuals to the thing they fear (e.g., plane flights), therapists have their choice of many methods, including systematic desensitization (SD) (Wolpe, 1958), imaginative implosion (Stampfl & Levis, 1967), and in vivo desensitization in the course of rational-emotive therapy (Ellis, 1962, 1971, 1973; Ellis & Whiteley, 1979; Ellis & Grieger, 1977). These seem to be radically different methods of desensitization, but as Teasdale (1977) points out, they have one thing in common: repeated presentation of a fear stimulus with no apparent disastrous consequence.

It seems that people with airplane (or other) phobias keep telling themselves, for one reason or another, "Going in a plane is too frightening, too painful; I can't stand it; I would practically fall apart at the seams if I had to experience this terrible event!" and they keep reindoctrinating themselves with this "fear" and reinforcing their belief in it by *not* going up in a plane. Every time they refuse to do so, they keep telling themselves (overtly or tacitly), "If I did fly, it *would* be horribly uncomfortable and now that I am avoiding flying, I can see how relatively comfortable I feel!" Moreover, by fearfully refusing to confront their phobia and *do* something to overcome it, it becomes almost impossible to get rid of it.

In virtually all kinds of desensitizing procedures, as Teasdale (1977) notes, they *do* something about their phobia: They actively confront it, either imaginatively or in vivo, and they *discover* that (1) the unpredictable event has more predictability than they originally thought it did; (2) nothing disastrous happens to them and they are *only* uncomfortable, and not, as they imagined, utterly *destroyed* by the confrontation; (3) they learn a technique such as SD, implosion therapy, or RET that gives them some possibility of *coping* with their anxiety in the future; (4) they learn that although they cannot control the feared event (the possibility of the plane's falling), they can definitely control some of their own *reactions* to it and therefore face a much "safer" kind of situation should they actually confront the feared object.

Let us make one other observation about the concept of discomfort anxiety (DA) in explaining and dealing with phobias. Emmelkamp, Kuipers, and Eggeraat (1978), in a study showing that in vivo desensitization works better with agoraphobics than do three different kinds of cognitive restructuring without in vivo retraining, point out that clinical agoraphobics probably differ from subjects in analog studies in that they have a higher degree of physiological arousal in anxiety-engendering situations (Lader, 1967) than do the former subjects. They note that "it is quite possible that cognitive restructuring constitutes an effective form of treatment for low physiological reactors (such as the subjects of analog studies), while such treatment will be effective for high physiological reactors (such as agoraphobics) only after the autonomic component has been reduced."

In a comment on the Emmelkamp et al. (1978) paper, I quite agree with their observation (Ellis, 1979). For if it is true that agoraphobics (and many other serious phobics) are high physiological reactors—and my own clinical findings for many years lead me to strongly support this hypothesis—then I would assume that they tend to feel more discomfort, and presumably more discomfort anxiety, than certain other disturbed individuals. Consequently, it seems likely they would tend to develop more phobias and hold on to them more strongly than would "lighter" or less physiologically involved phobics. The discomfort anxiety theory helps explain why agoraphobics are somewhat different from other phobics and why they are so difficult to treat.

In many important respects, then, the concept of discomfort anxiety seems to shed light on human disturbance and on psychotherapeutic processes. It especially leads the way toward creating and utilizing more effective, more elegant, and more long-lasting forms of psychological treatment. I suggest, for example, that many or most of the therapeutic methods used today are in themselves forms of indulgence, and that in the long run they reinforce people's discomfort anxiety and possibly do more harm than good. Take, for instance, muscular relaxation methods, which are so popular among behavior therapists. While there is no question that such techniques frequently work and result in considerable symptom removal, like all methods of therapy, they also have ideological implications, some of which seem to be iatrogenic:

1. Usually, as in Wolpe's (1958, 1973) systematic desensitization, relaxation is used in a gradual way to interrupt clients' feelings of anxiety. The very gradualness of this procedure, I suggest, may easily reaffirm these clients' beliefs that they *must* slowly, easily, and by comfortable degrees, tackle their anxieties, and that as soon as they experience any intense feelings of fear they *have* to relax their muscles and thereby distract themselves from these feelings. Such beliefs, of course, may well serve to increase, rather than to decrease, their discomfort anxiety.

2. Relaxation methods essentially consist of cognitive distraction rather than cognitive restructuring. If, for example, clients are afraid of elevators and they imagine themselves getting closer and closer to elevators and then, as they feel anxious about this imagined closeness, they focus on relaxing their muscles, they automatically distract themselves from the idea "I *must not* enter elevators; it would be *awful* if something happened to me when I rode in them!" They may well decrease their anxiety by this distraction procedure, but they usually have not *worked at* really *giving up* their irrational beliefs about riding in elevators. Relaxation and other forms of cognitive distraction are almost always much easier than actively combating and rethinking one's basic irrationalities. They consequently reinforce people's notions of the horror of work, for instance, and thus may increase their discomfort anxiety.

3. Cognitive distraction, though a viable method of psychotherapy, probably is not as effective in most instances as in vivo desensitization. By employing it with clients, the therapist avoids getting them to face the actual elevators or other irrationally feared objects, and thereby gives them an inelegant method of solving their problems. Again, it tends to sustain or augment their discomfort anxiety.

It is tempting for me to overemphasize the significance of discomfort anxiety and to relate all forms of emotional disturbance to this concept. Thus, humans tend to believe that they *must* perform well and have approval, that others *must* treat them properly, and that the conditions under which they live *must* be easy and enjoyable. When these three *mus*turbatory views are not affirmed by reality—which is often the case in this frustrating world—they usually conclude that they *can't stand* their own, others', or the world's imperfections and that it is *awful and terrible* that such unpleasantness is allowed to occur. In some respects, they seem to have low frustration tolerance (LFT) or discomfort anxiety as an aspect of virtually all their emotional disturbances—their self-downing, their hostility, and their self-pity. In a sense, then, we could say that virtually all "emotional" disturbances arise from LFT.

My clinical perception and judgment, however, tells me that this formulation omits some essential data about people and their disturbances. Although ego anxiety and discomfort anxiety are found in almost all individuals, and, as noted already, significantly interrelate and reinforce each other, I think it is best to view them as separate but interlocking behaviors. In that way, they have maximum explanatory and therapeutic usefulness.

REFERENCES

Abramson, L. Y., & Sackheim, H. A. (1977). A paradox in depression: Uncontrollability and self-blame. *Psychological Bulletin, 84,* 838–851.

Beck, A. T. (1967). *Depression.* New York: Hoeber-Harper.

Beck, A. T. (1976). *Cognitive therapy and the emotional disorders.* New York: International Universities Press.

Dollard, J., Doob, L., Miller, N. E., Mowrer, O.H., & Sears, R. R. (1939). *Frustration and aggression.* New Haven, CT: Yale University Press.

Ellis, A. (1962). *Reason and emotion in psychotherapy.* New York: Lyle Stuart.

Ellis, A. (1968). What really causes therapeutic change? *Voices, 4*(2), 90–97.

Ellis, A. (1970). The cognitive element in experiential and relationship psychotherapy. *Existential Psychiatry, 28,* 35–42.

Ellis, A. (1971). *Growth through reason.* Palo Alto, CA: Science and Behavior Books; Hollywood, CA: Wilshire Books.

Ellis, A. (1973). *Humanistic psychotherapy: The rational-emotive approach.* New York: Julian Press and McGraw-Hill Paperbacks.

Ellis, A. (1974). Cognitive aspects of abreactive therapy. *Voices, 10*(1), 48–56.

Ellis, A. (1976). The biological basis of human irrationality. *Journal of Individual Psychology, 32,* 145–168.

Ellis, A. (1979). A note on the treatment of agoraphobics with cognitive modification versus prolonged exposure *in vivo. Behavior Research and Therapy, 17*(2), 162–163.

Selections from the Writings of Albert Ellis Ph.D.

Ellis, A., & Grieger, R. (1977). *Handbook of rational-emotive therapy.* New York: Springer Publishing Co.

Ellis, A., & Harper, R. A. (1975). *A new guide to rational living.* Englewood Cliffs, NJ: Prentice-Hall; Hollywood, CA: Wilshire Books.

Ellis, A., & Whiteley, J. M. (Eds.). (1979). *Theoretical and empirical foundations of rational-emotive therapy.* Monterey, CA: Brooks/Cole.

Emmelkamp, P. M. G., Kuipers, A. C., & Eggeraat, J. B. (1978). Cognitive modification versus prolonged exposure *in vivo:* A comparison with agoraphobics as subjects. *Behaviour Therapy and Research, 16,* 33–41.

Freud, S. *Standard edition of the complete psychological works of Sigmund Freud.* London: Hogarth, 1965.

Gantt, W. H. (1944). Experimental basis for neurotic behavior. *Psychosomatic Medicine Monographs,* Nos. 3 & 4.

Hamilton, G. V. (1925). *An introduction to objective psychopathology.* St. Louis: C. V. Mosby.

Janov, A. (1970). *The primal scream.* New York: Delta.

Jones, R. G. (1968). *A factored measure of Ellis' irrational belief system, with personality and maladjustment correlates.* Unpublished doctoral dissertation, Texas Technological University, Lubbock, TX.

Lader, M. H. (1967). Palmer skin conductance measures in anxiety and phobic states. *Journal of Psychosomatic Research, 11,* 271–281.

Levitt, E. E., & Lubin, B. (1975). *Depression,* New York: Springer Publishing Co.

Lidell, H. S. (1944). Conditioned reflex method and experimental neurosis. In J. McV. Hunt (Ed.), *Personality and the behavior disorders.* New York: Ronald.

Low, A. A. (1952). *Mental health through will training.* Boston: Christopher.

Marks, I. M., Viswanathan, R., Lipsedge, M. S., & Gardner, R. (1972). Enhanced relief by flooding during waning diazepam effect. *British Journal of Psychiatry, 121,* 493–505.

Masserman, J. H. (1943). *Behavior and neurosis.* Chicago: University of Chicago Press.

Mineka, S., & Kihlstrom, J. F. (1978). Unpredictable and uncontrollable events: A new perspective on experimental neurosis. *Journal of Abnormal Psychology, 87,* 256–271.

Pavlov, I. P. (1927). *Conditioned reflexes.* London: Oxford University Press.

Rehm, L. P. (1977). A self-control model of depression. *Behavior Therapy, 8,* 787–804.

Seligman, M. E. P. (1975). *Helplessness.* San Francisco: W. H. Freeman.

Stampfl, P. G., & Levis, D. J. (1967). Essentials of implosive therapy. *Journal of Abnormal Psychology, 72,* 496–503.

Sutton-Simon, K. (1979). A study of irrational ideas of individuals with fears of heights, with social anxiety, and with fear of heights plus social anxieties. *Cognitive Therapy and Research, 3*(2), 193–204.

Teasdale, J. D. (1977). Psychological treatment of phobias. In N. S.

Sutherland (Ed.), *Tutorial essays in psychology* (Vol. 1). Hillsdale, NJ: Erlbaum.

Weekes, C. (1969). *Hope and help for your nerves.* New York: Hawthorne.

Weekes, C. (1972). *Peace from nervous suffering.* New York: Hawthorne.

Weekes, C. (1977). *Simple effective treatment of agoraphobia.* New York: Hawthorne.

Wolpe, J. (1958). *Psychotherapy by reciprocal inhibition.* Stanford, CA: Stanford University Press.

Wolpe, J. (1973). *The practice of behavior therapy.* New York: Pergamon.

Wolpe, J. (1978). Cognition and causation in human behavior and its therapy. *American Psychologist, 33,* 437–446.

CHAPTER 19

AN ACTIVE-DIRECTIVE PSYCHOTHERAPY

EDITOR'S COMMENTARY:

Ellis explained changes in style and content in this selection. He especially pointed out differences between his comments made in the 1962 edition of Reason and Emotion in Psychotherapy *and the more recent 1994 revision. Yet, Ellis argued that individual human disturbance evolved from early parental influences, from society, and from one's own constructions. Ellis gave examples of how he originally demanded that homework be completed by a client (the so-called appeal to authority, namely, Ellis) to a more collaborative construction of what was to be accomplished, how it was to be done, and so on. Above all, Ellis argued that being active-directive was seldom rejected by clients. Today, a more careful distinction might be made between being "quietly" active rather than active in ways that could seem threatening to a client—especially a passive-dependent client.*

Excerpted from *Reason and Emotion in Psychotherapy,*
Birch Lane Press, 1994

1. REBT takes the stand, in theory and in practice, that both the therapist and the client had better be quite active in the course of therapy. Although the client's attitudes can definitely change when the therapist is relatively passive, it is assumed that he or she can be more effectively helped if the therapist is at least partly didactic.

2. REBT holds that people often hold on to their ideas very strongly and rigidly; and that therefore they had often better be vigorously persuaded by a therapist that they can give them up and arrive at less self-defeating Beliefs.

3. Irrational Beliefs (iBs) that people upset themselves with what are largely premises and certainly not facts. They therefore can be actively challenged by an effective therapist. And illogical deductions that are made from (sensible and self-defeating) Beliefs can also be shown to be invalid and self-defeating—if the therapist actively demonstrates this to his or her clients.[1]

4. According to REBT, people largely construct their main irrationalities—that is, their musts and demands about achieving their preferences—but they are also strongly influenced (because they are highly suggestible) by their parents and their culture. Therefore their therapists had better exert a fairly strong influence to help them counteract the many other strong influences on them.[2]

5. REBT goes along with Kurt Goldstein, A. H. Maslow, and Carl Rogers, that people have innate self-changing and self-actualizing tendencies. But it also holds that they have strong innate self-defeating, musturbatory tendencies and that the latter frequently get in the way of and block the former. Only, often, with outside therapeutic teaching help, are they likely to be able to decrease their self-defeating and enhance their self-actualizing tendencies.[3]

6. In the case of some very disturbed and rigid clients—particularly personality disorders—a dramatic, no-nonsense attitude by the therapist may almost be necessary for real help to take place.

7. Clients actively discourage themselves about their ability to change. Consequently, active encouragement on the part of their therapists proves to be very useful and sometimes even necessary.

8. Many therapists seem to be afraid that they will lose most of their clients if they directly go after their nonsense and try to help them change it. I have rarely found this to be true in using REBT. If therapists think they *need* their clients' approval they will tend to be passive and namby-pamby. This rarely does either them or their clients much good! Active-directive therapists are hardly that needy or weak.

9. A great deal of resistance by clients may result from their quite sensibly resisting the poor techniques of psychoanalytic and other therapists. With more efficient therapy, they will probably resist much less.[4]

10. Clients persist, over the years, in adopting, creating, and maintaining bad habits. Without realizing that they are doing so, they really work very persistently and vigorously to make themselves get and stay disturbed. Therefore, therapists can often vigorously persist at teaching them how and encouraging them to change.

11. Clients' activity is just as important as that of their therapists. Here is how I ushered in the cognitive-behavior revolution in the 1950s and summarized what I had been doing in the first edition of *Reason and Emotion in Psychotherapy*. "Vigorous verbal rethinking will usually lead to changed motor behavior; and forcefully repatterned sensory-motor activity will usually lead to changed ideation. But the quickest and most deep-rooted behavioral modification will usually follow from a *combined* attack on the old dysfunctional ways of thinking-doing."[5]

12. Disturbed clients have forcefully upset themselves, usually for many years, and often have a powerful tendency to hang on to their self-defeating thoughts, feelings, and behaviors. So active-directive, and sometimes forceful, therapy is frequently in order.

13. As pointed out in the last chapter of the original edition of *Reason and Emotion in Psychotherapy*, much of the resistance of clients is probably biologically based and results from their easily resisting all kinds of change, including favorable change. Therefore, therapists can acknowledge this fact and work quite hard to help clients overcome their natural resistance.[6]

14. Resistance often stems from the clients' low frustration tolerance (LFT) and discomfort disturbance. Therefore therapists had better show them clearly that this is so and show them how to tackle and to overcome their LFT.[7]

15. Much resistance may result from the clients being defensive and feeling too uncomfortable, because of shame or embarrassment, to tackle some of their main problems. REBT actively-directively deals with this form of resistance by showing clients, right from the start, that they do not have to feel ashamed of anything, nor put themselves down as humans no matter how badly they perform. It therefore often swiftly helps them to overcome this form of resistance.[8]

16. Many clients at first refuse to acknowledge that they are angry, anxious, or otherwise emotionally upset. So the therapist's active persistence in showing them that they really do have these feelings often helps them accept them and to work against them.

17. To change their thoughts, feelings, and behaviors people almost always have to act against them as well as to think and feel against them. Consequently, although therapists may not forcefully assign homework, they had often better strongly collaborate with clients to accept it and work at carrying it out.

18. A combined verbal and behavioral disputing of the client's dysfunctional thoughts, feelings, and acts will usually be much better than either one of these forms of disputation. Therefore, effective therapists had better do their best to see that clients work in both these highly important areas.[9]

As might be expected, some of the material that I outlined in this chapter of the original *Reason and Emotion in Psychotherapy* is now out of date and has been corrected in modern REBT. Here are some of the changes that I have made:

I emphasized that people usually become neurotic because they take over their irrational Beliefs from their parents and then actively repropagandize themselves. This is partly true. But it is probably more true that people largely accept the goals and standards of their parents and culture and then creatively *construct* their absolutistic shoulds and musts about these standards. So modern REBT mainly holds that they largely upset themselves and then "constructively" continue to upset themselves with the same basic musts.

I say that people's triple-headed indoctrination with irrational Beliefs—from their parents, their society, and their own creation—makes their musts very strong. Actually, the musts are strong because they largely flow from *strong* preferences, and people easily and naturally hang on to these. Their milder goals and preferences, however, which they largely learn from others, as well as construct themselves, are often not that strong, and they less often musturbate about them.

Also, the standards and values that we learn and construct—such as the values of love, success, comfort, and safety—are often sensible preferences and aid our survival and happiness. But we then creatively demand that we *must* at all times achieve these values and we thereby practically guarantee that we will frequently make ourselves anxious, depressed, self-hating, enraged, and self-pitying.

We construct and reconstruct almost everything we do—including our neuroses! We do so because that is our biological nature. We, like other animals, largely construct our lives by unconsciously or tacitly reacting to the Activating Events we experience. But, as humans, we have the ability to do a good deal of conscious, aware, cognitive, emotive, and behavioral reconstruction, and that is what REBT active-directively tries to enhance.[10]

On pages 198 to 204 of *Reason and Emotion in Psychotherapy*, I keep indicating that I and other rational emotive behavior therapists actively *give* homework assignments and forcefully get after clients to carry these out. The second part of this statement is true, because in my individual and group therapy I check on my clients' assignments, discover what they are telling themselves if they are not doing them, and see that they are reassigned. However, I (and other REBT practitioners) rarely *give* homework or reassign it without *collaborating* with clients on what would be particularly suitable for each of them and without *agreeing* on what the homework is—and often *agreeing* on what reinforcers may be used if it is done and what penalties may be incurred if it isn't done. In group therapy, the other members also actively participate in suggesting what other members will do for homework and how later changes will be made.

Thus, Manny, a thirty-year-old, very shy virgin agreed with me and his therapy group that, for the first time in his life, he would talk to a woman at a popular New York bar. But when he failed to do so because of his extreme anxiety about other people at the bar seeing him get rejected, we agreed with him to change his assignment to merely talking over the phone to a woman who had placed an ad in a personals column. After doing this, he agreed to talk to a woman sitting next to him on a bus; and after succeeding, three weeks later, in doing so, he agreed again to try to pick up a woman at a bar even though others were watching him. He was able to try to do so three times in one night. He figured out for himself that he would only allow himself to order any kind of drink *after* he had talked to a woman; and that worked!

On page 199, I say, "An individual's disturbance largely [may] consist of the original irrational sentences he has been indoctrinated with in his childhood and that he has kept telling himself ever since that time." I now see that he largely indoctrinated himself with his shoulds and musts and that then he has kept telling them to himself or, more accurately, thinking them unconsciously on a profound underlying philosophical level, and acting on them, without too often actually voicing them to himself.

I presented several cases of actively using REBT with various of my early clients in the 1962 version of this chapter. So let me, with a few minor revisions, repeat these cases here.

When I was seeing a schizophrenic woman who had had no less than fifteen years of previous therapy with several competent therapists and who, when I saw her, was still exceptionally disturbed, I took all the client could give for several months. And she gave plenty! She would call me up literally in the middle of the night; would refuse to leave the therapeutic session when her time had expired; would yell at me in a loud tone of voice, so that any other waiting clients would hear; would phone me while other clients were being seen and would refuse to make the call brief, so that I finally would hang up on her. She frequently acted negative and hostile. I absorbed the hostility and obtained a fine degree of rapport with her; but still, from time to time, she would be overtly hostile.

One day, when she was refusing to leave my office when her session had expired, I deliberately raised my voice and said: "Now, look here: I've taken enough of your nonsense as far as not getting out of here on time is concerned. I've spoken to you nicely about this several times before, but apparently it hasn't done any good. Now I'm telling you once and for all: if you don't get out of here *pronto* whenever I signal that the session has come to an end, you can take yourself straight to another therapist. And that goes for those telephone calls and other annoyances of yours, too. If I ever so much as receive one single unnecessary call from you again, especially when I tell you that I am busy and cannot speak to you at the time, that's the end of our relationship. And I mean it! I've taken enough of your nonsense, and it seems to me that I've been pretty nice to you in the meantime. But enough is enough! Either, hereafter, you are going to show some respect for me and my way of working, or you can go to the devil and get another therapist. And, if you want, I'll be glad to recommend you to one right now."

My client, with a terribly shocked look, immediately became conciliatory and apologetically left. Thereafter, for a period of several months, I had no trouble with her. During this period, she also improved considerably, for the first time in her long history of psychotherapy. She then began to slip slowly back into her previous negative behavior toward me; and, after taking this for a few sessions, I again let her have it, right between the ears, and told her that I would refuse to see her again if she did not immediately change her ways. She quickly became much more considerate. I had little trouble with her thereafter, and she made even more improvements.

On two other occasions, with male clients, I told each one, after I had seen him only a few sessions: "Now let's stop this nonsense. You're giving me an obvious pack of lies and evasions, and at that rate we'll get absolutely no place. If you want to go on kidding yourself, and refraining from working to get better, that's your business. But my business is helping people get better, and I don't intend to waste time with those who keep giving me a lot of trouble. Now either you quit lying and evading or stew in your own damned neuroses for the rest of your life. Which shall it be?" In both of these instances, my clients made significant changes in their attitudes toward me, toward therapy, and toward themselves.

With this kind of highly active-directive, *unpampering* approach, I find that I can sometimes push negativistic and inert people into self-healing action when a passive, nondirective technique would merely encourage them to continue their defeatist and self-defeating tendencies forever.

I also find, in the course of REBT encounters, that persistent activity by the therapist often pays off. This is to be expected on theoretical grounds: since if an individual's disturbance largely consists of the irrational Beliefs he has kept telling himself for a long time, it is only to be expected that such persistently ingrained indoctrinations will require a considerable amount of, shall we say, persistent "outgraining." This seems to be true of most learned habits: once they are distinctly overlearned, then, even though they lead to unfortunate results, it is difficult to unlearn them and to learn different habits. Therefore, the habituated individual had better persist and persist in the unlearning and relearning process.

The REBT therapist, consequently, frequently keeps questioning, challenging, and reeducating his clients, until even the difficult customers (DCs) among them are ready to give up their dysfunctional behavior patterns and replace them with more functional philosophies and behaviors. If the therapist fails to persist, the clients often run back into their old hiding places, and refuse to be smoked out of their neurosis.

In one particularly difficult case, I was seeing a highly intelligent young woman teacher who had urinary and defecatory symptoms which seemed to be closely related to her sexual problems. However, she was loath to discuss sexual issues and, in spite of some probing on my part, she remained exceptionally vague about her sex life. She particularly insisted that she had never masturbated nor had any guilt in relation to masturbation. I was most doubtful about this, but could not get any additional information with repeated questioning.

Feeling that the client was definitely resisting, I determined to make an even more concerted frontal attack on her masturbatory feelings and actions. In spite of her insistence that she had never masturbated, I forced the issue and asked her if she knew what masturbation consisted of in females. She looked confused, so I said:

"Masturbation in females is not usually like it is commonly supposed to be in so-called dirty jokes or conversational innuendo. Do you know how it's actually done?"

She became quite flustered and finally blurted out: "Well, I've never used a candle, or anything like that."

"No doubt you haven't," I persisted, "but masturbation in females very rarely consists of using a candle or anything like that. What it usually consists of is using some kind of friction, such as manual friction, on the external sex organs or the clitoris. Have you ever done anything like that? I'm sure you must have, since almost all women do at one time or another. Maybe you pressed you thighs together, or rubbed against desks, or did things along that line. Can't you remember now?"

My client suddenly blushed furiously and became completely mute for almost ten minutes. After that, slowly, and at my continued insistence, she indicated that she had been masturbating for years. It was then easy to show her that she had known all along what she had been doing, but had refused to acknowledge this fact by pretending that masturbation consisted only of inserting objects into the vagina. This meant that she must have been exceptionally guilty about continuing to masturbate; and her guilt was, at least in part, causing her defecatory and urinary symptoms. The client quickly acknowledged this, stopped the self-downing she had been doing about masturbation and slowly began to improve, whereas previously we had been able to effect virtually no improvement.

In many other cases treated with REBT, I have found that persistence has paid off. When clients have insisted that they are not guilty, or angry, or anxious, I have kept confronting them, with evidence from their own behavior, that they probably are disturbed, and in most instances they have soon begun to admit that they are, but may insist that they do not know why. Or they insist that they are not telling themselves anything to make themselves disturbed. I often forcefully contend that they *do* know why and that they *are* believing some self-defeating ideas. Again, the more I persist, the more they usually admit that I am correct, and that they *can* help themselves by changing these ideas.

Another important method that frequently is used in REBT is the therapist's agreeing with the clients on specific homework assignments.

As an example of working out a specific assignment with a client, we may take the instance of Carmine, a twenty-seven-year-old male who was sent to therapy by his fiancée, who claimed that he didn't relate at all to their mutual friends, but would sit reading a newspaper or working on some accounting problem when they were visiting or being visited. After seeing this man for only two sessions, I saw that he was unusually inhibited and that he had been so ever since his early childhood. His mother had been exceptionally critical of everything he ever did; and his father had perfunctorily accepted his school successes (which were notable) but had not really shown any interest in him. As a result of feeling terribly "hurt" and horrified by his view of the reactions (or lack of reactions) of his parents, he had begun to distrust everyone and to relate in only a superficial manner.

On theoretical grounds, Carmine was shown that he was probably telling himself ideas like: "If I get too close to people, they may reject me, as my mother and father did; and that would be terrible!" and: "If I make myself relatively inaccessible to people and they *still* accept me, then I'll feel safe with them, and will be able to open up more to them later."

The client could not see, as yet, that he actually was holding these kinds of Beliefs, but was willing to admit that he might be. We therefore arranged the homework assignment of (a) his looking for his own specific self-defeating statements whenever he found himself in any kind of a social retreat, and (b) deliberately forcing himself, at these times of retreat, to enter into closer relations with other people, to stop reading his newspaper, and to say anything he had on his mind no matter how stupid it might seem.

After two weeks of agreeing with this assignment, Carmine came into his next session of therapy and reported: "I did what we arranged."

"Yes? And what happened?"

"Quite a lot! I found it much more difficult than I thought it would be to put it into effect. Really difficult!"

"But you did so, nevertheless?"

"Oh, yes. I kept doing, forcing myself to do so. Much more difficult than I expected, it was!"

"What was the difficulty, exactly?"

"First of all, finding those Beliefs. The ones you thought I was telling myself. I just couldn't see them at all at first. I seemed to be saying absolutely nothing to myself. But every time I found myself retreating from people, I said to myself: 'Now, even though you can't see it, I'm sure you have some irrational thoughts. What are they?' And I finally found them. And there were many of them! And they all seemed to say the same thing."

"What thing?"

"That I, uh, was going to be rejected."

"If you spoke up and participated with others, you mean?"

"Yes, if I related to them I was going to be rejected. And wouldn't that be perfectly awful if I was to be rejected. And there was no reason for me, uh, to take that, uh, awful thing, and be rejected in that awful manner."

"So you might as well shut your trap and stay off in your corner, away from the others."

"Yes, so I might as well shut my trap and stay off in my corner, away from the others."

"So you did see it?"

"Oh, yes! I certainly saw it. Many times, during the two weeks."

"And did you do the second part of the homework assignment?"

"The forcing myself to speak up and express myself?"

"Yes, that part."

"That was worse. That was really hard. Much harder than I thought it would be. But I did it."

"And—?"

"Oh, not bad at all. I spoke up several times; more than I've ever done before. Some people were very surprised. Phyllis was very surprised, too. But I spoke up. And, you know something?"

"What?"

"I even enjoyed it some of the times!"

"You enjoyed expressing yourself?"

"Yes. The Slotts were there one day, at Phyllis's place. And they were talking about the United Nations and political things that I really don't know very much about, because I think, you know, that I've actually avoided finding out much about that sort of thing in the past, knowing that I would be afraid to talk about it. Well, anyway, they were talking about this recent stuff that's been in the papers, and I had an idea about it that I thought I'd like to bring up, but I could see that, as I used to do, I was going to keep my mouth shut and say nothing, for fear of their all looking at me as if I was crazy and didn't know what I was talking about. But I said to myself, instead, 'Here's my chance to take the plunge, and do more of my homework!' And I spoke up and said my little piece, and they all looked at me, and I don't even know how it exactly went over, though nobody seemed to disagree very much. But, anyway, *I* knew that I had expressed myself for once, and that was the thing."

"And how did you feel after expressing yourself like that?"

"Remarkable! I don't remember when I last felt this way. I felt, uh, just remarkable—good, that is. It was really something to feel! But it was so *hard*. I almost didn't make it. And a couple of other times during the week I had to force myself again. But I did. And I was glad!"

"So your homework assignments paid off?"

"They did; they really did."

Within the next few weeks, largely as a result of doing his homework assignments, Carmine became less inhibited socially and was able to express himself more freely than he had ever been able to do before. It is doubtful whether, without this kind of homework assignment, he would have made so much progress so quickly.

In another instance, I arranged a specific assignment with Sonya, a twenty-year-old woman who had recently married and who was having considerable difficulty being affectionate to her mother-in-law. Her own mother and father had never been overtly affectionate to her, and she had always referred to them, from early childhood, as Jack and Barbara, rather than Dad and Mom. But her mother-in-law, whom she liked and wanted to be friendly with, was a very affectionate woman, who winced every time Sonya called her Mrs. Steen or Marion, and obviously wanted to be called Mom.

The client's problem was that she did not *feel* like calling her mother-in-law "Mom," and felt that she would be hypocritical if she did so just to remain on good terms with her. I showed her, however, that she was refusing to see things from the mother-in-law's frame of reference, and that she was moralistically viewing the woman as being horribly childish. If she undamningly accepted her mother-in-law, I convinced her, she would be helping herself, her husband, and her in-laws; and with this kind of unmoralistic attitude, she would have no difficulty in calling her mother-in-law "Mom" instead of "Mrs. Steen."

Sonya accepted this view in theory, but she still had great difficulty thinking of and addressing her mother-in-law as "Mom." Whereupon, we agreed on the specific assignment of calling Mrs. Steen on the phone every day for a two-week period, and beginning the conversation with "Hi, Mom," and forcing herself to get in two or three more "Moms" before their talk was over. She reluctantly said she would try this assignment, even though she still felt uncomfortable and somewhat hypocritical about it.

After this experiment had progressed for a week, I saw Sonya and asked her how she was doing with her psychotherapeutic homework.

"Oh, yes," she said, "I meant to tell you about that. After talking to my mother-in-law for only three days, I found that calling her 'Mom' was really easy. In fact, I kind of got to like the sound of the word. And, do you know what? I actually started using it with my own mother, too! And *she* seems to like it!"

"So now you have two *Moms* for the price of one!"

"Yes. And, just as you predicted, I really *feel* closer to my mother-in-law. And to my mother, as well! It didn't take long at all, did it?

"No, it certainly didn't. The feeling of closeness pretty quickly followed the action of saying the word *Mom*. That's what the French novelist, Stendhal, pointed out about love, well over a century ago: that if you act *as if* you are in love with another, you very likely soon *will be*. That's what happens to many of our feelings—that *after* we act on them we begin to feel them quite deeply."

"It worked out just like that in my case. And I'm very glad that it did, and that I kept doing my homework conscientiously. I never thought I'd go back to school through psychotherapy, but that's the way it's seemed to work out."

"Which is probably just the way it should, considering that effective psychotherapy and reeducation are often practically synonymous."

These are typical instances of the many ways in which highly active directive methods, including arranging for specific assignments, are used in REBT. While other schools of therapy, such as radical behavior therapy, employ somewhat similar techniques, REBT does so on theoretical grounds that are an integral part of its basic rationale.

If verbal *and* sensorimotor indoctrinations and self-constructions teach people to think irrationally and to feel disturbed, then the same kind of double-barreled restructuring can be helpful in reorganizing their thinking and emoting. Vigorous verbal rethinking will often lead to changed motor behavior; and forcefully repatterned sensorimotor activity will often lead to changed ideation. But the quickest and most deep-rooted behavioral modifications will usually follow from a *combined* verbal and sensorimotor attack on the old, dysfunctional ways of thinking-doing."

CHAPTER NOTES

1. Ellis, 1957a, 1957b, 1965c, 1971, 1973b, 1977a, 1985b, 1991p.
2. Bernard, 1991, 1993; Dryden, 1994a, 1994b; Dryden & Hill, 1993; Ellis, 1991p; Ellis & Dryden, 1987, 1990, 1991; Ellis *&* Harper, 1975; Walen, DiGiuseppe, *&* Dryden, 1992; Yankura & Dryden, 1991.
3. Dryden & Yankura, 1992; Ellis, 1973b, 1991a; Goldstein, 1954; Maslow, 1954, 1968; Rogers, 1951, 1961.
4. Ellis, 1982a, 1985b, 1994a, 1994b; Wachtel, 1982.
5. Ellis, 1959a, 1962a, 1982a; 1985b.
6. Ellis, 1962a, 1977a, 1985b; Ellis & Knaus, 1977; Hauck, 1974; Dryden *&* Gordon, 1993; Dryden & Hill, 1993; Knaus, 1974, 1983; Walen, DiGiuseppe, & Dryden, 1992.

7. Ellis, 1985b; Ellis & Abrahms, 1978; Ellis & Abrams, 1994; Ellis &
Dryden, 1987, 1990, 1991; Ellis & Knaus, 1977; Ellis & Velten, 1992.

8. Ellis, 1985b, 1991i, 1991n, 1991p, 1992c, 1992g, 1992j, 1993d, 1993e;
Hauck, 1992; Mills, 1993.

9. Dryden, 1994b; Dryden & Hill, 1993; Ellis, 1991a, 1991i, 1991n, 1991p,
1992g, 1992j, 1993d, 1993i, 1993l; Ellis & Abrahms, 1978; Ellis &
Dryden, 1987; Ibanez, 1960; Israeli, 1962; Walen, DiGiuseppe, &
Dryden, 1992; Wolfe, 1992.

10. Blau, 1993; Edelman, 1989, 1991; Ellis, 1957a, 1957b, 1965e, 1973b,
1985b, 1988e; Ruth, 1992.

11. Bernard, 1991, 1993; Blau, 1993; Dryden, 1994a; Dryden & Hill, 1992;
Ellis, 1957a, 1973a, 1977a, 1985b, 1988e, 1991p; Ellis & Abrams, 1994;
Ellis & Velten, 1992; Greenberg & Safran, 1987; Guidano, 1987, 1991;
Mahoney, 1991; Muran, 1991, 1993; Walen, DiGiuseppe, & Dryden,
1992; Wolfe, 1992.

CHAPTER 20

GUILT, RESPONSIBILITY AND PSYCHOTHERAPY

EDITOR'S COMMENTARY:

This short vignette is a very clear statement by Ellis concerning moral anxiety. He contrasted his arguments to those from Mowrer, and he even accepted that wrongdoing and/ or lack of responsibility differ from self-blame and self-acceptance (Ellis actually used the term "essence," a term he disdained in much of his writing). The short chapter probably deserved expansion since it was one leg of a tripod in his theory of anxiety—moral anxiety.

Excerpted from *Reason and Emotion in Psychotherapy,*
Birch Lane Press, 1994

In chapter 7 of the original edition of *Reason and Emotion in Psychotherapy,* I considered O. Hobart Mowrer's views on "sin" and psychotherapy and agreed with several of them. The main points in this chapter with which I still agree are the following:[1]

1. In opposition to the psychoanalytic position, I agree with Mowrer that psychotherapy had better be largely concerned with clients' sense of morality and wrongdoing. An effective therapist will help clients see that they

are acting immorally (destructively) to themselves and to others, that they can correct their unethical behavior in most instances, and that when they cannot or do not correct it they are still not bad or immoral *persons*. Rather, they are fallible humans who right now are behaving, or have in the past behaved, wrongly or badly, who had better change that behavior, but who can accept themselves, their essence, their being *whether or not* they act immorally or unethically (according to the rules of their society and to their personal rules and standards).

2. REBT teaches you to Dispute and surrender your thoughts and feelings of guilt, self-damnation, or what Mowrer calls "sin" and to divide them clearly into two separate parts: Part I is when you sensibly acknowledge, "I have done the wrong thing and I am responsible for them doing it. I'm determined to correct my wrongdoings, to make restitution for them, and to stop repeating them in the future." Part 2 is when you illegitimately and self-sabotagingly add, "Therefore, I am a bastard, a sinner, a no-goodnik, a valueless person for doing this wrong deed!"[2]

3. Although humans are never likely to determine any absolute, final, or God-given standard of morals or ethics, they can fairly easily agree, in any given community, on what is "right" and what is "wrong" and can therefore rate or measure their thoughts, feelings, and acts as "good" or "bad." They can also often see that certain of their behaviors are self- and society-helping and can deem those behaviors to be "good." And they can observe that others' behaviors are self- and society-sabotaging and can deem these to be "bad." In the final analysis "right" and "wrong" acts in any community are established by some kind of consensus; and it is not too difficult for people in a community to arrive at this kind of consensus, and then to make certain special exceptions to it.

4. To have a sensible, rational philosophy of morality, you will tend to believe, "If I do this particular act, it will be wrong or immoral" and, "Therefore, I'd preferably better try not to do it and not repeat it." But you never have to add, "If I do commit or keep committing a wrong or immoral act, I am an immoral, generally bad person."

5. When you call yourself a "sinner" or an "immoral person" you rate or evaluate your entire essence or being in terms of one or more of your acts and this is unhealthy or self-defeating for several reasons:

a. It is an arrant overgeneralization, because *you* hardly *are* any of your *performances.*[3]

b. When you denigrate your*self* for your mistaken *acts* you strongly and wrongly imply that you are so essentially bad that you have little or no ability to improve these acts in the present and future.

c. Being biased by your negative self-evaluation, you will often create a self-fulfilling prophecy and actually *make yourself* continue to act immorally and mistakenly in the future.

d. You will tend to obsess about your present and past wrongdoings and therefore render yourself ineffective at accurately observing and rating these poor acts, waste your energy in recriminations, and make yourself less capable of changing them now and later.

e. You may see yourself as a *bad individual* who deserves to be punished for your wrong behaviors, and will therefore sometimes actually keep acting bad in order to bring about this "deserved" punishment.

f. You will often be so horrified about your poor behaviors that you will not want to admit that you really acted so bad and will sometimes rationalize about your immoralities and repress knowledge of them, so that you refuse to see how bad your acts actually are and therefore not be ready to correct or change them.

g. Once you condemn yourself, your whole being, for making mistakes or for "sinning," you almost always make yourself anxious, depressed, and self-damning; and you often recognize that you feel this way and even that you have made yourself feel this way with your perfectionist standards. You then may take your disturbed emotional Consequence (C), feelings of worthlessness, and make it into a secondary Activating Event (A), "I see that I feel worthless and depressed." You may then irrationally tell yourself at B, your Belief System, "I must not be depressed! It's awful that I've made myself depressed!" You thus bring on a secondary symptom of feeling depressed about your depression. You then feel so disturbed that you may act worse than ever, and often create more mistakes and "sins!"

h. Even when people go for therapy, because they feel so guilty about their wrong acts and feel so worthless for having committed them, they very frequently worry about whether they will do well in therapy and make the mistake of not following some of the principles that their therapist is showing them how to use. They then make themselves guilty about their lack of therapeutic comprehension or progress and, on a tertiary level, become even more disturbed—and therefore more prone to bad behavior!

6. You preferably should not use words like "sin" and "sinner," because they imply absolute, God-given (or devil-given) standards that help you to condemn your self, your entire being, for some of your mistaken acts. Instead, you had better acknowledge that you committed wrongdoings and acted irresponsibly and that you are usually culpable or responsible for your poor behaviors, but that you are a fallible human who is allowed to make mistakes, even serious ones, and had better correct them if you can; but that you are never totally damnable for making these grave errors. Instead of damning and punishing yourself for your acts, it would be better if you made restitution to your victims (or their relatives) and concentrated on acting less immorally in the present and future.[4]

The words *sin* and *sinner* are also best avoided because, as Stevan Nielsen [personal communication, 1994] points out, they can be used preferentially but usually have absolutistic and musturbatory overtones. Thus, "sin" can merely mean a violation of a rule—a transgression, a breach, or an infraction. That is fine, because there are certainly social and individual rules and we humans often violate them. We only make this breach a neurotic problem, however, when we insist that the violated rule is *sacred* and that we *absolutely must* not breach it. When we call our wrongdoing a "sin," we imply (in our Judeo-Christian culture) that conforming to the rule *is* "sacred" and that any violation of it *is* "horrible." We also imply that we *preferably* should not be a "wrongdoer" or "mistake maker" but that we *absolutely must* never be a (thoroughly worthless) "sinner." So I quite agree with Stevan Nielsen—who is a clinical psychologist and a Mormon elder—that, especially when we use REBT, we had better avoid the words *sin* and *sinner*.

As Stevan Nielsen also points out [personal communication] "insistence on viewing one's behavior as 'sin' and viewing oneself as a 'sinner' makes little sense unless one also makes room in one's thinking for the concepts of 'repentance' and 'forgiveness,' including forgiving the self for making a mistake. Just as the notion of behavior without considering the possibility or, even, the likelihood of that behavior changing is irrational, so, also, the notion of 'sin' (just another form of behavior, albeit, an undesirable behavior) is irrational without, again, allowance for change—for repentance."

These are some of the main points in chapter 7, which I originally titled "Sin and Psychotherapy," with which I still strongly agree. Now let me consider some of my disagreements with other points in the chapter and outline how I would tend to correct them today.

I originally agreed with Mowrer, on page 132 of the original *Reason and Emotion in Psychotherapy,* "that the only basic solution to the problem of emotional disturbance is the correction or cessation of the disturbed person's immoral actions." However, I no longer agree with Mowrer in this respect. Emotional disturbance, such as neurosis, doesn't stem from immoral behavior but from people's absolutistic demands *about* that behavior—as well as from their unconditional demands about their and others' behaviors and about the world. However, some disturbance, such as endogenous depression, bipolar depression, and obsessive-compulsive disorder, have strong biological components. So correcting their immoral behavior will help many people to feel less disturbed. But it will hardly cure all their emotional problems![5]

I say, on page 135, that if people "objectively" and nondamningly believe, "If I do this act it will be wrong" and "Therefore how do I *not* do it?" they will tend to be less immoral and healthier than if they believe, "If I do this immoral act I will be a sinner, a blackguard, a worthless person." True, but some people, such as psychopaths, do not damn themselves for their misdeeds and still easily commit them.

I also point out (pp. 136–137) that when one excoriates oneself for one's wrongdoings, one will "often implosively drive himself to more misdeeds in order, sooner or later, to bring punishment for those sins on his own head." Occasionally, yes. But not too often!

I again say that blaming oneself for one's wrongdoings inevitably leads to damning others for their misdeeds and to making oneself hostile to them. Often—but hardly inevitably!

I make a more serious error on page 138 when I state: "Blaming . . . is the essence of virtually all emotional disturbances and, as I tell my clients on many occasions, if I can induce them never, under any circumstances, to blame or punish anyone, including and especially themselves, it will be virtually impossible for them ever to become seriously disturbed." No, it won't! They can easily disturb themselves by creating low frustration tolerance (LFT) or discomfort disturbance—by insisting that they *must* not be uncomfortable and *must* have everything they want when they want it. They can also have biologically based disturbances, such as endogenous depression, obsessive-compulsive disorder, borderline personality disorder, and psychosis.[6]

On page 139 I state that self-damning can easily produce powerful anxiety and "concomitant breakdown states" in which people cannot clearly think of anything, least of all constructively changing themselves. Another exaggeration! Self-downing about immoral and incompetent acts often leads to anxiety but rarely to breakdown states—unless one has strong innate tendencies to have "nervous breakdowns," personality disorders, or psychotic states. Nonetheless, self-castigation is often pernicious—and quite avoidable if one uses REBT to ward it off.

On page 145 I overstate my case again by stating that healthy and happy humans "should have a clear-cut sense of wrongdoing, and... not only try to understand the origin of [their] antisocial behavior but... do something effective to become more morally oriented." I mean *preferably should,* not *absolutely should.* In *Reason and Emotion in Psychotherapy* I often use *should* and *must* loosely, which I stopped doing in my later writings on REBT. *Conditional* shoulds and musts are all right: such as, "If I want to survive, I *should* and *must* eat and breathe." For surviving almost always *necessitates* eating and breathing. But, of course, I don't *have* to survive and only *choose* to do so. If I *choose* to practice as a physician I normally *must* finish medical school and *must* get a license. But I can choose not to practice medicine and then don't *need* a degree or license. So there are many legitimate *contingent* shoulds and musts but (as far as we know) no *absolute,* under *all* conditions at *all* times, necessities. These absolutistic demands, says REBT, largely lead to neurosis, and may be Disputed and changed to sensible preferences.

On page 146 I proclaim: "The concept of sin is the direct and indirect cause of virtually all neurotic disturbance." It would have been preferable had I stated, "Neurosis largely (not completely) stems from (1) damning yourself (your *self*) for your mistakes and wrongdoings (which we preferably had better not call 'sins'); (2) damning other people for their immoralities and inadequacies; and (3) damning the world for its failure to give you everything you want and nothing that you don't want. A deep-seated sense of 'sin' and guilt encourages much, but hardly all, human neurosis."

Because REBT teaches people to have unconditional positive regard (self-acceptance) for themselves and others it is sometimes accused of having no morality and of encouraging irresponsible behavior. Not so! Because it aims to help clients—and other people—to relate well to others and to avoid being penalized by their social group, it normally has no special moral rules but tends to adopt those of the community or culture in which the individual lives.

Even if social rules are "unreasonable" or "irrational"—such as laws that ban sex relations among consenting adults—REBT practitioners usually advise people to see that they are not severely penalized for being caught flouting such rules. If they consciously choose to be martyrs, and deliberately perform illegal acts to help change the undue restrictions of their community, that is okay—as long as they are willing to take the penalty for their "crimes," But they had better weigh the risks and choose to act accordingly.

So unless individuals are mentally deficient, psychotic, or otherwise incapable of following moral and personal rules, REBT holds them quite responsible for their "sins." It nonetheless accepts the "sinner" but not his or her "sin." This still seems to me a quite sensible form of morality!

CHAPTER NOTES

1. Mowrer, 1960a, 1960b.
2. Burns, 1993; Ellis, 1957a, 1958b, 1960, 1972c, 1976c, 1990b, 1992c, 1994c, 1994e; Ellis & Dryden, 1987, 1990g, 1990h, 1992c; Ellis & Harper, 1961a, 1961b, 1975; FitzMaurice, 1989; R. Franklin, 1993; Hauck, 1992; T. Miller, 1988; Mills, 1993.
3. Bourland & Johnston, 1991; De Bono, 1991; FitzMaurice, 1989; Hayakawa, 1965; W. Johnson, 1946; Korzybski, 1933, 1951.
4. Beck, 1991; Burns, 1990; Ellis, 1965a, 1965b, 1965c, 1971, 1973b, 1977a, 1985b, 1988e, 1991i, 1992c, 1994e; Ellis & Dryden, 1987, 1990, 1991.
5. J. Adler, 1994; Begley, 1994; Cowley, 1994; Eysenck, 1967; Eysenck & Ellis, 1993; Gazzinga, 1993; Franklin, 1987; Lipchik & Gefner, 1994; Meehl, 1962; Rosenthal, 1971; Wegner, 1994; Zaidel, 1994.
6. Bellak, 1994; Cloninger, Svrakic, & Przybek, 1994; Ellis, 1965b, 1979a, 1980a, 1994b; Langley, 1993; Silver & Rosenbluth, 1992.

CHAPTER 21

HOW AND WHEN
FAITH-BELIEF
HELPS PSYCHOTHERAPY

EDITOR'S COMMENTARY:

Ellis wrote that he had better admit that religion and spiritual beliefs sometimes do help a person with his or her mental health and he even allowed for an assumption that a spiritual realm existed. He still argued for probabilistic atheism for himself but he allowed that gullible people often could benefit from religious or spiritual beliefs!

Excerpted from *Road to Tolerance,*
Prometheus, 2004

Some writers have for many years claimed that people's holding definite religious, supernatural, mystical, and spiritual views may admittedly sabotage their physical well-being and mental health. But they have meant that "bad" or "false" or "fraudulent" philosophies lead to this kind of outcome.

In the last few decades, the relationship of people's turning to religion and/or spirituality has received vastly increased attention and study; the consensus of almost innumerable articles and books in the field seems to be that "wrong" religious and spiritual views can hinder, while "good" ones may enhance people's physical and mental health and increase their happiness. At least *some* believers, especially disturbed ones, appear to benefit—or *say* they benefit—from their religious faith.

Much can be said for and against this allegation, for proreligionists can "discover" that a "spiritual" view bolsters mental health, and antireligionists can prejudicially "find" that it sabotages it. Who is to support unbiased claims in either direction? Virtually no one.

As I first pointed out almost forty years ago, self-ratings of how much you have benefited from *any* of your values are easily prejudiced by the values themselves. Thus, if you are conservative about marriage, you will often claim to researchers that your own marriage is "good" or "happy," while if you hold liberal views on marriage and divorce, you may more honestly tell researchers that your own marriage is "poor" or "unhappy." Many studies have shown—as I indicated in my 1965 critique, "The Validity of Personality Questionnaires"—that respondents who want to favorably impress researchers lie on their tests, while other respondents give more truthful answers when they are not ashamed of their more honest responses.

Almost all the many studies of the mental health of religious and nonreligious respondents are not to be trusted and may well be misleading. Most of them "show" that religious subjects say that they received definite benefits from following religious or spiritual attitudes—such as increased confidence, competence, productivity, and emotional well-being. They *say* they enhanced their lives, and most of them really believe that they did. But did they actually do so—or did they consciously and unconsciously exaggerate these "findings?" Who can accurately say? My guess—like that of many scientific researchers—is that many of the conservative respondents exaggerated the virtues of their religious attitudes and blithely ignored the disadvantages of either religious or spiritualized views.

Let me, however, give the Devil his due. Let me assume that many— perhaps millions—of people who say that religio-spiritual philosophies have enhanced their lives have distinctly benefited as they have reported. For one thing, their *thinking* they have benefited will often make their feelings valid. Thus, as I have mentioned before, if you devoutly *think* that Jesus or the Devil is helpfully on your side, even if this is only your delusion, you may *help yourself by* giving in to this delusion. As Shakespeare noted, "There's nothing either good or bad but thinking makes it so." Some of the worst delusions actually work. Moreover, if you are *profoundly convinced* that anything, including religious faith, will give you more confidence to do things, your *conviction* may lead you to *act* in a more productive way. People who *believe* that they can get a better job frequently push themselves and get one.

Let me assume that something beyond empiricism does exist and that your belief in this supernatural "thing" is not empirically justified or "true," but it helps you "spiritually" and awards you better mental and physical health and happiness. Assume that your religious or spiritual convictions are somehow "true"—that God or Jesus or Allah really does exist and your acknowledging his existence distinctly helps you live a "fuller" life.

Now try to assume the opposite: that there is nothing supernatural and no "spirits" in the world but that your *believing* that there are and worshipping the (false) dictates of a (nonexistent) deity somehow enhances your life— gives you, for example, a goal or purpose to live for.

In both these (conflicting) cases, you may win Pascal's wager—for you benefit either (1) by the existing God or (2) by the nonexisting but firmly dreamed of God. So what have you got to lose? You might as well *accept* God's existence—or not accept it but still act *as if* he existed.

This is what I think the majority of people do. They can't be sure that anything supernatural exists, but they also can't prove that it doesn't—so they choose to allege that because it *may* exist, it really does. They *choose* to be deists or theists. More skeptical people; however, choose to believe that supernatural beings most probably don't exist—since if they did, there would be *some* empirical evidence proving that they do—but they still retain some safety by acknowledging that they *may* possibly exist so they can accept their existence and still think it is possibly an illusion. Still more skeptical people think (as I do) that supernatural "things" most probably *don't* exist, so let's assume that they don't. Finally, dogmatic atheists believe that spiritual "things" absolutely don't exist and even *can't* exist. Apparently, people are able to *choose* their degrees of skepticism about spirits and gods.

Why do I choose to be a probabilistic atheist, who is *almost* certain that supernatural entities don't exist but nonetheless *may*? For several reasons:

1. Probabilistic atheism *most probably* is, as far as I (or any reasonable person) can *see*, factual or "true."
2. It is a non-safety-seeking, *honest* position to take. It represents *my* personal views.
3. It unbigotedly recognizes that gods, devils, and angels *could* possibly exist because even laws of probability are not *sacred*. Anything *could* happen even against the "laws" of probability.
4. Dogmatic, absolute atheism *is* unprovable and is a bigotry in itself, so I certainly don't want to subscribe to that.
5. Probabilistic atheism allows me—and others—to stop arguing about unprovable and undisprovable gods and get on with more important

life problems. It saves needless discussion and bickering.

6. It accords with the *known* facts, keeps looking for the unknown ones, but doesn't obsess about them.

7. It enables me (and others) to *want* but not *need* perfectionism and certainty.

8. It surrenders the emotionally disturbed, sadistic, and very improbable idea that if there were gods, they would never forgive those of us who refuse to believe in them and roast us in hell forever. It paradoxically avoids making gods into human devils!

9. It gives me (and others) the freedom, the real freedom, to choose our own hypotheses, thoughts, feelings, and behaviors and to widen our possibilities of living.

I think that these are good reasons for keeping my probabilistically based atheism instead of some more caviling position. People denigrate me for holding it, but I can take their opposition without cringing.

Back to my question: Does faith actually help religious and spiritual people to improve their mental health? Yes, I'd better admit: With *some* gullible people it *sometimes* does. They think that they would be too uncomfortable taking the atheistic position that there is so little possibility of supernaturalism existing that they might as well *assume* that it does not—and they tell themselves, "I'll be safe and assume that supernatural entities *may* exist, that they may be helpful to me if they do, and that therefore I'd better believe in this and ask for their help." They then take a compromising, weak way out of this question, while people like me more honestly choose the atheistic way. If these middle-of-the-road compromisers are correct and there *is* a vengeful God who will punish nonbelievers, I'll risk taking that (improbable) consequence!

CHAPTER 22

AN EXAMPLE OF WHERE REBT HAS NOT PERSONALLY WORKED FOR ME

EDITOR'S COMMENTARY:

The title of this selection seemed overly broad when, in fact, Ellis meant that his usual high frustration tolerance (HFT) yielded to LFT or DA (discomfort anxiety). He provided an example of the breakdown. The selection was really not an indication of where REBT did not work, but where one of its techniques did not work for Ellis; he yielded to low frustration tolerance and discomfort anxiety.

Excerpted from *REBT; It Works for Me - It Can Work for You*, Prometheus, 2004

Normally, I have fairly high frustration tolerance (HFT), which I have increased over the years by using REBT on myself. This is evidenced by my publishing more than seventy-five books and some eight hundred articles, giving over eighty professional and public workshops a year in New York and throughout the world, regularly supervising ten interns and therapists in REBT, and having sessions every week with about seventy individual and group therapy clients. Pretty good for an old man! In fact, in my eighty-ninth year, I published five new books and more than a dozen articles. So I hardly indulge in my natural low frustration tolerance (LFT) and procrastination, but make strong efforts to override them.

317

Nonetheless, I still at times suffer from abysmal LFT—and my use of REBT hardly removes it. Take, for example, what happened to me in August 1999. I was scheduled to give workshops from 10:00 AM to 5:00 PM in Colorado Springs. To make sure I arrived in time, I planned on taking a flight on one of the largest airlines from New York directly to Colorado Springs the afternoon before. We were scheduled to leave New York at 5:00 PM, stop over briefly in Dallas, and then arrive at our destination at 9:00 PM. I deliberately took this flight because it was the only one that went, with an interim stop, directly to Colorado Springs. So, presumably, I couldn't miss getting there Thursday night, in good time to be fresh for my workshops on Friday.

No such luck. The airline never told us passengers what happened to our plane, but after a two-hour delay, the airline finally got us on a substitute plane that was to leave LaGuardia Airport at 7:00 PM. Then, during our delay in taking off, a thunderstorm occurred while we were about to leave LaGuardia. All plane traffic was halted, and we finally left New York at 9:00 PM—several hours late.

The pilots did their best, but by the time we arrived in Dallas, it was midnight Dallas time, so the airline quite unethically, I thought, canceled our continuing flight to Colorado Springs. We were stuck for the night in Dallas. I explained to the airline agent that I had to open my workshop in Colorado Springs at 10:00 AM the next morning and therefore had to have an early flight to that city. He lied to me, said there was no early morning flight and that I would have to take an 11:00 AM flight and arrive, at the earliest, at 12:15 PM, long after my workshop was scheduled to begin. Actually, there was a 6:30 AM flight from Dallas to Colorado Springs, but because it was on a rival airline the agent wrongly told me it didn't exist. So he put me up in a flea-bag hotel for the night in Dallas and cooked my goose good! Not only was the hotel third rate, but about a hundred small ants were crawling on the floor of my bathroom. I spent a good deal of the night killing them.

Fortunately, I called the people for whom I was giving the workshops in Colorado Springs; they got on the phone to the airlines, and I was able to get on a plane at 6:30 AM for Denver and then on to Colorado Springs—for an extra $550 (and after about three hours of sleep on Thursday night). I arrived at my conference at 10:30 AM, so I still missed some of my workshop time. But at least I gave most of my presentations.

To make matters still worse, I was supposed to fly on Friday night, after my workshops, back to New York on the same delinquent airline that had unethically given me so much trouble on Thursday. As a result of their poor scheduling, they gave me only forty-five minutes to connect in Denver with my New York leg, and my leg to Denver was a half-hour late. I had to run a fantastic distance at the Denver airport to catch my New York plane. I, and my bedraggled luggage, finally made the New York plane, just as they were closing the doors to take off. I was lucky and the last one to make the plane.

What frustrations on this trip, for which this well-known airline was reprehensibly responsible. Thus: (1) My original plane got unexpectedly lost. (2) We were therefore two hours late in starting. (3) We consequently sat on the field another hour waiting for a thunderstorm to pass. (4) We were three hours late to Dallas. (5) The airline unethically canceled our duly scheduled flight to Colorado Springs—for no good reason that I could see. (6) The agent lied to me about there being no early flight Friday morning to my destination. (7) The airline put me up for the night in a flea-bag motel, which had hundreds of ants in the bathroom.

Frankly, I was incensed. I obsessively awfulized. I tried to use my best REBT, but it didn't work. I foolishly vowed to never use that infamous airline again. My usual high frustration tolerance failed me and for two days, including my trip back to New York and the following day, I inwardly seethed. As soon as I returned, I wrote the airline a scathing note and demanded monetary remuneration.

Finally, I went over the dismal events of the trip, saw that the airline was wrong and its unethical agent was highly fallible, but that those kinds of mistakes were not *horrible* and sometimes inevitably occurred. I then got back some measure of my higher frustration tolerance. I damned the *behavior* of the airline and its agent, but stopped blaming the airline *itself* or the personhood of the agent. At last, my REBT began to work again. I have even traveled on that wrongheaded airline again since that time, with, fortunately, much better results. My ill-fated trip was indeed bad but I could *stand* it, learn from it, and still survive. My frustration tolerance was, for a while, rudely interrupted— but not forever.

CHAPTER 23

THE ALPHA AND OMEGA:
TEN RULES FOR ACHIEVING
PERSONAL HAPPINESS

EDITOR'S COMMENTARY:

It seems fitting to summarize the revolution with ten rules Ellis thought to be important for personal happiness. A short survey of Ellis's writing through 1976 show that he was prone toward lists. The lists were often presented with numbers or as bullets. The evolution has moved, then, from his pre-academic period with LAMP and then graduate studies to his keen interest in matters sexual and amative to theory foundation. Thereafter he refined his theory and applied it. As ideas and research came in from colleagues (especially in closely allied areas such as CBT), Ellis's last efforts were to show how he applied the theory to himself. The list below is presented for the reader to consider how Ellis's ideas evolved—or if they evolved—from the revolution in the mid-1950s to his publications in 2004.

Excerpted from *A Guide to Personal Happiness,*
Wilshire Books, 1966

1. *Decide to strive primarily for your own happiness.* This is your right as a human; and, as we have noted throughout this book, there are many advantages to doing so. Consider the virtues of giving primary value to your own existence and your own enjoyment. And if you think that these virtues are worth it, decide—yes, *decide*—to strive for them.

2. Decide to put other people's happiness a close second to your own. Since you will probably choose to live among other people and to try to get along with them, and since your own happiness will, therefore, be tied up with that of these others, you had better decide to consider seriously the rights and privileges of all other humans and, in particular, to put some of them a close second to yourself. Enlightened self-interest includes the interest of others.

3. Decide that you largely control your own emotional destiny. As a human living in a social group, you are never completely autonomous but give away some control to others. But you can still decide to think your own thoughts and feel your own emotions. Decide, therefore, which reactions and feelings you want to experience.

4. When you feel disturbed or act self-defeatingly, look for your disturbance-creating Beliefs. Find the absolutistics *shoulds, musts,* and *commands* with which you needlessly upset yourself. Assume that you implicitly or explicitly hold and strongly believe in these *musts* and look into your head and heart to find them.

5. Actively dispute and surrender your self-sabotaging musts. Don't merely parrot their irrationality, but use the scientific method to prove their falseness.

6. Figure out a set of rational Beliefs that will help you live happily and keep reviewing them. Teach yourself to understand and believe that "Nothing is *awful*," "I *can* stand what I don't like!" "I am never a rotten, worthless individual, no matter how badly I behave!" and similar self-helping rational beliefs.

7. Use several other cognitive methods of surrendering your irrational Beliefs—such as, thinking homework, problem solving, semantic precision, referenting, imaging, bibliotherapy, and the use of humor.

8. Work directly on your emotions to change them from inappropriate to appropriate feelings. Use several or all of the methods outlined elsewhere, such as rational-emotive imagery, unconditional self-acceptance, shame-attacking exercises, self-disclosure exercises, role-playing, and the use of forceful and dramatic self-statements to feel more appropriately.

9. Forcefully act against your irrational Beliefs and inappropriate feelings. Use several or all of the behavioral methods outlined elsewhere to change your feelings, beliefs, and actions. For example, give yourself homework assignments that make you face the things you needlessly fear and perform useful tasks that you foolishly avoid. Use self-management procedures to reward yourself for effective behavior and to penalize yourself for self-defeating performances. At times, consider using relaxation and other methods of physical distraction, skill training, and the use of stimulus-control methods to help yourself lead a less disturbed, happier life.

10. *Resolve to change, acknowledge that change means hard work, and keep working to implement your resolutions.* The ability to choose your own emotional destiny or to use will power consists of (1) a strong resolution to change; (2) determination to work at the process of change; and (3) actual work to implement that process. Only *practice* makes perfect; and, as we say in RET, there's rarely any gain without pain! Careful thought plus work and practice are the essence of achieving personal happiness.

INDEX